FANTASTIC FOUR

Eternal Flame

On Doctor Doom and Victorious' wedding day, Victorious revealed her recent liaison with the Human Torch. An enraged Doom attacked all those present, including the Fantastic Four. As special punishment, Doom blasted the Human Torch with a device that left him burning brighter and hotter than ever before and unable to turn off his flames.

Back at the Fantastic Four's new home, the rebuilt Baxter Building in New York City, Mr. Fantastic promised to find a cure for the Torch's condition. But the team was soon attacked by several different versions of Kang the Conqueror, who targeted the team throughout the past and the present. The time-travelers were seeking a mysterious prize left behind by Nathaniel Richards, Mr. Fantastic's late father. By working together with their past selves, the Fantastic Four were able to defeat Kang and retrieve the prize for themselves—a hologram of Nathaniel that revealed a startling secret. Reed has a half sister!

The Fantastic Four created by Stan Lee & Jack Kirby

COLLECTION EDITOR: **Jennifer Grünwald**
ASSISTANT EDITOR: **Daniel Kirchhoffer**
ASSISTANT MANAGING EDITOR: **Maia Loy**
ASSOCIATE MANAGER, TALENT RELATIONS: **Lisa Montalbano**

VP PRODUCTION & SPECIAL PROJECTS: **Jeff Youngquist**
BOOK DESIGNERS: **Sarah Spadaccini** with **Adam Del Re**
SVP PRINT, SALES & MARKETING: **David Gabriel**
EDITOR IN CHIEF: **C.B. Cebulski**

FANTASTIC FOUR VOL. 9: ETERNAL FLAME. Contains material originally published in magazine form as FANTASTIC FOUR (2018) #36-39, FANTASTIC FOUR: ROAD TRIP (2020) #1 and FANTASTIC FOUR: GRIMM NOIR (2020) #1. First printing 2021. ISBN 978-1-302-92626-7. Published by MARVEL WORLDWIDE, INC., a subsidiary of MARVEL ENTERTAINMENT, LLC. OFFICE OF PUBLICATION: 1290 Avenue of the Americas, New York, NY 10104. © 2021 MARVEL. No similarity between any of the names, characters, persons, and/or institutions in this book with those of any living or dead person or institution is intended, and any such similarity which may exist is purely coincidental. **Printed in Canada.** KEVIN FEIGE, Chief Creative Officer; DAN BUCKLEY, President, Marvel Entertainment; JOE QUESADA, EVP & Creative Director; DAVID BOGART, Associate Publisher & SVP of Talent Affairs; TOM BREVOORT, VP, Executive Editor; NICK LOWE, Executive Editor, VP of Content, Digital Publishing; DAVID GABRIEL, VP of Print & Digital Publishing; JEFF YOUNGQUIST, VP of Production & Special Projects; ALEX MORALES, Director of Publishing Operations; DAN EDINGTON, Managing Editor; RICKEY PURDIN, Director of Talent Relations; JENNIFER GRÜNWALD, Senior Editor, Special Projects; SUSAN CRESPI, Production Manager; STAN LEE, Chairman Emeritus. For information regarding advertising in Marvel Comics or on Marvel.com, please contact Vit DeBellis, Custom Solutions & Integrated Advertising Manager, at vdebellis@marvel.com. For Marvel subscription inquiries, please call 888-511-5480. **Manufactured between 12/24/2021 and 1/25/2022 by SOLISCO PRINTERS, SCOTT, QC, CANADA.**

10 9 8 7 6 5 4 3 2 1

Eternal Flame

——————— FANTASTIC FOUR #36-37 ———————

Dan Slott
WRITER

Nico Leon
ARTIST

Dono Sánchez-Almara
COLOR ARTIST

Mark Brooks (#36) and
Terry Dodson & Rachel Dodson (#37)
COVER ARTISTS

——————— FANTASTIC FOUR #38-39 ———————

Dan Slott
WRITER

Francesco Manna
ARTIST

Jesus Aburtov
COLOR ARTIST

Terry Dodson & Rachel Dodson
COVER ARTISTS

——————— FANTASTIC FOUR: GRIMM NOIR ———————

Gerry Duggan & Ron Garney
STORYTELLERS

Matt Milla
COLOR ARTIST

Terry Dodson & Rachel Dodson
COVER ARTISTS

——————— FANTASTIC FOUR: ROAD TRIP ———————

Christopher Cantwell
WRITER

Filipe Andrade
ARTIST

Chris O'Halloran
COLOR ARTIST

Valerio Giangiordano & Tamra Bonvillain
COVER ARTISTS

——————————————————————————

VC's Joe Caramagna
LETTERER

Martin Biro &
Shannon Andrews Ballesteros
ASSISTANT EDITORS

Alanna Smith &
Annalise Bissa
ASSOCIATE EDITORS

Tom Brevoort
EDITOR

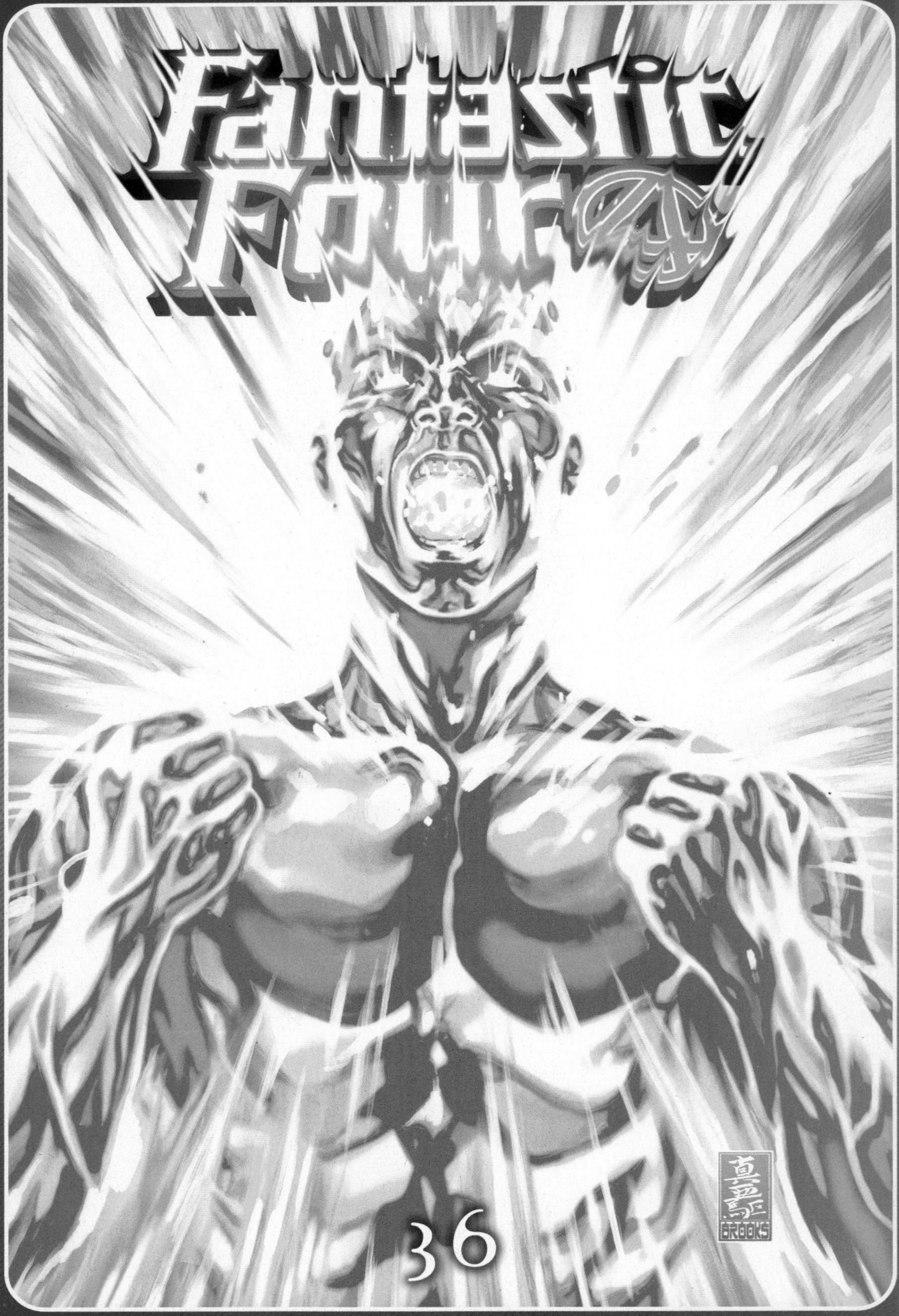
Fantastic Four
36
BROOKS

"Flame On"

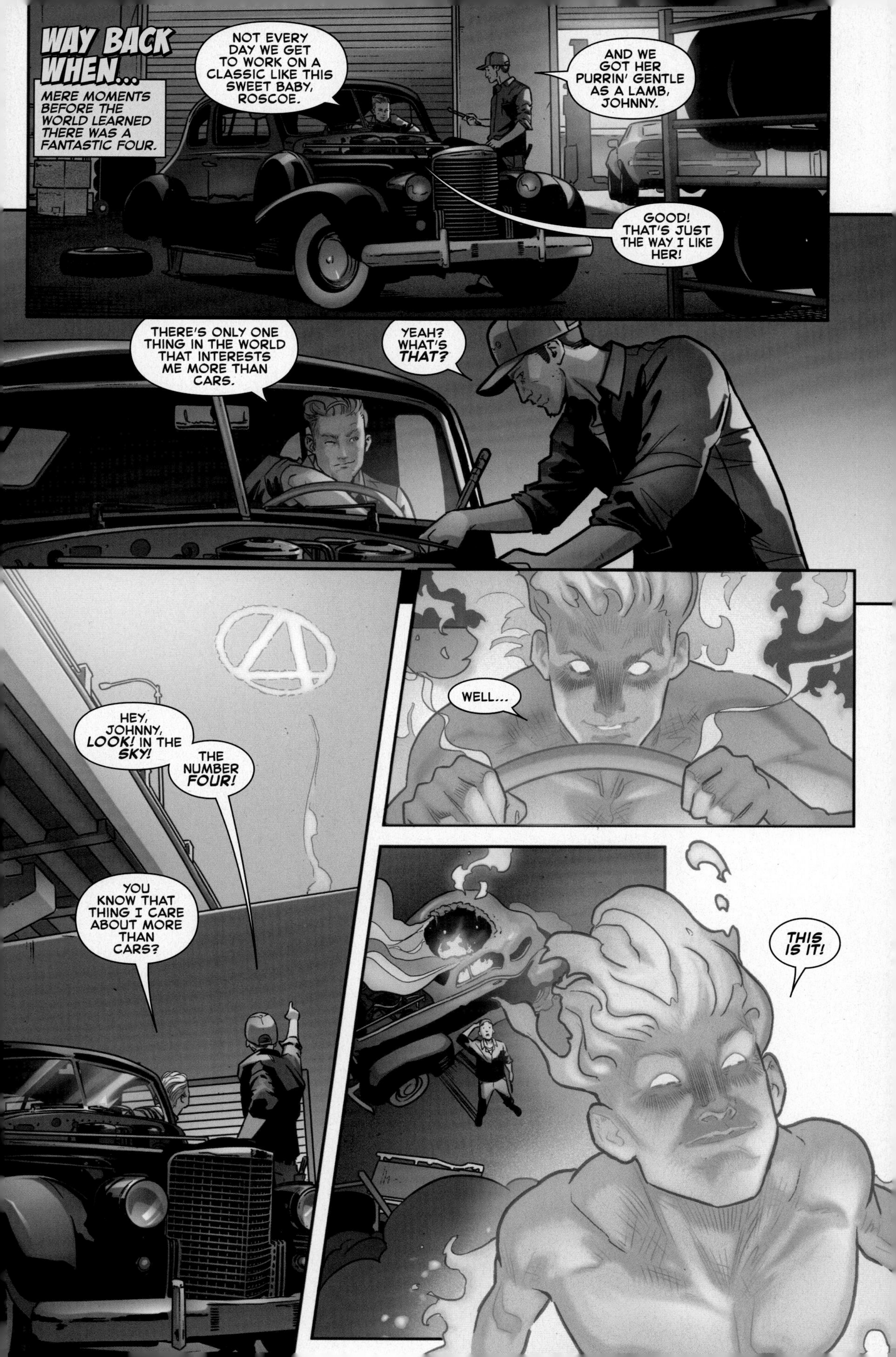
WAY BACK WHEN...
MERE MOMENTS BEFORE THE WORLD LEARNED THERE WAS A FANTASTIC FOUR.
NOT EVERY DAY WE GET TO WORK ON A CLASSIC LIKE THIS SWEET BABY, ROSCOE.
AND WE GOT HER PURRIN' GENTLE AS A LAMB, JOHNNY.
GOOD! THAT'S JUST THE WAY I LIKE HER!
THERE'S ONLY ONE THING IN THE WORLD THAT INTERESTS ME MORE THAN CARS.
YEAH? WHAT'S THAT?
HEY, JOHNNY, LOOK! IN THE SKY!
THE NUMBER FOUR!
YOU KNOW THAT THING I CARE ABOUT MORE THAN CARS?
WELL...
THIS IS IT!

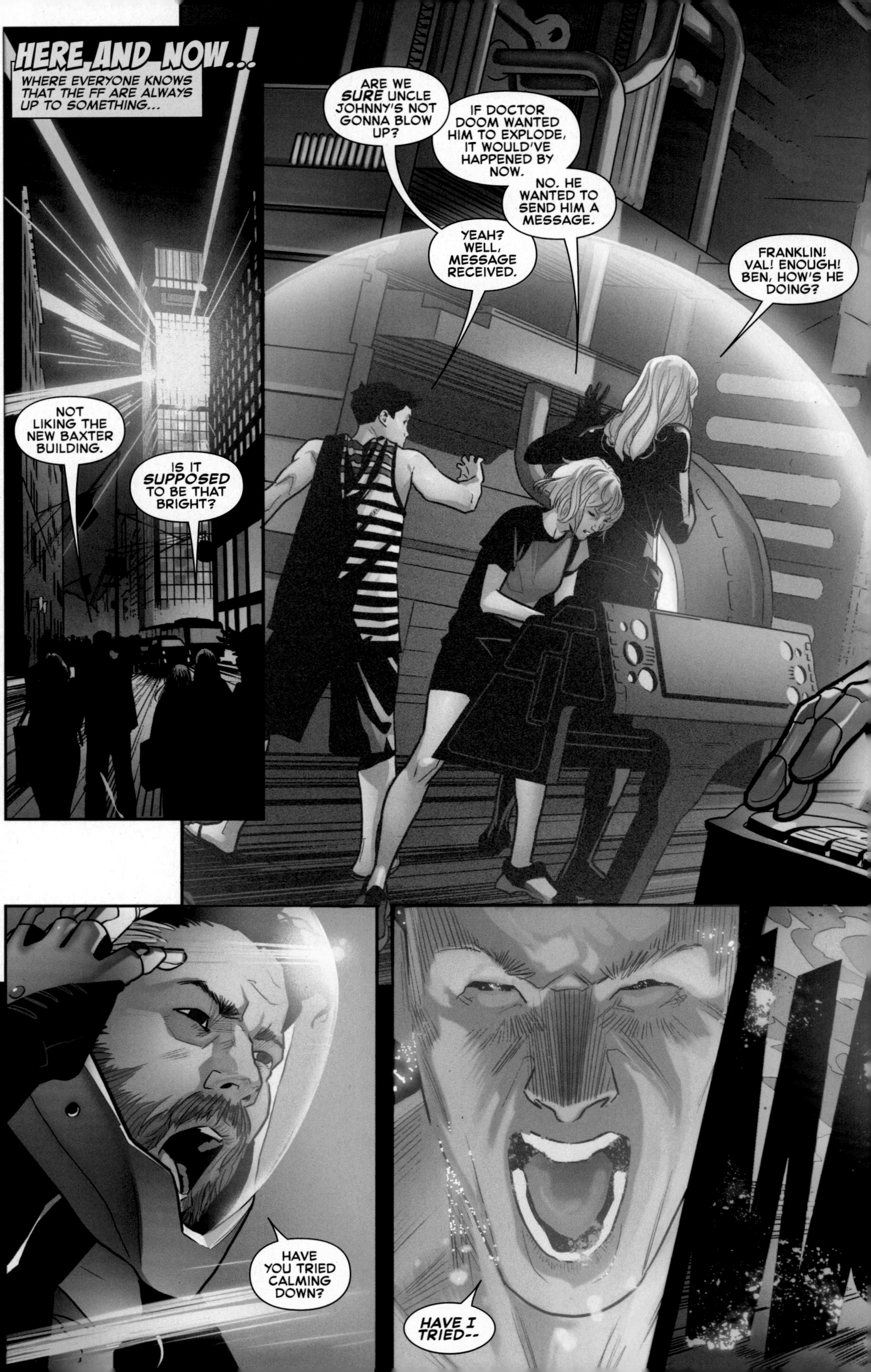
HERE AND NOW...!
WHERE EVERYONE KNOWS THAT THE FF ARE ALWAYS UP TO SOMETHING...
NOT LIKING THE NEW BAXTER BUILDING.
IS IT SUPPOSED TO BE THAT BRIGHT?
ARE WE SURE UNCLE JOHNNY'S NOT GONNA BLOW UP?
IF DOCTOR DOOM WANTED HIM TO EXPLODE, IT WOULD'VE HAPPENED BY NOW.
NO. HE WANTED TO SEND HIM A MESSAGE.
YEAH? WELL, MESSAGE RECEIVED.
FRANKLIN! VAL! ENOUGH! BEN, HOW'S HE DOING?
HAVE YOU TRIED CALMING DOWN?
HAVE I TRIED--

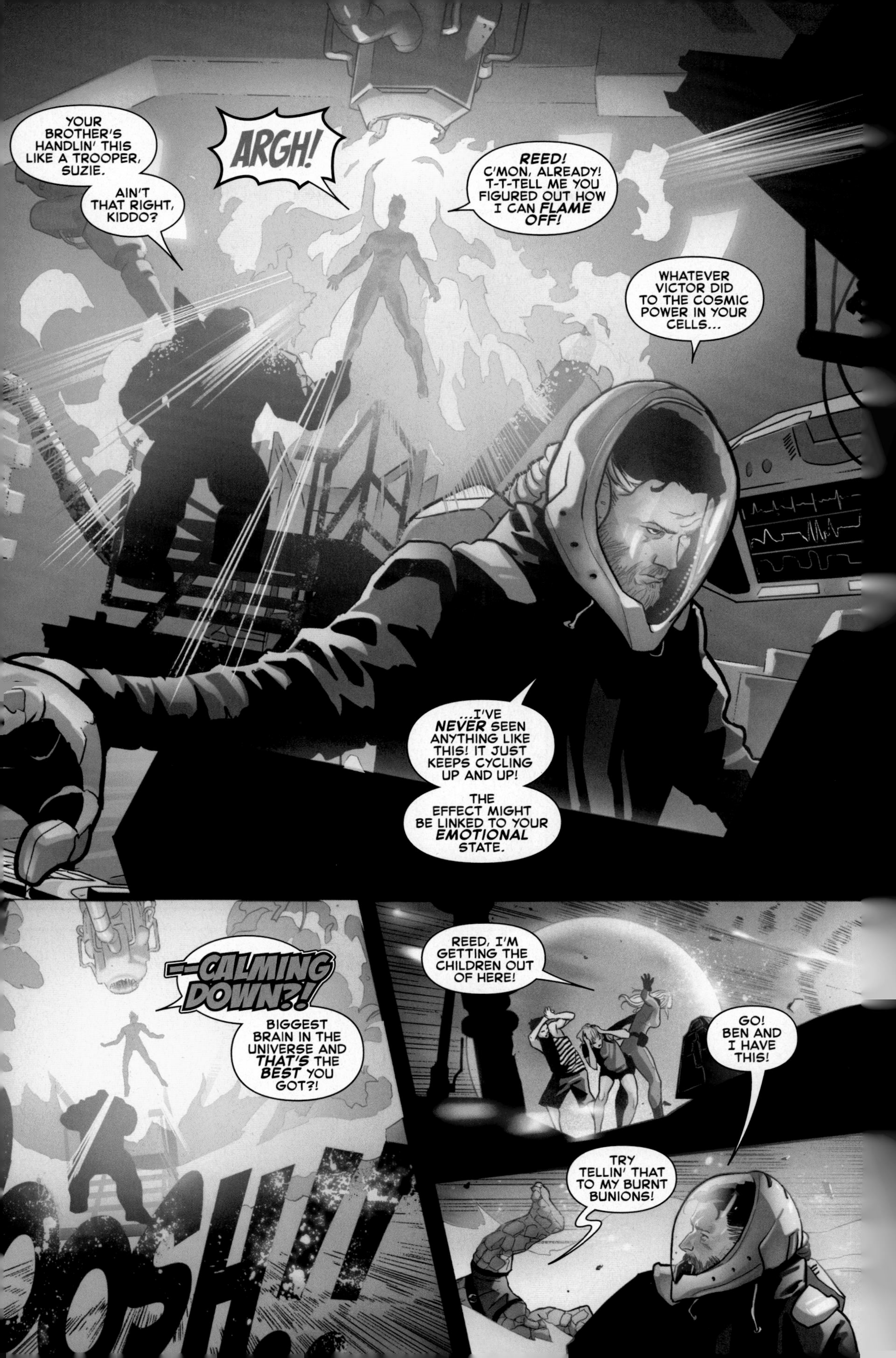

YOUR BROTHER'S HANDLIN' THIS LIKE A TROOPER, SUZIE.
AIN'T THAT RIGHT, KIDDO?
ARGH!
REED! C'MON, ALREADY! T-T-TELL ME YOU FIGURED OUT HOW I CAN FLAME OFF!
WHATEVER VICTOR DID TO THE COSMIC POWER IN YOUR CELLS...
...I'VE NEVER SEEN ANYTHING LIKE THIS! IT JUST KEEPS CYCLING UP AND UP!
THE EFFECT MIGHT BE LINKED TO YOUR EMOTIONAL STATE.
--CALMING DOWN?!
BIGGEST BRAIN IN THE UNIVERSE AND THAT'S THE BEST YOU GOT?!
REED, I'M GETTING THE CHILDREN OUT OF HERE!
GO! BEN AND I HAVE THIS!
TRY TELLIN' THAT TO MY BURNT BUNIONS!

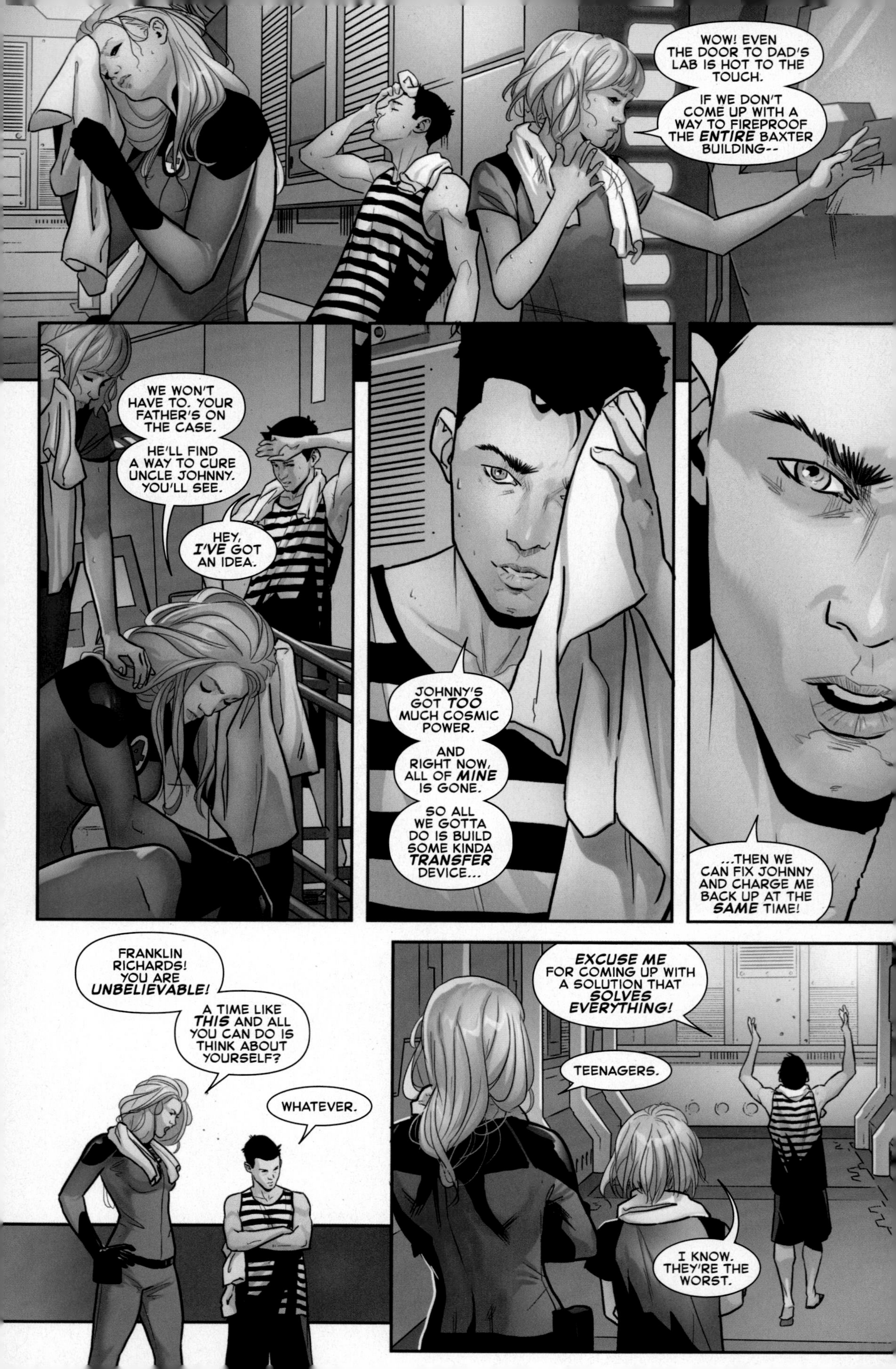
WOW! EVEN THE DOOR TO DAD'S LAB IS HOT TO THE TOUCH.
IF WE DON'T COME UP WITH A WAY TO FIREPROOF THE ENTIRE BAXTER BUILDING--
WE WON'T HAVE TO. YOUR FATHER'S ON THE CASE.
HE'LL FIND A WAY TO CURE UNCLE JOHNNY. YOU'LL SEE.
HEY, I'VE GOT AN IDEA.
JOHNNY'S GOT TOO MUCH COSMIC POWER.
AND RIGHT NOW, ALL OF MINE IS GONE.
SO ALL WE GOTTA DO IS BUILD SOME KINDA TRANSFER DEVICE...
...THEN WE CAN FIX JOHNNY AND CHARGE ME BACK UP AT THE SAME TIME!
FRANKLIN RICHARDS! YOU ARE UNBELIEVABLE!
A TIME LIKE THIS AND ALL YOU CAN DO IS THINK ABOUT YOURSELF?
WHATEVER.
EXCUSE ME FOR COMING UP WITH A SOLUTION THAT SOLVES EVERYTHING!
TEENAGERS.
I KNOW. THEY'RE THE WORST.

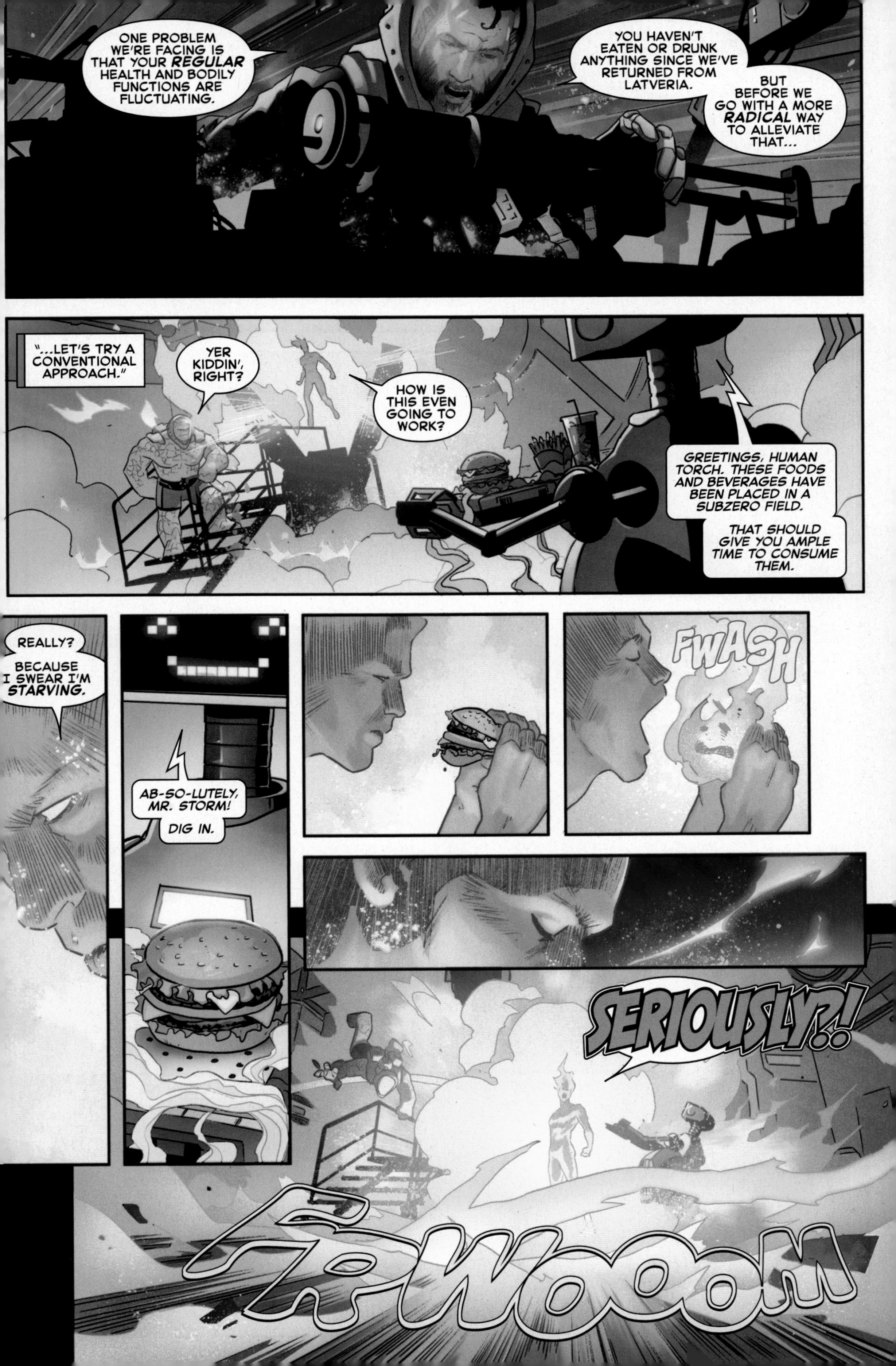
ONE PROBLEM WE'RE FACING IS THAT YOUR REGULAR HEALTH AND BODILY FUNCTIONS ARE FLUCTUATING.
YOU HAVEN'T EATEN OR DRUNK ANYTHING SINCE WE'VE RETURNED FROM LATVERIA.
BUT BEFORE WE GO WITH A MORE RADICAL WAY TO ALLEVIATE THAT...
"...LET'S TRY A CONVENTIONAL APPROACH."
YER KIDDIN', RIGHT?
HOW IS THIS EVEN GOING TO WORK?
GREETINGS, HUMAN TORCH. THESE FOODS AND BEVERAGES HAVE BEEN PLACED IN A SUBZERO FIELD.
THAT SHOULD GIVE YOU AMPLE TIME TO CONSUME THEM.
REALLY?
BECAUSE I SWEAR I'M STARVING.
AB-SO-LUTELY, MR. STORM!
DIG IN.
FWASH
SERIOUSLY?!
FWOOOM

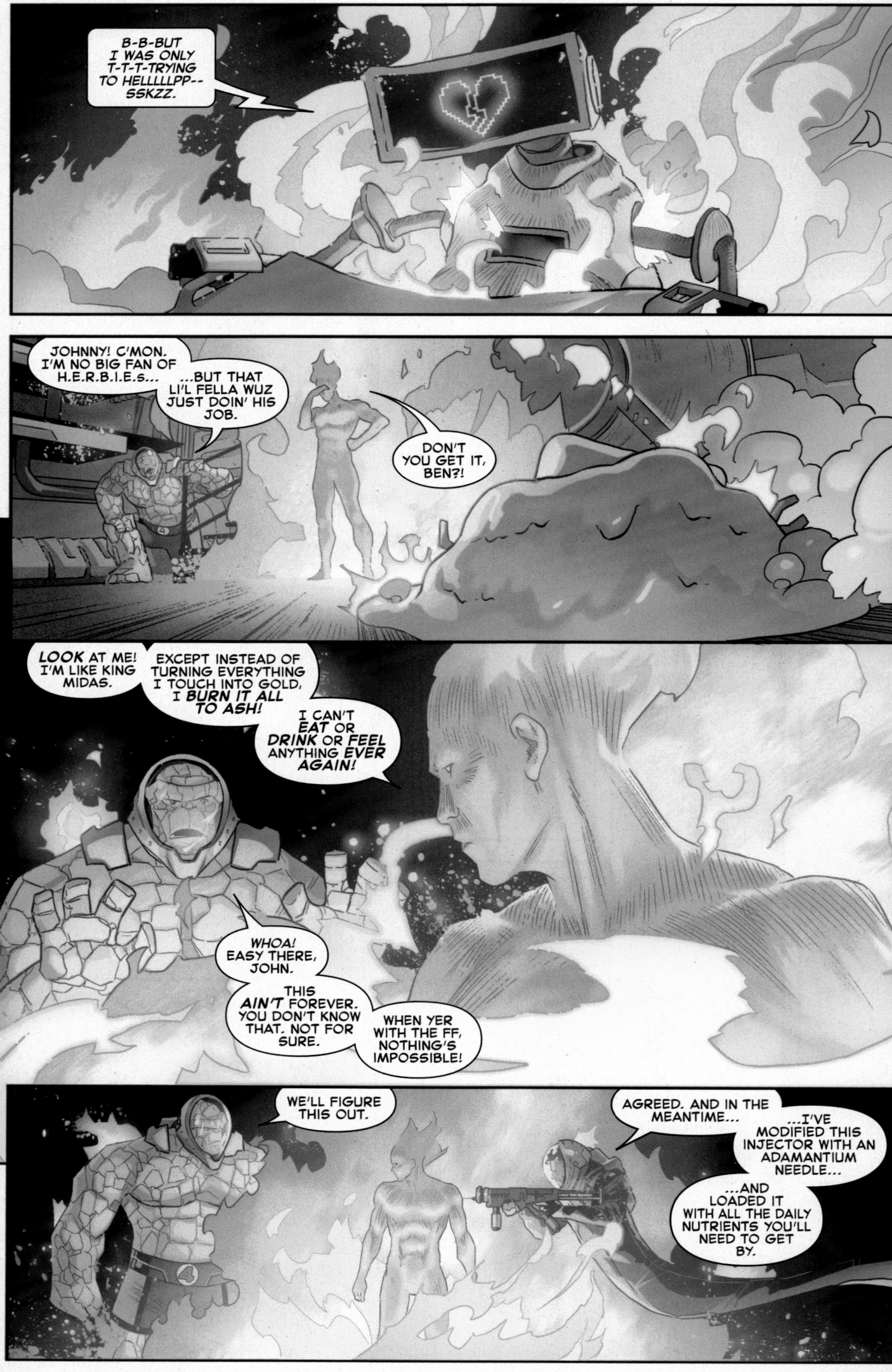
B-B-BUT I WAS ONLY T-T-T-TRYING TO HELLLLLPP-- SSKZZ.
JOHNNY! C'MON. I'M NO BIG FAN OF H.E.R.B.I.E.s...
...BUT THAT LI'L FELLA WUZ JUST DOIN' HIS JOB.
DON'T YOU GET IT, BEN?!
LOOK AT ME! I'M LIKE KING MIDAS.
EXCEPT INSTEAD OF TURNING EVERYTHING I TOUCH INTO GOLD, I BURN IT ALL TO ASH!
I CAN'T EAT OR DRINK OR FEEL ANYTHING EVER AGAIN!
WHOA! EASY THERE, JOHN.
THIS AIN'T FOREVER. YOU DON'T KNOW THAT. NOT FOR SURE.
WHEN YER WITH THE FF, NOTHING'S IMPOSSIBLE!
WE'LL FIGURE THIS OUT.
AGREED. AND IN THE MEANTIME...
...I'VE MODIFIED THIS INJECTOR WITH AN ADAMANTIUM NEEDLE...
...AND LOADED IT WITH ALL THE DAILY NUTRIENTS YOU'LL NEED TO GET BY.

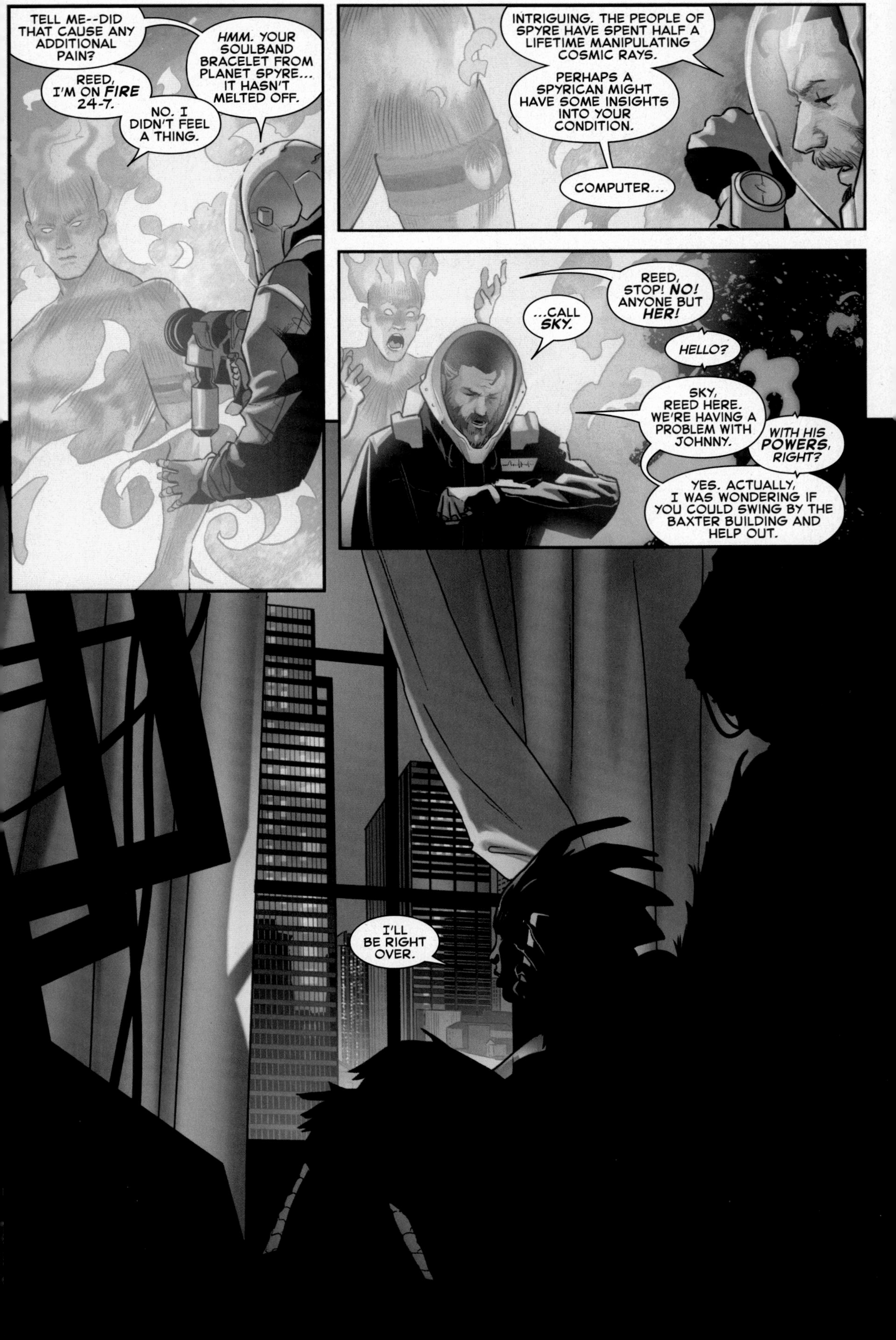
TELL ME--DID THAT CAUSE ANY ADDITIONAL PAIN?
REED, I'M ON *FIRE* 24-7.
NO. I DIDN'T FEEL A THING.
HMM. YOUR SOULBAND BRACELET FROM PLANET SPYRE... IT HASN'T MELTED OFF.
INTRIGUING. THE PEOPLE OF SPYRE HAVE SPENT HALF A LIFETIME MANIPULATING COSMIC RAYS.
PERHAPS A SPYRICAN MIGHT HAVE SOME INSIGHTS INTO YOUR CONDITION.
COMPUTER...
...CALL *SKY.*
REED, STOP! *NO!* ANYONE BUT *HER!*
HELLO?
SKY, REED HERE. WE'RE HAVING A PROBLEM WITH JOHNNY.
WITH HIS POWERS, RIGHT?
YES. ACTUALLY, I WAS WONDERING IF YOU COULD SWING BY THE BAXTER BUILDING AND HELP OUT.
I'LL BE RIGHT OVER.

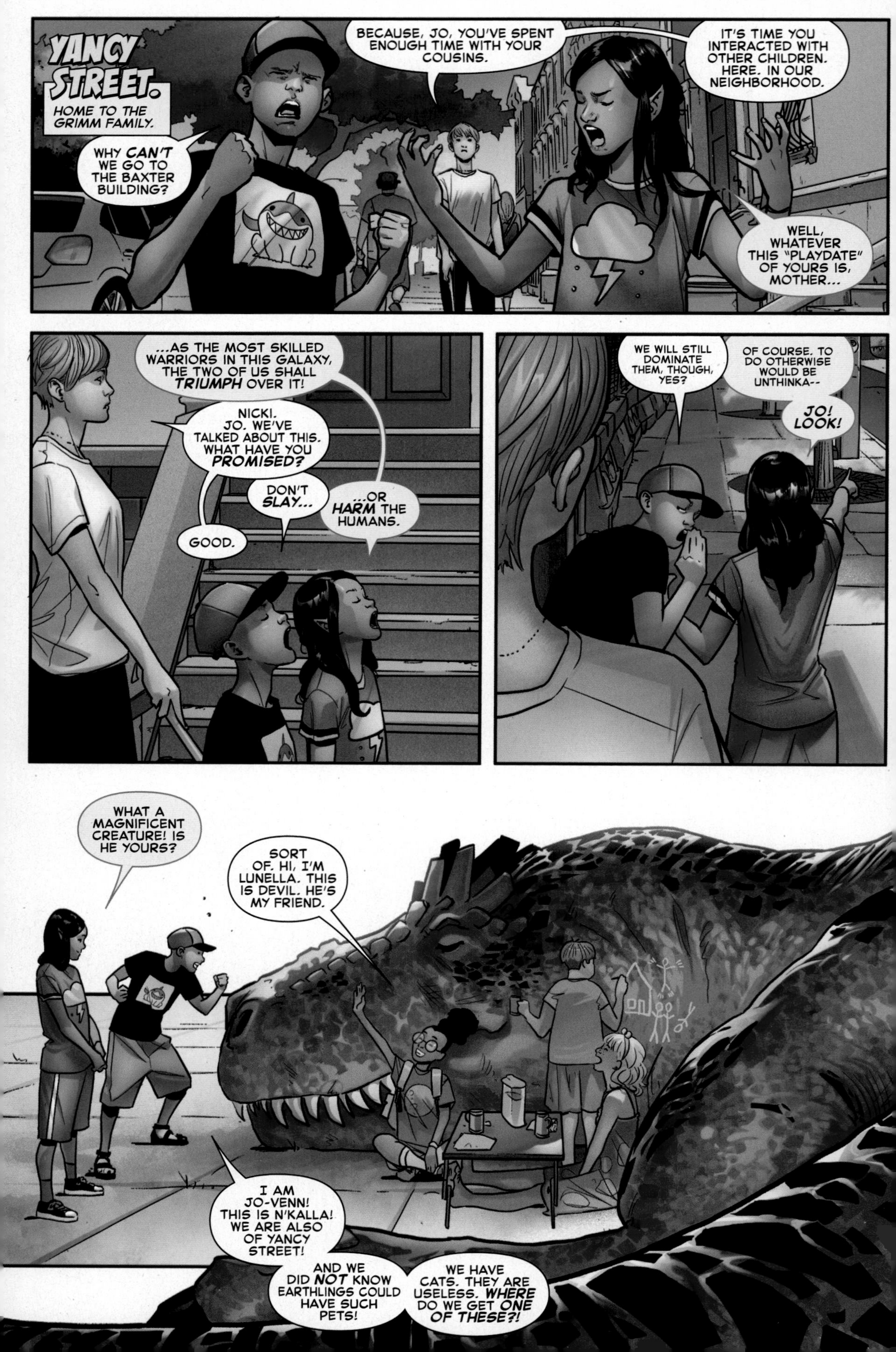
YANCY STREET.
HOME TO THE GRIMM FAMILY.
WHY CAN'T WE GO TO THE BAXTER BUILDING?
BECAUSE, JO, YOU'VE SPENT ENOUGH TIME WITH YOUR COUSINS.
IT'S TIME YOU INTERACTED WITH OTHER CHILDREN. HERE. IN OUR NEIGHBORHOOD.
WELL, WHATEVER THIS "PLAYDATE" OF YOURS IS, MOTHER...
...AS THE MOST SKILLED WARRIORS IN THIS GALAXY, THE TWO OF US SHALL TRIUMPH OVER IT!
NICKI. JO. WE'VE TALKED ABOUT THIS. WHAT HAVE YOU PROMISED?
DON'T SLAY...
...OR HARM THE HUMANS.
GOOD.
WE WILL STILL DOMINATE THEM, THOUGH, YES?
OF COURSE. TO DO OTHERWISE WOULD BE UNTHINKA--
JO! LOOK!
WHAT A MAGNIFICENT CREATURE! IS HE YOURS?
SORT OF. HI, I'M LUNELLA. THIS IS DEVIL. HE'S MY FRIEND.
I AM JO-VENN! THIS IS N'KALLA! WE ARE ALSO OF YANCY STREET!
AND WE DID NOT KNOW EARTHLINGS COULD HAVE SUCH PETS!
WE HAVE CATS. THEY ARE USELESS. WHERE DO WE GET ONE OF THESE?!

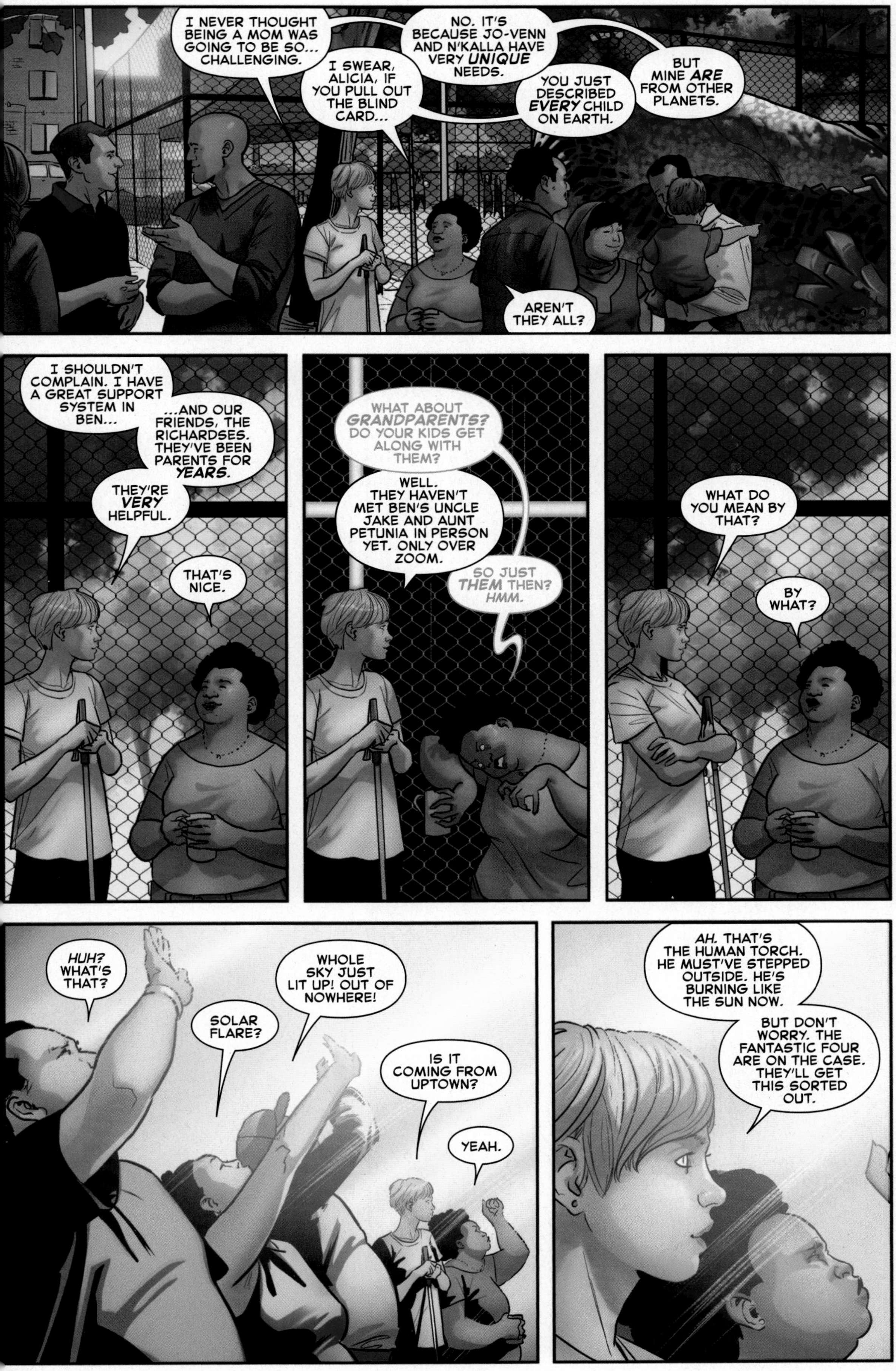

I NEVER THOUGHT BEING A MOM WAS GOING TO BE SO... CHALLENGING.
I SWEAR, ALICIA, IF YOU PULL OUT THE BLIND CARD...
NO. IT'S BECAUSE JO-VENN AND N'KALLA HAVE VERY UNIQUE NEEDS.
YOU JUST DESCRIBED EVERY CHILD ON EARTH.
BUT MINE ARE FROM OTHER PLANETS.
AREN'T THEY ALL?
I SHOULDN'T COMPLAIN. I HAVE A GREAT SUPPORT SYSTEM IN BEN...
...AND OUR FRIENDS, THE RICHARDSES. THEY'VE BEEN PARENTS FOR YEARS.
THEY'RE VERY HELPFUL.
THAT'S NICE.
WHAT ABOUT GRANDPARENTS? DO YOUR KIDS GET ALONG WITH THEM?
WELL. THEY HAVEN'T MET BEN'S UNCLE JAKE AND AUNT PETUNIA IN PERSON YET. ONLY OVER ZOOM.
SO JUST THEM THEN? HMM.
WHAT DO YOU MEAN BY THAT?
BY WHAT?
HUH? WHAT'S THAT?
SOLAR FLARE?
WHOLE SKY JUST LIT UP! OUT OF NOWHERE!
IS IT COMING FROM UPTOWN?
YEAH.
AH. THAT'S THE HUMAN TORCH. HE MUST'VE STEPPED OUTSIDE. HE'S BURNING LIKE THE SUN NOW.
BUT DON'T WORRY. THE FANTASTIC FOUR ARE ON THE CASE. THEY'LL GET THIS SORTED OUT.

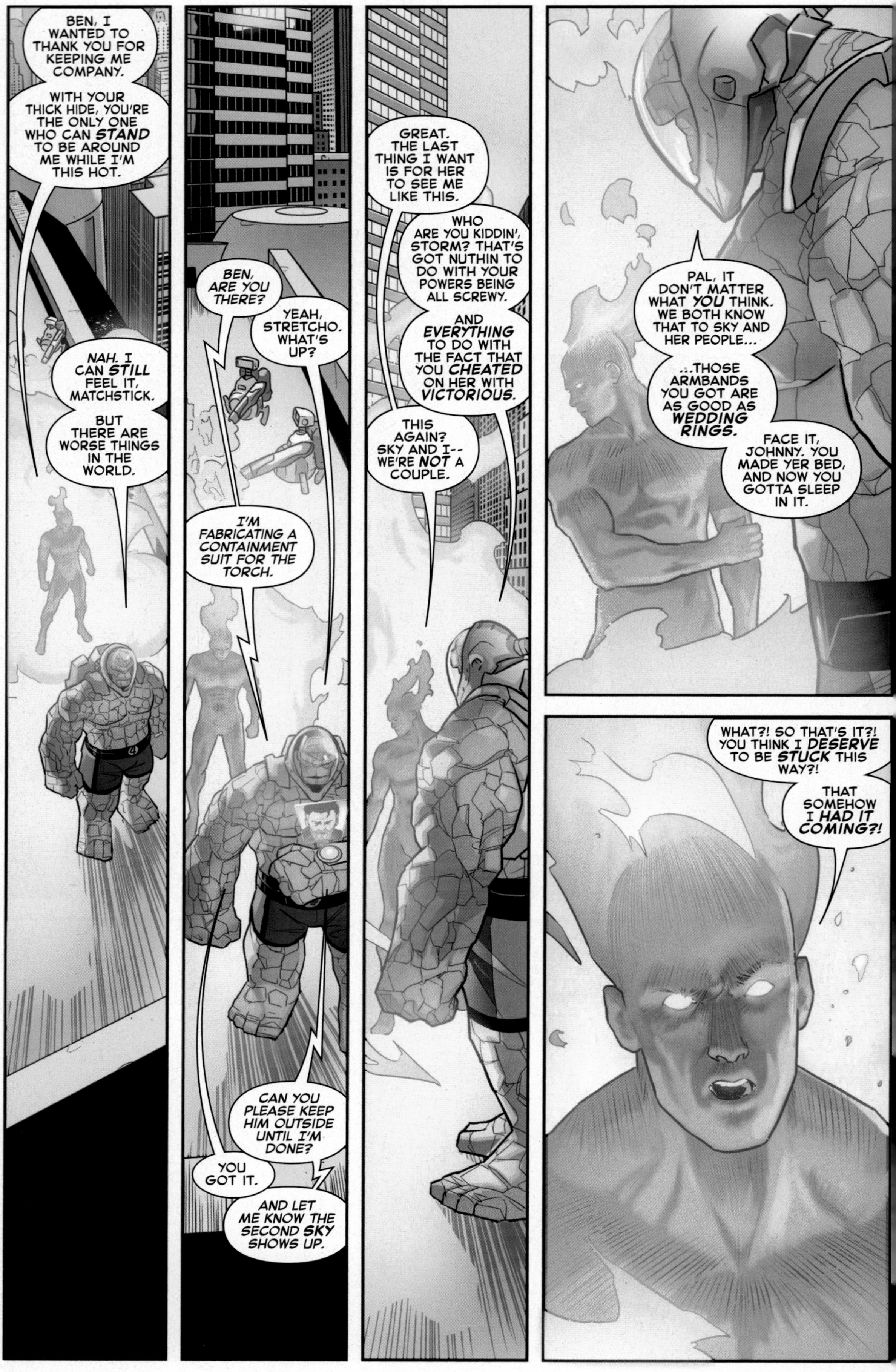
BEN, I WANTED TO THANK YOU FOR KEEPING ME COMPANY.
WITH YOUR THICK HIDE, YOU'RE THE ONLY ONE WHO CAN STAND TO BE AROUND ME WHILE I'M THIS HOT.
NAH. I CAN STILL FEEL IT, MATCHSTICK.
BUT THERE ARE WORSE THINGS IN THE WORLD.
BEN, ARE YOU THERE?
YEAH, STRETCHO. WHAT'S UP?
I'M FABRICATING A CONTAINMENT SUIT FOR THE TORCH.
CAN YOU PLEASE KEEP HIM OUTSIDE UNTIL I'M DONE?
YOU GOT IT.
AND LET ME KNOW THE SECOND SKY SHOWS UP.
GREAT. THE LAST THING I WANT IS FOR HER TO SEE ME LIKE THIS.
WHO ARE YOU KIDDIN', STORM? THAT'S GOT NUTHIN TO DO WITH YOUR POWERS BEING ALL SCREWY.
AND EVERYTHING TO DO WITH THE FACT THAT YOU CHEATED ON HER WITH VICTORIOUS.
THIS AGAIN? SKY AND I-- WE'RE NOT A COUPLE.
PAL, IT DON'T MATTER WHAT YOU THINK. WE BOTH KNOW THAT TO SKY AND HER PEOPLE...
...THOSE ARMBANDS YOU GOT ARE AS GOOD AS WEDDING RINGS.
FACE IT, JOHNNY. YOU MADE YER BED, AND NOW YOU GOTTA SLEEP IN IT.
WHAT?! SO THAT'S IT?! YOU THINK I DESERVE TO BE STUCK THIS WAY?!
THAT SOMEHOW I HAD IT COMING?!

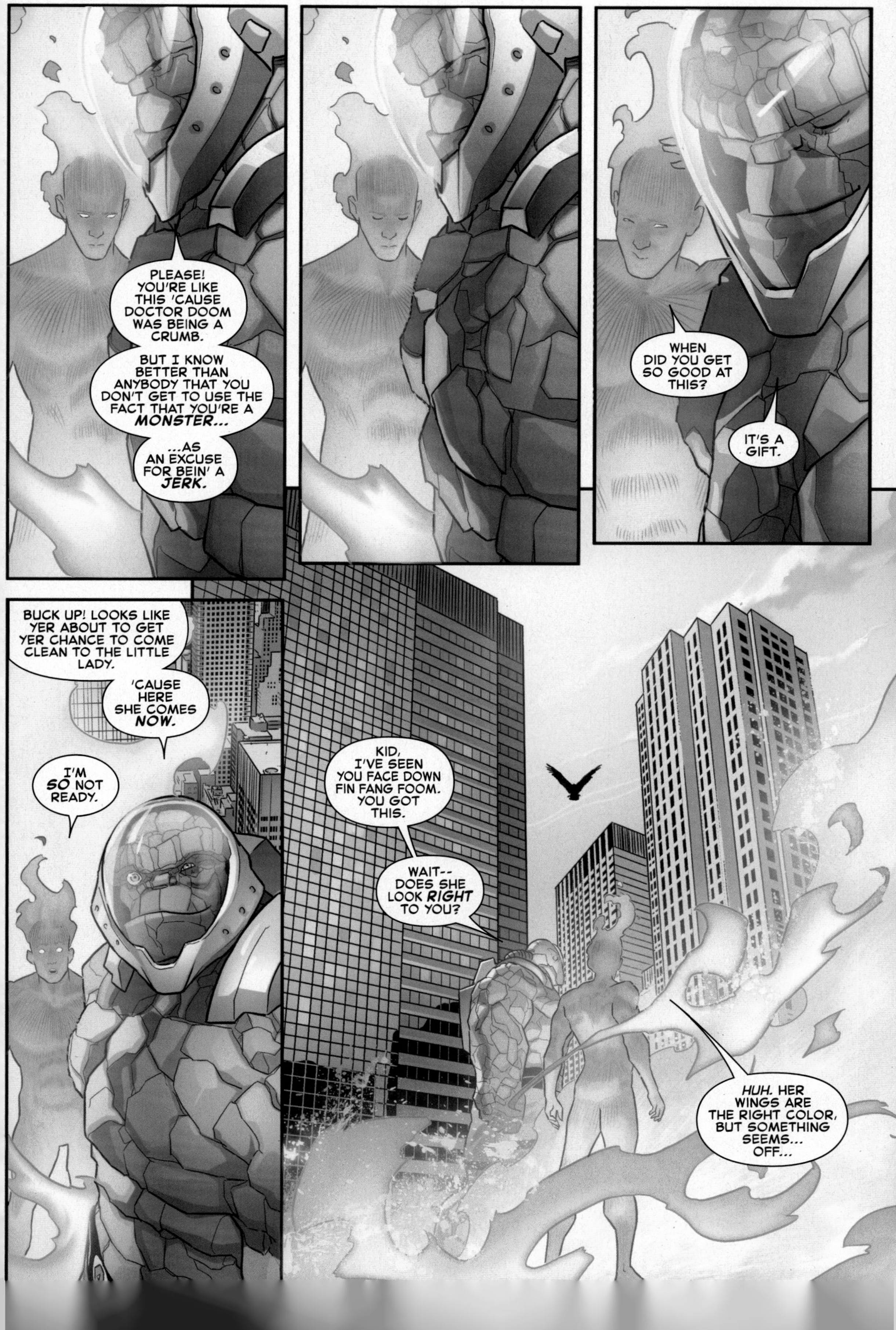
PLEASE! YOU'RE LIKE THIS 'CAUSE DOCTOR DOOM WAS BEING A CRUMB.
BUT I KNOW BETTER THAN ANYBODY THAT YOU DON'T GET TO USE THE FACT THAT YOU'RE A ***MONSTER...***
...AS AN EXCUSE FOR BEIN' A ***JERK.***
WHEN DID YOU GET SO GOOD AT THIS?
IT'S A GIFT.
BUCK UP! LOOKS LIKE YER ABOUT TO GET YER CHANCE TO COME CLEAN TO THE LITTLE LADY.
'CAUSE HERE SHE COMES ***NOW.***
I'M ***SO*** NOT READY.
KID, I'VE SEEN YOU FACE DOWN FIN FANG FOOM. YOU GOT THIS.
WAIT-- DOES SHE LOOK ***RIGHT*** TO YOU?
HUH. HER WINGS ARE THE RIGHT COLOR, BUT SOMETHING SEEMS... OFF...

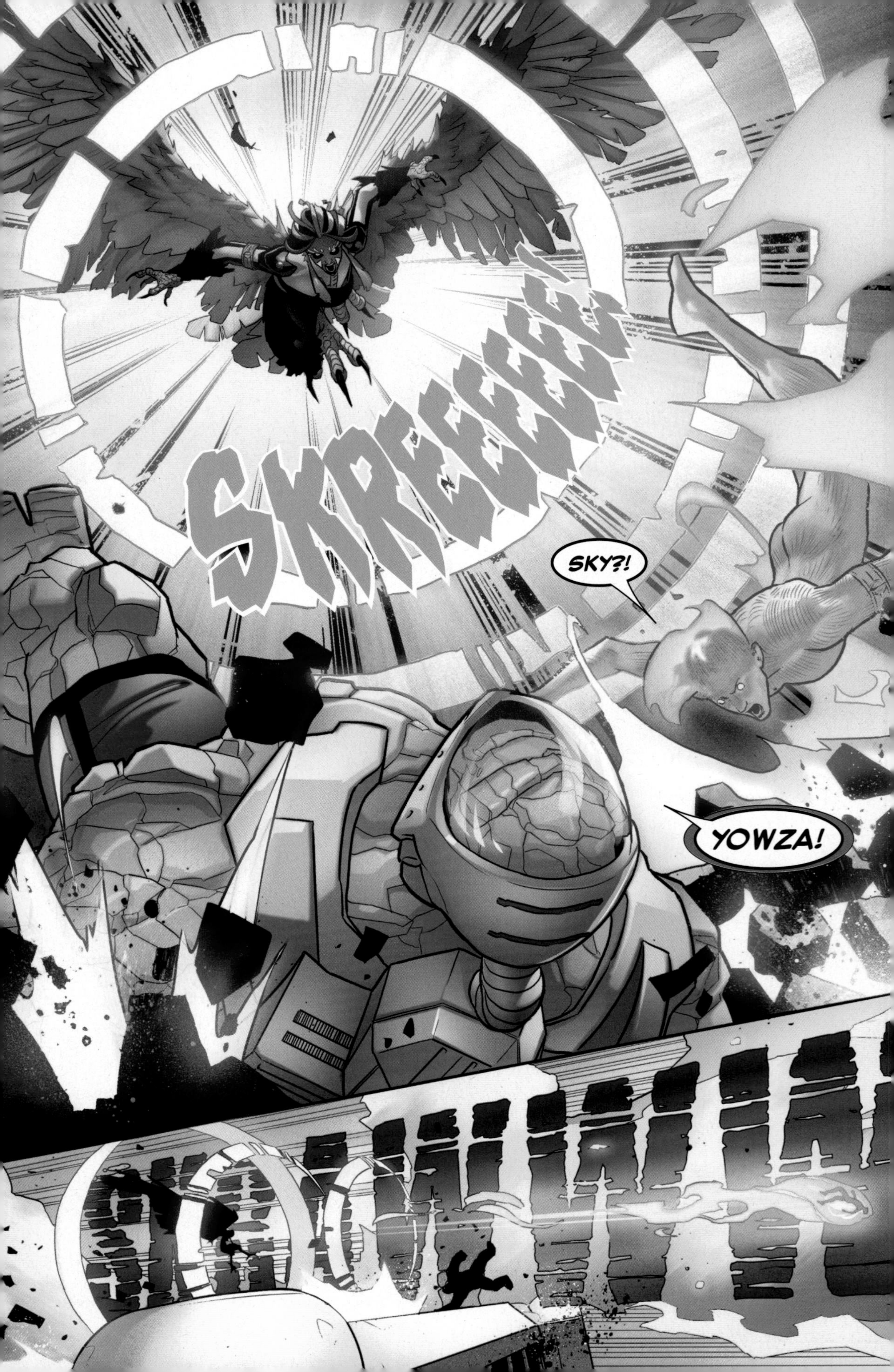
SKREEEEEE
SKY?!
YOWZA!

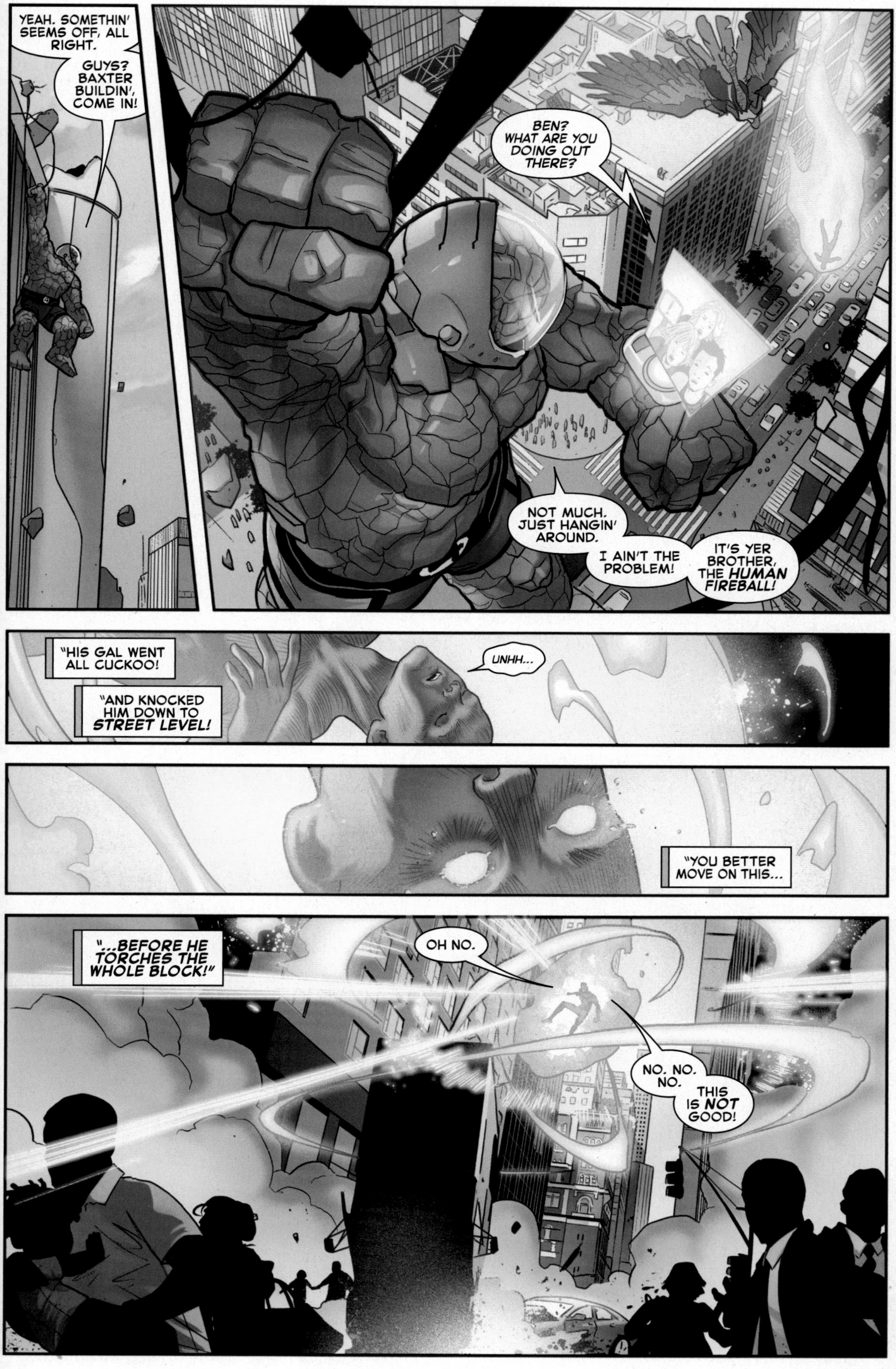
YEAH. SOMETHIN' SEEMS OFF, ALL RIGHT.
GUYS? BAXTER BUILDIN', COME IN!
BEN? WHAT ARE YOU DOING OUT THERE?
NOT MUCH. JUST HANGIN' AROUND.
I AIN'T THE PROBLEM!
IT'S YER BROTHER, THE HUMAN FIREBALL!
"HIS GAL WENT ALL CUCKOO!
"AND KNOCKED HIM DOWN TO STREET LEVEL!
UNHH...
"YOU BETTER MOVE ON THIS...
"...BEFORE HE TORCHES THE WHOLE BLOCK!"
OH NO.
NO. NO. NO.
THIS IS NOT GOOD!

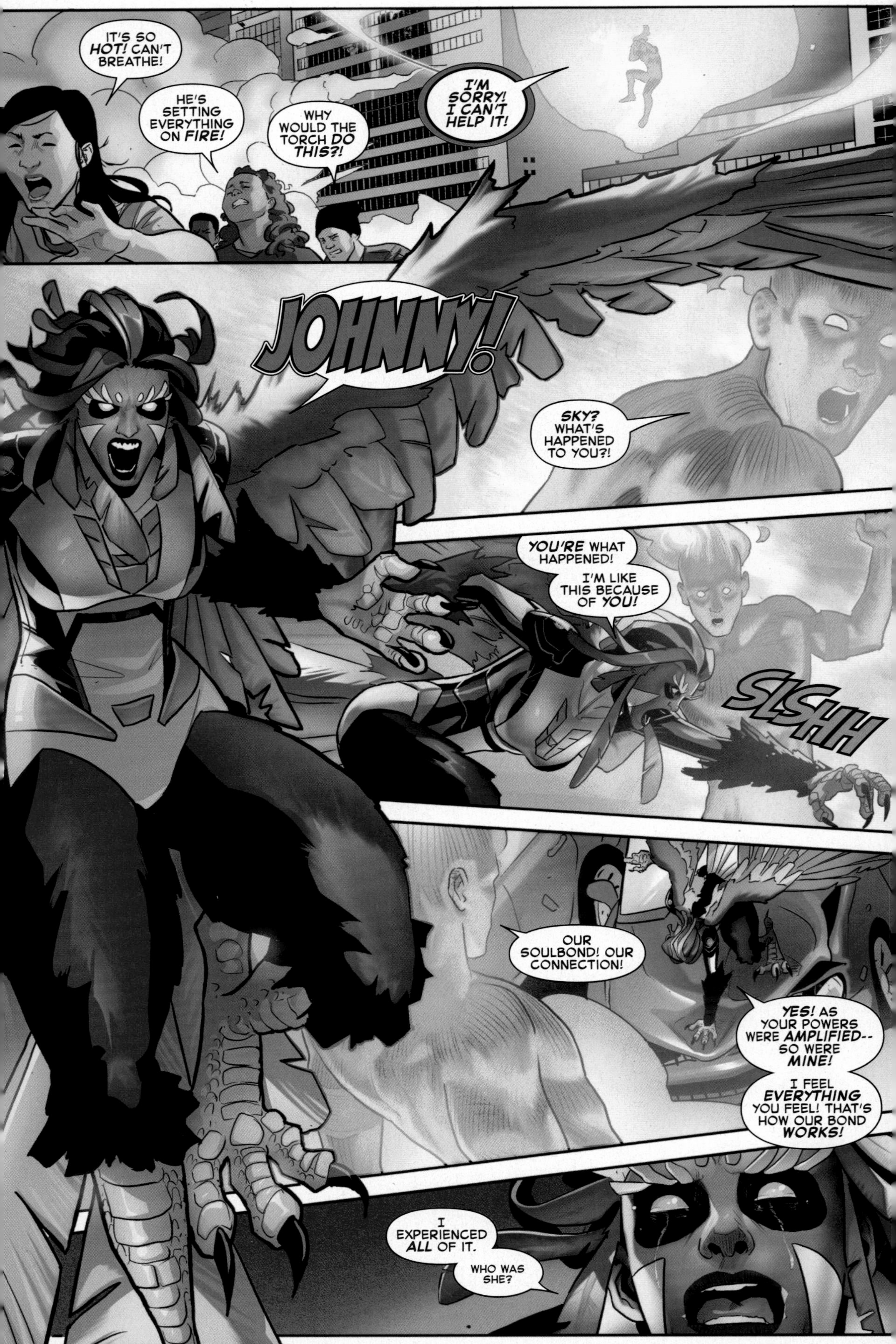
IT'S SO HOT! CAN'T BREATHE!
HE'S SETTING EVERYTHING ON FIRE!
WHY WOULD THE TORCH DO THIS?!
I'M SORRY! I CAN'T HELP IT!
JOHNNY!
SKY? WHAT'S HAPPENED TO YOU?!
YOU'RE WHAT HAPPENED!
I'M LIKE THIS BECAUSE OF YOU!
SLSHH
OUR SOULBOND! OUR CONNECTION!
YES! AS YOUR POWERS WERE AMPLIFIED-- SO WERE MINE!
I FEEL EVERYTHING YOU FEEL! THAT'S HOW OUR BOND WORKS!
I EXPERIENCED ALL OF IT.
WHO WAS SHE?

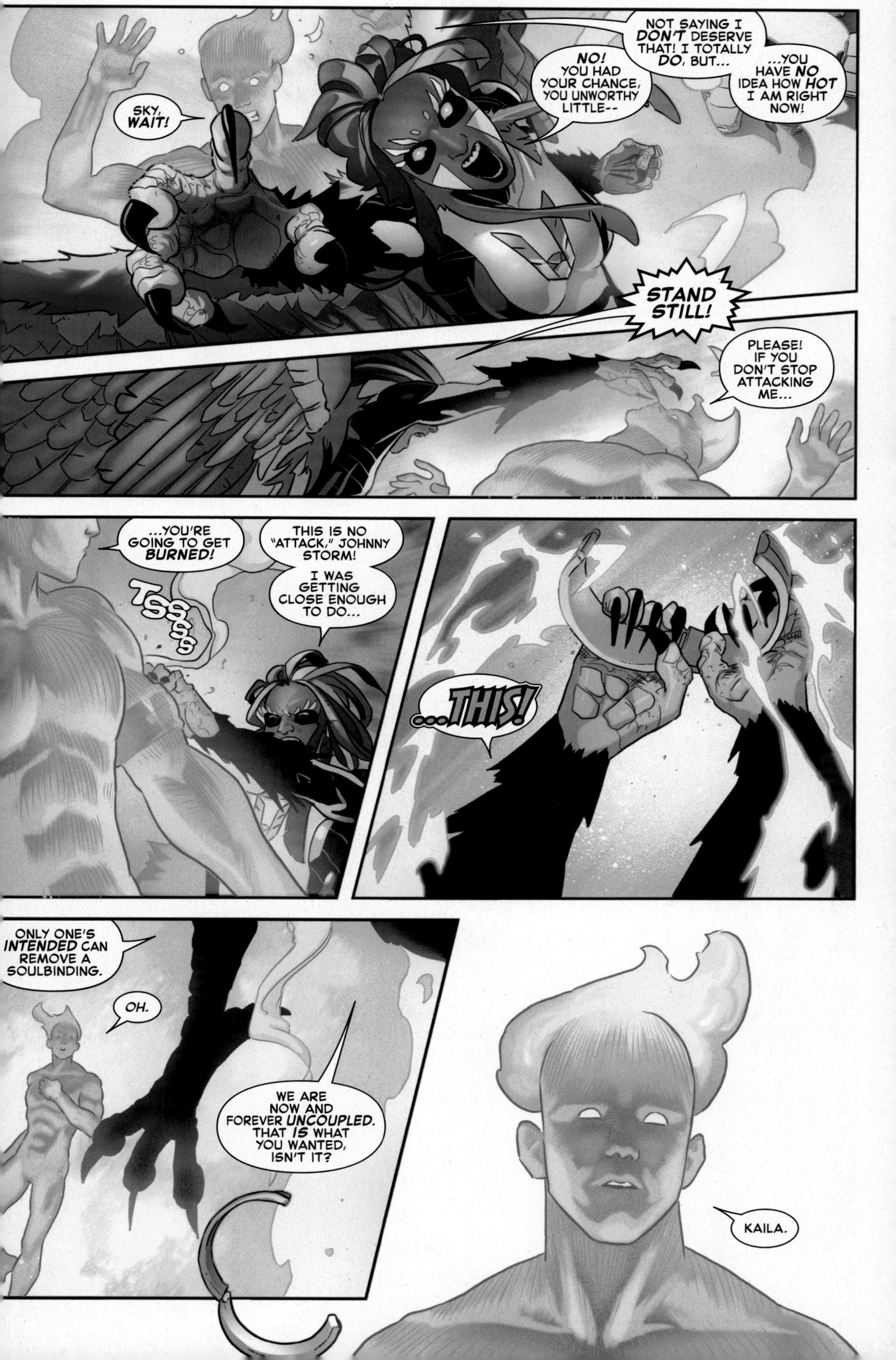

SKY, WAIT!
NO! YOU HAD YOUR CHANCE, YOU UNWORTHY LITTLE--
NOT SAYING I DON'T DESERVE THAT! I TOTALLY DO, BUT...
...YOU HAVE NO IDEA HOW HOT I AM RIGHT NOW!
STAND STILL!
PLEASE! IF YOU DON'T STOP ATTACKING ME...
...YOU'RE GOING TO GET BURNED!
TSSSS
THIS IS NO "ATTACK," JOHNNY STORM!
I WAS GETTING CLOSE ENOUGH TO DO...
...THIS!
ONLY ONE'S INTENDED CAN REMOVE A SOULBINDING.
OH.
WE ARE NOW AND FOREVER UNCOUPLED. THAT IS WHAT YOU WANTED, ISN'T IT?
KAILA.

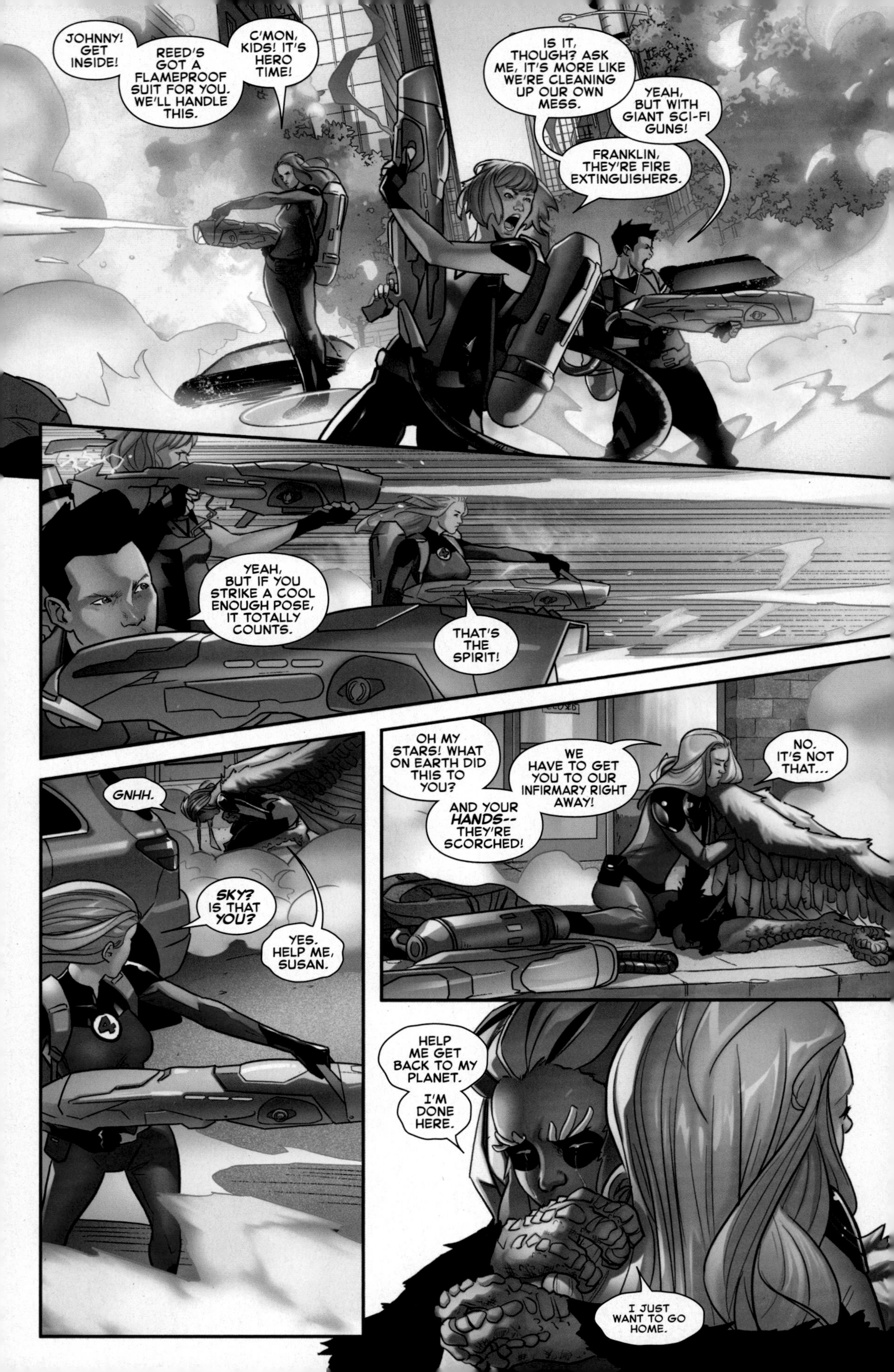
JOHNNY! GET INSIDE!
REED'S GOT A FLAMEPROOF SUIT FOR YOU. WE'LL HANDLE THIS.
C'MON, KIDS! IT'S HERO TIME!
IS IT, THOUGH? ASK ME, IT'S MORE LIKE WE'RE CLEANING UP OUR OWN MESS.
YEAH, BUT WITH GIANT SCI-FI GUNS!
FRANKLIN, THEY'RE FIRE EXTINGUISHERS.
YEAH, BUT IF YOU STRIKE A COOL ENOUGH POSE, IT TOTALLY COUNTS.
THAT'S THE SPIRIT!
GNHH.
SKY? IS THAT YOU?
YES. HELP ME, SUSAN.
OH MY STARS! WHAT ON EARTH DID THIS TO YOU?
AND YOUR HANDS-- THEY'RE SCORCHED!
WE HAVE TO GET YOU TO OUR INFIRMARY RIGHT AWAY!
NO. IT'S NOT THAT...
HELP ME GET BACK TO MY PLANET.
I'M DONE HERE.
I JUST WANT TO GO HOME.

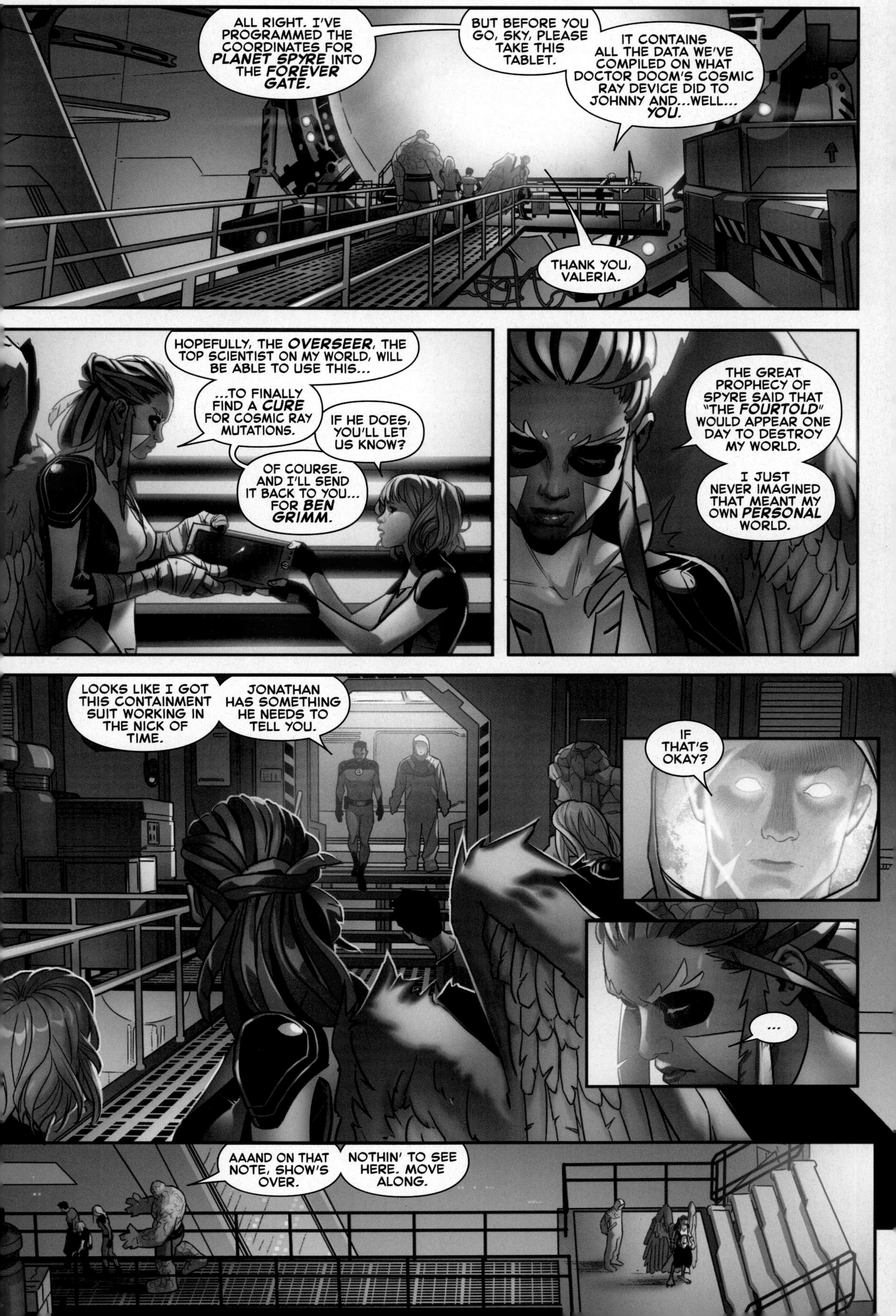
ALL RIGHT. I'VE PROGRAMMED THE COORDINATES FOR PLANET SPYRE INTO THE FOREVER GATE.
BUT BEFORE YOU GO, SKY, PLEASE TAKE THIS TABLET.
IT CONTAINS ALL THE DATA WE'VE COMPILED ON WHAT DOCTOR DOOM'S COSMIC RAY DEVICE DID TO JOHNNY AND...WELL... YOU.
THANK YOU, VALERIA.
HOPEFULLY, THE OVERSEER, THE TOP SCIENTIST ON MY WORLD, WILL BE ABLE TO USE THIS...
...TO FINALLY FIND A CURE FOR COSMIC RAY MUTATIONS.
IF HE DOES, YOU'LL LET US KNOW?
OF COURSE. AND I'LL SEND IT BACK TO YOU... FOR BEN GRIMM.
THE GREAT PROPHECY OF SPYRE SAID THAT "THE FOURTOLD" WOULD APPEAR ONE DAY TO DESTROY MY WORLD.
I JUST NEVER IMAGINED THAT MEANT MY OWN PERSONAL WORLD.
LOOKS LIKE I GOT THIS CONTAINMENT SUIT WORKING IN THE NICK OF TIME.
JONATHAN HAS SOMETHING HE NEEDS TO TELL YOU.
IF THAT'S OKAY?
...
AAAND ON THAT NOTE, SHOW'S OVER.
NOTHIN' TO SEE HERE. MOVE ALONG.

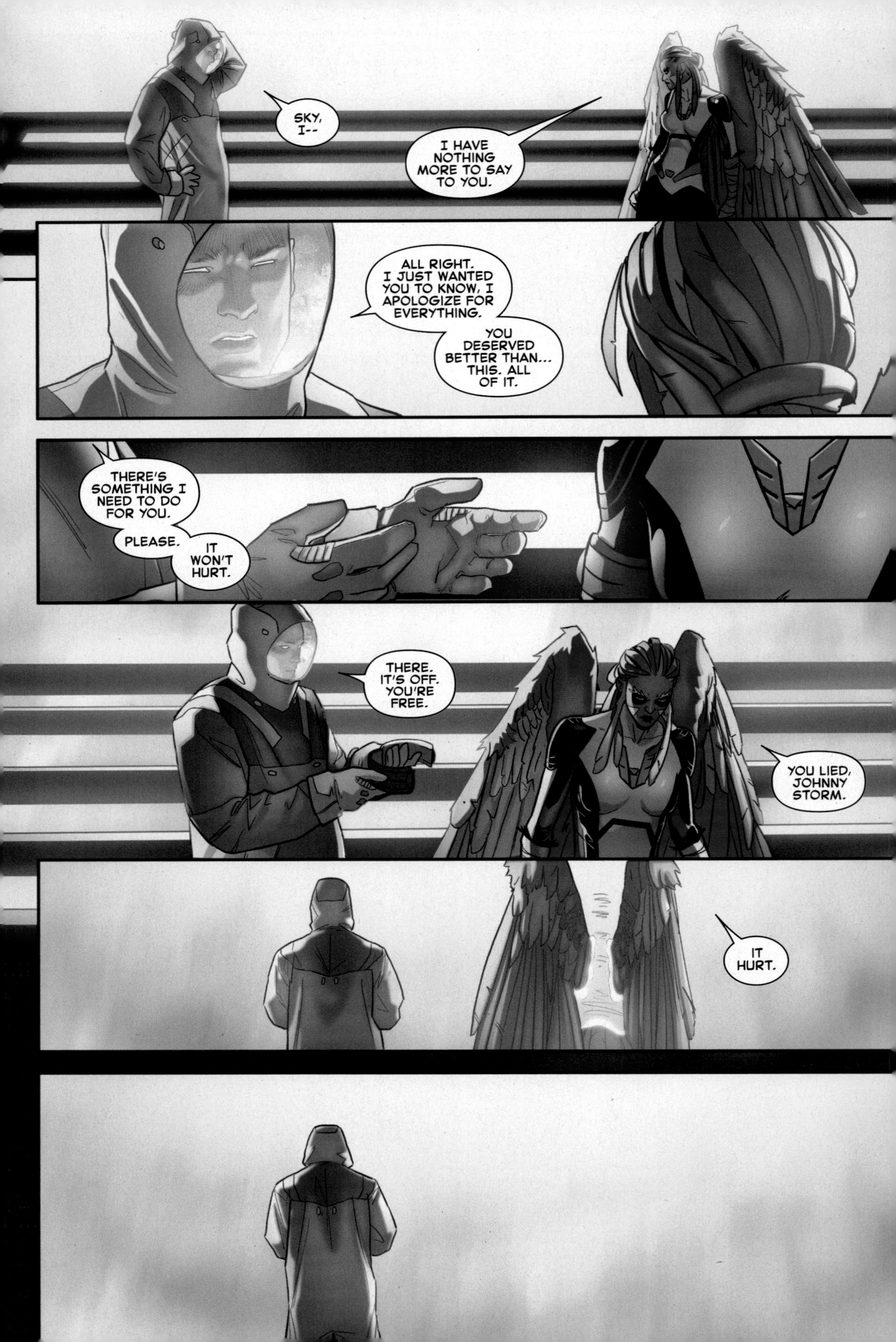
SKY, I--
I HAVE NOTHING MORE TO SAY TO YOU.
ALL RIGHT. I JUST WANTED YOU TO KNOW, I APOLOGIZE FOR EVERYTHING.
YOU DESERVED BETTER THAN... THIS. ALL OF IT.
THERE'S SOMETHING I NEED TO DO FOR YOU.
PLEASE.
IT WON'T HURT.
THERE. IT'S OFF. YOU'RE FREE.
YOU LIED, JOHNNY STORM.
IT HURT.

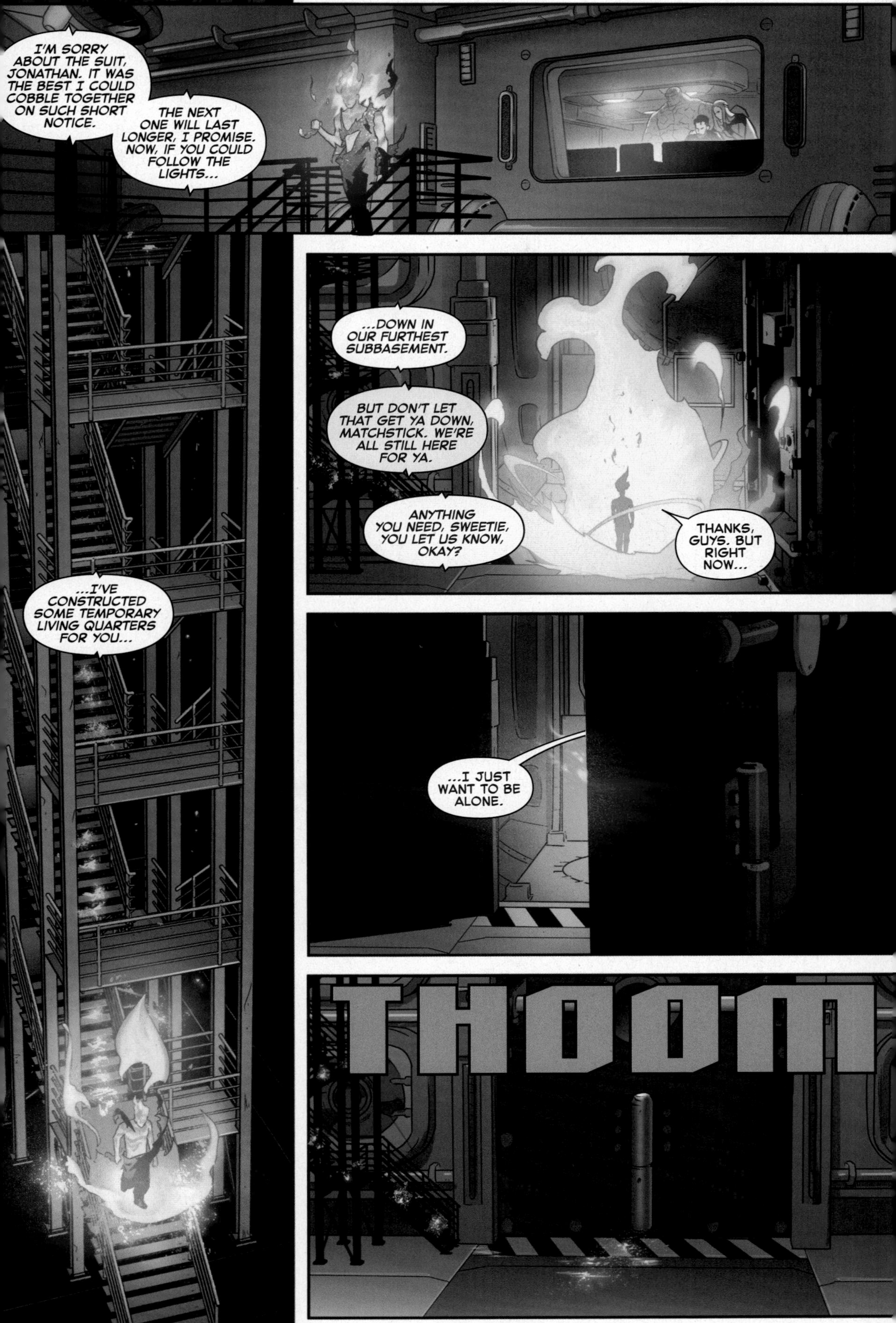
I'M SORRY ABOUT THE SUIT, JONATHAN. IT WAS THE BEST I COULD COBBLE TOGETHER ON SUCH SHORT NOTICE.
THE NEXT ONE WILL LAST LONGER, I PROMISE. NOW, IF YOU COULD FOLLOW THE LIGHTS...
...I'VE CONSTRUCTED SOME TEMPORARY LIVING QUARTERS FOR YOU...
...DOWN IN OUR FURTHEST SUBBASEMENT.
BUT DON'T LET THAT GET YA DOWN, MATCHSTICK. WE'RE ALL STILL HERE FOR YA.
ANYTHING YOU NEED, SWEETIE, YOU LET US KNOW, OKAY?
THANKS, GUYS. BUT RIGHT NOW...
...I JUST WANT TO BE ALONE.
THOOM

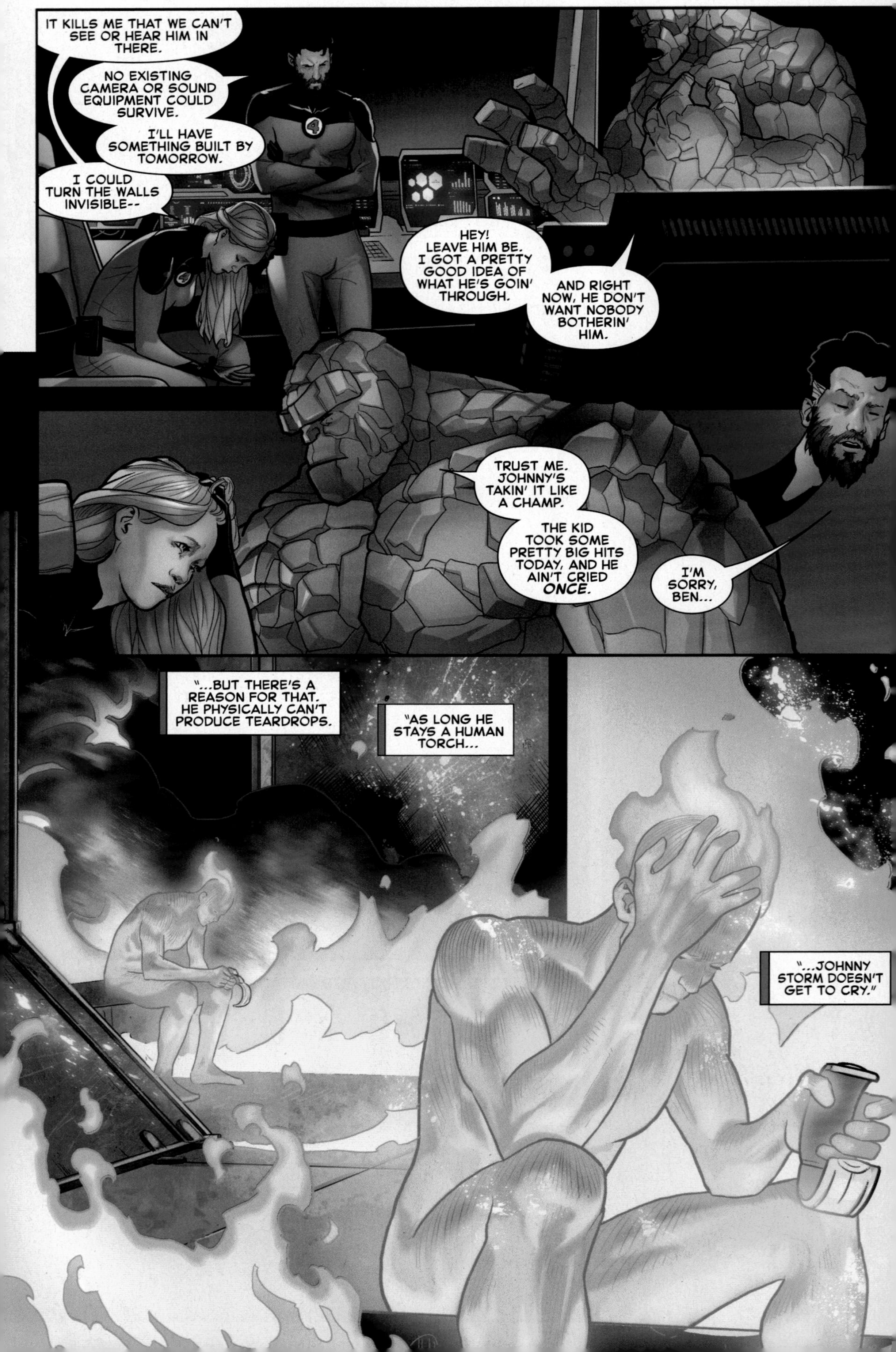
IT KILLS ME THAT WE CAN'T SEE OR HEAR HIM IN THERE.
NO EXISTING CAMERA OR SOUND EQUIPMENT COULD SURVIVE.
I'LL HAVE SOMETHING BUILT BY TOMORROW.
I COULD TURN THE WALLS INVISIBLE--
HEY! LEAVE HIM BE. I GOT A PRETTY GOOD IDEA OF WHAT HE'S GOIN' THROUGH.
AND RIGHT NOW, HE DON'T WANT NOBODY BOTHERIN' HIM.
TRUST ME. JOHNNY'S TAKIN' IT LIKE A CHAMP.
THE KID TOOK SOME PRETTY BIG HITS TODAY, AND HE AIN'T CRIED *ONCE.*
I'M SORRY, BEN...
"...BUT THERE'S A REASON FOR THAT. HE PHYSICALLY CAN'T PRODUCE TEARDROPS.
"AS LONG HE STAYS A HUMAN TORCH...
"...JOHNNY STORM DOESN'T GET TO CRY."

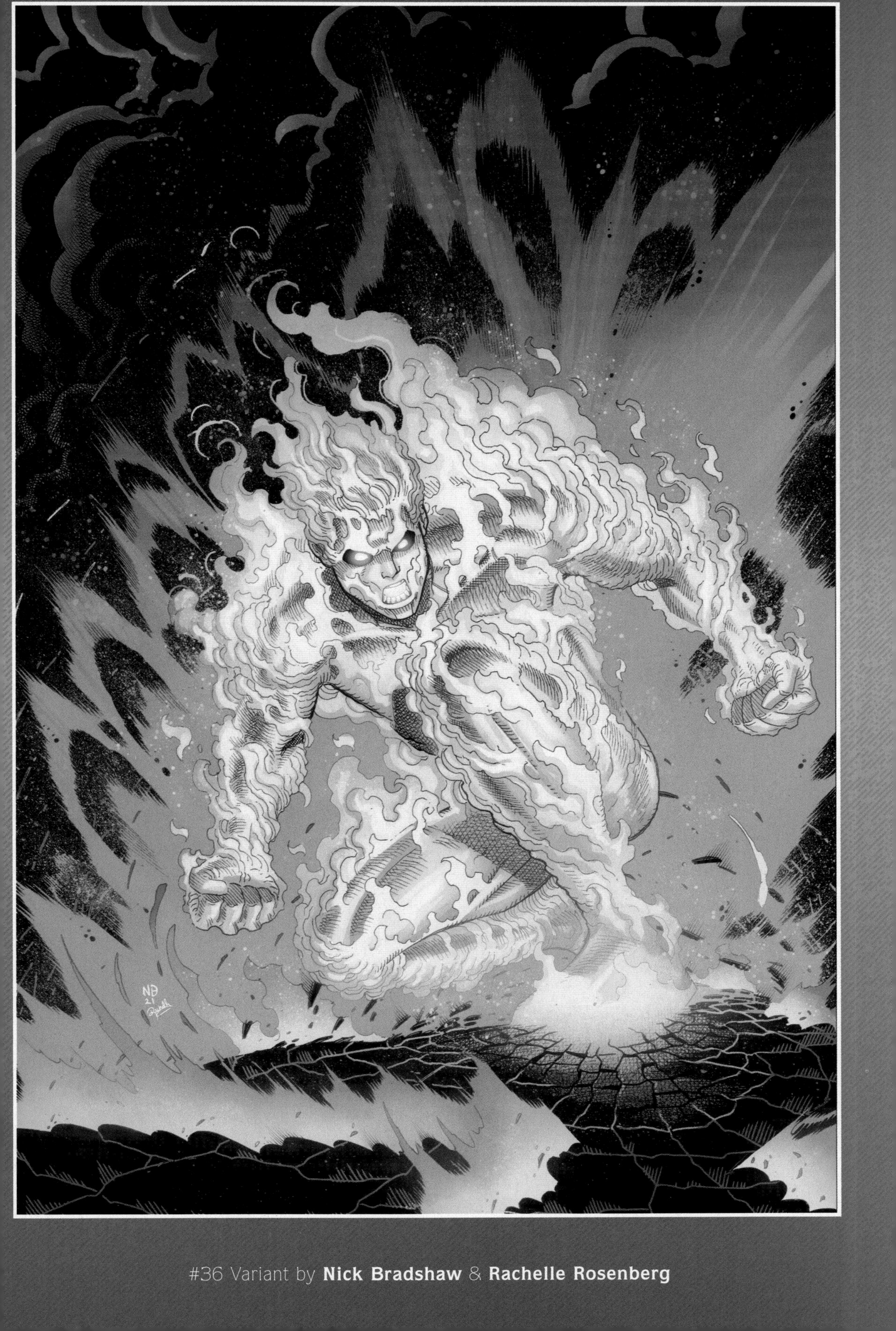

#36 Variant by **Nick Bradshaw** & **Rachelle Rosenberg**

37

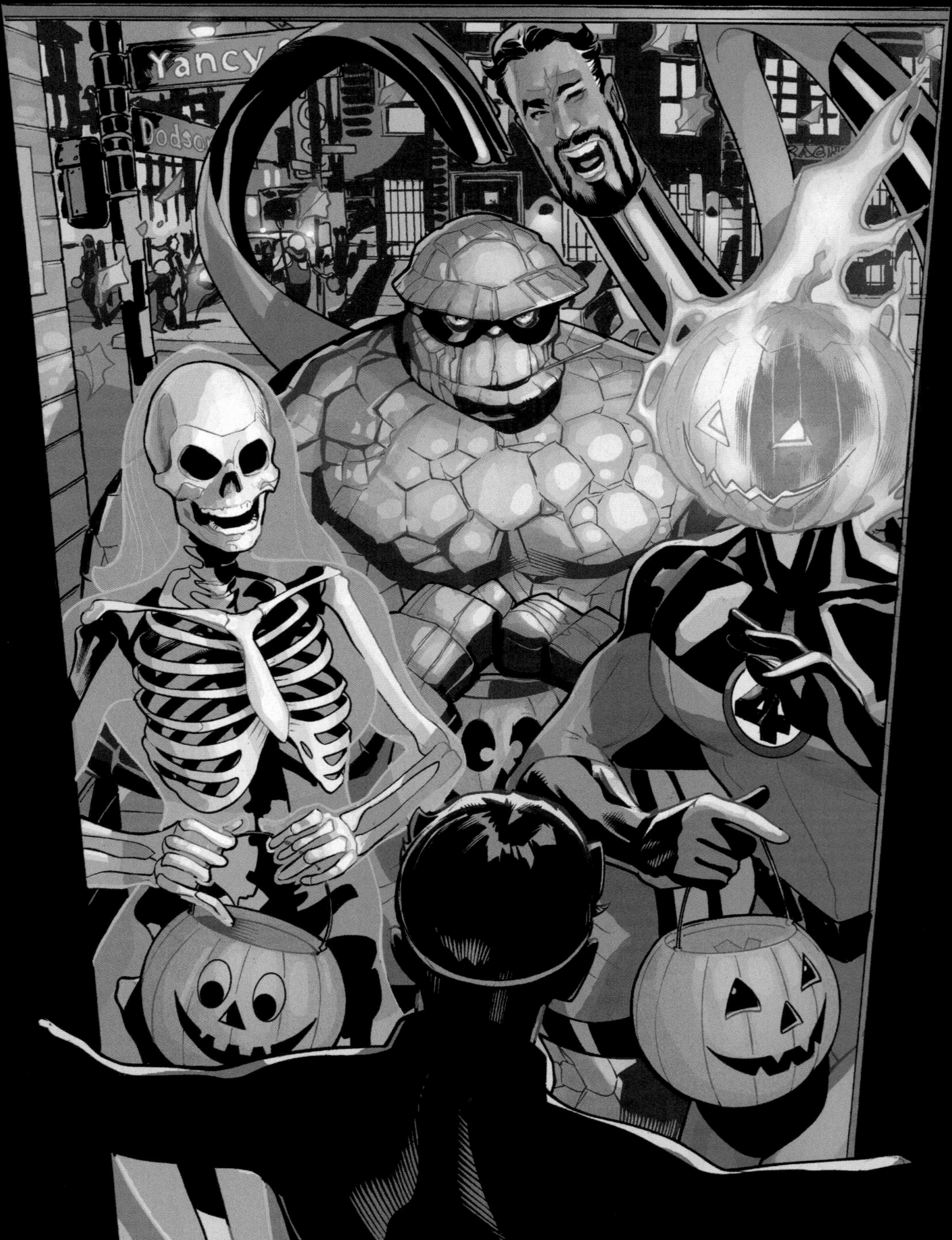
Yancy
Dodso

"There Are Monsters on Yancy Street"

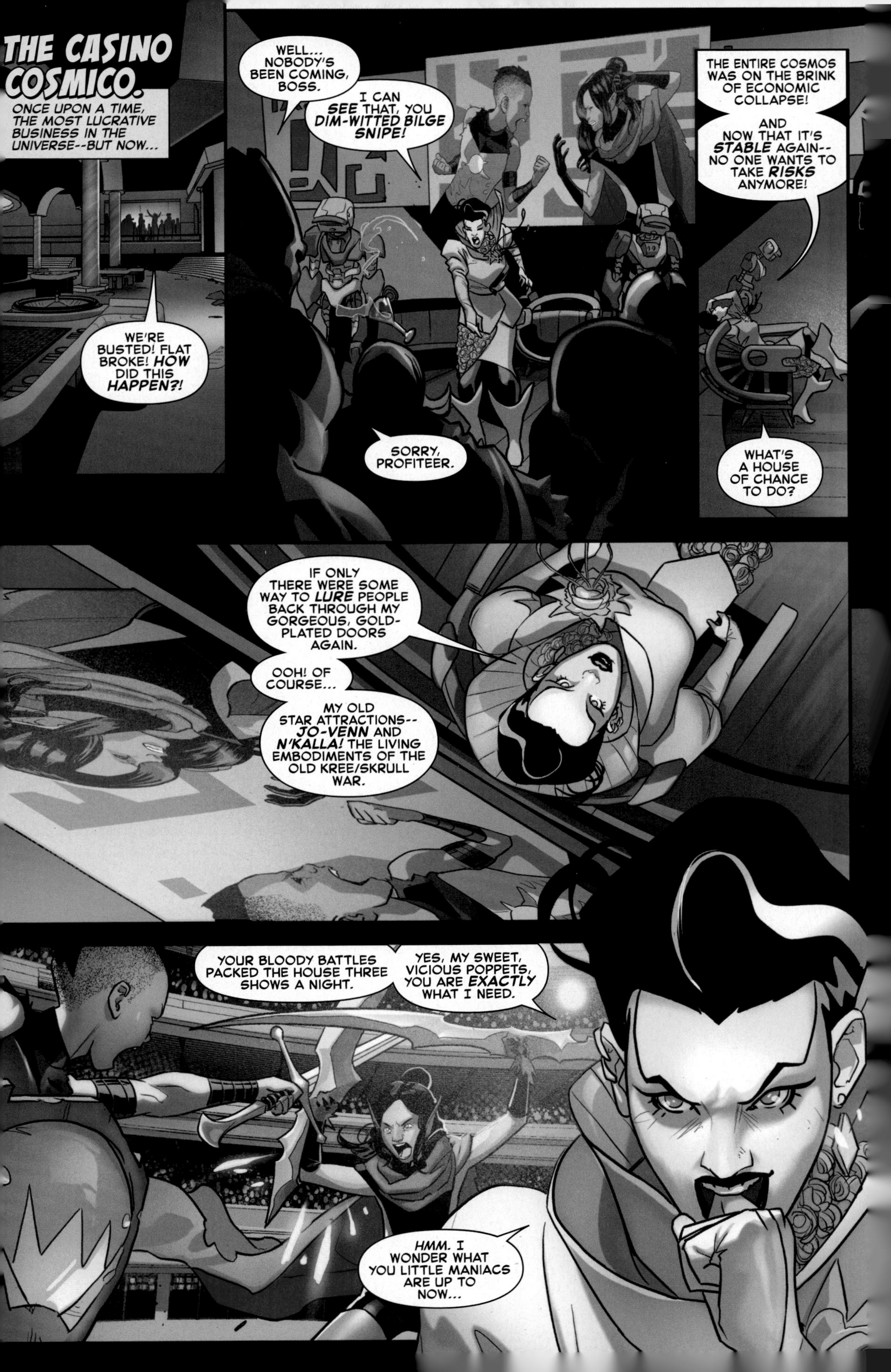
THE CASINO COSMICO.
ONCE UPON A TIME, THE MOST LUCRATIVE BUSINESS IN THE UNIVERSE--BUT NOW...
WE'RE BUSTED! FLAT BROKE! HOW DID THIS HAPPEN?!
WELL... NOBODY'S BEEN COMING, BOSS.
I CAN SEE THAT, YOU DIM-WITTED BILGE SNIPE!
SORRY, PROFITEER.
THE ENTIRE COSMOS WAS ON THE BRINK OF ECONOMIC COLLAPSE!
AND NOW THAT IT'S STABLE AGAIN-- NO ONE WANTS TO TAKE RISKS ANYMORE!
WHAT'S A HOUSE OF CHANCE TO DO?
IF ONLY THERE WERE SOME WAY TO LURE PEOPLE BACK THROUGH MY GORGEOUS, GOLD-PLATED DOORS AGAIN.
OOH! OF COURSE...
MY OLD STAR ATTRACTIONS-- JO-VENN AND N'KALLA! THE LIVING EMBODIMENTS OF THE OLD KREE/SKRULL WAR.
YOUR BLOODY BATTLES PACKED THE HOUSE THREE SHOWS A NIGHT.
YES, MY SWEET, VICIOUS POPPETS, YOU ARE EXACTLY WHAT I NEED.
HMM. I WONDER WHAT YOU LITTLE MANIACS ARE UP TO NOW...

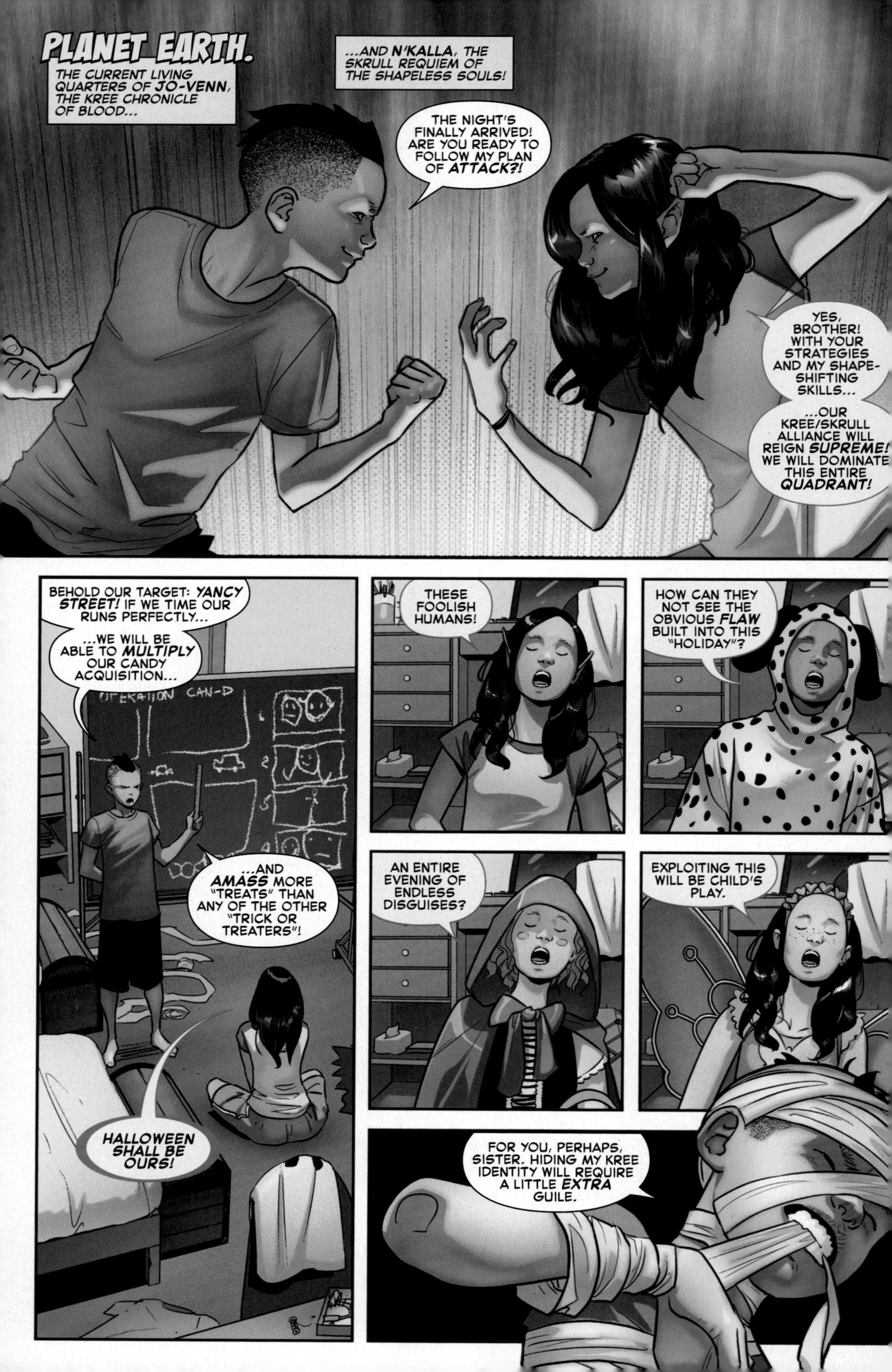
PLANET EARTH.
THE CURRENT LIVING QUARTERS OF JO-VENN, THE KREE CHRONICLE OF BLOOD...
...AND N'KALLA, THE SKRULL REQUIEM OF THE SHAPELESS SOULS!
THE NIGHT'S FINALLY ARRIVED! ARE YOU READY TO FOLLOW MY PLAN OF ATTACK?!
YES, BROTHER! WITH YOUR STRATEGIES AND MY SHAPE-SHIFTING SKILLS...
...OUR KREE/SKRULL ALLIANCE WILL REIGN SUPREME! WE WILL DOMINATE THIS ENTIRE QUADRANT!
BEHOLD OUR TARGET: YANCY STREET! IF WE TIME OUR RUNS PERFECTLY...
...WE WILL BE ABLE TO MULTIPLY OUR CANDY ACQUISITION...
OPERATION CAN-D
...AND AMASS MORE "TREATS" THAN ANY OF THE OTHER "TRICK OR TREATERS"!
HALLOWEEN SHALL BE OURS!
THESE FOOLISH HUMANS!
HOW CAN THEY NOT SEE THE OBVIOUS FLAW BUILT INTO THIS "HOLIDAY"?
AN ENTIRE EVENING OF ENDLESS DISGUISES?
EXPLOITING THIS WILL BE CHILD'S PLAY.
FOR YOU, PERHAPS, SISTER. HIDING MY KREE IDENTITY WILL REQUIRE A LITTLE EXTRA GUILE.

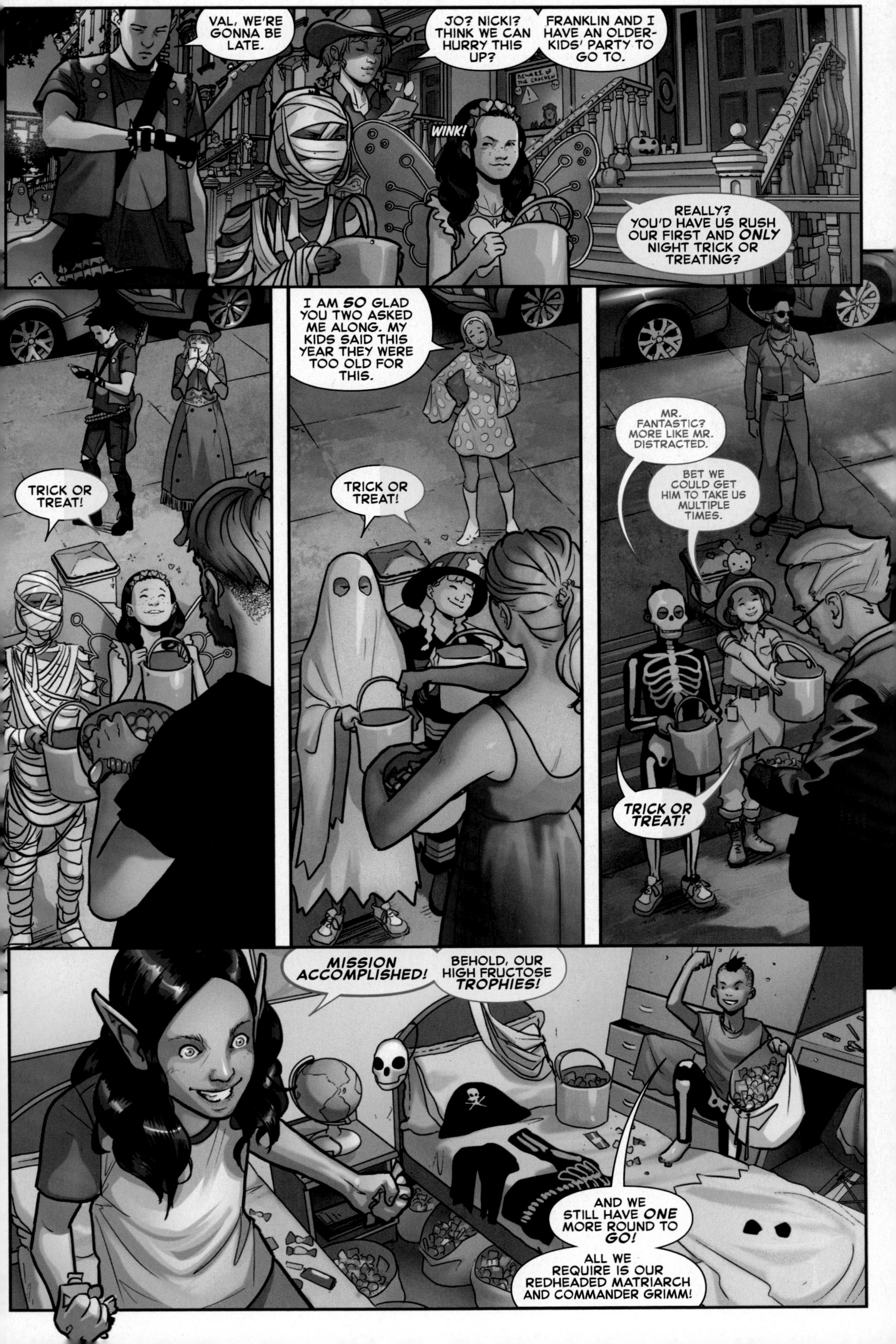
VAL, WE'RE GONNA BE LATE.
JO? NICKI? THINK WE CAN HURRY THIS UP?
FRANKLIN AND I HAVE AN OLDER-KIDS' PARTY TO GO TO.
BEWARE OF THE CRACKEN
WINK!
REALLY? YOU'D HAVE US RUSH OUR FIRST AND ONLY NIGHT TRICK OR TREATING?
TRICK OR TREAT!
I AM SO GLAD YOU TWO ASKED ME ALONG. MY KIDS SAID THIS YEAR THEY WERE TOO OLD FOR THIS.
TRICK OR TREAT!
MR. FANTASTIC? MORE LIKE MR. DISTRACTED.
BET WE COULD GET HIM TO TAKE US MULTIPLE TIMES.
TRICK OR TREAT!
MISSION ACCOMPLISHED!
BEHOLD, OUR HIGH FRUCTOSE TROPHIES!
AND WE STILL HAVE ONE MORE ROUND TO GO!
ALL WE REQUIRE IS OUR REDHEADED MATRIARCH AND COMMANDER GRIMM!

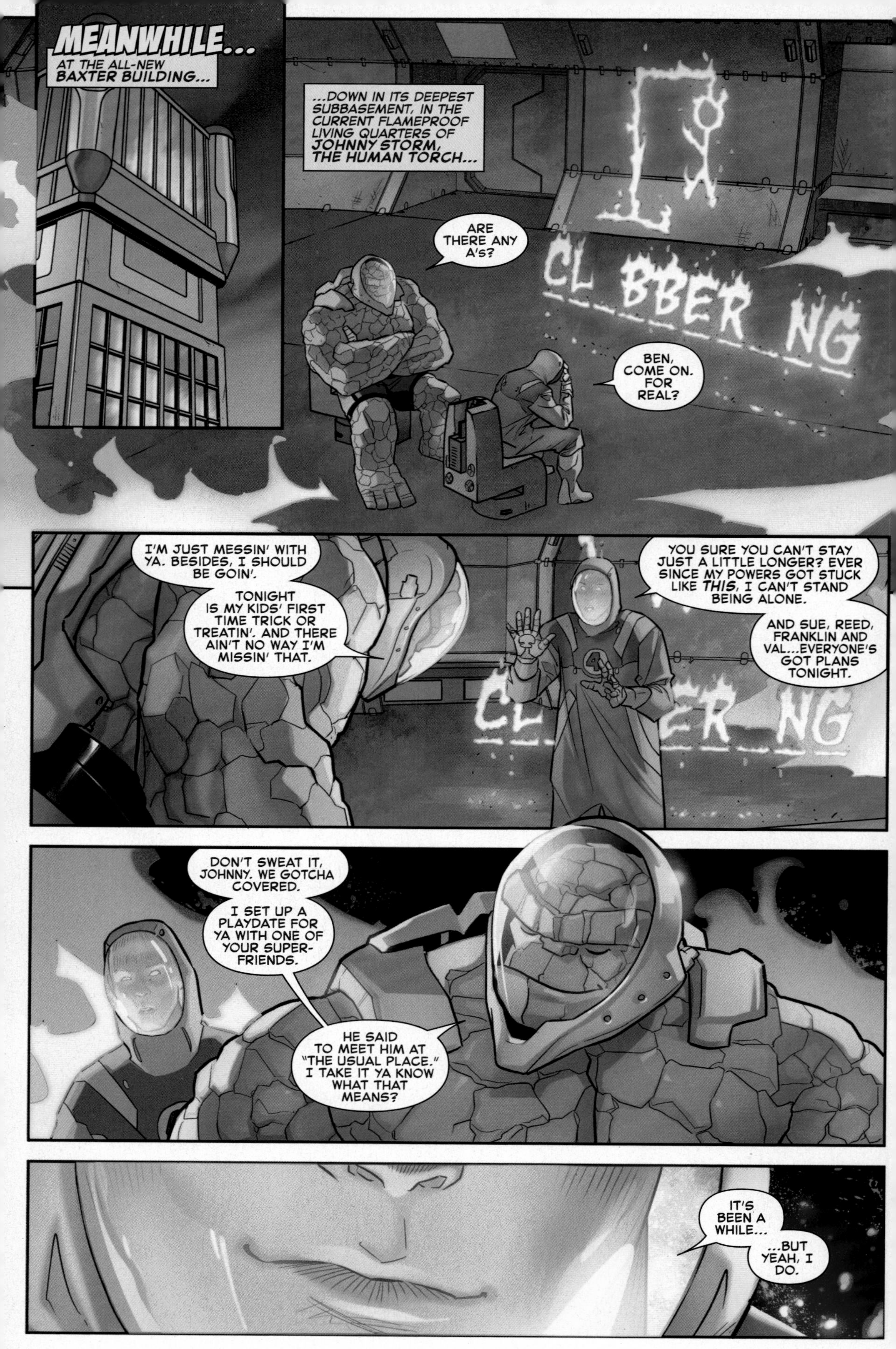
MEANWHILE...
AT THE ALL-NEW BAXTER BUILDING...
...DOWN IN ITS DEEPEST SUBBASEMENT, IN THE CURRENT FLAMEPROOF LIVING QUARTERS OF JOHNNY STORM, THE HUMAN TORCH...
ARE THERE ANY A's?
CL BBER NG
BEN, COME ON. FOR REAL?
I'M JUST MESSIN' WITH YA. BESIDES, I SHOULD BE GOIN'.
TONIGHT IS MY KIDS' FIRST TIME TRICK OR TREATIN'. AND THERE AIN'T NO WAY I'M MISSIN' THAT.
YOU SURE YOU CAN'T STAY JUST A LITTLE LONGER? EVER SINCE MY POWERS GOT STUCK LIKE THIS, I CAN'T STAND BEING ALONE.
AND SUE, REED, FRANKLIN AND VAL...EVERYONE'S GOT PLANS TONIGHT.
DON'T SWEAT IT, JOHNNY. WE GOTCHA COVERED.
I SET UP A PLAYDATE FOR YA WITH ONE OF YOUR SUPER-FRIENDS.
HE SAID TO MEET HIM AT "THE USUAL PLACE." I TAKE IT YA KNOW WHAT THAT MEANS?
IT'S BEEN A WHILE...
...BUT YEAH, I DO.

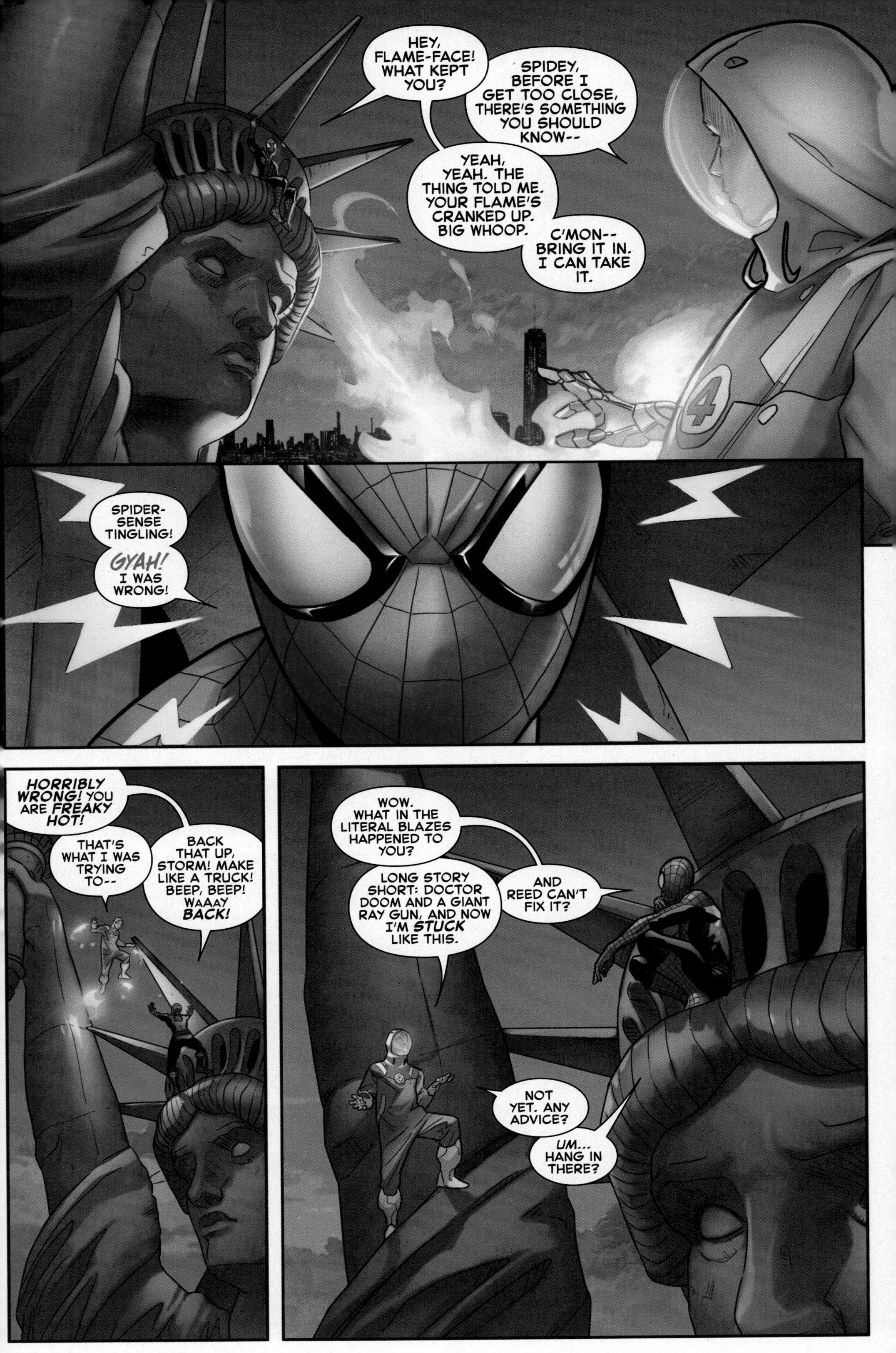
HEY, FLAME-FACE! WHAT KEPT YOU?
SPIDEY, BEFORE I GET TOO CLOSE, THERE'S SOMETHING YOU SHOULD KNOW--
YEAH, YEAH. THE THING TOLD ME. YOUR FLAME'S CRANKED UP. BIG WHOOP.
C'MON-- BRING IT IN. I CAN TAKE IT.
SPIDER-SENSE TINGLING!
GYAH! I WAS WRONG!
HORRIBLY WRONG! YOU ARE FREAKY HOT!
THAT'S WHAT I WAS TRYING TO--
BACK THAT UP, STORM! MAKE LIKE A TRUCK! BEEP, BEEP! WAAAY BACK!
WOW. WHAT IN THE LITERAL BLAZES HAPPENED TO YOU?
LONG STORY SHORT: DOCTOR DOOM AND A GIANT RAY GUN, AND NOW I'M STUCK LIKE THIS.
AND REED CAN'T FIX IT?
NOT YET. ANY ADVICE?
UM... HANG IN THERE?

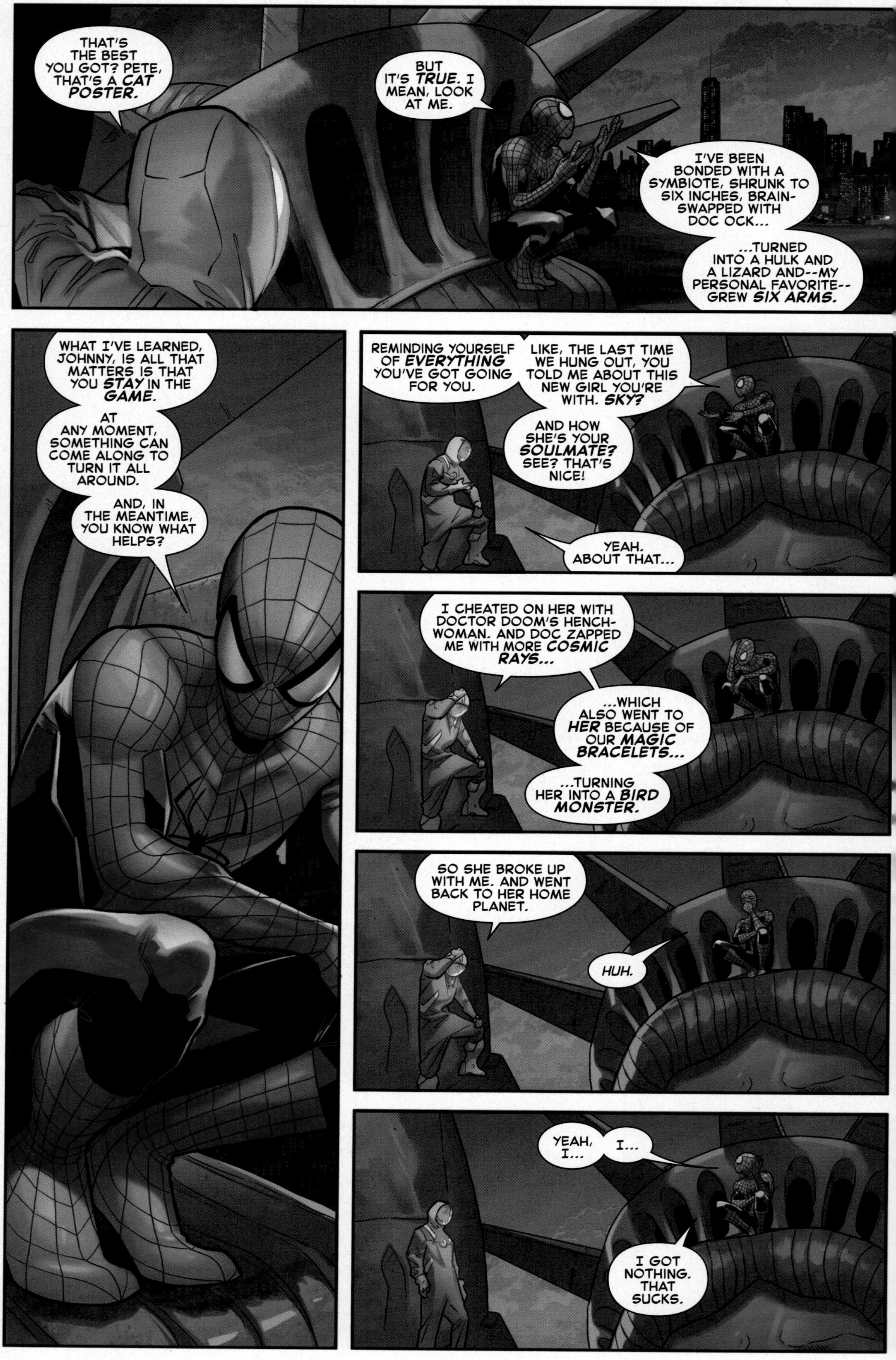
THAT'S THE BEST YOU GOT? PETE, THAT'S A CAT POSTER.
BUT IT'S TRUE. I MEAN, LOOK AT ME.
I'VE BEEN BONDED WITH A SYMBIOTE, SHRUNK TO SIX INCHES, BRAIN-SWAPPED WITH DOC OCK...
...TURNED INTO A HULK AND A LIZARD AND--MY PERSONAL FAVORITE--GREW SIX ARMS.
WHAT I'VE LEARNED, JOHNNY, IS ALL THAT MATTERS IS THAT YOU STAY IN THE GAME.
AT ANY MOMENT, SOMETHING CAN COME ALONG TO TURN IT ALL AROUND.
AND, IN THE MEANTIME, YOU KNOW WHAT HELPS?
REMINDING YOURSELF OF EVERYTHING YOU'VE GOT GOING FOR YOU.
LIKE, THE LAST TIME WE HUNG OUT, YOU TOLD ME ABOUT THIS NEW GIRL YOU'RE WITH. SKY?
AND HOW SHE'S YOUR SOULMATE? SEE? THAT'S NICE!
YEAH. ABOUT THAT...
I CHEATED ON HER WITH DOCTOR DOOM'S HENCH-WOMAN. AND DOC ZAPPED ME WITH MORE COSMIC RAYS...
...WHICH ALSO WENT TO HER BECAUSE OF OUR MAGIC BRACELETS...
...TURNING HER INTO A BIRD MONSTER.
SO SHE BROKE UP WITH ME. AND WENT BACK TO HER HOME PLANET.
HUH.
YEAH, I...
I...
I GOT NOTHING. THAT SUCKS.

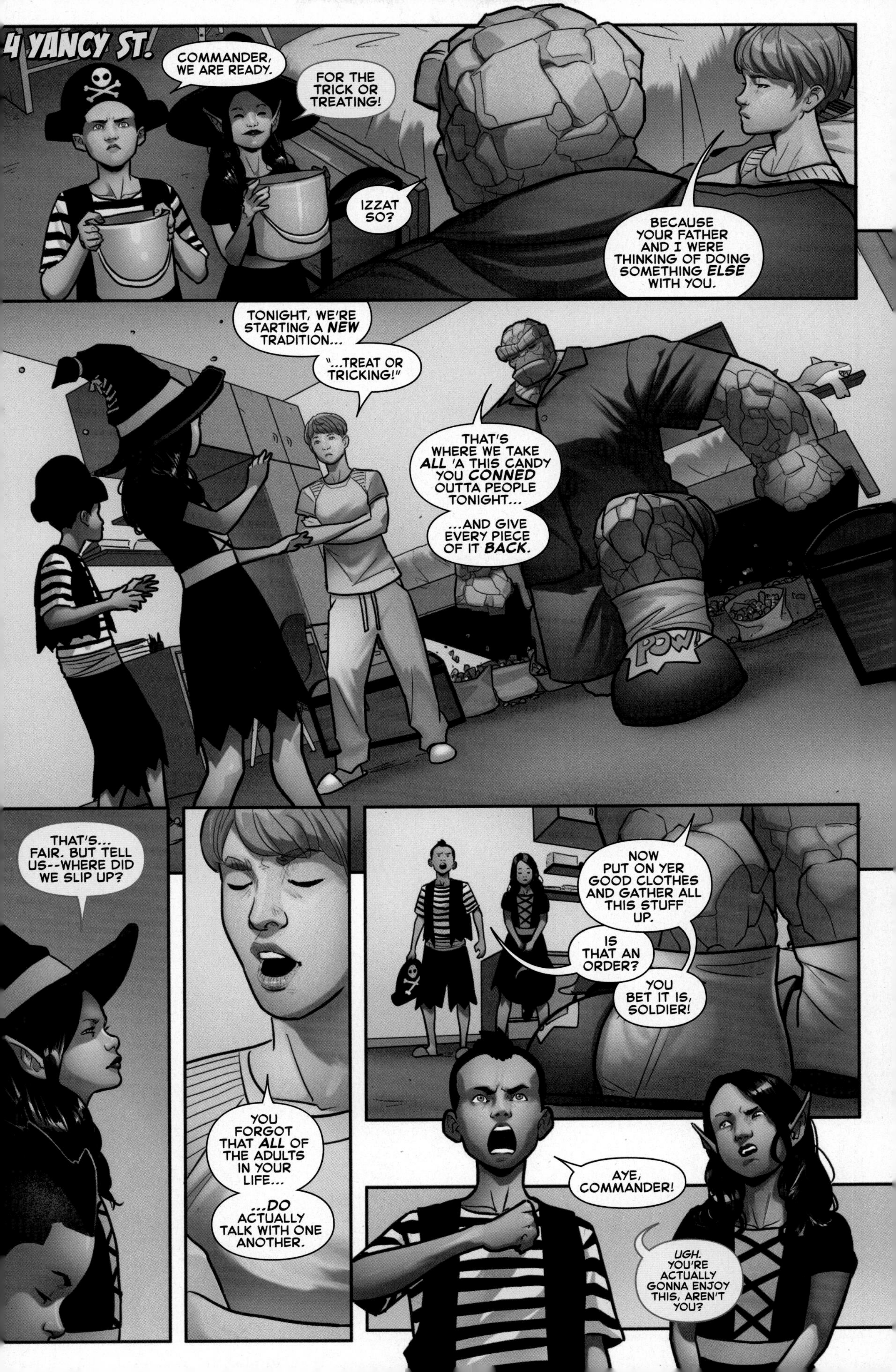
4 YANCY ST!
COMMANDER, WE ARE READY.
FOR THE TRICK OR TREATING!
IZZAT SO?
BECAUSE YOUR FATHER AND I WERE THINKING OF DOING SOMETHING ELSE WITH YOU.
TONIGHT, WE'RE STARTING A NEW TRADITION...
"...TREAT OR TRICKING!"
THAT'S WHERE WE TAKE ALL 'A THIS CANDY YOU CONNED OUTTA PEOPLE TONIGHT...
...AND GIVE EVERY PIECE OF IT BACK.
POW!
THAT'S... FAIR. BUT TELL US--WHERE DID WE SLIP UP?
YOU FORGOT THAT ALL OF THE ADULTS IN YOUR LIFE...
...DO ACTUALLY TALK WITH ONE ANOTHER.
NOW PUT ON YER GOOD CLOTHES AND GATHER ALL THIS STUFF UP.
IS THAT AN ORDER?
YOU BET IT IS, SOLDIER!
AYE, COMMANDER!
UGH. YOU'RE ACTUALLY GONNA ENJOY THIS, AREN'T YOU?

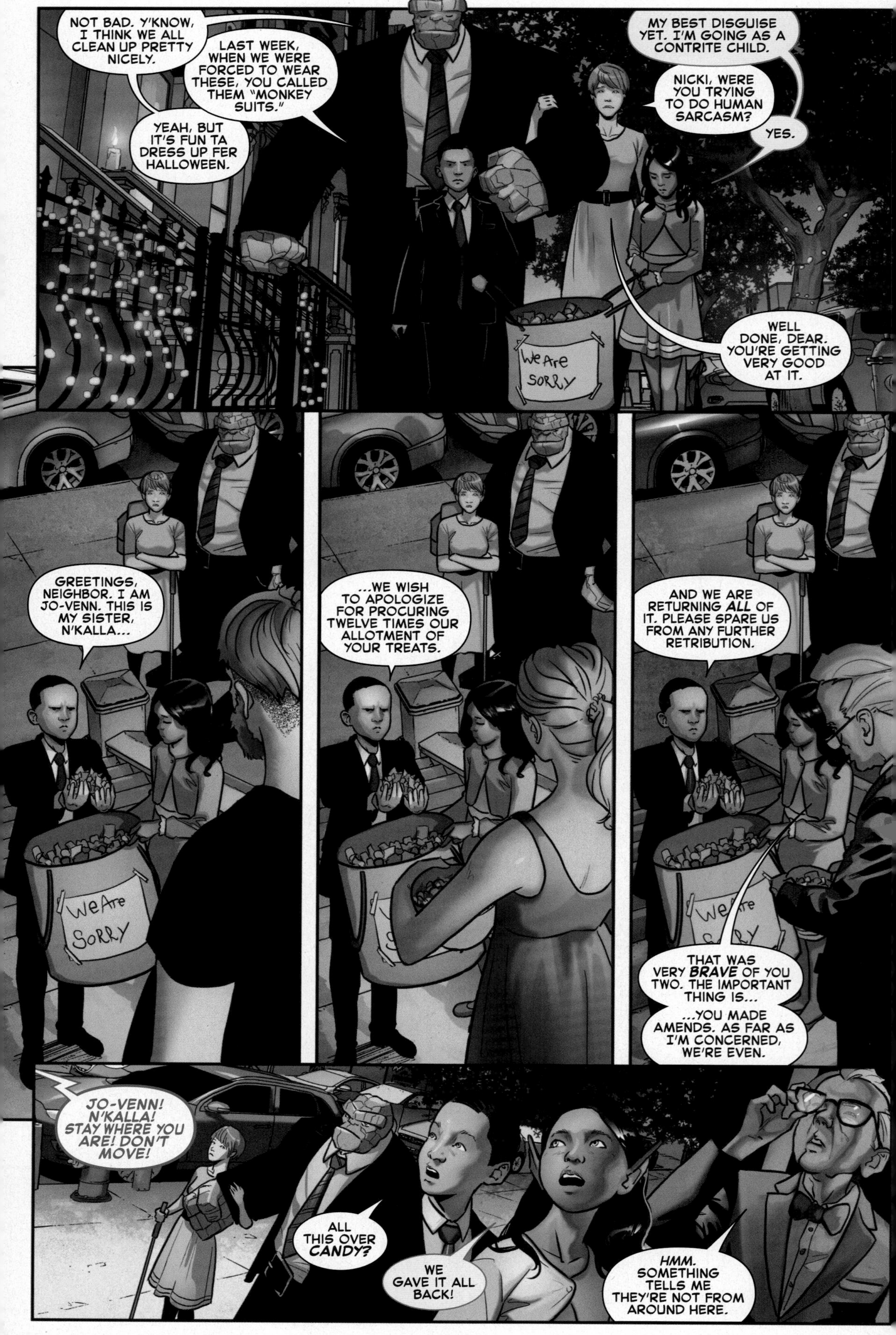
NOT BAD. Y'KNOW, I THINK WE ALL CLEAN UP PRETTY NICELY.
LAST WEEK, WHEN WE WERE FORCED TO WEAR THESE, YOU CALLED THEM "MONKEY SUITS."
YEAH, BUT IT'S FUN TA DRESS UP FER HALLOWEEN.
MY BEST DISGUISE YET. I'M GOING AS A CONTRITE CHILD.
NICKI, WERE YOU TRYING TO DO HUMAN SARCASM?
YES.
WELL DONE, DEAR. YOU'RE GETTING VERY GOOD AT IT.
We Are SORRY
GREETINGS, NEIGHBOR. I AM JO-VENN. THIS IS MY SISTER, N'KALLA...
We Are SORRY
...WE WISH TO APOLOGIZE FOR PROCURING TWELVE TIMES OUR ALLOTMENT OF YOUR TREATS.
AND WE ARE RETURNING *ALL* OF IT. PLEASE SPARE US FROM ANY FURTHER RETRIBUTION.
THAT WAS VERY ***BRAVE*** OF YOU TWO. THE IMPORTANT THING IS...
...YOU MADE AMENDS. AS FAR AS I'M CONCERNED, WE'RE EVEN.
JO-VENN! N'KALLA! STAY WHERE YOU ARE! DON'T MOVE!
ALL THIS OVER ***CANDY?***
WE GAVE IT ALL BACK!
HMM. SOMETHING TELLS ME THEY'RE NOT FROM AROUND HERE.

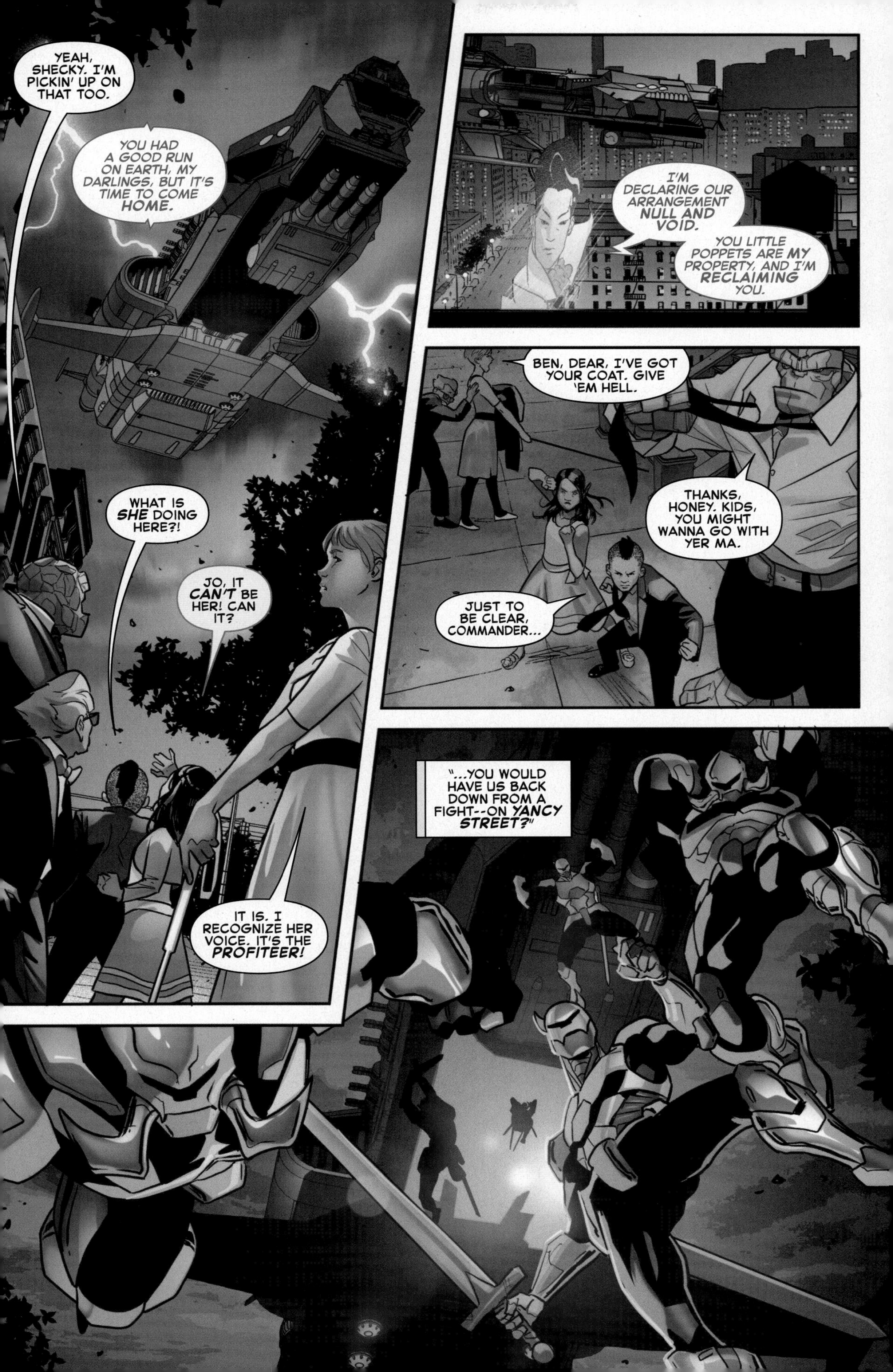
YEAH, SHECKY. I'M PICKIN' UP ON THAT TOO.
YOU HAD A GOOD RUN ON EARTH, MY DARLINGS, BUT IT'S TIME TO COME HOME.
I'M DECLARING OUR ARRANGEMENT NULL AND VOID.
YOU LITTLE POPPETS ARE MY PROPERTY, AND I'M RECLAIMING YOU.
WHAT IS SHE DOING HERE?!
JO, IT CAN'T BE HER! CAN IT?
IT IS. I RECOGNIZE HER VOICE. IT'S THE PROFITEER!
BEN, DEAR, I'VE GOT YOUR COAT. GIVE 'EM HELL.
THANKS, HONEY. KIDS, YOU MIGHT WANNA GO WITH YER MA.
JUST TO BE CLEAR, COMMANDER...
"...YOU WOULD HAVE US BACK DOWN FROM A FIGHT--ON YANCY STREET?"

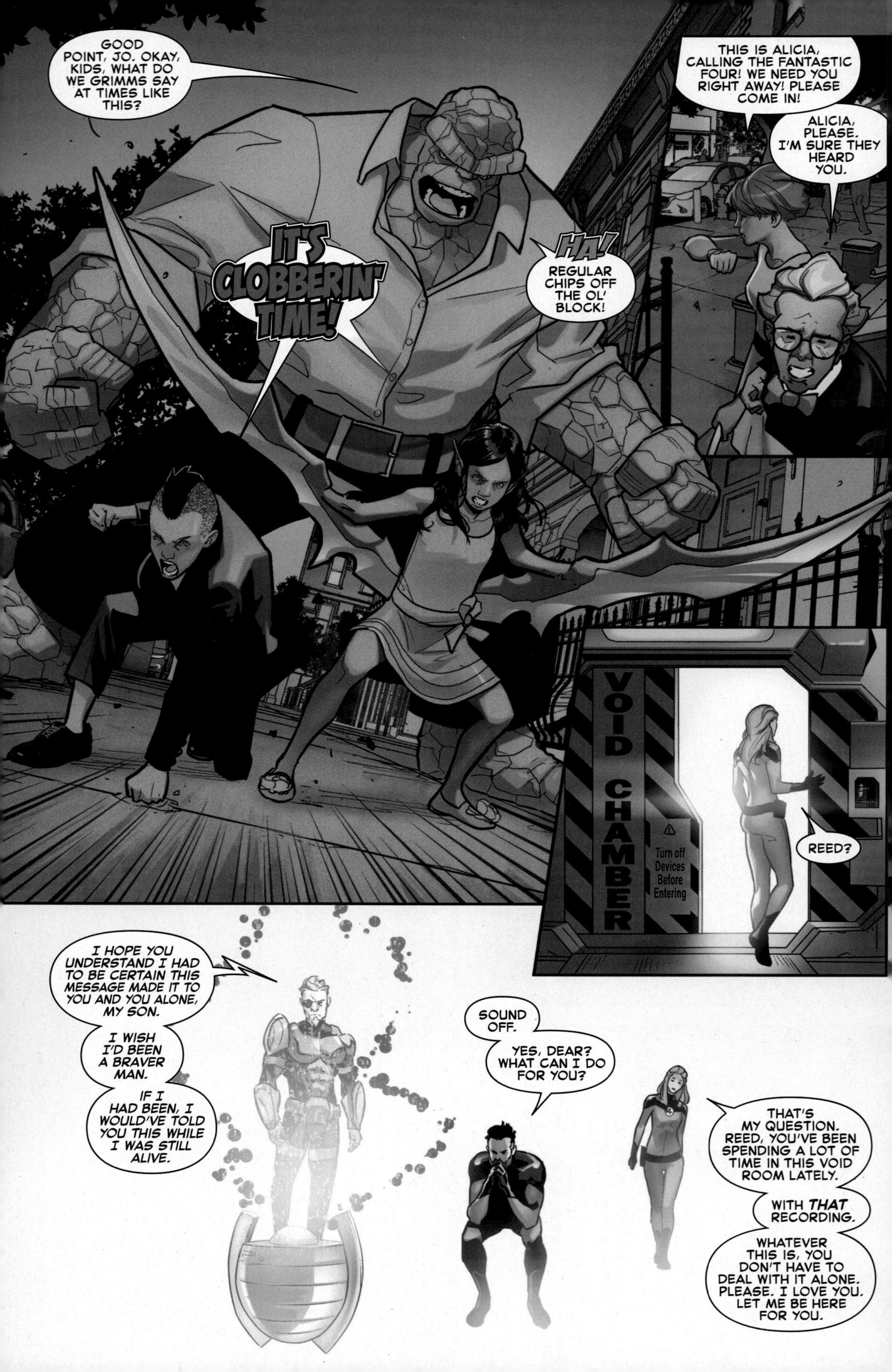
GOOD POINT, JO. OKAY, KIDS, WHAT DO WE GRIMMS SAY AT TIMES LIKE THIS?
IT'S CLOBBERIN' TIME!
HA! REGULAR CHIPS OFF THE OL' BLOCK!
THIS IS ALICIA, CALLING THE FANTASTIC FOUR! WE NEED YOU RIGHT AWAY! PLEASE COME IN!
ALICIA, PLEASE. I'M SURE THEY HEARD YOU.
VOID CHAMBER
Turn off Devices Before Entering
REED?
I HOPE YOU UNDERSTAND I HAD TO BE CERTAIN THIS MESSAGE MADE IT TO YOU AND YOU ALONE, MY SON.
I WISH I'D BEEN A BRAVER MAN.
IF I HAD BEEN, I WOULD'VE TOLD YOU THIS WHILE I WAS STILL ALIVE.
SOUND OFF.
YES, DEAR? WHAT CAN I DO FOR YOU?
THAT'S MY QUESTION. REED, YOU'VE BEEN SPENDING A LOT OF TIME IN THIS VOID ROOM LATELY.
WITH THAT RECORDING.
WHATEVER THIS IS, YOU DON'T HAVE TO DEAL WITH IT ALONE. PLEASE. I LOVE YOU. LET ME BE HERE FOR YOU.

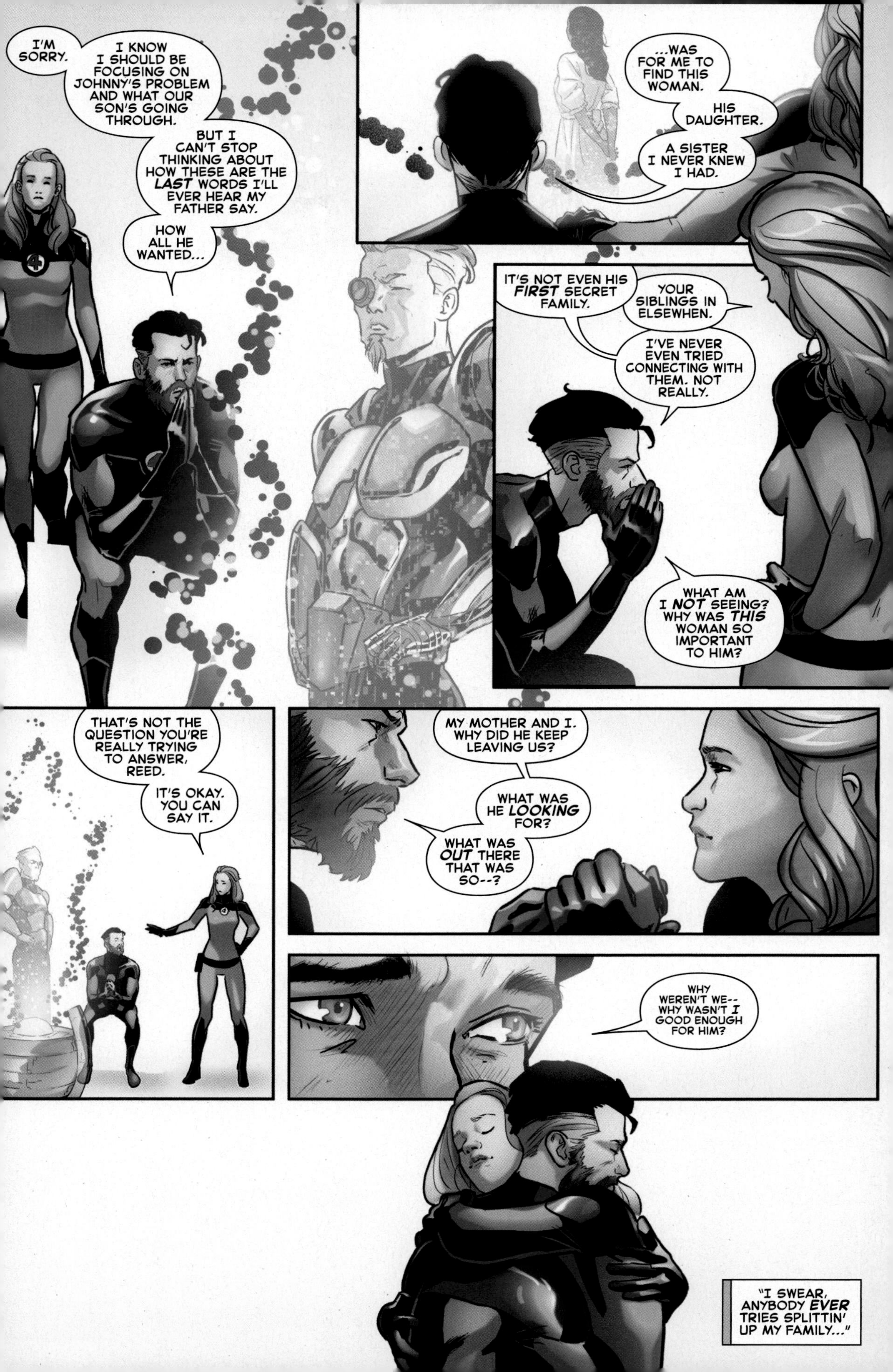
I'M SORRY.
I KNOW I SHOULD BE FOCUSING ON JOHNNY'S PROBLEM AND WHAT OUR SON'S GOING THROUGH.
BUT I CAN'T STOP THINKING ABOUT HOW THESE ARE THE LAST WORDS I'LL EVER HEAR MY FATHER SAY.
HOW ALL HE WANTED...
...WAS FOR ME TO FIND THIS WOMAN.
HIS DAUGHTER.
A SISTER I NEVER KNEW I HAD.
IT'S NOT EVEN HIS FIRST SECRET FAMILY.
YOUR SIBLINGS IN ELSEWHEN.
I'VE NEVER EVEN TRIED CONNECTING WITH THEM. NOT REALLY.
WHAT AM I NOT SEEING? WHY WAS THIS WOMAN SO IMPORTANT TO HIM?
THAT'S NOT THE QUESTION YOU'RE REALLY TRYING TO ANSWER, REED.
IT'S OKAY. YOU CAN SAY IT.
MY MOTHER AND I. WHY DID HE KEEP LEAVING US?
WHAT WAS HE LOOKING FOR?
WHAT WAS OUT THERE THAT WAS SO--?
WHY WEREN'T WE-- WHY WASN'T I GOOD ENOUGH FOR HIM?
"I SWEAR, ANYBODY EVER TRIES SPLITTIN' UP MY FAMILY..."

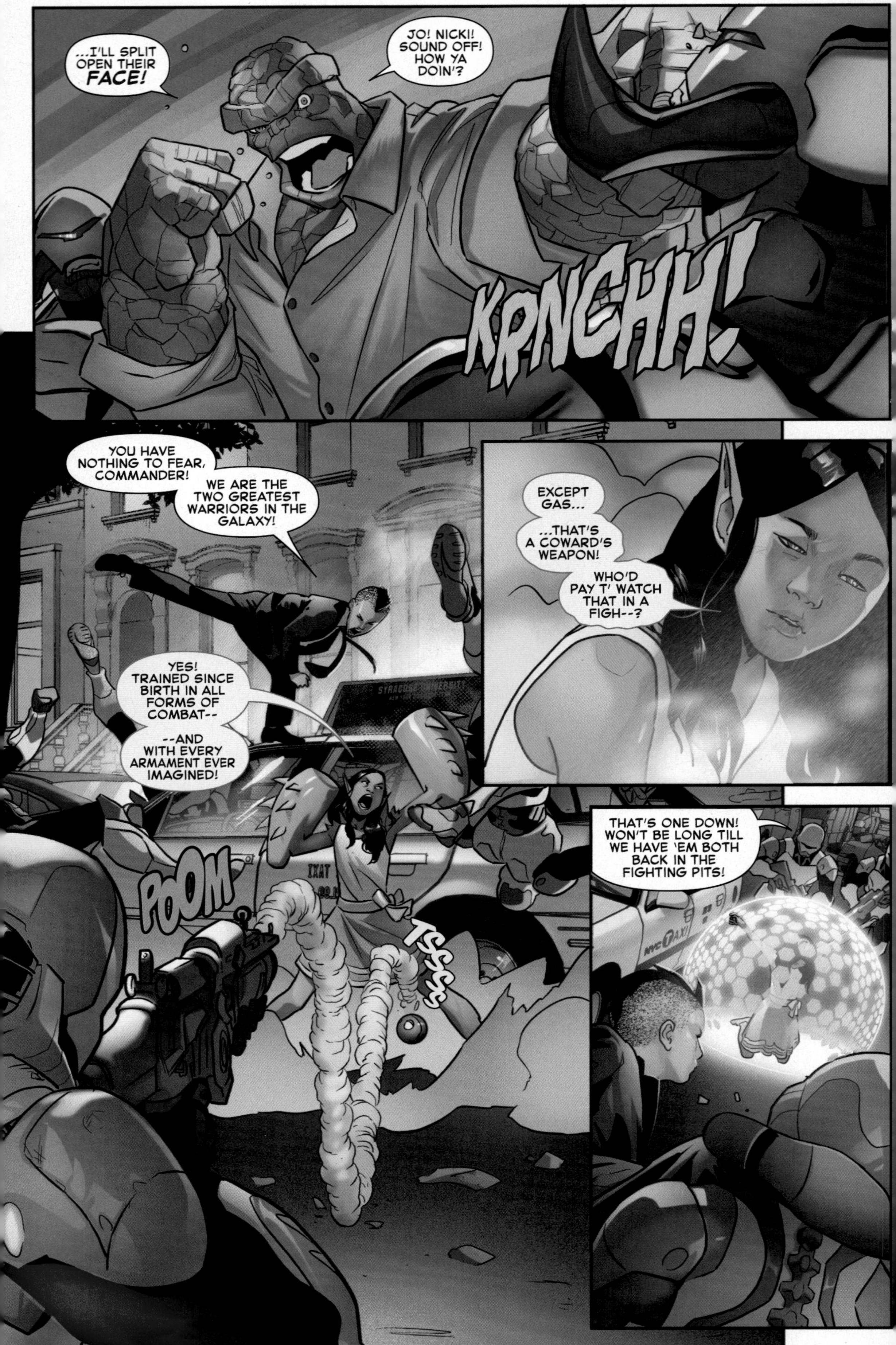
...I'LL SPLIT OPEN THEIR FACE!
JO! NICKI! SOUND OFF! HOW YA DOIN'?
KRNCHH!
YOU HAVE NOTHING TO FEAR, COMMANDER!
WE ARE THE TWO GREATEST WARRIORS IN THE GALAXY!
YES! TRAINED SINCE BIRTH IN ALL FORMS OF COMBAT--
--AND WITH EVERY ARMAMENT EVER IMAGINED!
POOM
TSSSS
EXCEPT GAS...
...THAT'S A COWARD'S WEAPON!
WHO'D PAY T' WATCH THAT IN A FIGH--?
THAT'S ONE DOWN! WON'T BE LONG TILL WE HAVE 'EM BOTH BACK IN THE FIGHTING PITS!

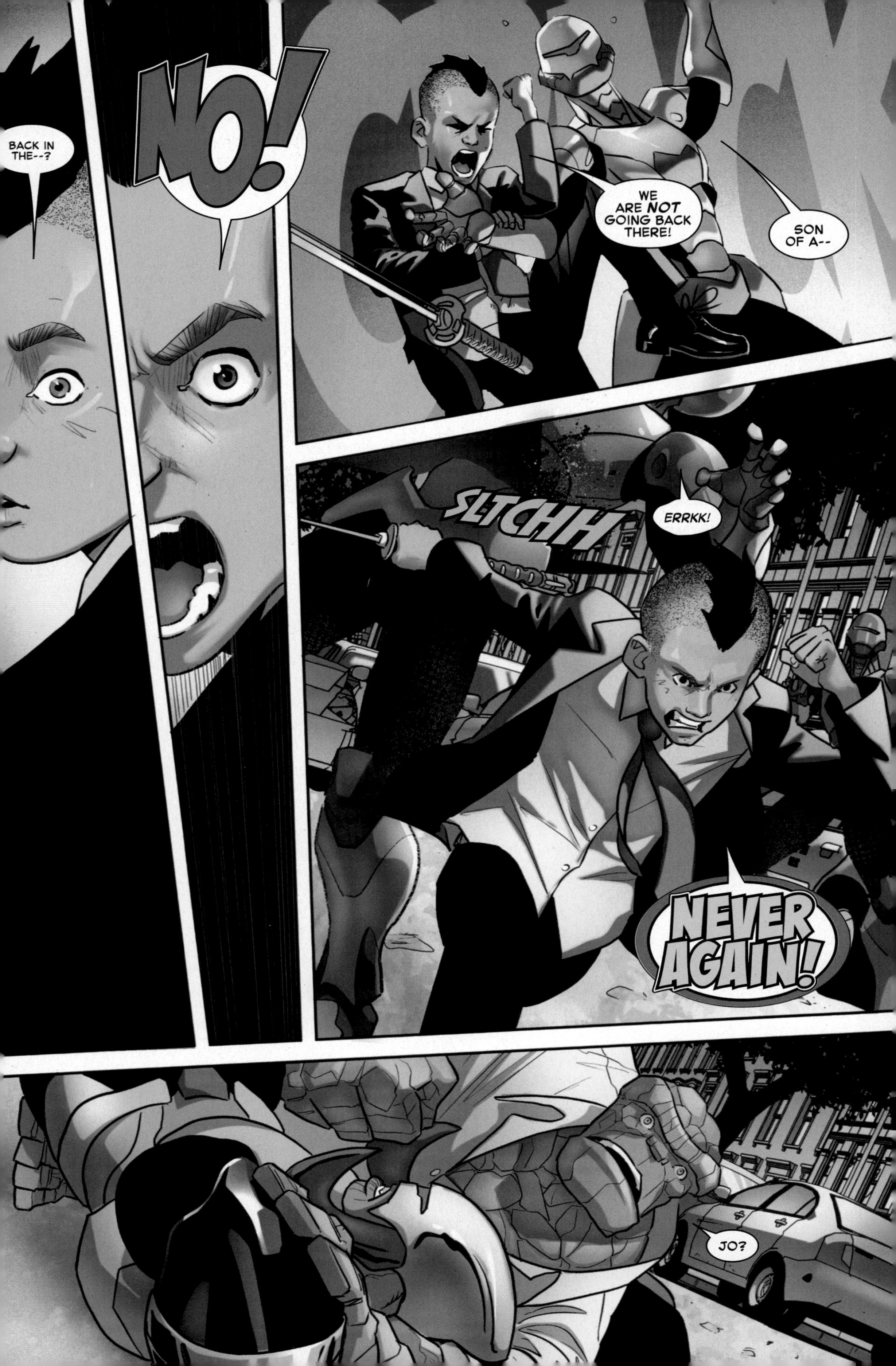
BACK IN THE--?
NO!
WE ARE NOT GOING BACK THERE!
SON OF A--
SLTCHH
ERRKK!
NEVER AGAIN!
JO?

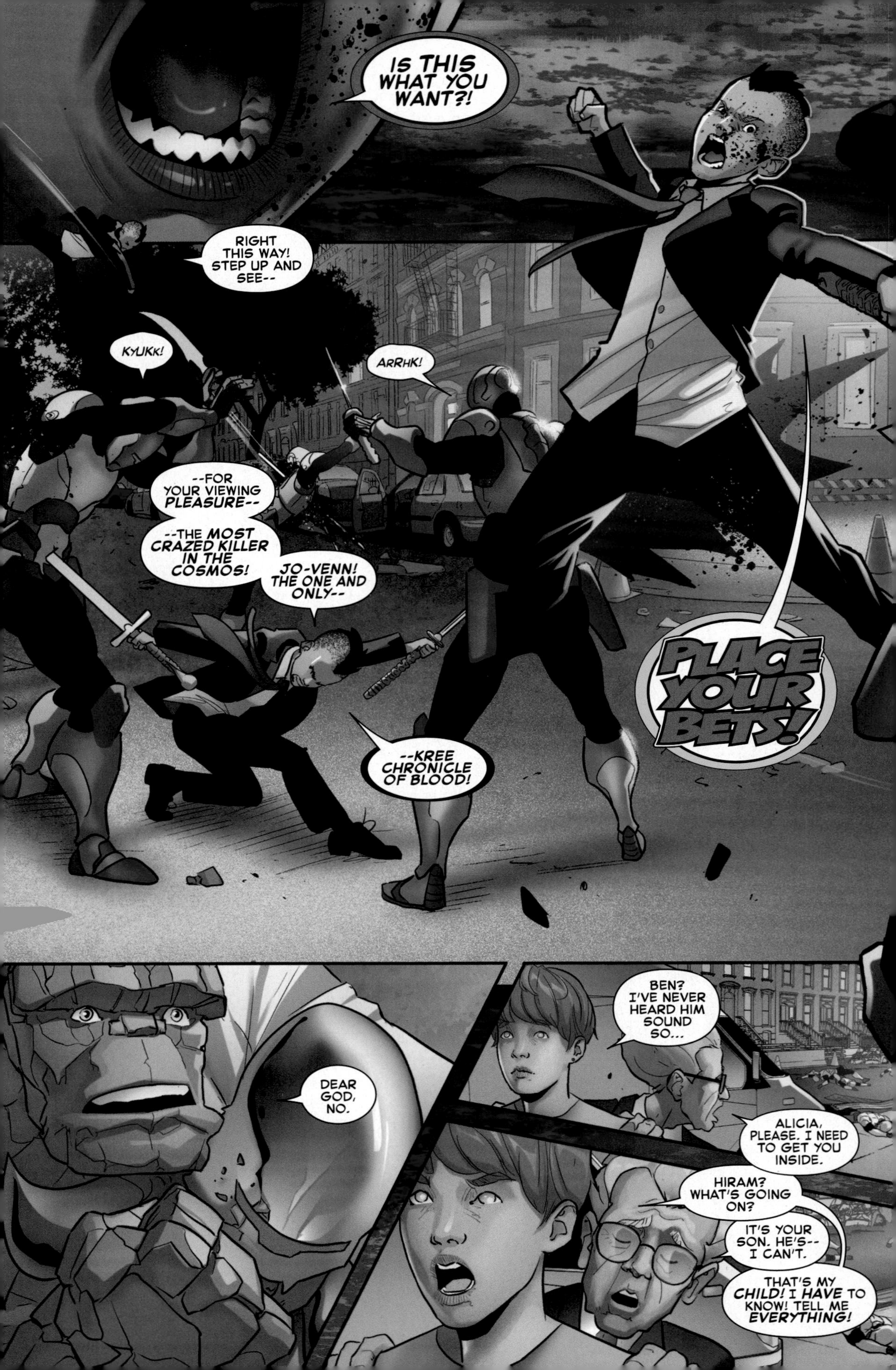
IS THIS WHAT YOU WANT?!
RIGHT THIS WAY! STEP UP AND SEE--
KYUKK!
ARRHK!
--FOR YOUR VIEWING PLEASURE--
--THE MOST CRAZED KILLER IN THE COSMOS!
JO-VENN! THE ONE AND ONLY--
--KREE CHRONICLE OF BLOOD!
PLACE YOUR BETS!
DEAR GOD, NO.
BEN? I'VE NEVER HEARD HIM SOUND SO...
ALICIA, PLEASE. I NEED TO GET YOU INSIDE.
HIRAM? WHAT'S GOING ON?
IT'S YOUR SON. HE'S-- I CAN'T.
THAT'S MY CHILD! I HAVE TO KNOW! TELL ME EVERYTHING!

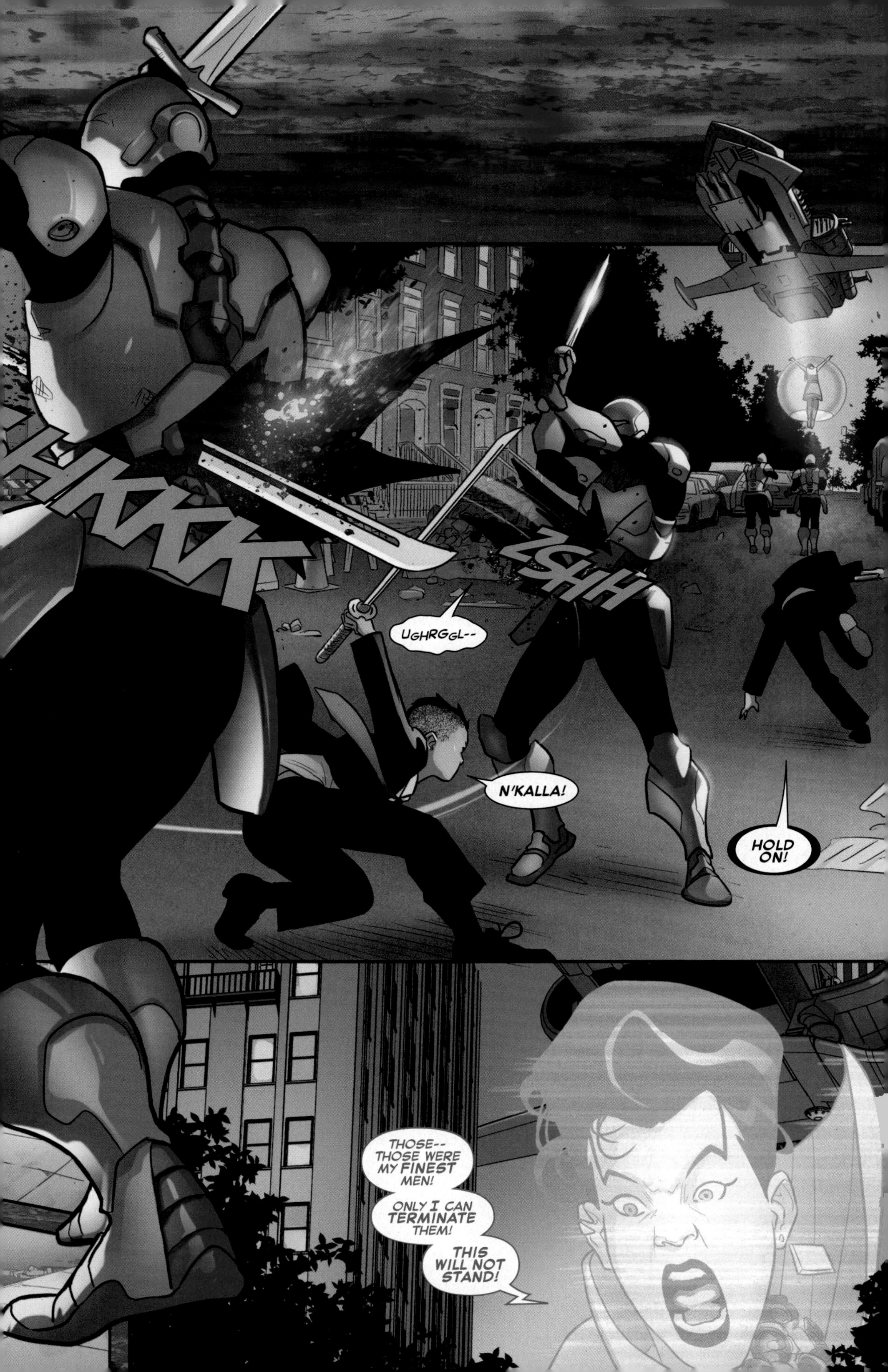

SHKKKK
ZSHH
UGHRGGL--
N'KALLA!
HOLD ON!
THOSE-- THOSE WERE MY FINEST MEN!
ONLY I CAN TERMINATE THEM!
THIS WILL NOT STAND!

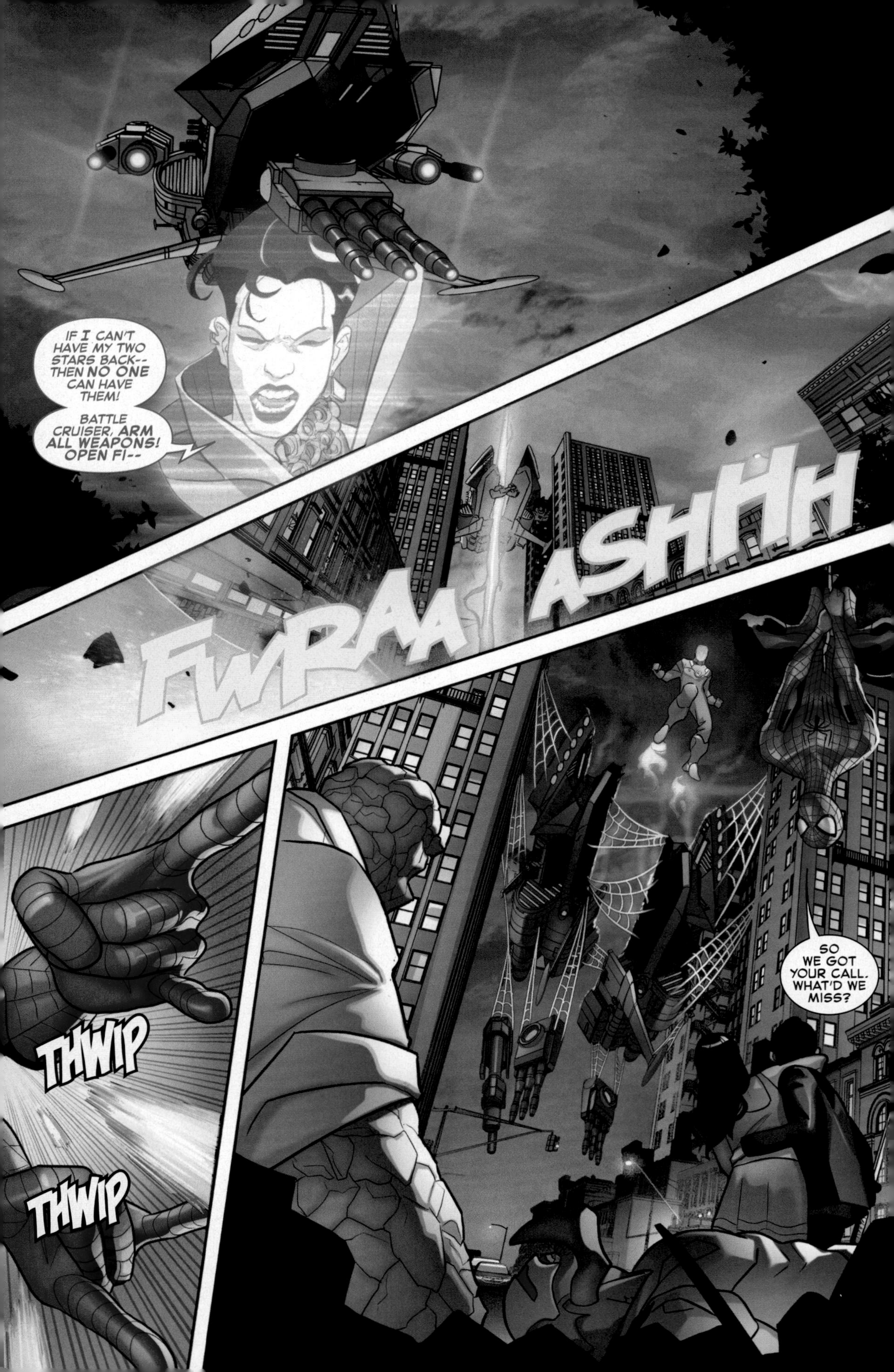
IF I CAN'T HAVE MY TWO STARS BACK-- THEN NO ONE CAN HAVE THEM!
BATTLE CRUISER, ARM ALL WEAPONS! OPEN FI--
FWRAAASHHH
SO WE GOT YOUR CALL. WHAT'D WE MISS?
THWIP
THWIP

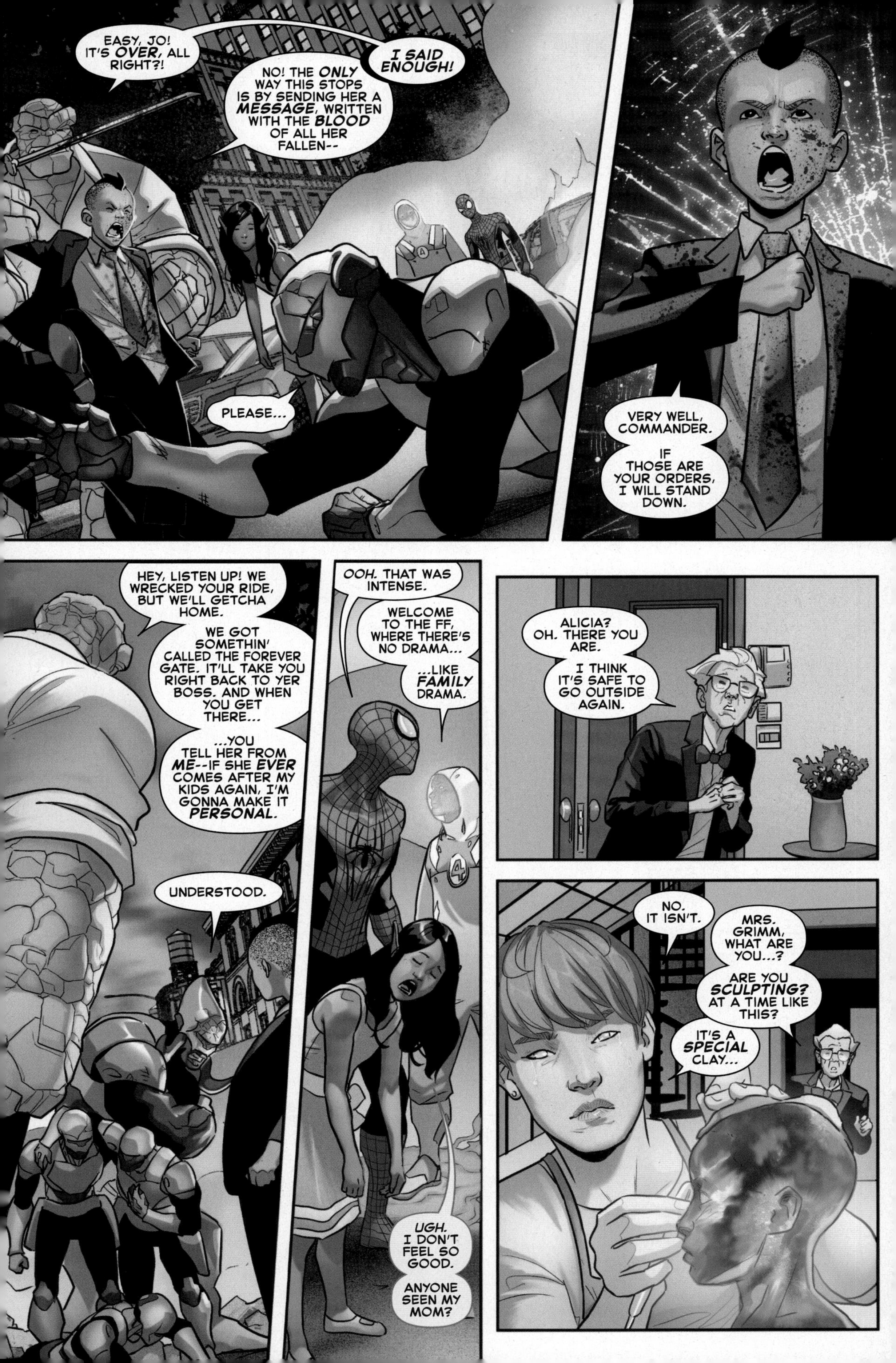

EASY, JO! IT'S OVER, ALL RIGHT?!
I SAID ENOUGH!
NO! THE ONLY WAY THIS STOPS IS BY SENDING HER A MESSAGE, WRITTEN WITH THE BLOOD OF ALL HER FALLEN--
PLEASE...
VERY WELL, COMMANDER.
IF THOSE ARE YOUR ORDERS, I WILL STAND DOWN.
HEY, LISTEN UP! WE WRECKED YOUR RIDE, BUT WE'LL GETCHA HOME.
WE GOT SOMETHIN' CALLED THE FOREVER GATE. IT'LL TAKE YOU RIGHT BACK TO YER BOSS. AND WHEN YOU GET THERE...
...YOU TELL HER FROM ME--IF SHE EVER COMES AFTER MY KIDS AGAIN, I'M GONNA MAKE IT PERSONAL.
UNDERSTOOD.
OOH. THAT WAS INTENSE.
WELCOME TO THE FF, WHERE THERE'S NO DRAMA...
...LIKE FAMILY DRAMA.
UGH. I DON'T FEEL SO GOOD.
ANYONE SEEN MY MOM?
ALICIA? OH. THERE YOU ARE.
I THINK IT'S SAFE TO GO OUTSIDE AGAIN.
NO. IT ISN'T.
MRS. GRIMM, WHAT ARE YOU...?
ARE YOU SCULPTING? AT A TIME LIKE THIS?
IT'S A SPECIAL CLAY...

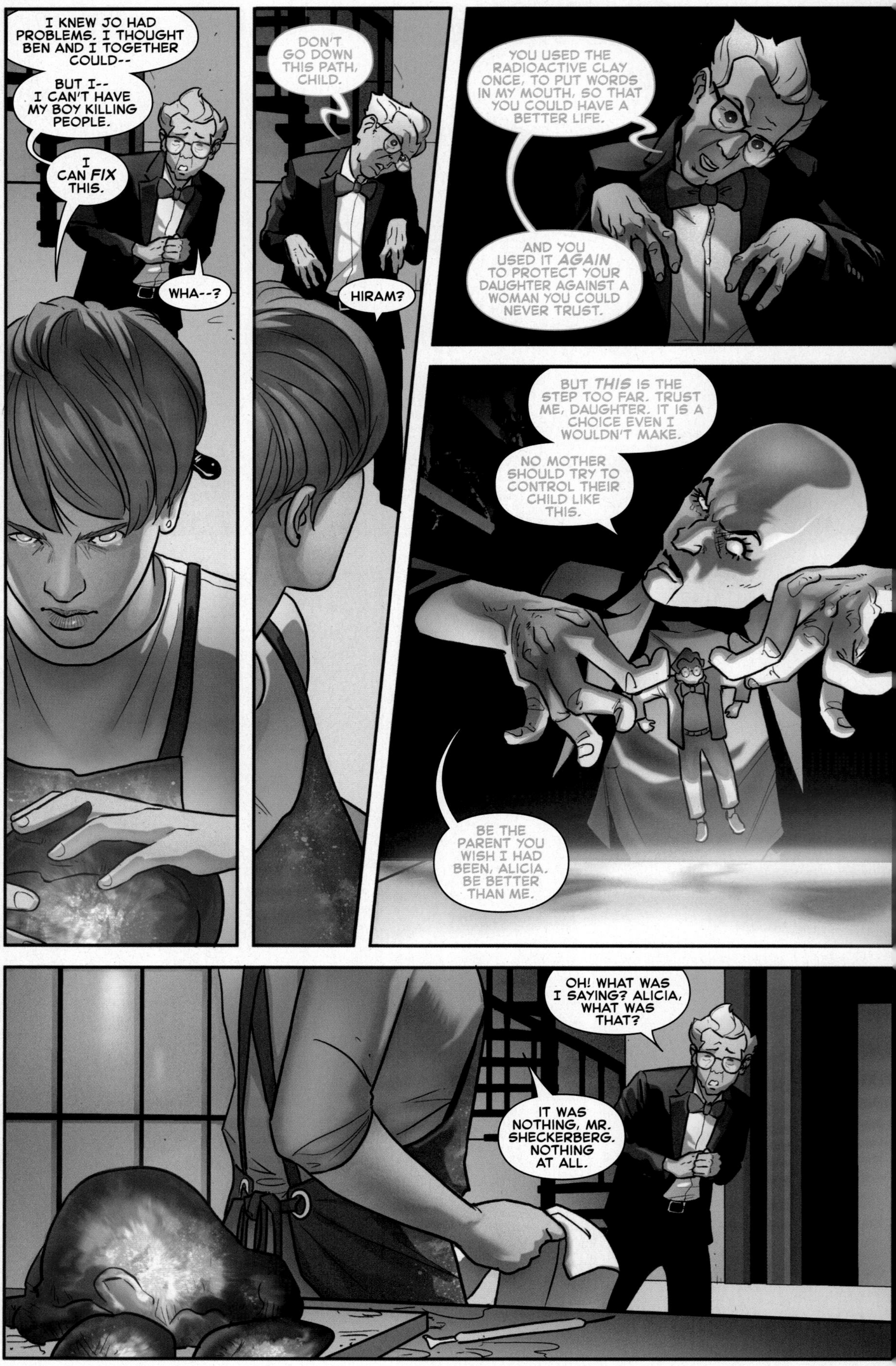
I KNEW JO HAD PROBLEMS. I THOUGHT BEN AND I TOGETHER COULD--
BUT I-- I CAN'T HAVE MY BOY KILLING PEOPLE.
I CAN FIX THIS.
WHA--?
DON'T GO DOWN THIS PATH, CHILD.
HIRAM?
YOU USED THE RADIOACTIVE CLAY ONCE, TO PUT WORDS IN MY MOUTH, SO THAT YOU COULD HAVE A BETTER LIFE.
AND YOU USED IT AGAIN TO PROTECT YOUR DAUGHTER AGAINST A WOMAN YOU COULD NEVER TRUST.
BUT THIS IS THE STEP TOO FAR. TRUST ME, DAUGHTER. IT IS A CHOICE EVEN I WOULDN'T MAKE.
NO MOTHER SHOULD TRY TO CONTROL THEIR CHILD LIKE THIS.
BE THE PARENT YOU WISH I HAD BEEN, ALICIA. BE BETTER THAN ME.
OH! WHAT WAS I SAYING? ALICIA, WHAT WAS THAT?
IT WAS NOTHING, MR. SHECKERBERG. NOTHING AT ALL.

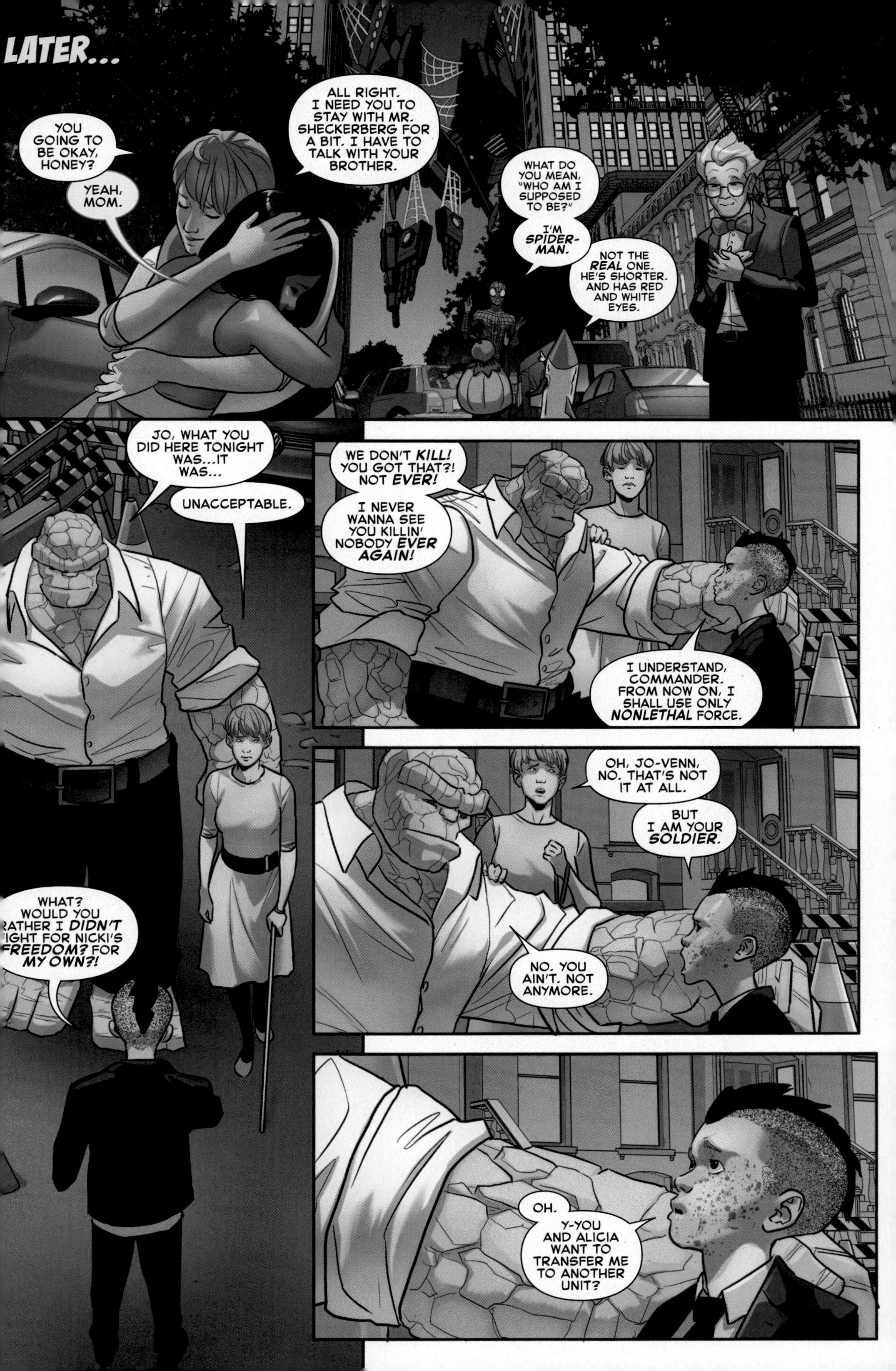
LATER...
YOU GOING TO BE OKAY, HONEY?
YEAH, MOM.
ALL RIGHT. I NEED YOU TO STAY WITH MR. SHECKERBERG FOR A BIT. I HAVE TO TALK WITH YOUR BROTHER.
WHAT DO YOU MEAN, "WHO AM I SUPPOSED TO BE?"
I'M SPIDER-MAN.
NOT THE REAL ONE. HE'S SHORTER. AND HAS RED AND WHITE EYES.
JO, WHAT YOU DID HERE TONIGHT WAS...IT WAS...
UNACCEPTABLE.
WHAT? WOULD YOU RATHER I DIDN'T FIGHT FOR NICKI'S FREEDOM? FOR MY OWN?!
WE DON'T KILL! YOU GOT THAT?! NOT EVER!
I NEVER WANNA SEE YOU KILLIN' NOBODY EVER AGAIN!
I UNDERSTAND, COMMANDER. FROM NOW ON, I SHALL USE ONLY NONLETHAL FORCE.
OH, JO-VENN, NO. THAT'S NOT IT AT ALL.
BUT I AM YOUR SOLDIER.
NO. YOU AIN'T. NOT ANYMORE.
OH.
Y-YOU AND ALICIA WANT TO TRANSFER ME TO ANOTHER UNIT?

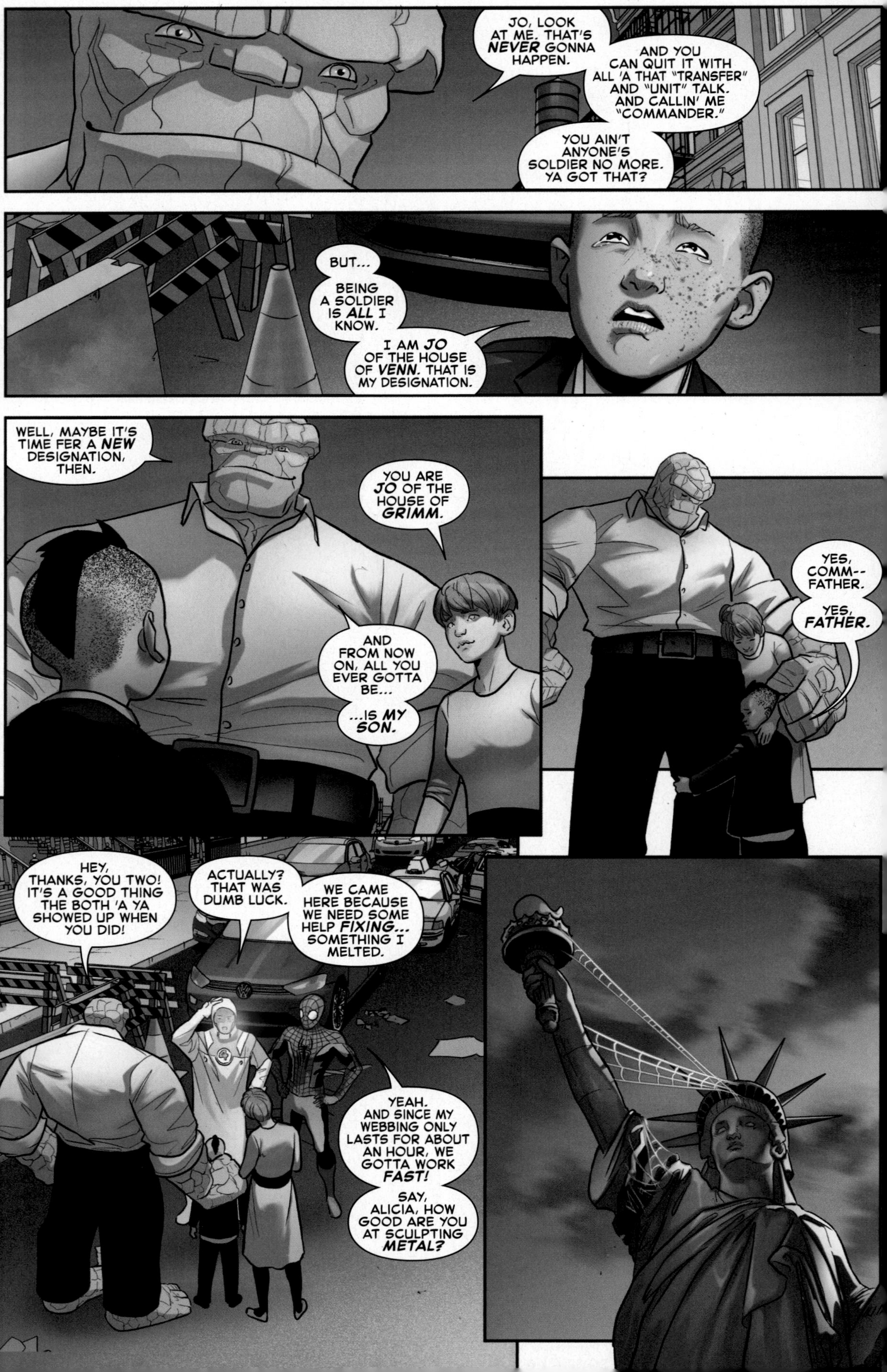
JO, LOOK AT ME. THAT'S NEVER GONNA HAPPEN.
AND YOU CAN QUIT IT WITH ALL 'A THAT "TRANSFER" AND "UNIT" TALK. AND CALLIN' ME "COMMANDER."
YOU AIN'T ANYONE'S SOLDIER NO MORE. YA GOT THAT?
BUT...
BEING A SOLDIER IS ALL I KNOW.
I AM JO OF THE HOUSE OF VENN. THAT IS MY DESIGNATION.
WELL, MAYBE IT'S TIME FER A NEW DESIGNATION, THEN.
YOU ARE JO OF THE HOUSE OF GRIMM.
AND FROM NOW ON, ALL YOU EVER GOTTA BE...
...IS MY SON.
YES, COMM-- FATHER.
YES, FATHER.
HEY, THANKS, YOU TWO! IT'S A GOOD THING THE BOTH 'A YA SHOWED UP WHEN YOU DID!
ACTUALLY? THAT WAS DUMB LUCK.
WE CAME HERE BECAUSE WE NEED SOME HELP FIXING... SOMETHING I MELTED.
YEAH. AND SINCE MY WEBBING ONLY LASTS FOR ABOUT AN HOUR, WE GOTTA WORK FAST!
SAY, ALICIA, HOW GOOD ARE YOU AT SCULPTING METAL?

38

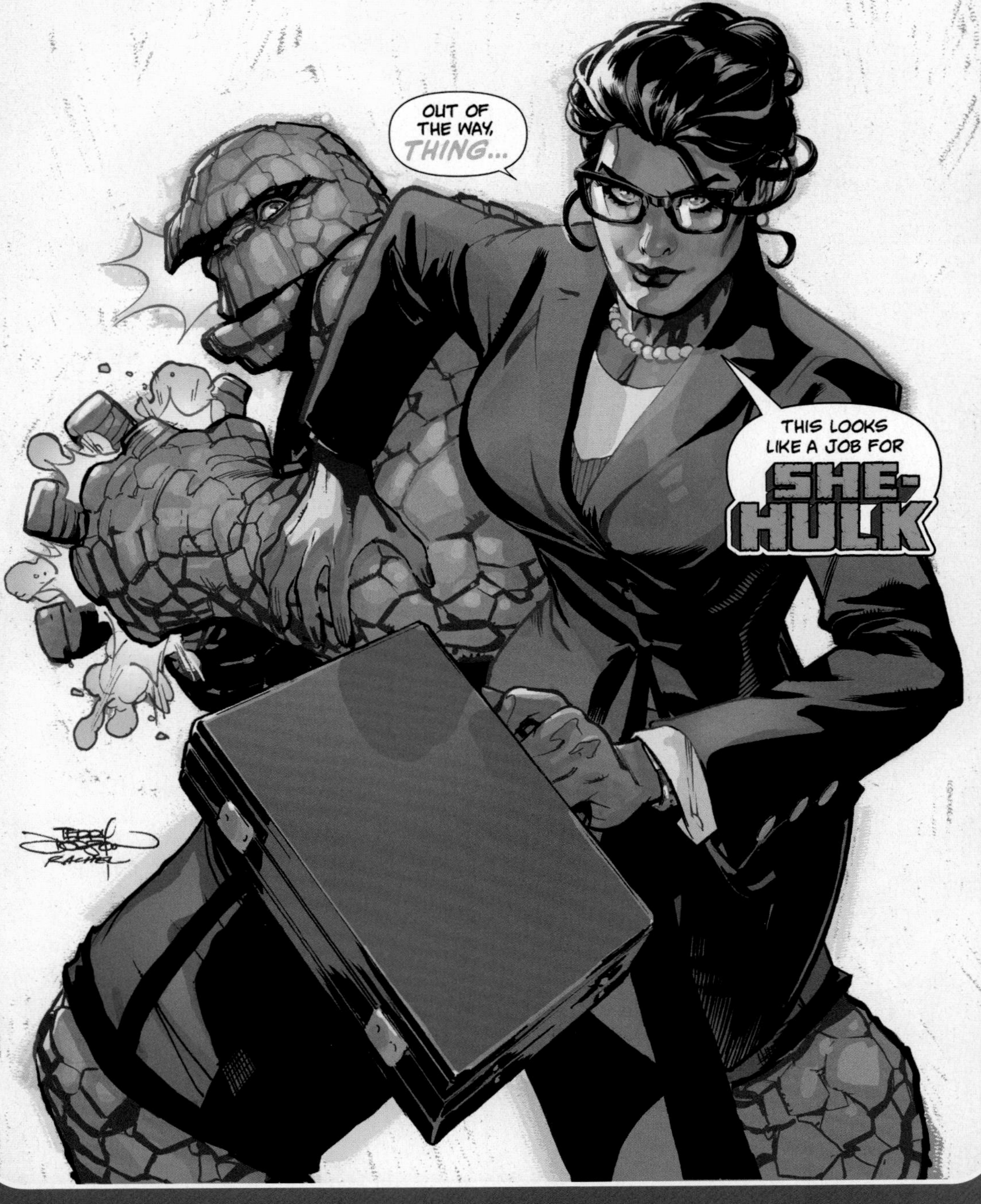
OUT OF THE WAY, THING...
THIS LOOKS LIKE A JOB FOR SHE-HULK

"Family Crisis"

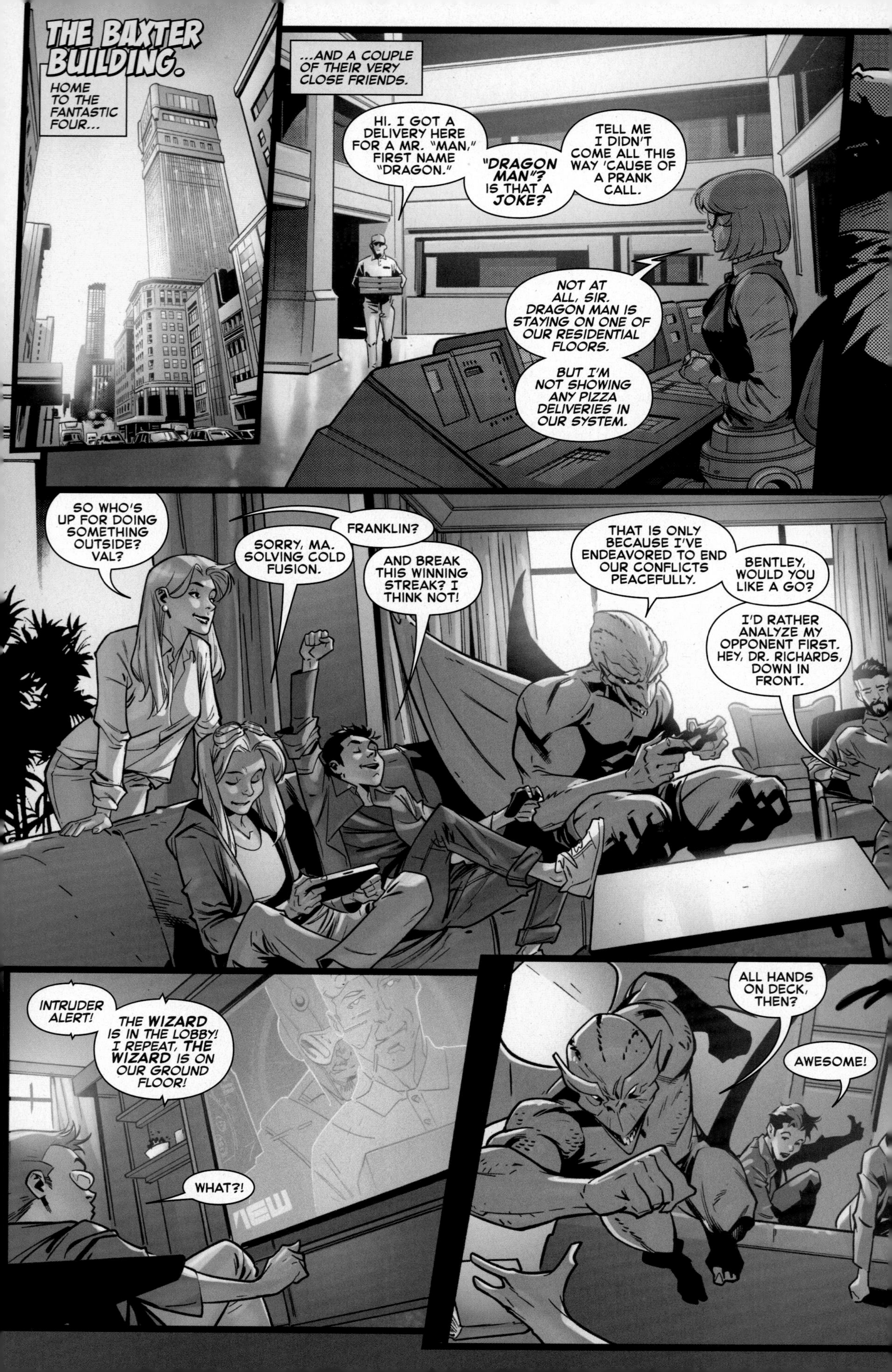
THE BAXTER BUILDING.
HOME TO THE FANTASTIC FOUR...
...AND A COUPLE OF THEIR VERY CLOSE FRIENDS.
HI. I GOT A DELIVERY HERE FOR A MR. "MAN," FIRST NAME "DRAGON."
"DRAGON MAN"? IS THAT A JOKE?
TELL ME I DIDN'T COME ALL THIS WAY 'CAUSE OF A PRANK CALL.
NOT AT ALL, SIR. DRAGON MAN IS STAYING ON ONE OF OUR RESIDENTIAL FLOORS.
BUT I'M NOT SHOWING ANY PIZZA DELIVERIES IN OUR SYSTEM.
SO WHO'S UP FOR DOING SOMETHING OUTSIDE? VAL?
SORRY, MA. SOLVING COLD FUSION.
FRANKLIN?
AND BREAK THIS WINNING STREAK? I THINK NOT!
THAT IS ONLY BECAUSE I'VE ENDEAVORED TO END OUR CONFLICTS PEACEFULLY.
BENTLEY, WOULD YOU LIKE A GO?
I'D RATHER ANALYZE MY OPPONENT FIRST. HEY, DR. RICHARDS, DOWN IN FRONT.
INTRUDER ALERT!
THE WIZARD IS IN THE LOBBY! I REPEAT, THE WIZARD IS ON OUR GROUND FLOOR!
WHAT?!
ALL HANDS ON DECK, THEN?
AWESOME!

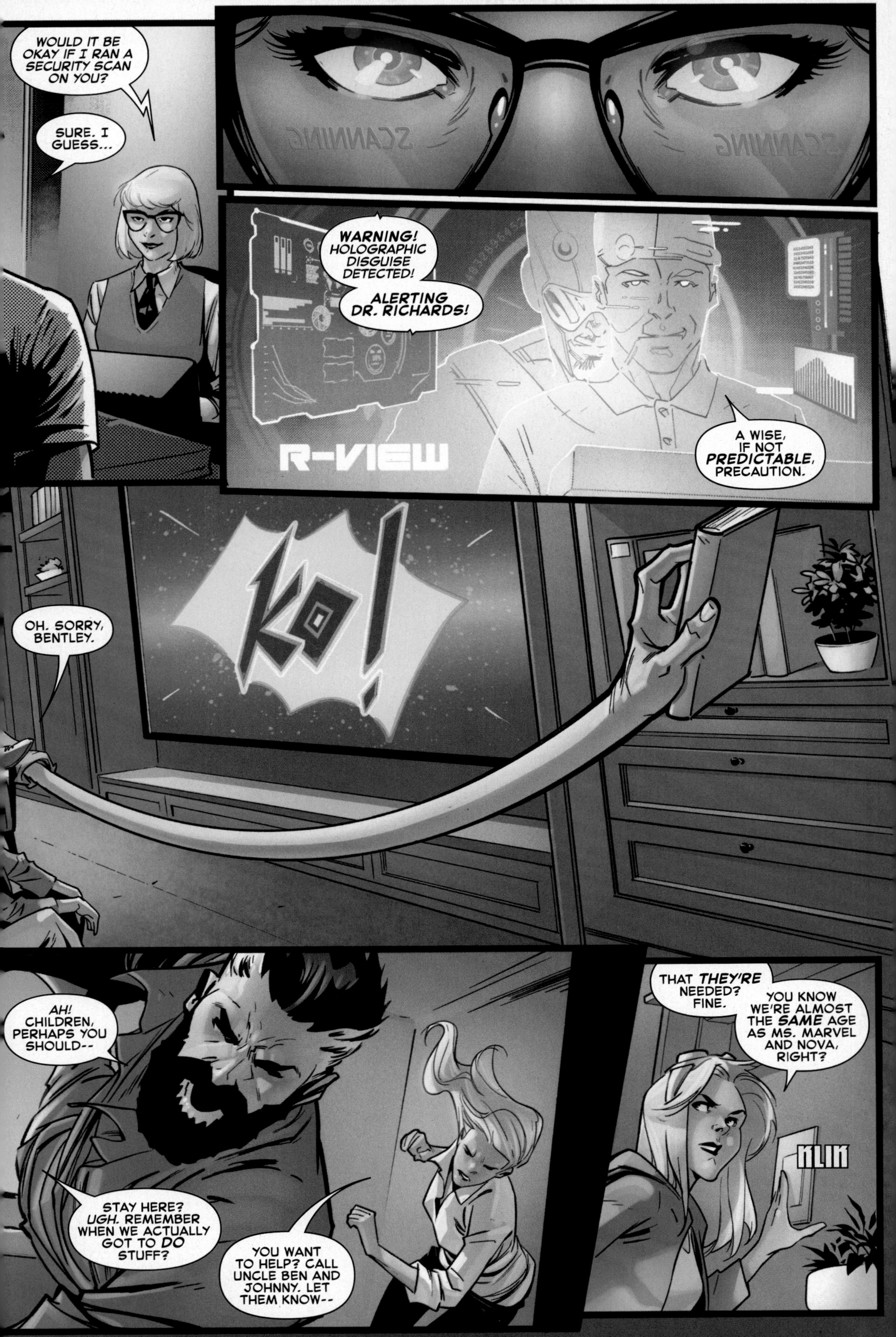
WOULD IT BE OKAY IF I RAN A SECURITY SCAN ON YOU?
SURE. I GUESS...
SCANNING
SCANNING
WARNING! HOLOGRAPHIC DISGUISE DETECTED!
ALERTING DR. RICHARDS!
R-VIEW
A WISE, IF NOT *PREDICTABLE*, PRECAUTION.
KO!
OH. SORRY, BENTLEY.
AH! CHILDREN, PERHAPS YOU SHOULD--
STAY HERE? *UGH.* REMEMBER WHEN WE ACTUALLY GOT TO *DO* STUFF?
YOU WANT TO HELP? CALL UNCLE BEN AND JOHNNY. LET THEM KNOW--
THAT *THEY'RE* NEEDED? FINE.
YOU KNOW WE'RE ALMOST THE *SAME* AGE AS MS. MARVEL AND NOVA, RIGHT?
KLIK

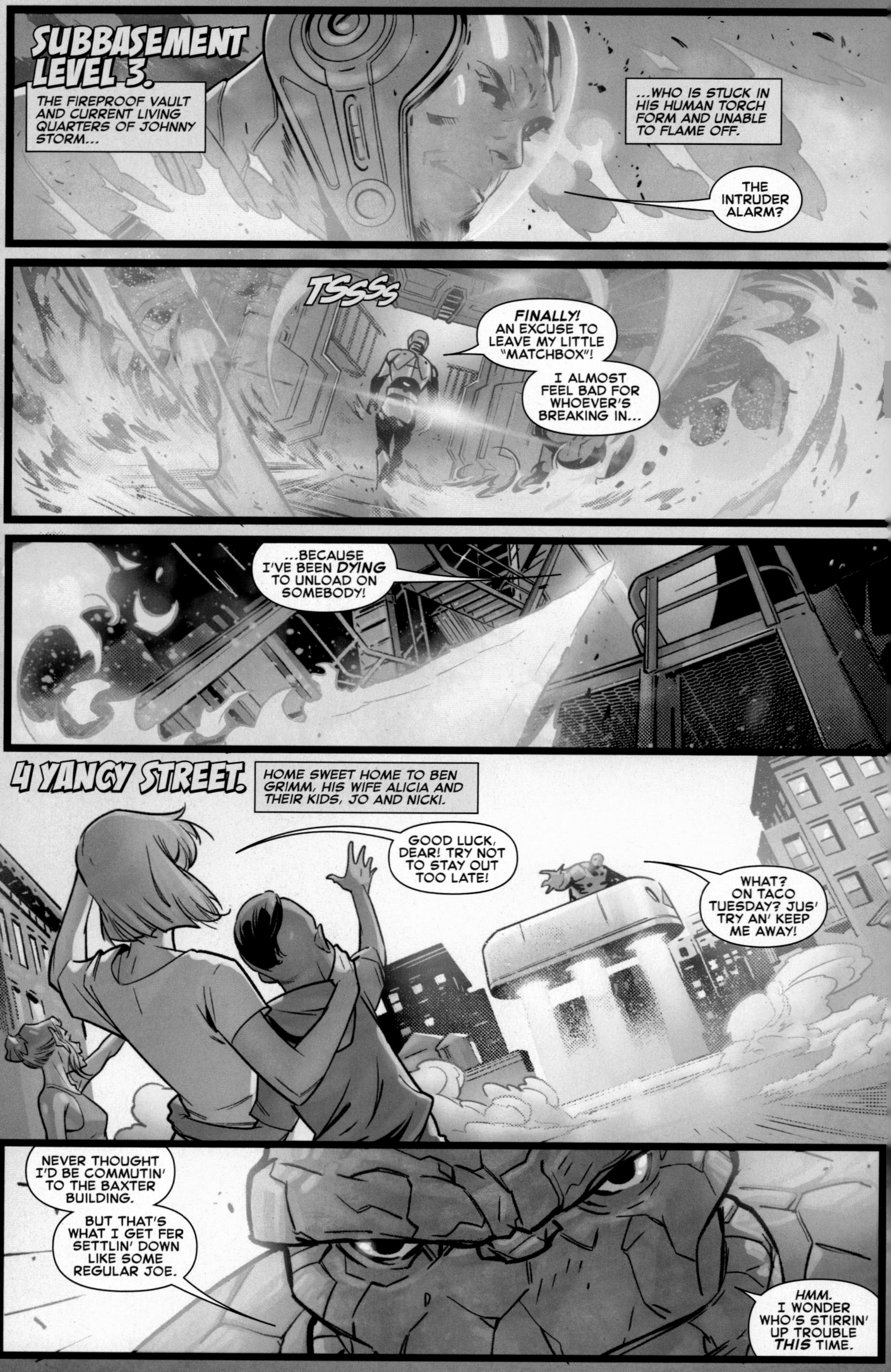
SUBBASEMENT LEVEL 3.
THE FIREPROOF VAULT AND CURRENT LIVING QUARTERS OF JOHNNY STORM...
...WHO IS STUCK IN HIS HUMAN TORCH FORM AND UNABLE TO FLAME OFF.
THE INTRUDER ALARM?
TSSSS
FINALLY! AN EXCUSE TO LEAVE MY LITTLE "MATCHBOX"!
I ALMOST FEEL BAD FOR WHOEVER'S BREAKING IN...
...BECAUSE I'VE BEEN DYING TO UNLOAD ON SOMEBODY!
4 YANCY STREET.
HOME SWEET HOME TO BEN GRIMM, HIS WIFE ALICIA AND THEIR KIDS, JO AND NICKI.
GOOD LUCK, DEAR! TRY NOT TO STAY OUT TOO LATE!
WHAT? ON TACO TUESDAY? JUS' TRY AN' KEEP ME AWAY!
NEVER THOUGHT I'D BE COMMUTIN' TO THE BAXTER BUILDING.
BUT THAT'S WHAT I GET FER SETTLIN' DOWN LIKE SOME REGULAR JOE.
HMM. I WONDER WHO'S STIRRIN' UP TROUBLE THIS TIME.

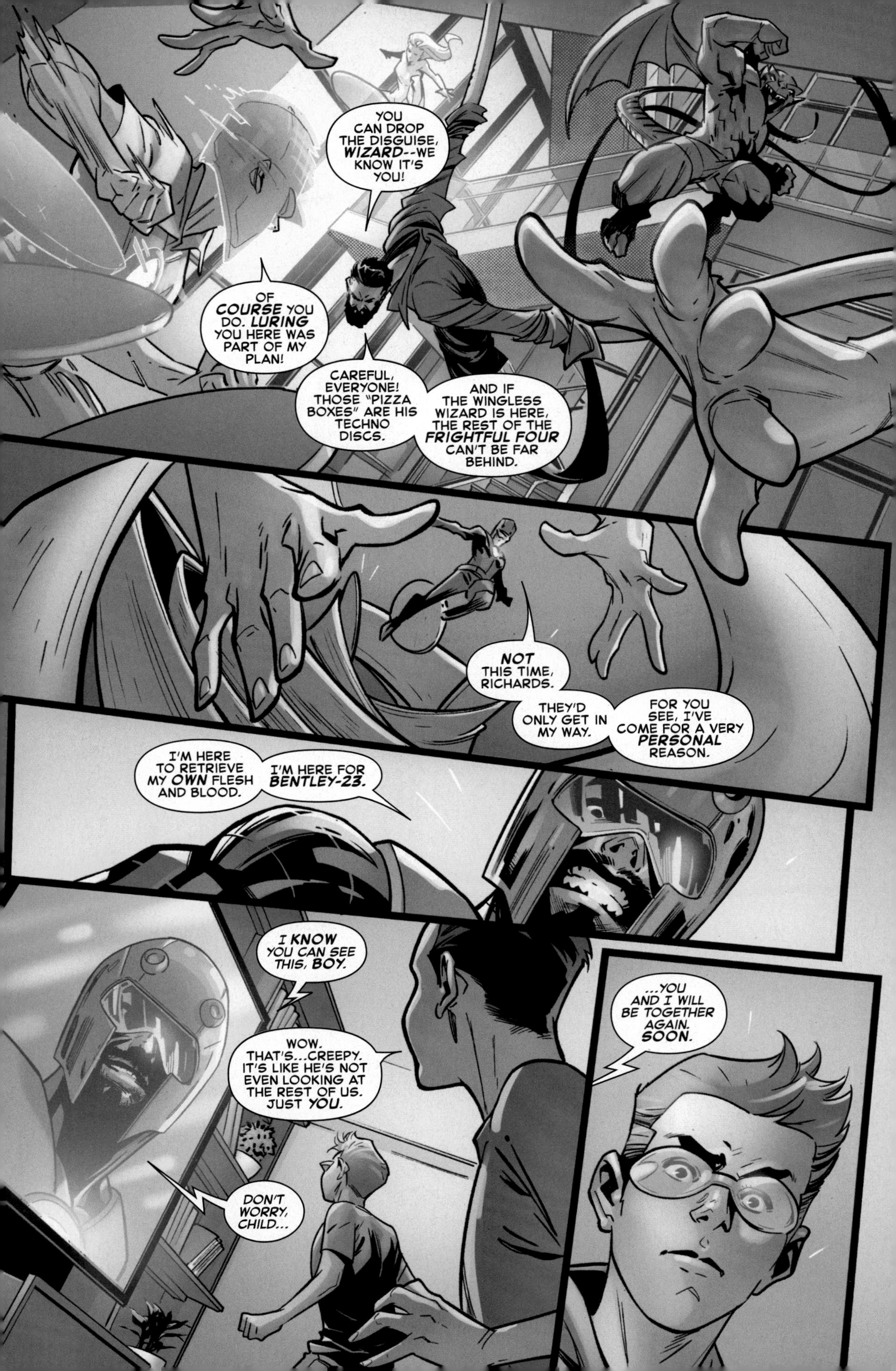
YOU CAN DROP THE DISGUISE, WIZARD--WE KNOW IT'S YOU!
OF COURSE YOU DO. LURING YOU HERE WAS PART OF MY PLAN!
CAREFUL, EVERYONE! THOSE "PIZZA BOXES" ARE HIS TECHNO DISCS.
AND IF THE WINGLESS WIZARD IS HERE, THE REST OF THE FRIGHTFUL FOUR CAN'T BE FAR BEHIND.
NOT THIS TIME, RICHARDS.
THEY'D ONLY GET IN MY WAY.
FOR YOU SEE, I'VE COME FOR A VERY PERSONAL REASON.
I'M HERE TO RETRIEVE MY OWN FLESH AND BLOOD.
I'M HERE FOR BENTLEY-23.
I KNOW YOU CAN SEE THIS, BOY.
WOW. THAT'S...CREEPY. IT'S LIKE HE'S NOT EVEN LOOKING AT THE REST OF US. JUST YOU.
DON'T WORRY, CHILD...
...YOU AND I WILL BE TOGETHER AGAIN. SOON.

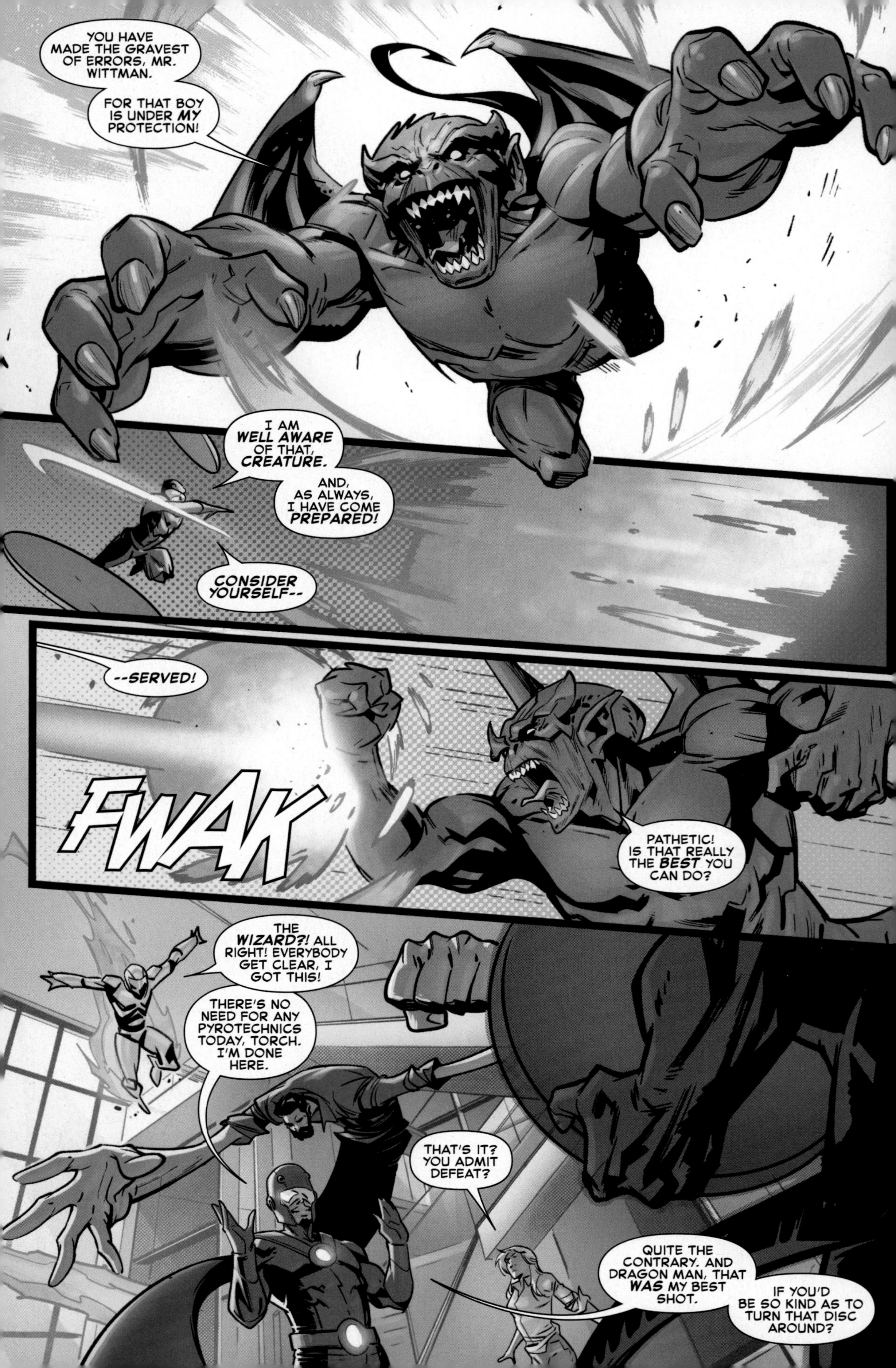
YOU HAVE MADE THE GRAVEST OF ERRORS, MR. WITTMAN.
FOR THAT BOY IS UNDER MY PROTECTION!
I AM WELL AWARE OF THAT, CREATURE.
AND, AS ALWAYS, I HAVE COME PREPARED!
CONSIDER YOURSELF--
--SERVED!
FWAK
PATHETIC! IS THAT REALLY THE BEST YOU CAN DO?
THE WIZARD?! ALL RIGHT! EVERYBODY GET CLEAR, I GOT THIS!
THERE'S NO NEED FOR ANY PYROTECHNICS TODAY, TORCH. I'M DONE HERE.
THAT'S IT? YOU ADMIT DEFEAT?
QUITE THE CONTRARY. AND DRAGON MAN, THAT WAS MY BEST SHOT.
IF YOU'D BE SO KIND AS TO TURN THAT DISC AROUND?

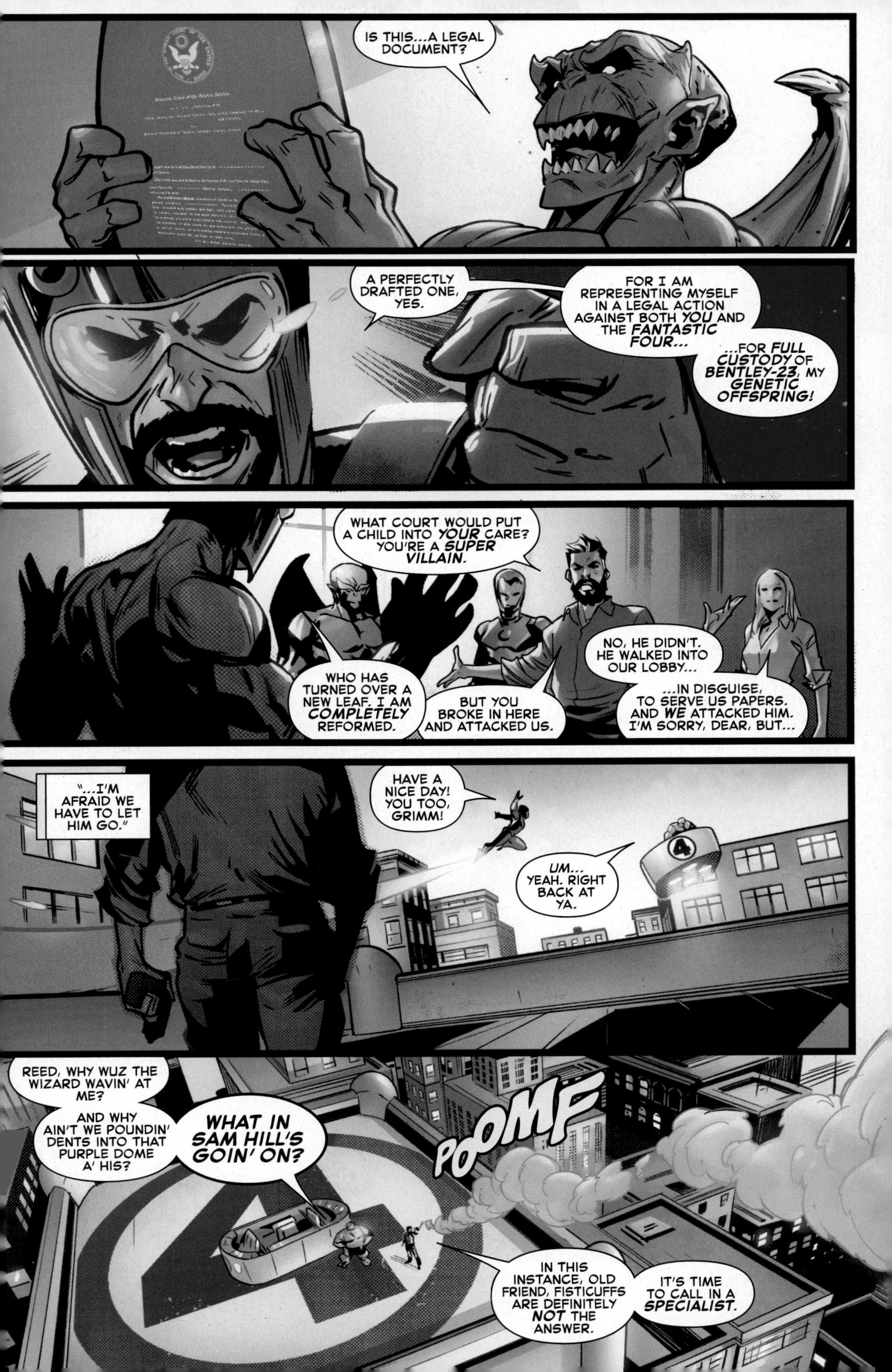
IS THIS...A LEGAL DOCUMENT?
A PERFECTLY DRAFTED ONE, YES.
FOR I AM REPRESENTING MYSELF IN A LEGAL ACTION AGAINST BOTH YOU AND THE FANTASTIC FOUR...
...FOR FULL CUSTODY OF BENTLEY-23, MY GENETIC OFFSPRING!
WHAT COURT WOULD PUT A CHILD INTO YOUR CARE? YOU'RE A SUPER VILLAIN.
WHO HAS TURNED OVER A NEW LEAF. I AM COMPLETELY REFORMED.
BUT YOU BROKE IN HERE AND ATTACKED US.
NO, HE DIDN'T. HE WALKED INTO OUR LOBBY...
...IN DISGUISE, TO SERVE US PAPERS. AND WE ATTACKED HIM. I'M SORRY, DEAR, BUT...
"...I'M AFRAID WE HAVE TO LET HIM GO."
HAVE A NICE DAY! YOU TOO, GRIMM!
UM... YEAH. RIGHT BACK AT YA.
REED, WHY WUZ THE WIZARD WAVIN' AT ME?
AND WHY AIN'T WE POUNDIN' DENTS INTO THAT PURPLE DOME A' HIS?
WHAT IN SAM HILL'S GOIN' ON?
POOMF
IN THIS INSTANCE, OLD FRIEND, FISTICUFFS ARE DEFINITELY NOT THE ANSWER.
IT'S TIME TO CALL IN A SPECIALIST.

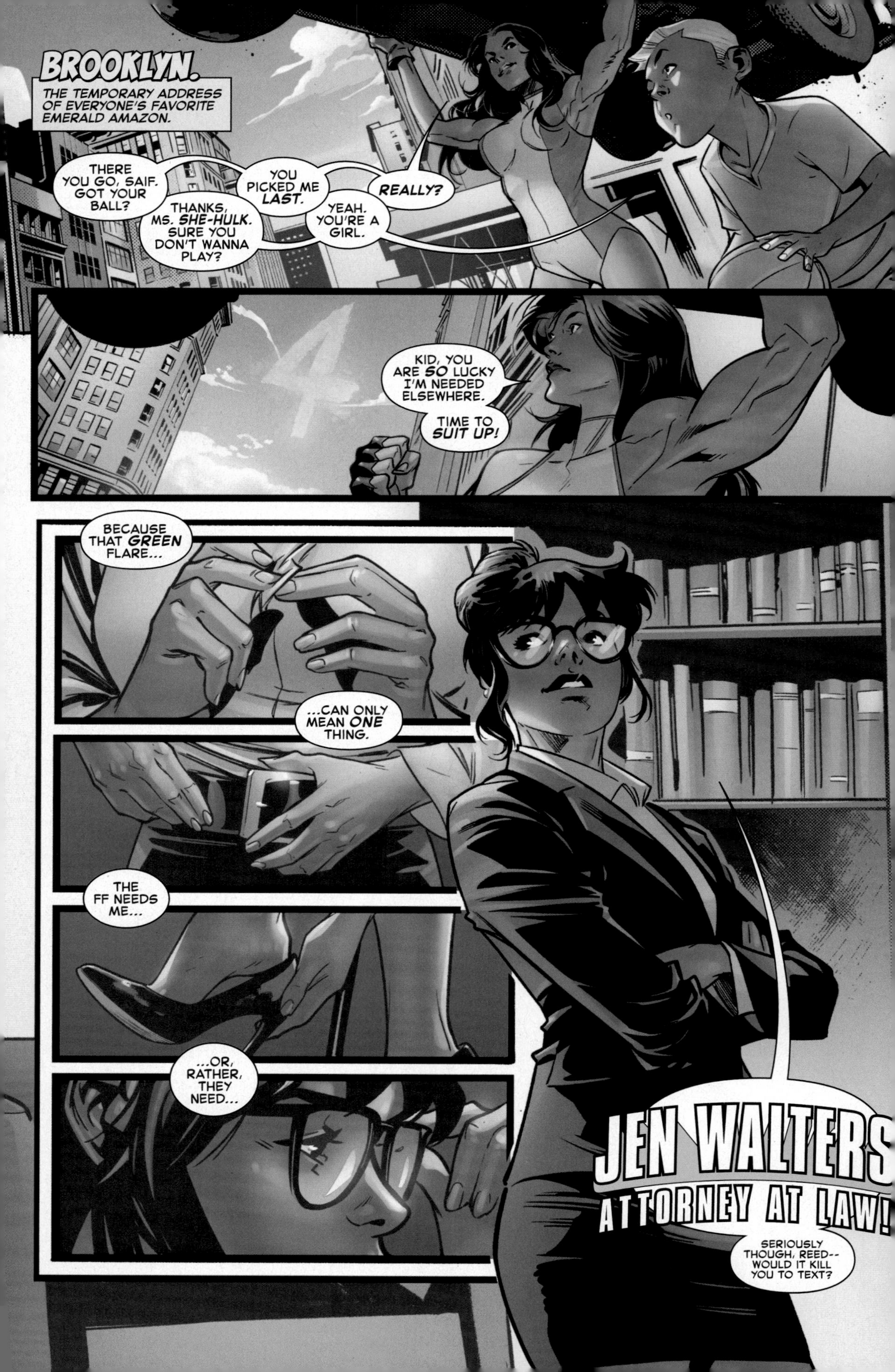
BROOKLYN.
THE TEMPORARY ADDRESS OF EVERYONE'S FAVORITE EMERALD AMAZON.
THERE YOU GO, SAIF. GOT YOUR BALL?
THANKS, MS. SHE-HULK. SURE YOU DON'T WANNA PLAY?
YOU PICKED ME LAST.
YEAH. YOU'RE A GIRL.
REALLY?
KID, YOU ARE SO LUCKY I'M NEEDED ELSEWHERE.
TIME TO SUIT UP!
BECAUSE THAT GREEN FLARE...
...CAN ONLY MEAN ONE THING.
THE FF NEEDS ME...
...OR, RATHER, THEY NEED...
JEN WALTERS
ATTORNEY AT LAW!
SERIOUSLY THOUGH, REED--WOULD IT KILL YOU TO TEXT?

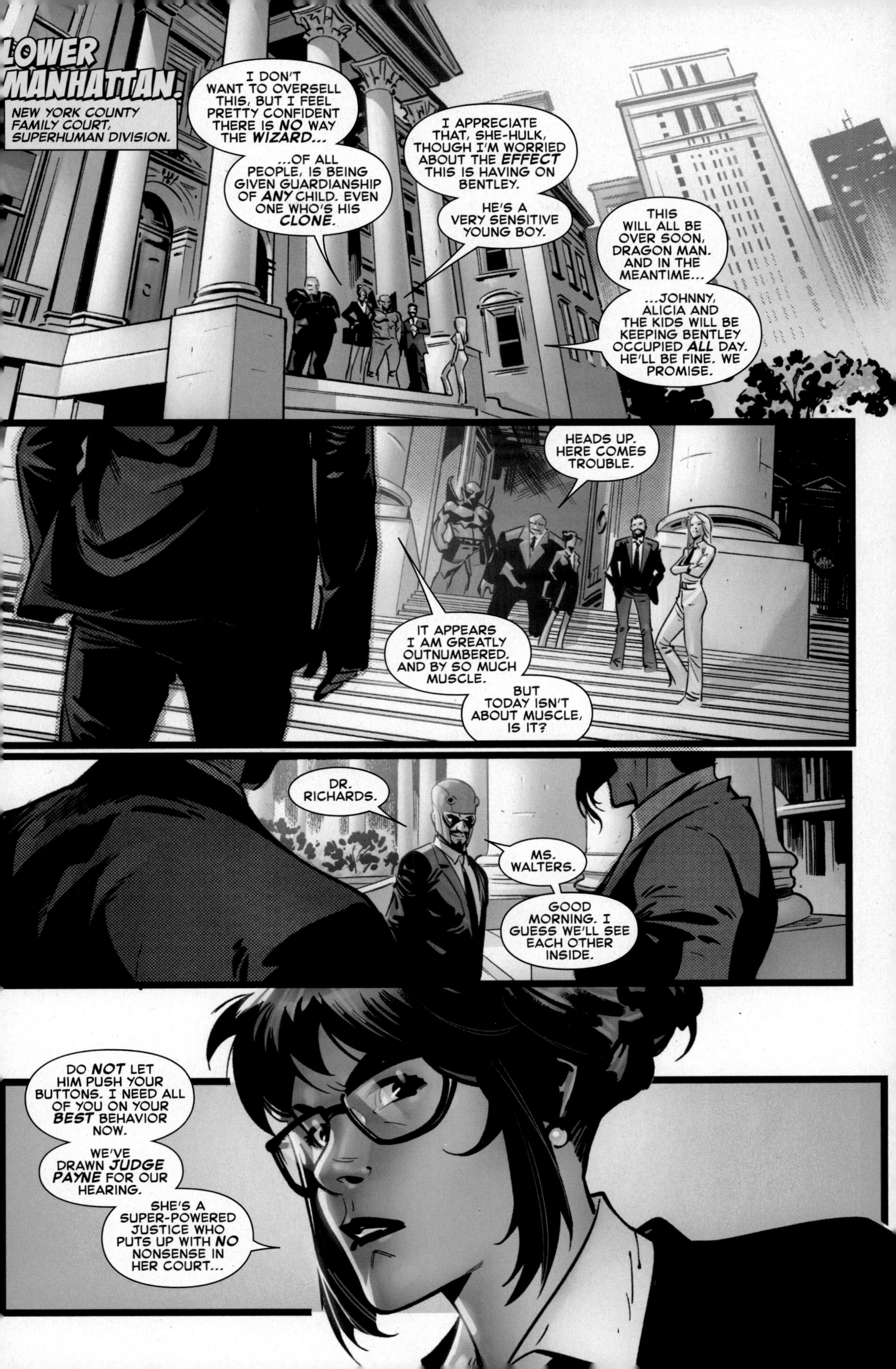
LOWER MANHATTAN.
NEW YORK COUNTY FAMILY COURT, SUPERHUMAN DIVISION.
I DON'T WANT TO OVERSELL THIS, BUT I FEEL PRETTY CONFIDENT THERE IS NO WAY THE WIZARD...
...OF ALL PEOPLE, IS BEING GIVEN GUARDIANSHIP OF ANY CHILD. EVEN ONE WHO'S HIS CLONE.
I APPRECIATE THAT, SHE-HULK, THOUGH I'M WORRIED ABOUT THE EFFECT THIS IS HAVING ON BENTLEY.
HE'S A VERY SENSITIVE YOUNG BOY.
THIS WILL ALL BE OVER SOON, DRAGON MAN. AND IN THE MEANTIME...
...JOHNNY, ALICIA AND THE KIDS WILL BE KEEPING BENTLEY OCCUPIED ALL DAY. HE'LL BE FINE. WE PROMISE.
HEADS UP. HERE COMES TROUBLE.
IT APPEARS I AM GREATLY OUTNUMBERED. AND BY SO MUCH MUSCLE.
BUT TODAY ISN'T ABOUT MUSCLE, IS IT?
DR. RICHARDS.
MS. WALTERS.
GOOD MORNING. I GUESS WE'LL SEE EACH OTHER INSIDE.
DO NOT LET HIM PUSH YOUR BUTTONS. I NEED ALL OF YOU ON YOUR BEST BEHAVIOR NOW.
WE'VE DRAWN JUDGE PAYNE FOR OUR HEARING.
SHE'S A SUPER-POWERED JUSTICE WHO PUTS UP WITH NO NONSENSE IN HER COURT...

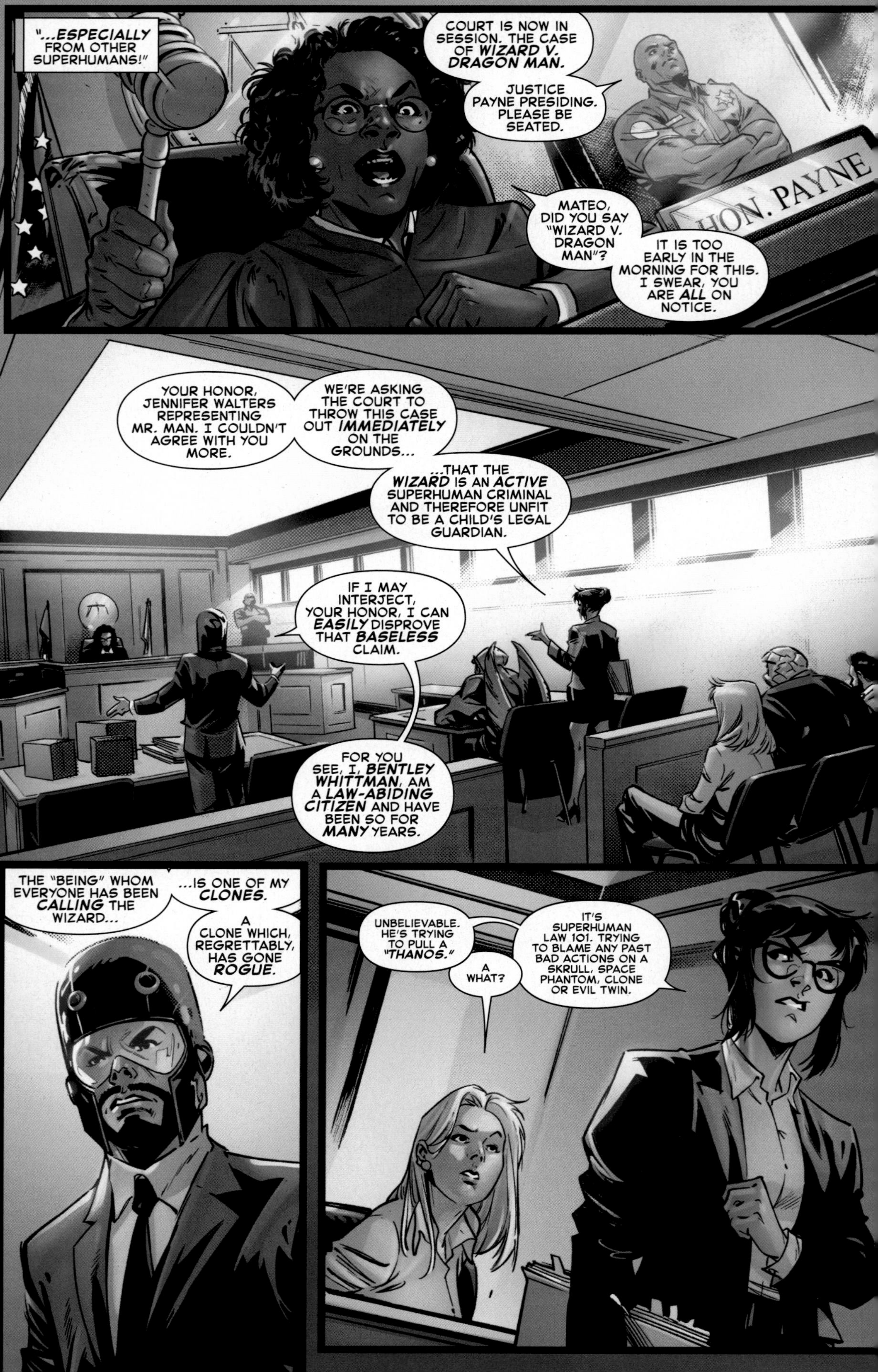
"...ESPECIALLY FROM OTHER SUPERHUMANS!"
COURT IS NOW IN SESSION. THE CASE OF WIZARD V. DRAGON MAN.
JUSTICE PAYNE PRESIDING. PLEASE BE SEATED.
HON. PAYNE
MATEO, DID YOU SAY "WIZARD V. DRAGON MAN"?
IT IS TOO EARLY IN THE MORNING FOR THIS. I SWEAR, YOU ARE ALL ON NOTICE.
YOUR HONOR, JENNIFER WALTERS REPRESENTING MR. MAN. I COULDN'T AGREE WITH YOU MORE.
WE'RE ASKING THE COURT TO THROW THIS CASE OUT IMMEDIATELY ON THE GROUNDS...
...THAT THE WIZARD IS AN ACTIVE SUPERHUMAN CRIMINAL AND THEREFORE UNFIT TO BE A CHILD'S LEGAL GUARDIAN.
IF I MAY INTERJECT, YOUR HONOR, I CAN EASILY DISPROVE THAT BASELESS CLAIM.
FOR YOU SEE, I, BENTLEY WHITTMAN, AM A LAW-ABIDING CITIZEN AND HAVE BEEN SO FOR MANY YEARS.
THE "BEING" WHOM EVERYONE HAS BEEN CALLING THE WIZARD...
...IS ONE OF MY CLONES.
A CLONE WHICH, REGRETTABLY, HAS GONE ROGUE.
UNBELIEVABLE. HE'S TRYING TO PULL A "THANOS."
A WHAT?
IT'S SUPERHUMAN LAW 101. TRYING TO BLAME ANY PAST BAD ACTIONS ON A SKRULL, SPACE PHANTOM, CLONE OR EVIL TWIN.

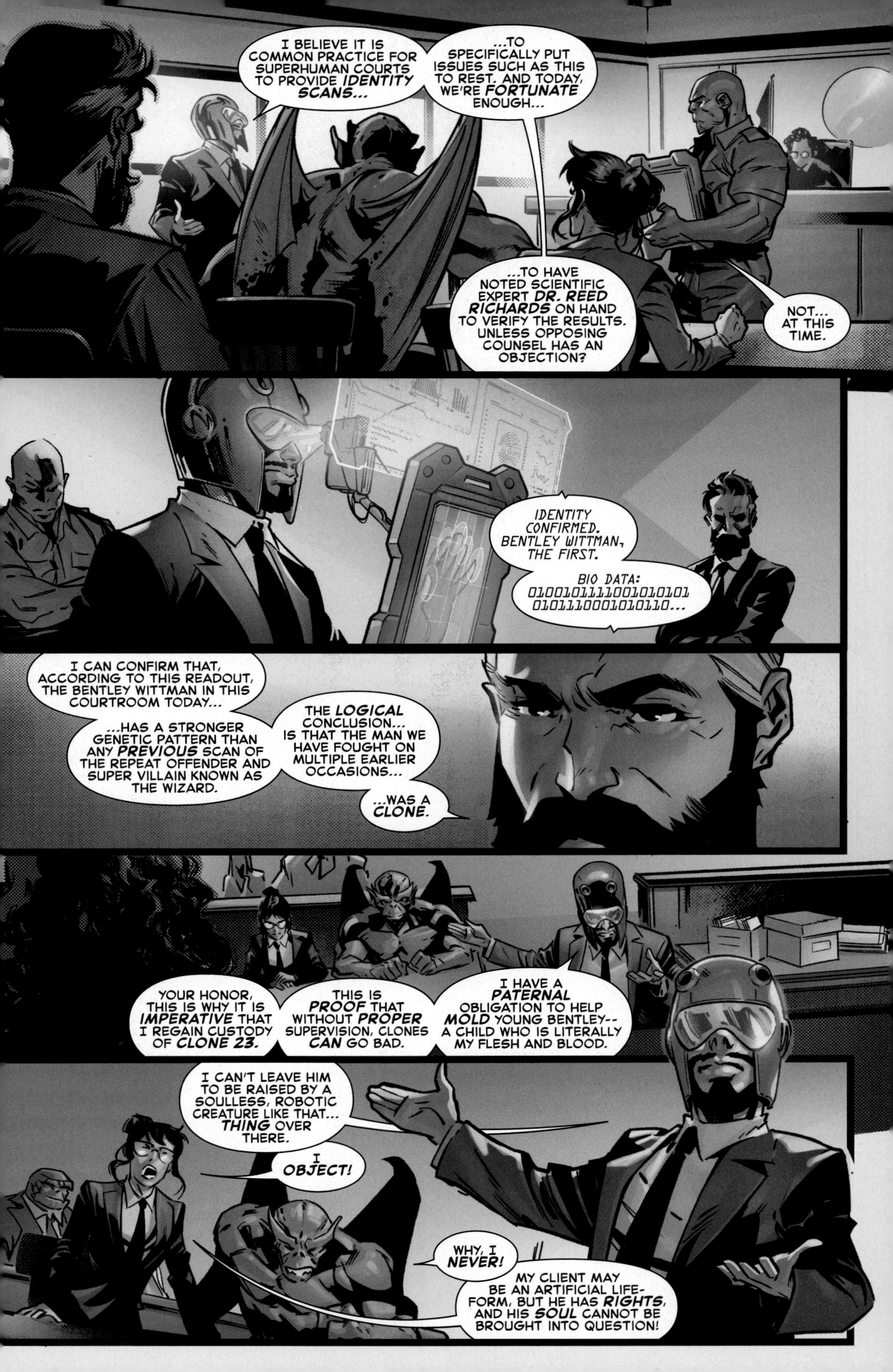
I BELIEVE IT IS COMMON PRACTICE FOR SUPERHUMAN COURTS TO PROVIDE IDENTITY SCANS...
...TO SPECIFICALLY PUT ISSUES SUCH AS THIS TO REST. AND TODAY, WE'RE FORTUNATE ENOUGH...
...TO HAVE NOTED SCIENTIFIC EXPERT DR. REED RICHARDS ON HAND TO VERIFY THE RESULTS. UNLESS OPPOSING COUNSEL HAS AN OBJECTION?
NOT... AT THIS TIME.
IDENTITY CONFIRMED. BENTLEY WITTMAN, THE FIRST.
BIO DATA: 01001011111001010101 0101110001010110...
I CAN CONFIRM THAT, ACCORDING TO THIS READOUT, THE BENTLEY WITTMAN IN THIS COURTROOM TODAY...
...HAS A STRONGER GENETIC PATTERN THAN ANY PREVIOUS SCAN OF THE REPEAT OFFENDER AND SUPER VILLAIN KNOWN AS THE WIZARD.
THE LOGICAL CONCLUSION... IS THAT THE MAN WE HAVE FOUGHT ON MULTIPLE EARLIER OCCASIONS...
...WAS A CLONE.
YOUR HONOR, THIS IS WHY IT IS IMPERATIVE THAT I REGAIN CUSTODY OF CLONE 23.
THIS IS PROOF THAT WITHOUT PROPER SUPERVISION, CLONES CAN GO BAD.
I HAVE A PATERNAL OBLIGATION TO HELP MOLD YOUNG BENTLEY-- A CHILD WHO IS LITERALLY MY FLESH AND BLOOD.
I CAN'T LEAVE HIM TO BE RAISED BY A SOULLESS, ROBOTIC CREATURE LIKE THAT... THING OVER THERE.
I OBJECT!
WHY, I NEVER!
MY CLIENT MAY BE AN ARTIFICIAL LIFE-FORM, BUT HE HAS RIGHTS, AND HIS SOUL CANNOT BE BROUGHT INTO QUESTION!

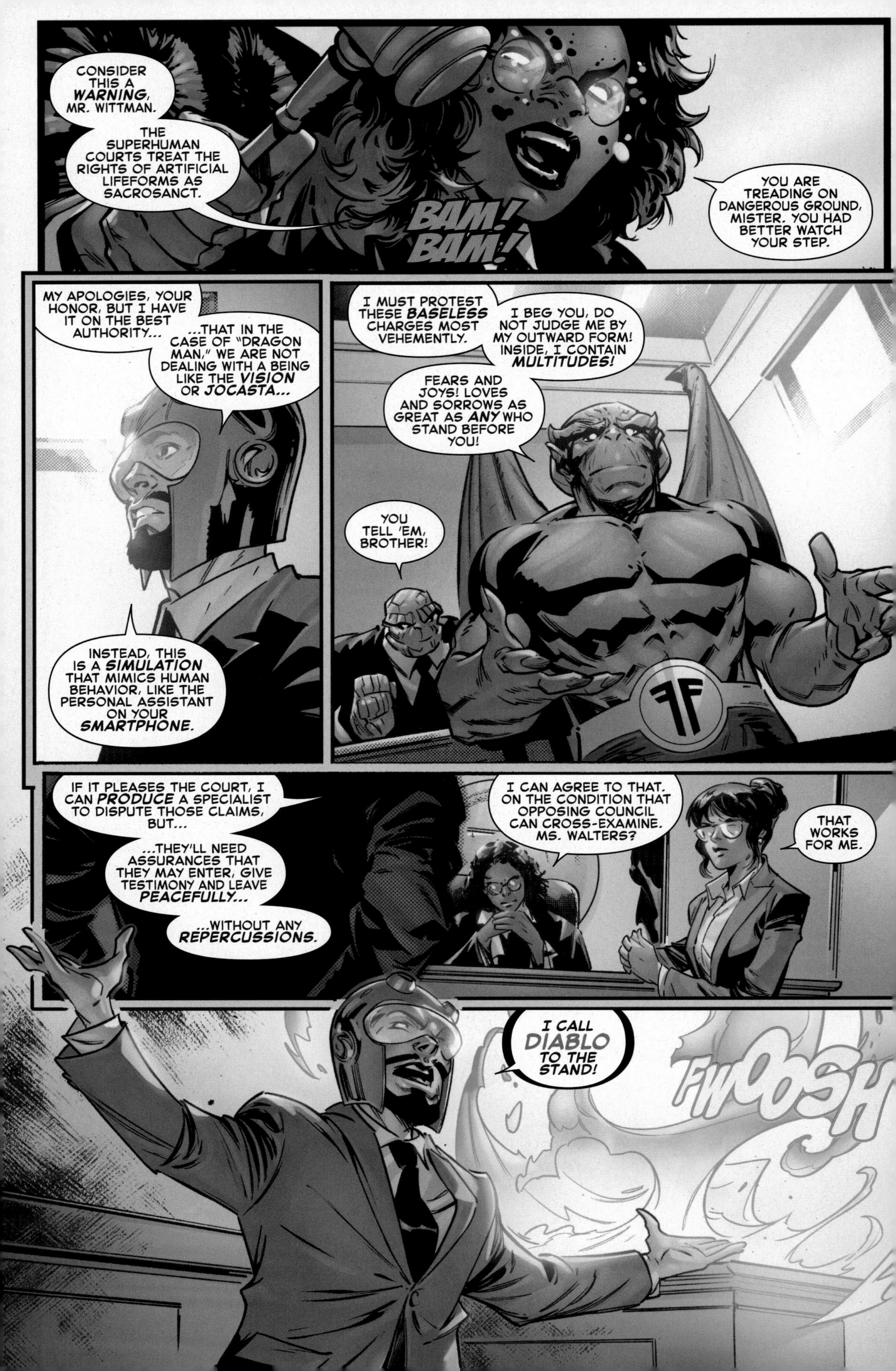
CONSIDER THIS A WARNING, MR. WITTMAN.
THE SUPERHUMAN COURTS TREAT THE RIGHTS OF ARTIFICIAL LIFEFORMS AS SACROSANCT.
BAM! BAM!
YOU ARE TREADING ON DANGEROUS GROUND, MISTER. YOU HAD BETTER WATCH YOUR STEP.
MY APOLOGIES, YOUR HONOR, BUT I HAVE IT ON THE BEST AUTHORITY...
...THAT IN THE CASE OF "DRAGON MAN," WE ARE NOT DEALING WITH A BEING LIKE THE VISION OR JOCASTA...
INSTEAD, THIS IS A SIMULATION THAT MIMICS HUMAN BEHAVIOR, LIKE THE PERSONAL ASSISTANT ON YOUR SMARTPHONE.
I MUST PROTEST THESE BASELESS CHARGES MOST VEHEMENTLY.
I BEG YOU, DO NOT JUDGE ME BY MY OUTWARD FORM! INSIDE, I CONTAIN MULTITUDES!
FEARS AND JOYS! LOVES AND SORROWS AS GREAT AS ANY WHO STAND BEFORE YOU!
YOU TELL 'EM, BROTHER!
IF IT PLEASES THE COURT, I CAN PRODUCE A SPECIALIST TO DISPUTE THOSE CLAIMS, BUT...
...THEY'LL NEED ASSURANCES THAT THEY MAY ENTER, GIVE TESTIMONY AND LEAVE PEACEFULLY...
...WITHOUT ANY REPERCUSSIONS.
I CAN AGREE TO THAT. ON THE CONDITION THAT OPPOSING COUNCIL CAN CROSS-EXAMINE. MS. WALTERS?
THAT WORKS FOR ME.
I CALL DIABLO TO THE STAND!
FWOOSH

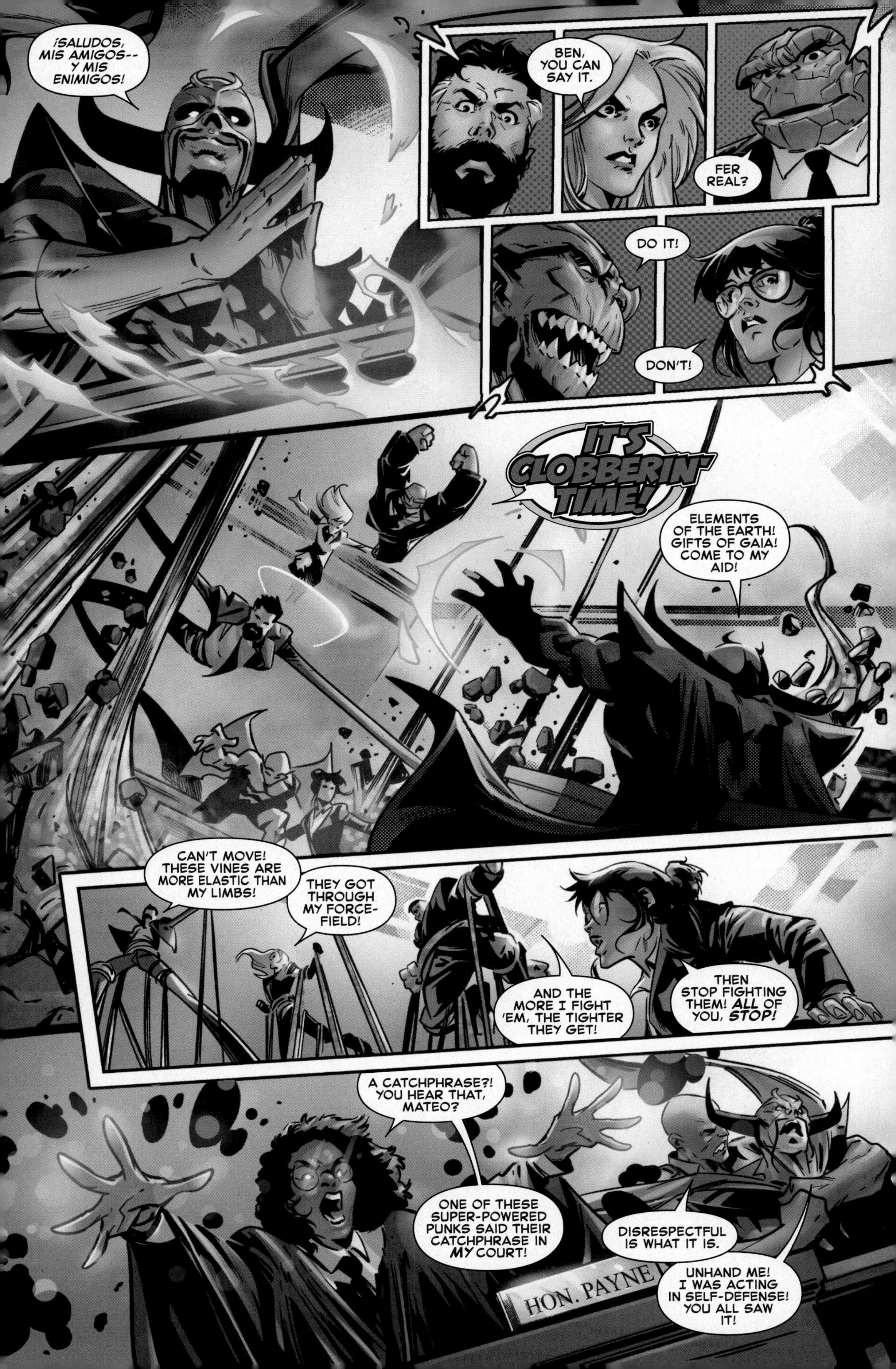

¡SALUDOS, MIS AMIGOS-- Y MIS ENIMIGOS!
BEN, YOU CAN SAY IT.
FER REAL?
DO IT!
DON'T!
IT'S CLOBBERIN' TIME!
ELEMENTS OF THE EARTH! GIFTS OF GAIA! COME TO MY AID!
CAN'T MOVE! THESE VINES ARE MORE ELASTIC THAN MY LIMBS!
THEY GOT THROUGH MY FORCE-FIELD!
AND THE MORE I FIGHT 'EM, THE TIGHTER THEY GET!
THEN STOP FIGHTING THEM! ALL OF YOU, STOP!
A CATCHPHRASE?! YOU HEAR THAT, MATEO?
ONE OF THESE SUPER-POWERED PUNKS SAID THEIR CATCHPHRASE IN MY COURT!
DISRESPECTFUL IS WHAT IT IS.
UNHAND ME! I WAS ACTING IN SELF-DEFENSE! YOU ALL SAW IT!
HON. PAYNE

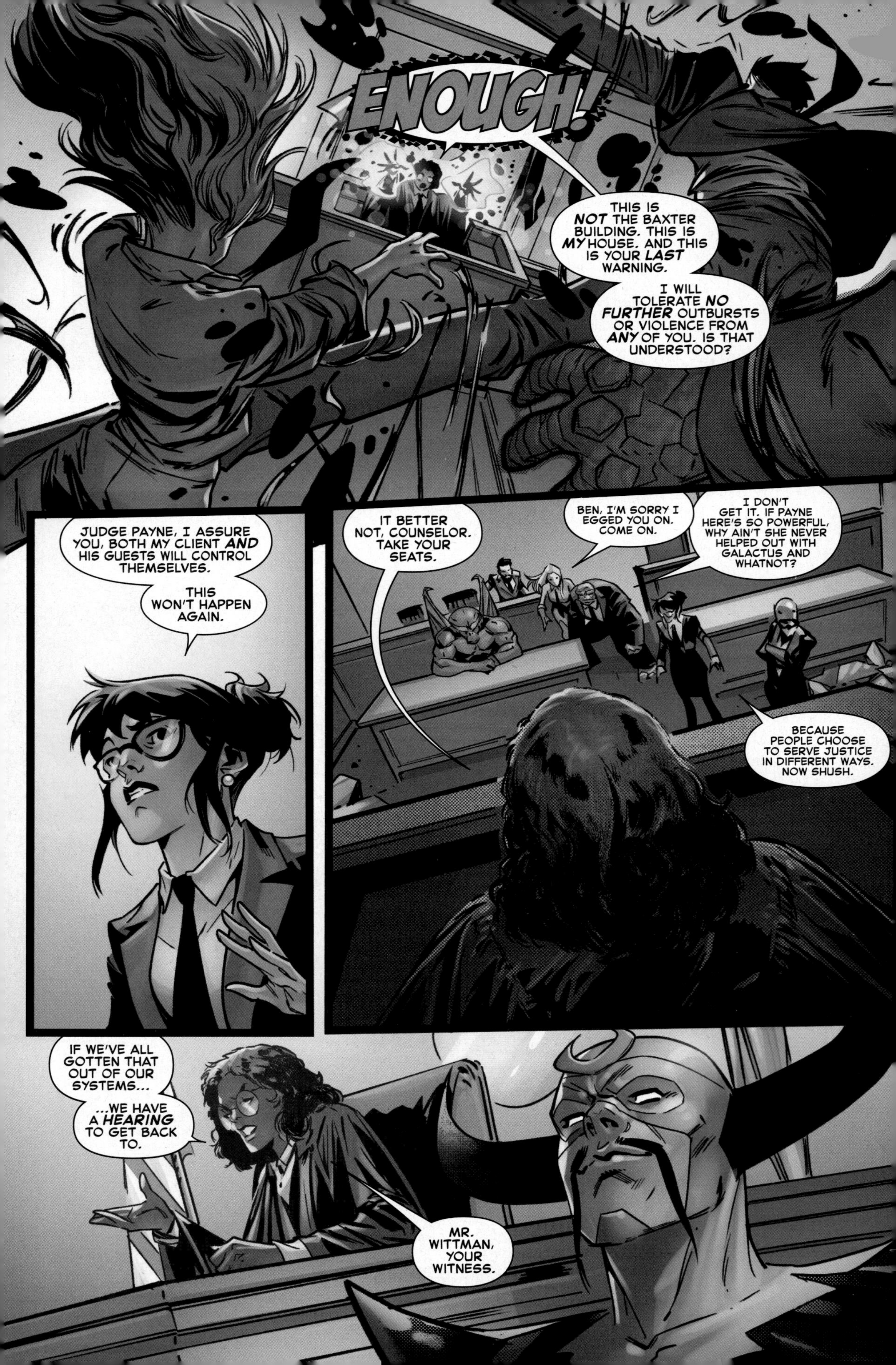
ENOUGH!
THIS IS NOT THE BAXTER BUILDING. THIS IS MY HOUSE. AND THIS IS YOUR LAST WARNING.
I WILL TOLERATE NO FURTHER OUTBURSTS OR VIOLENCE FROM ANY OF YOU. IS THAT UNDERSTOOD?
JUDGE PAYNE, I ASSURE YOU, BOTH MY CLIENT AND HIS GUESTS WILL CONTROL THEMSELVES.
THIS WON'T HAPPEN AGAIN.
IT BETTER NOT, COUNSELOR. TAKE YOUR SEATS.
BEN, I'M SORRY I EGGED YOU ON. COME ON.
I DON'T GET IT. IF PAYNE HERE'S SO POWERFUL, WHY AIN'T SHE NEVER HELPED OUT WITH GALACTUS AND WHATNOT?
BECAUSE PEOPLE CHOOSE TO SERVE JUSTICE IN DIFFERENT WAYS. NOW SHUSH.
IF WE'VE ALL GOTTEN THAT OUT OF OUR SYSTEMS...
...WE HAVE A HEARING TO GET BACK TO.
MR. WITTMAN, YOUR WITNESS.

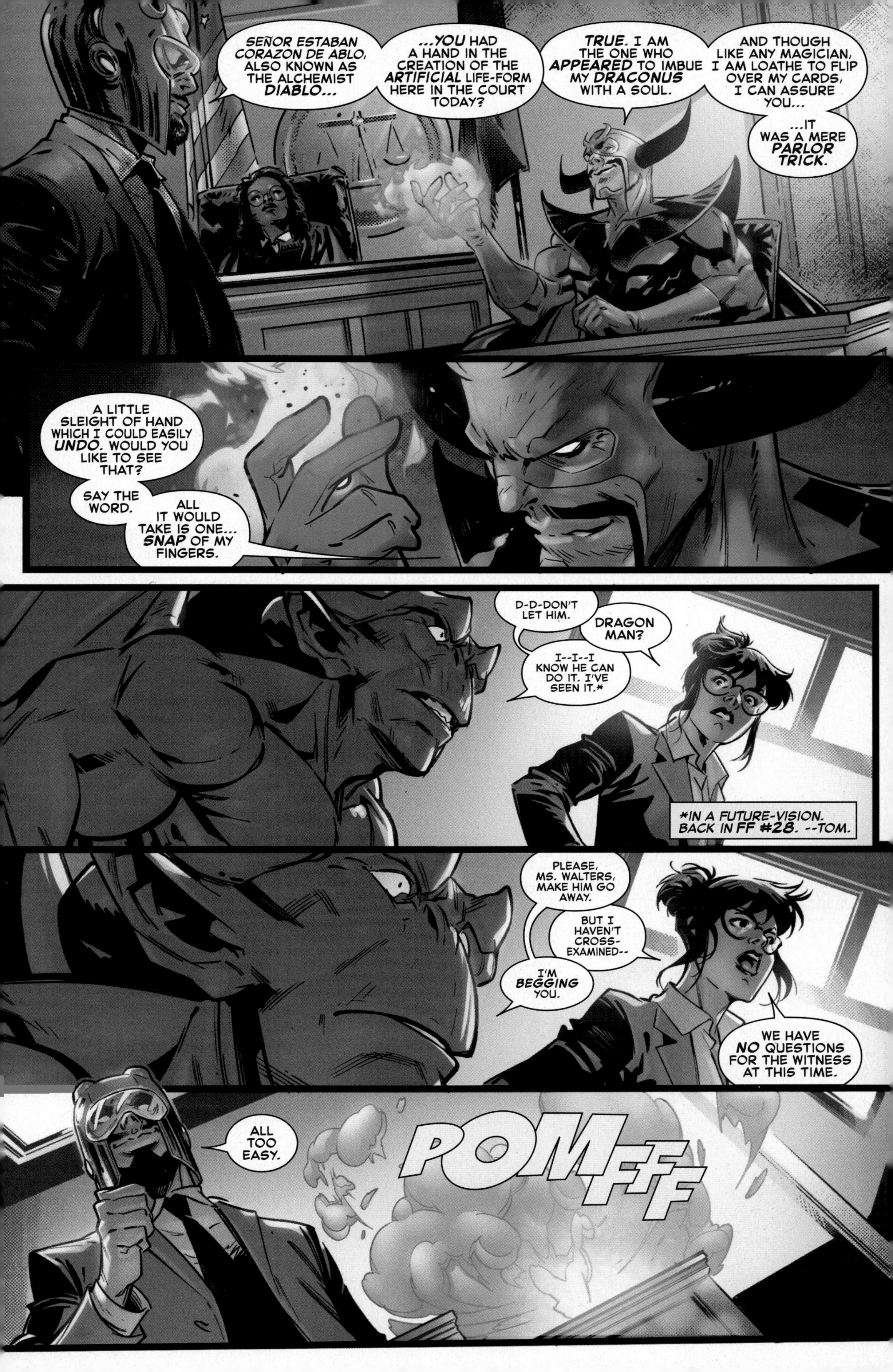
SEÑOR ESTABAN CORAZON DE ABLO, ALSO KNOWN AS THE ALCHEMIST DIABLO...
...YOU HAD A HAND IN THE CREATION OF THE ARTIFICIAL LIFE-FORM HERE IN THE COURT TODAY?
TRUE. I AM THE ONE WHO APPEARED TO IMBUE MY DRACONUS WITH A SOUL.
AND THOUGH LIKE ANY MAGICIAN, I AM LOATHE TO FLIP OVER MY CARDS, I CAN ASSURE YOU...
...IT WAS A MERE PARLOR TRICK.
A LITTLE SLEIGHT OF HAND WHICH I COULD EASILY UNDO. WOULD YOU LIKE TO SEE THAT?
SAY THE WORD.
ALL IT WOULD TAKE IS ONE... SNAP OF MY FINGERS.
D-D-DON'T LET HIM.
DRAGON MAN?
I--I--I KNOW HE CAN DO IT. I'VE SEEN IT.*
*IN A FUTURE-VISION. BACK IN FF #28. --TOM.
PLEASE, MS. WALTERS, MAKE HIM GO AWAY.
BUT I HAVEN'T CROSS-EXAMINED--
I'M BEGGING YOU.
WE HAVE NO QUESTIONS FOR THE WITNESS AT THIS TIME.
ALL TOO EASY.
POMFFF

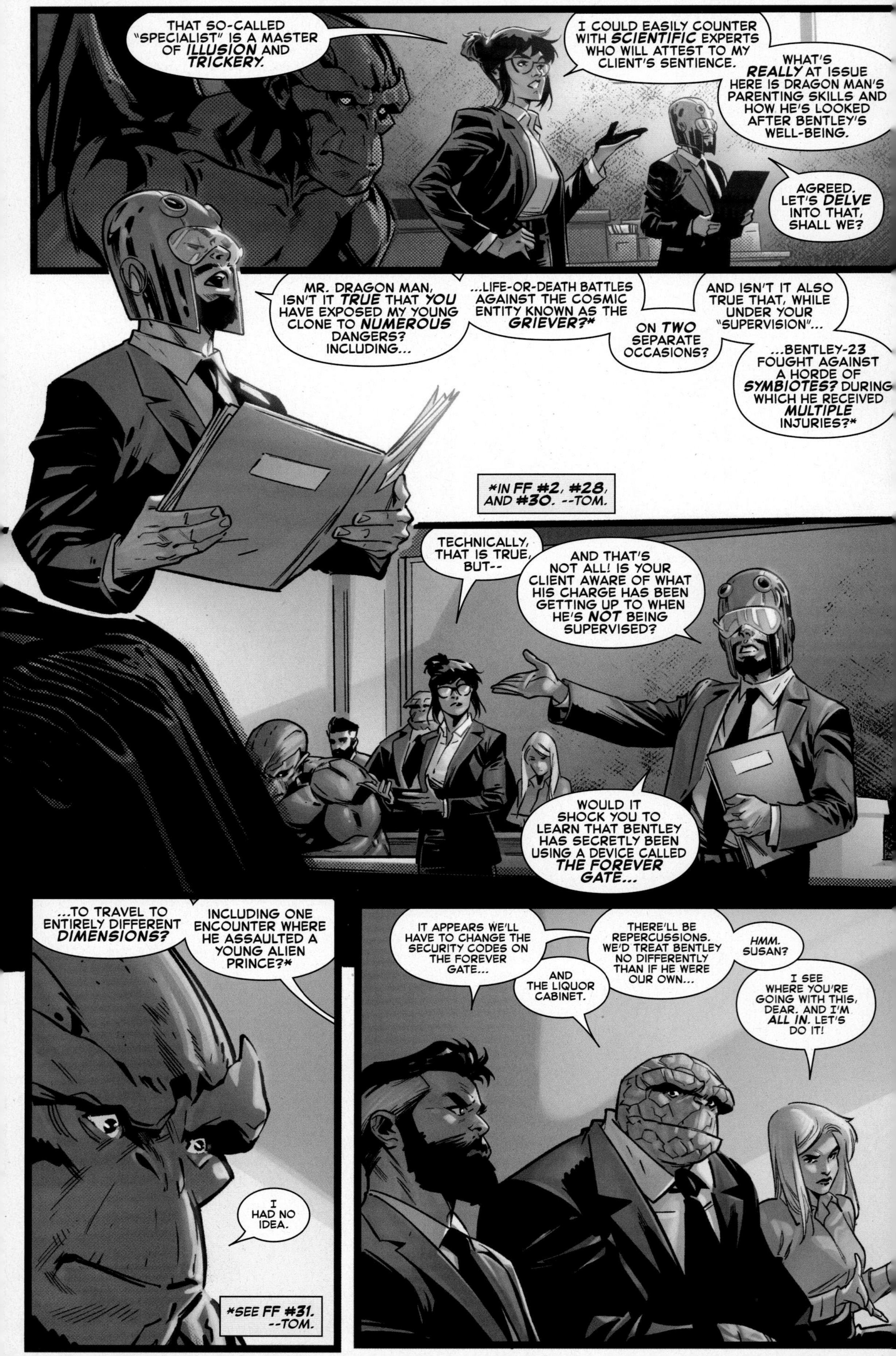
THAT SO-CALLED "SPECIALIST" IS A MASTER OF ILLUSION AND TRICKERY.
I COULD EASILY COUNTER WITH SCIENTIFIC EXPERTS WHO WILL ATTEST TO MY CLIENT'S SENTIENCE.
WHAT'S REALLY AT ISSUE HERE IS DRAGON MAN'S PARENTING SKILLS AND HOW HE'S LOOKED AFTER BENTLEY'S WELL-BEING.
AGREED. LET'S DELVE INTO THAT, SHALL WE?
MR. DRAGON MAN, ISN'T IT TRUE THAT YOU HAVE EXPOSED MY YOUNG CLONE TO NUMEROUS DANGERS? INCLUDING...
...LIFE-OR-DEATH BATTLES AGAINST THE COSMIC ENTITY KNOWN AS THE GRIEVER?*
ON TWO SEPARATE OCCASIONS?
AND ISN'T IT ALSO TRUE THAT, WHILE UNDER YOUR "SUPERVISION"...
...BENTLEY-23 FOUGHT AGAINST A HORDE OF SYMBIOTES? DURING WHICH HE RECEIVED MULTIPLE INJURIES?*
*IN FF #2, #28, AND #30. --TOM.
TECHNICALLY, THAT IS TRUE, BUT--
AND THAT'S NOT ALL! IS YOUR CLIENT AWARE OF WHAT HIS CHARGE HAS BEEN GETTING UP TO WHEN HE'S NOT BEING SUPERVISED?
WOULD IT SHOCK YOU TO LEARN THAT BENTLEY HAS SECRETLY BEEN USING A DEVICE CALLED THE FOREVER GATE...
...TO TRAVEL TO ENTIRELY DIFFERENT DIMENSIONS?
INCLUDING ONE ENCOUNTER WHERE HE ASSAULTED A YOUNG ALIEN PRINCE?*
I HAD NO IDEA.
*SEE FF #31. --TOM.
IT APPEARS WE'LL HAVE TO CHANGE THE SECURITY CODES ON THE FOREVER GATE...
AND THE LIQUOR CABINET.
THERE'LL BE REPERCUSSIONS. WE'D TREAT BENTLEY NO DIFFERENTLY THAN IF HE WERE OUR OWN...
HMM. SUSAN?
I SEE WHERE YOU'RE GOING WITH THIS, DEAR. AND I'M ALL IN. LET'S DO IT!

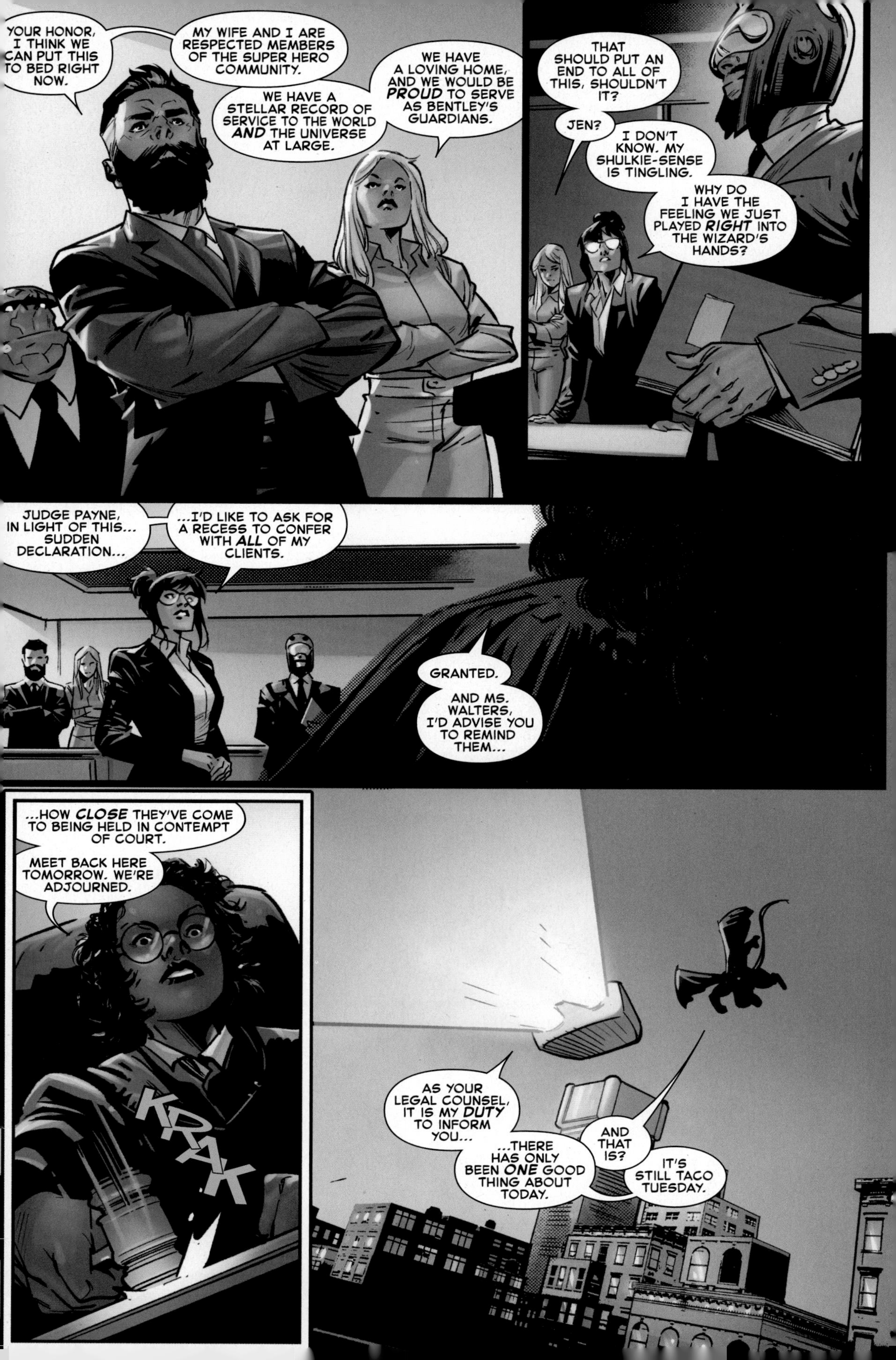
YOUR HONOR, I THINK WE CAN PUT THIS TO BED RIGHT NOW.
MY WIFE AND I ARE RESPECTED MEMBERS OF THE SUPER HERO COMMUNITY.
WE HAVE A STELLAR RECORD OF SERVICE TO THE WORLD AND THE UNIVERSE AT LARGE.
WE HAVE A LOVING HOME, AND WE WOULD BE PROUD TO SERVE AS BENTLEY'S GUARDIANS.
THAT SHOULD PUT AN END TO ALL OF THIS, SHOULDN'T IT?
JEN?
I DON'T KNOW. MY SHULKIE-SENSE IS TINGLING.
WHY DO I HAVE THE FEELING WE JUST PLAYED RIGHT INTO THE WIZARD'S HANDS?
JUDGE PAYNE, IN LIGHT OF THIS... SUDDEN DECLARATION...
...I'D LIKE TO ASK FOR A RECESS TO CONFER WITH ALL OF MY CLIENTS.
GRANTED.
AND MS. WALTERS, I'D ADVISE YOU TO REMIND THEM...
...HOW CLOSE THEY'VE COME TO BEING HELD IN CONTEMPT OF COURT.
MEET BACK HERE TOMORROW. WE'RE ADJOURNED.
KRAK
AS YOUR LEGAL COUNSEL, IT IS MY DUTY TO INFORM YOU...
AND THAT IS?
...THERE HAS ONLY BEEN ONE GOOD THING ABOUT TODAY.
IT'S STILL TACO TUESDAY.

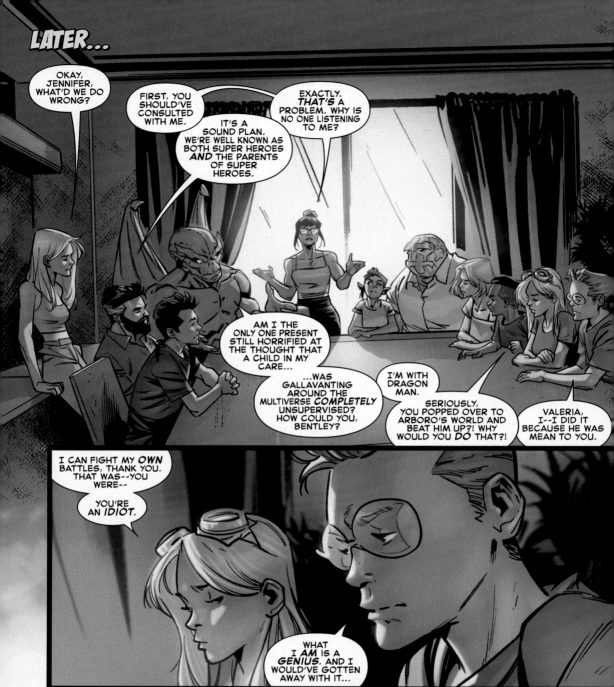

OKAY, JENNIFER, WHAT'D WE DO WRONG?

FIRST, YOU SHOULD'VE CONSULTED WITH ME.

IT'S A SOUND PLAN. WE'RE WELL KNOWN AS BOTH SUPER HEROES *AND* THE PARENTS OF SUPER HEROES.

EXACTLY. *THAT'S* A PROBLEM. WHY IS NO ONE LISTENING TO ME?

AM I THE ONLY ONE PRESENT STILL HORRIFIED AT THE THOUGHT THAT A CHILD IN MY CARE...

...WAS GALLAVANTING AROUND THE MULTIVERSE *COMPLETELY* UNSUPERVISED? HOW COULD YOU, BENTLEY?

I'M WITH DRAGON MAN.

SERIOUSLY, YOU POPPED OVER TO ARBORO'S WORLD AND BEAT HIM UP?! WHY WOULD YOU *DO* THAT?!

VALERIA, I--I DID IT BECAUSE HE WAS MEAN TO YOU.

I CAN FIGHT MY *OWN* BATTLES, THANK YOU. THAT WAS--YOU WERE--

YOU'RE AN *IDIOT*.

WHAT I *AM* IS A *GENIUS*. AND I WOULD'VE GOTTEN AWAY WITH IT...

...IF THE *WIZARD* HADN'T RATTED ME OUT. HOW DID HE *DO* THAT?

WAIT. WHAT DID HE SAY BEFORE?

"I KNOW YOU CAN SEE THIS, BOY." NOT *HEAR* THIS. *SEE* THIS. HMM.

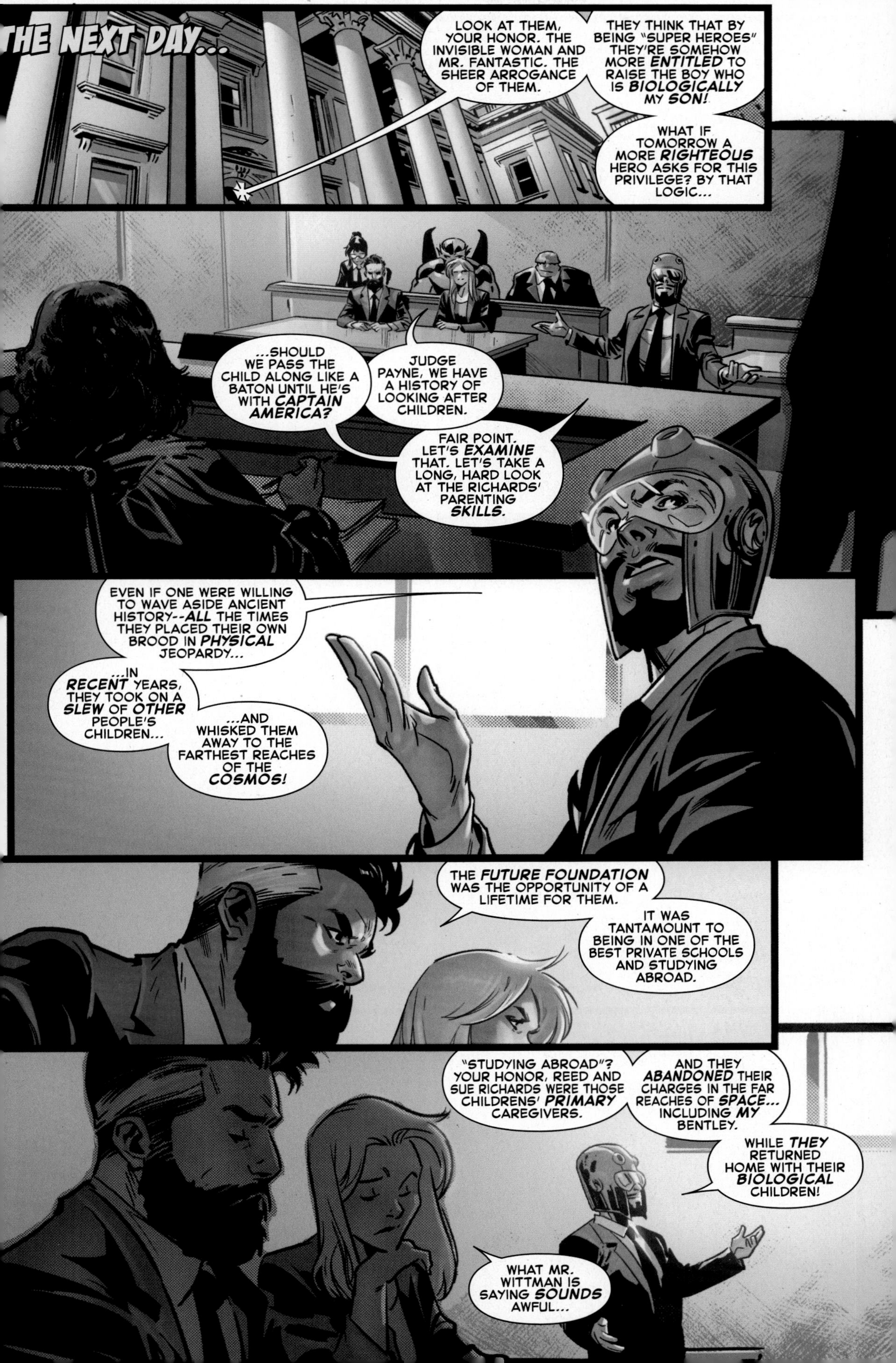
THE NEXT DAY...
LOOK AT THEM, YOUR HONOR. THE INVISIBLE WOMAN AND MR. FANTASTIC. THE SHEER ARROGANCE OF THEM.
THEY THINK THAT BY BEING "SUPER HEROES" THEY'RE SOMEHOW MORE ENTITLED TO RAISE THE BOY WHO IS BIOLOGICALLY MY SON!
WHAT IF TOMORROW A MORE RIGHTEOUS HERO ASKS FOR THIS PRIVILEGE? BY THAT LOGIC...
...SHOULD WE PASS THE CHILD ALONG LIKE A BATON UNTIL HE'S WITH CAPTAIN AMERICA?
JUDGE PAYNE, WE HAVE A HISTORY OF LOOKING AFTER CHILDREN.
FAIR POINT. LET'S EXAMINE THAT. LET'S TAKE A LONG, HARD LOOK AT THE RICHARDS' PARENTING SKILLS.
EVEN IF ONE WERE WILLING TO WAVE ASIDE ANCIENT HISTORY--ALL THE TIMES THEY PLACED THEIR OWN BROOD IN PHYSICAL JEOPARDY...
...IN RECENT YEARS, THEY TOOK ON A SLEW OF OTHER PEOPLE'S CHILDREN...
...AND WHISKED THEM AWAY TO THE FARTHEST REACHES OF THE COSMOS!
THE FUTURE FOUNDATION WAS THE OPPORTUNITY OF A LIFETIME FOR THEM.
IT WAS TANTAMOUNT TO BEING IN ONE OF THE BEST PRIVATE SCHOOLS AND STUDYING ABROAD.
"STUDYING ABROAD"? YOUR HONOR, REED AND SUE RICHARDS WERE THOSE CHILDRENS' PRIMARY CAREGIVERS.
AND THEY ABANDONED THEIR CHARGES IN THE FAR REACHES OF SPACE... INCLUDING MY BENTLEY.
WHILE THEY RETURNED HOME WITH THEIR BIOLOGICAL CHILDREN!
WHAT MR. WITTMAN IS SAYING SOUNDS AWFUL...

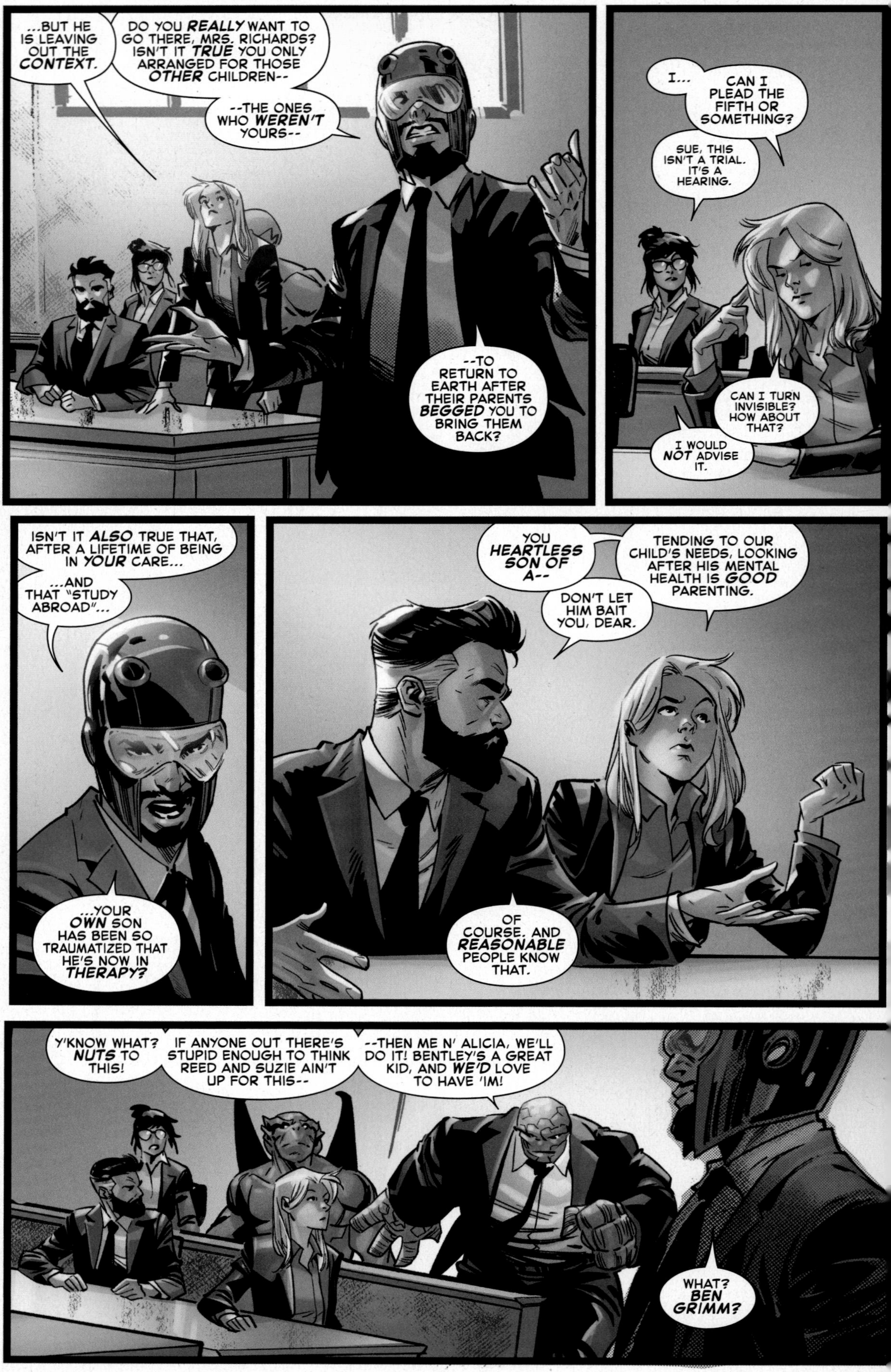
...BUT HE IS LEAVING OUT THE CONTEXT.
DO YOU REALLY WANT TO GO THERE, MRS. RICHARDS? ISN'T IT TRUE YOU ONLY ARRANGED FOR THOSE OTHER CHILDREN--
--THE ONES WHO WEREN'T YOURS--
--TO RETURN TO EARTH AFTER THEIR PARENTS BEGGED YOU TO BRING THEM BACK?
I...
CAN I PLEAD THE FIFTH OR SOMETHING?
SUE, THIS ISN'T A TRIAL. IT'S A HEARING.
CAN I TURN INVISIBLE? HOW ABOUT THAT?
I WOULD NOT ADVISE IT.
ISN'T IT ALSO TRUE THAT, AFTER A LIFETIME OF BEING IN YOUR CARE...
...AND THAT "STUDY ABROAD"...
...YOUR OWN SON HAS BEEN SO TRAUMATIZED THAT HE'S NOW IN THERAPY?
YOU HEARTLESS SON OF A--
DON'T LET HIM BAIT YOU, DEAR.
TENDING TO OUR CHILD'S NEEDS, LOOKING AFTER HIS MENTAL HEALTH IS GOOD PARENTING.
OF COURSE. AND REASONABLE PEOPLE KNOW THAT.
Y'KNOW WHAT? NUTS TO THIS!
IF ANYONE OUT THERE'S STUPID ENOUGH TO THINK REED AND SUZIE AIN'T UP FOR THIS--
--THEN ME N' ALICIA, WE'LL DO IT! BENTLEY'S A GREAT KID, AND WE'D LOVE TO HAVE 'IM!
WHAT? BEN GRIMM?

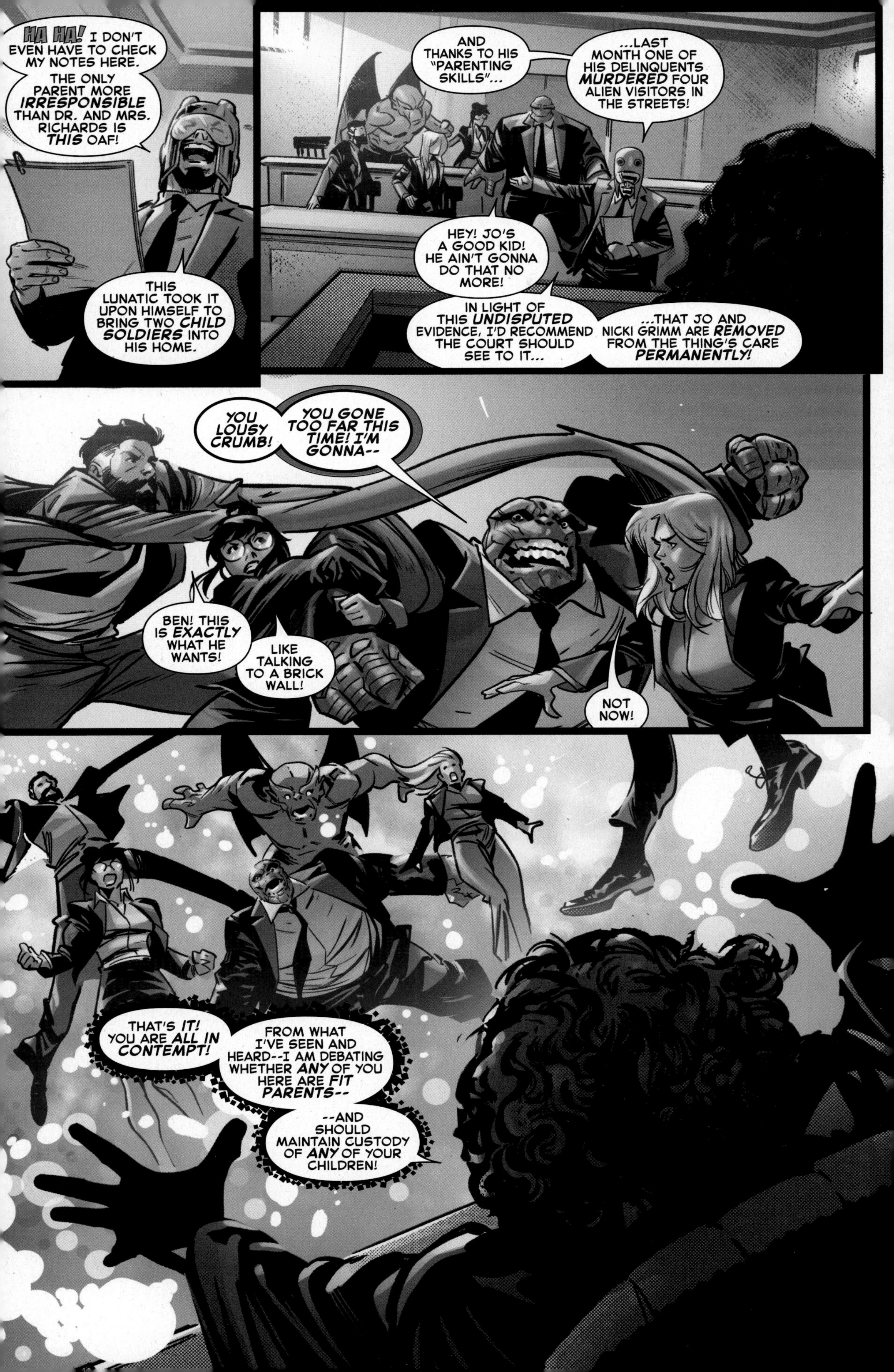
HA HA! I DON'T EVEN HAVE TO CHECK MY NOTES HERE.
THE ONLY PARENT MORE IRRESPONSIBLE THAN DR. AND MRS. RICHARDS IS THIS OAF!
THIS LUNATIC TOOK IT UPON HIMSELF TO BRING TWO CHILD SOLDIERS INTO HIS HOME.
AND THANKS TO HIS "PARENTING SKILLS"...
...LAST MONTH ONE OF HIS DELINQUENTS MURDERED FOUR ALIEN VISITORS IN THE STREETS!
HEY! JO'S A GOOD KID! HE AIN'T GONNA DO THAT NO MORE!
IN LIGHT OF THIS UNDISPUTED EVIDENCE, I'D RECOMMEND THE COURT SHOULD SEE TO IT...
...THAT JO AND NICKI GRIMM ARE REMOVED FROM THE THING'S CARE PERMANENTLY!
YOU LOUSY CRUMB!
YOU GONE TOO FAR THIS TIME! I'M GONNA--
BEN! THIS IS EXACTLY WHAT HE WANTS!
LIKE TALKING TO A BRICK WALL!
NOT NOW!
THAT'S IT! YOU ARE ALL IN CONTEMPT!
FROM WHAT I'VE SEEN AND HEARD--I AM DEBATING WHETHER ANY OF YOU HERE ARE FIT PARENTS--
--AND SHOULD MAINTAIN CUSTODY OF ANY OF YOUR CHILDREN!

39

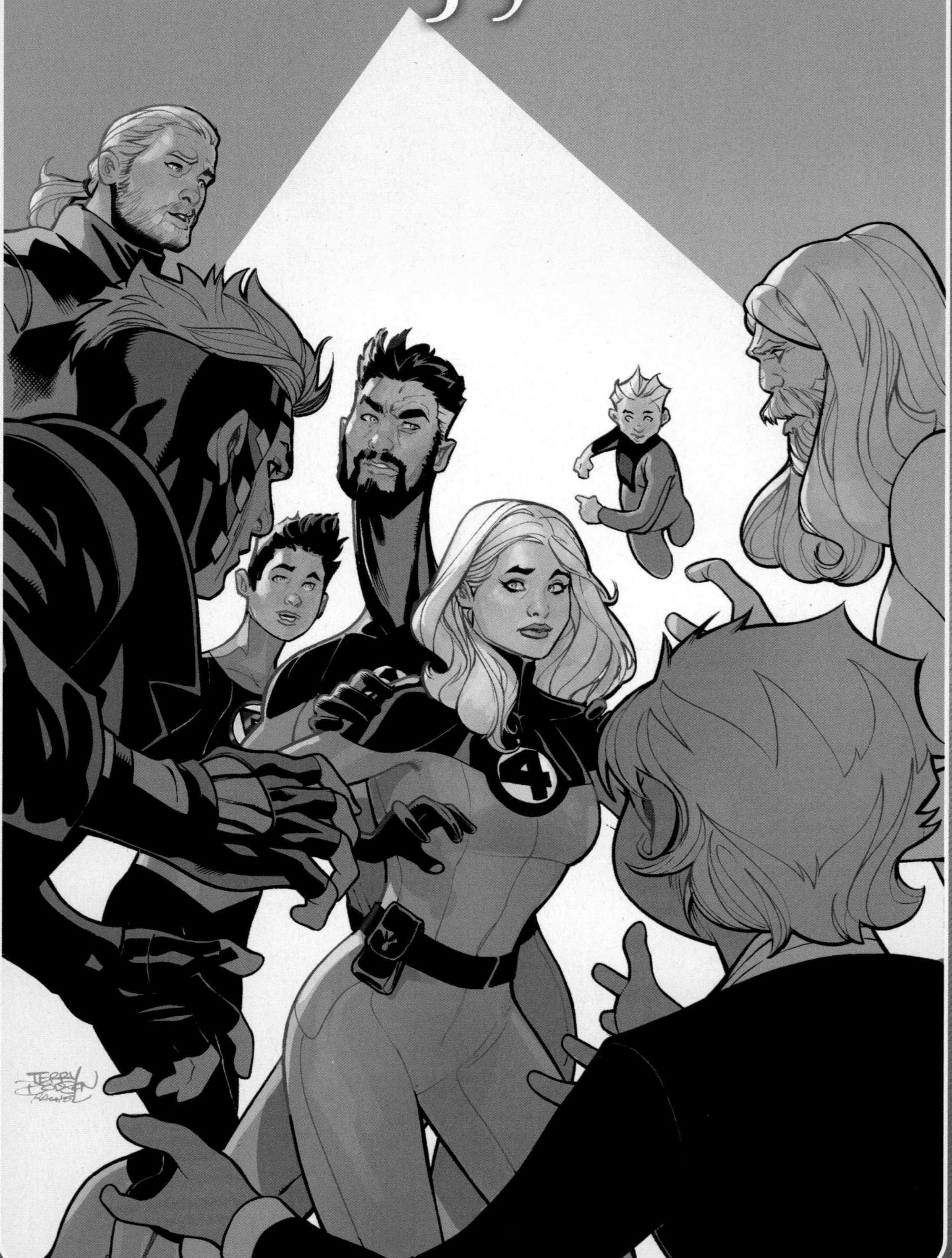

“Free Bentley”

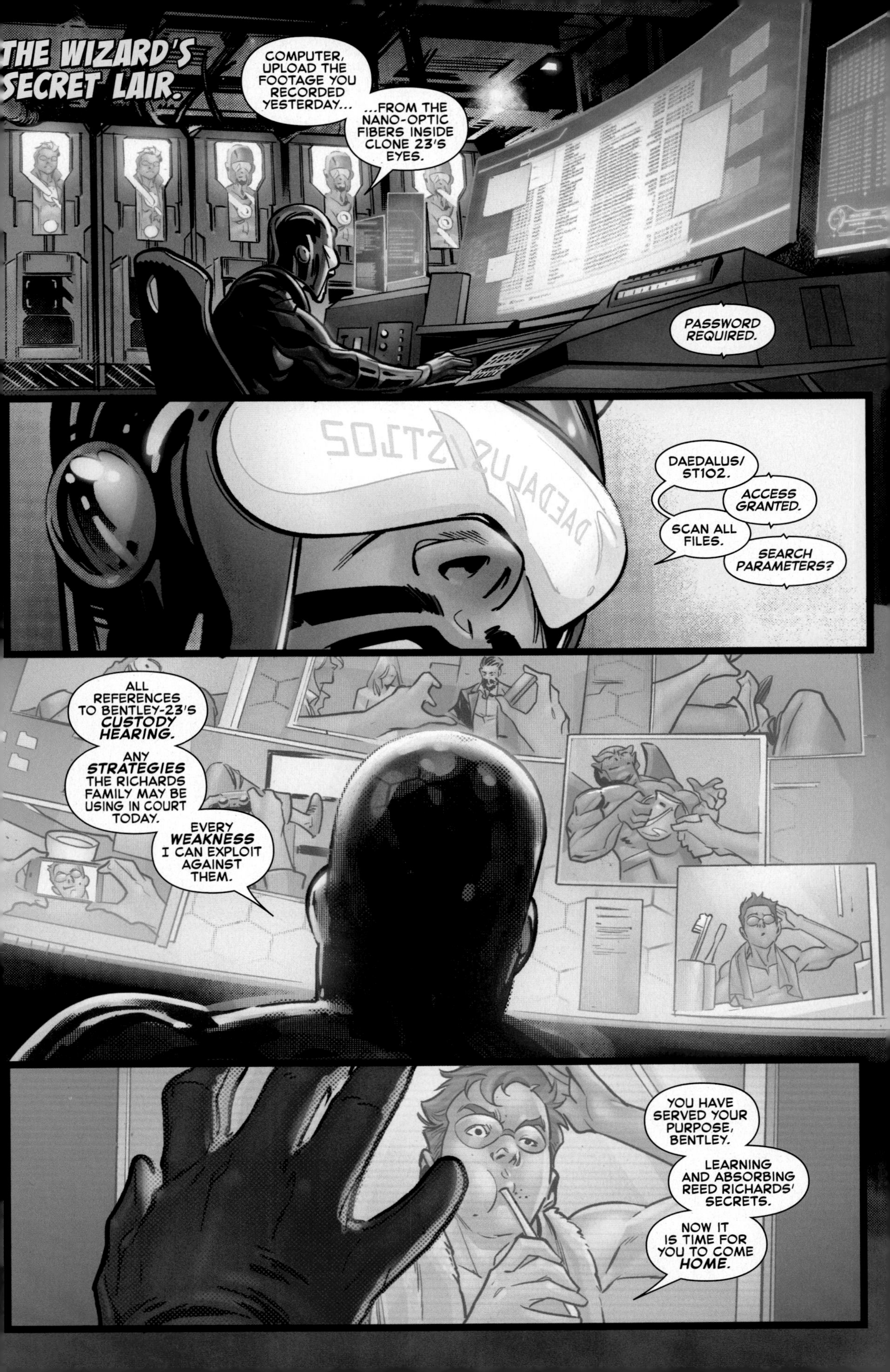
THE WIZARD'S SECRET LAIR.
COMPUTER, UPLOAD THE FOOTAGE YOU RECORDED YESTERDAY...
...FROM THE NANO-OPTIC FIBERS INSIDE CLONE 23'S EYES.
PASSWORD REQUIRED.
DAEDALUS/ST102
DAEDALUS/ ST102.
ACCESS GRANTED.
SCAN ALL FILES.
SEARCH PARAMETERS?
ALL REFERENCES TO BENTLEY-23'S CUSTODY HEARING.
ANY STRATEGIES THE RICHARDS FAMILY MAY BE USING IN COURT TODAY.
EVERY WEAKNESS I CAN EXPLOIT AGAINST THEM.
YOU HAVE SERVED YOUR PURPOSE, BENTLEY.
LEARNING AND ABSORBING REED RICHARDS' SECRETS.
NOW IT IS TIME FOR YOU TO COME HOME.

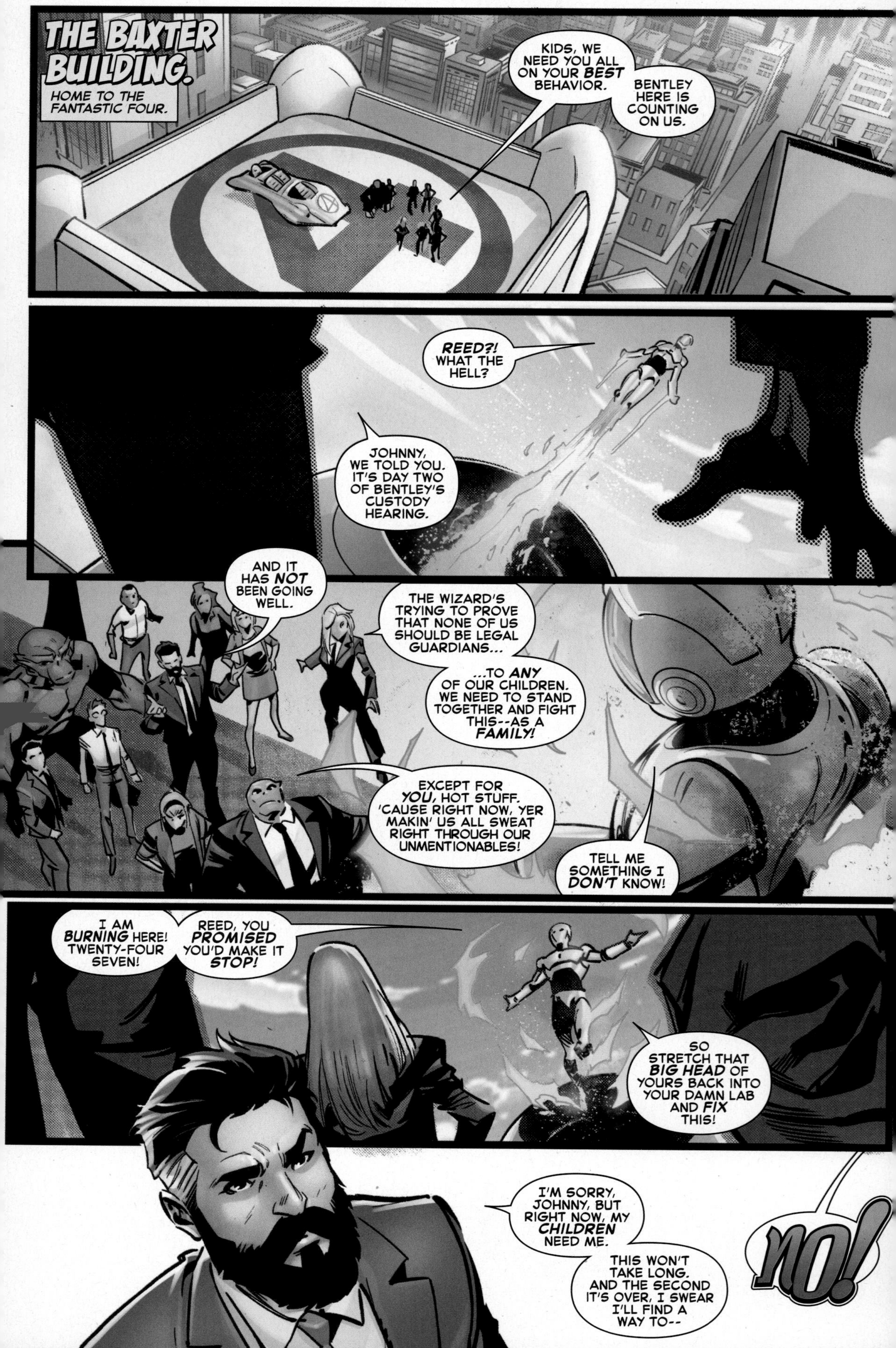
THE BAXTER BUILDING.
HOME TO THE FANTASTIC FOUR.
KIDS, WE NEED YOU ALL ON YOUR BEST BEHAVIOR.
BENTLEY HERE IS COUNTING ON US.
REED?! WHAT THE HELL?
JOHNNY, WE TOLD YOU. IT'S DAY TWO OF BENTLEY'S CUSTODY HEARING.
AND IT HAS NOT BEEN GOING WELL.
THE WIZARD'S TRYING TO PROVE THAT NONE OF US SHOULD BE LEGAL GUARDIANS...
...TO ANY OF OUR CHILDREN. WE NEED TO STAND TOGETHER AND FIGHT THIS--AS A FAMILY!
EXCEPT FOR YOU, HOT STUFF. 'CAUSE RIGHT NOW, YER MAKIN' US ALL SWEAT RIGHT THROUGH OUR UNMENTIONABLES!
TELL ME SOMETHING I DON'T KNOW!
I AM BURNING HERE! TWENTY-FOUR SEVEN!
REED, YOU PROMISED YOU'D MAKE IT STOP!
SO STRETCH THAT BIG HEAD OF YOURS BACK INTO YOUR DAMN LAB AND FIX THIS!
I'M SORRY, JOHNNY, BUT RIGHT NOW, MY CHILDREN NEED ME.
THIS WON'T TAKE LONG. AND THE SECOND IT'S OVER, I SWEAR I'LL FIND A WAY TO--
NO!

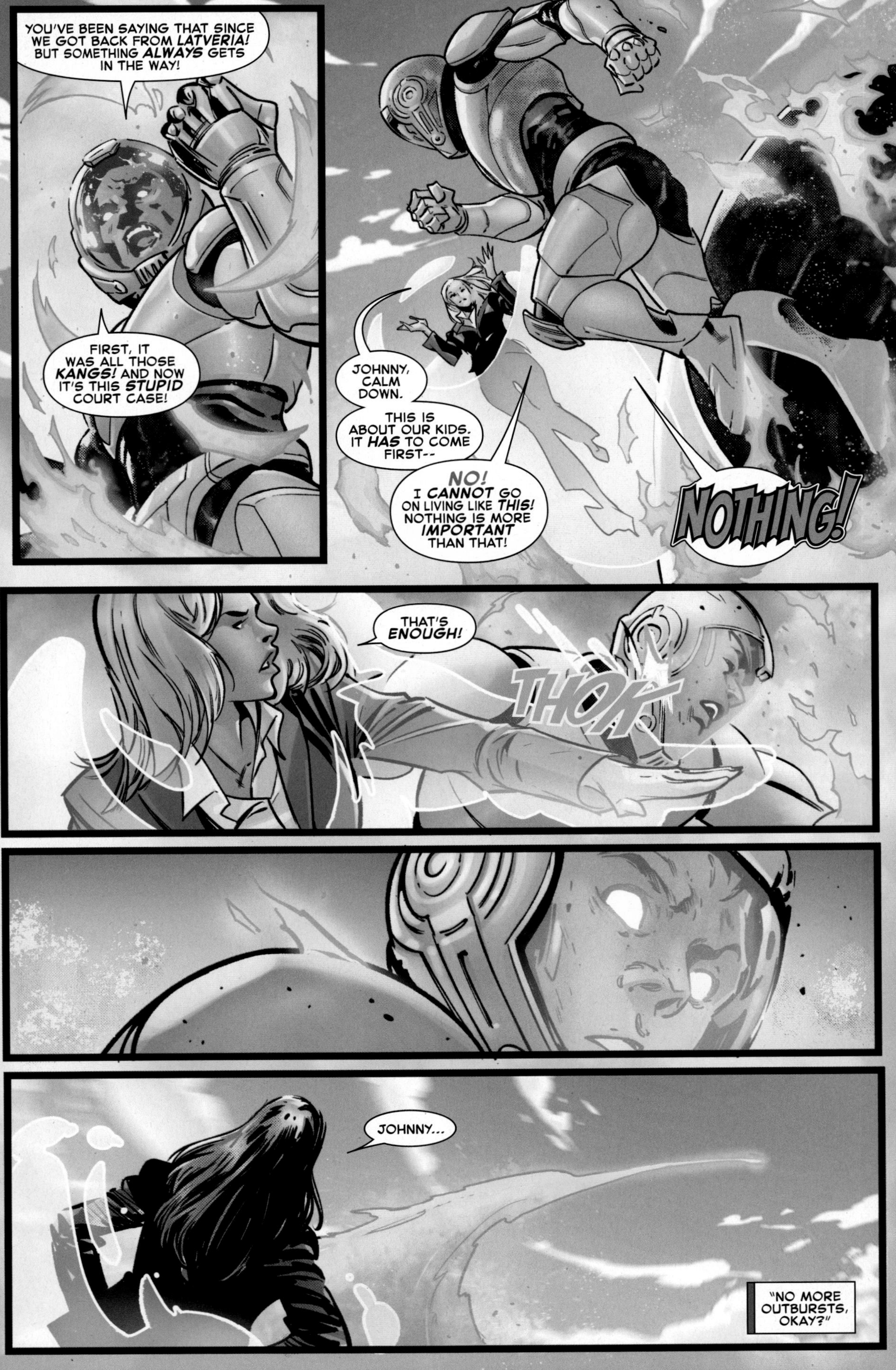
YOU'VE BEEN SAYING THAT SINCE WE GOT BACK FROM LATVERIA! BUT SOMETHING ALWAYS GETS IN THE WAY!
FIRST, IT WAS ALL THOSE KANGS! AND NOW IT'S THIS STUPID COURT CASE!
JOHNNY, CALM DOWN.
THIS IS ABOUT OUR KIDS. IT HAS TO COME FIRST--
NO! I CANNOT GO ON LIVING LIKE THIS! NOTHING IS MORE IMPORTANT THAN THAT!
NOTHING!
THAT'S ENOUGH!
THOK
JOHNNY...
"NO MORE OUTBURSTS, OKAY?"

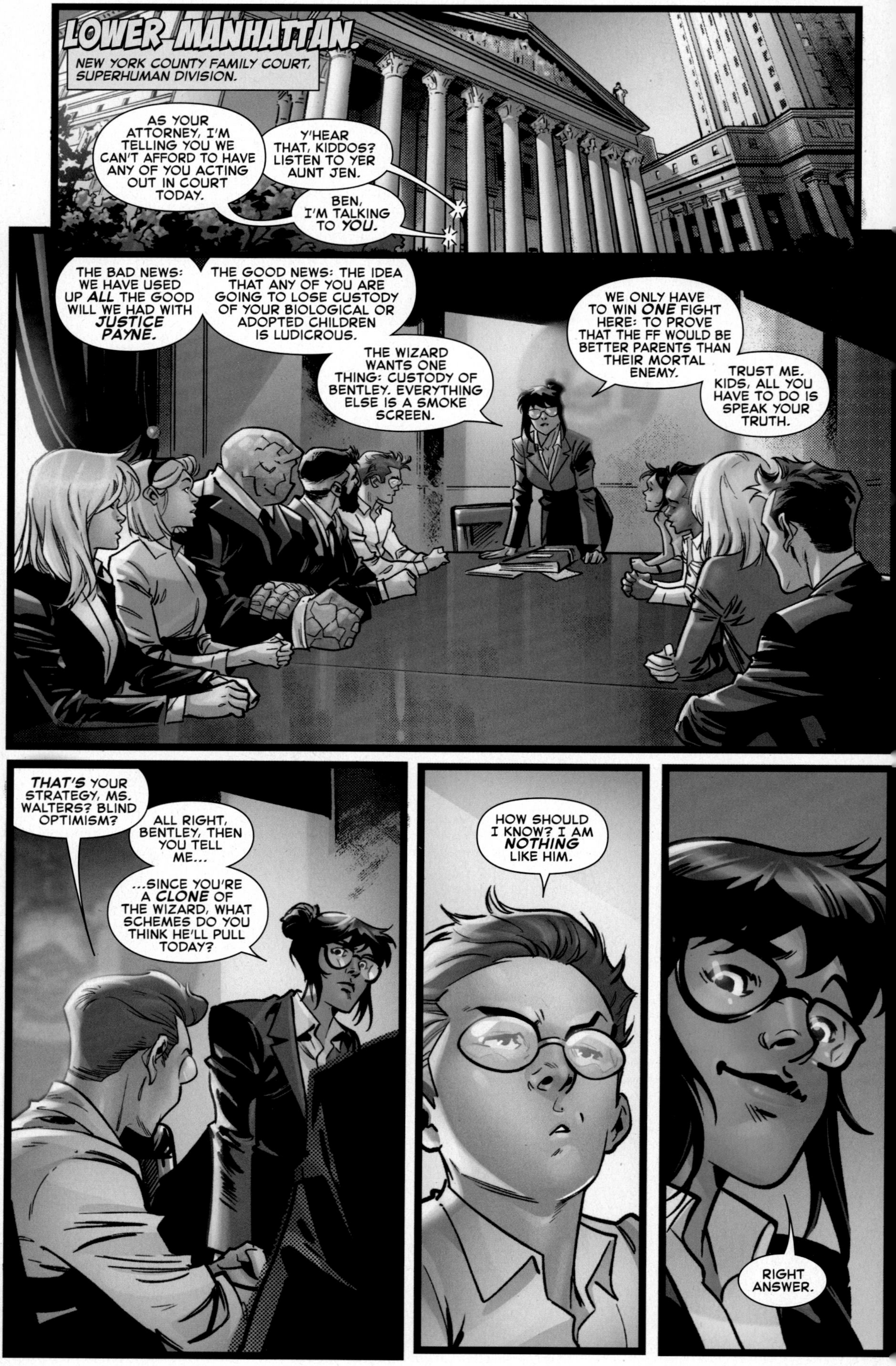
LOWER MANHATTAN.
NEW YORK COUNTY FAMILY COURT, SUPERHUMAN DIVISION.
AS YOUR ATTORNEY, I'M TELLING YOU WE CAN'T AFFORD TO HAVE ANY OF YOU ACTING OUT IN COURT TODAY.
Y'HEAR THAT, KIDDOS? LISTEN TO YER AUNT JEN.
BEN, I'M TALKING TO *YOU.*
THE BAD NEWS: WE HAVE USED UP *ALL* THE GOOD WILL WE HAD WITH *JUSTICE PAYNE.*
THE GOOD NEWS: THE IDEA THAT ANY OF YOU ARE GOING TO LOSE CUSTODY OF YOUR BIOLOGICAL OR ADOPTED CHILDREN IS LUDICROUS.
THE WIZARD WANTS ONE THING: CUSTODY OF BENTLEY. EVERYTHING ELSE IS A SMOKE SCREEN.
WE ONLY HAVE TO WIN *ONE* FIGHT HERE: TO PROVE THAT THE FF WOULD BE BETTER PARENTS THAN THEIR MORTAL ENEMY.
TRUST ME. KIDS, ALL YOU HAVE TO DO IS SPEAK YOUR TRUTH.
THAT'S YOUR STRATEGY, MS. WALTERS? BLIND OPTIMISM?
ALL RIGHT, BENTLEY, THEN YOU TELL ME...
...SINCE YOU'RE A *CLONE* OF THE WIZARD, WHAT SCHEMES DO YOU THINK HE'LL PULL TODAY?
HOW SHOULD I KNOW? I AM *NOTHING* LIKE HIM.
RIGHT ANSWER.

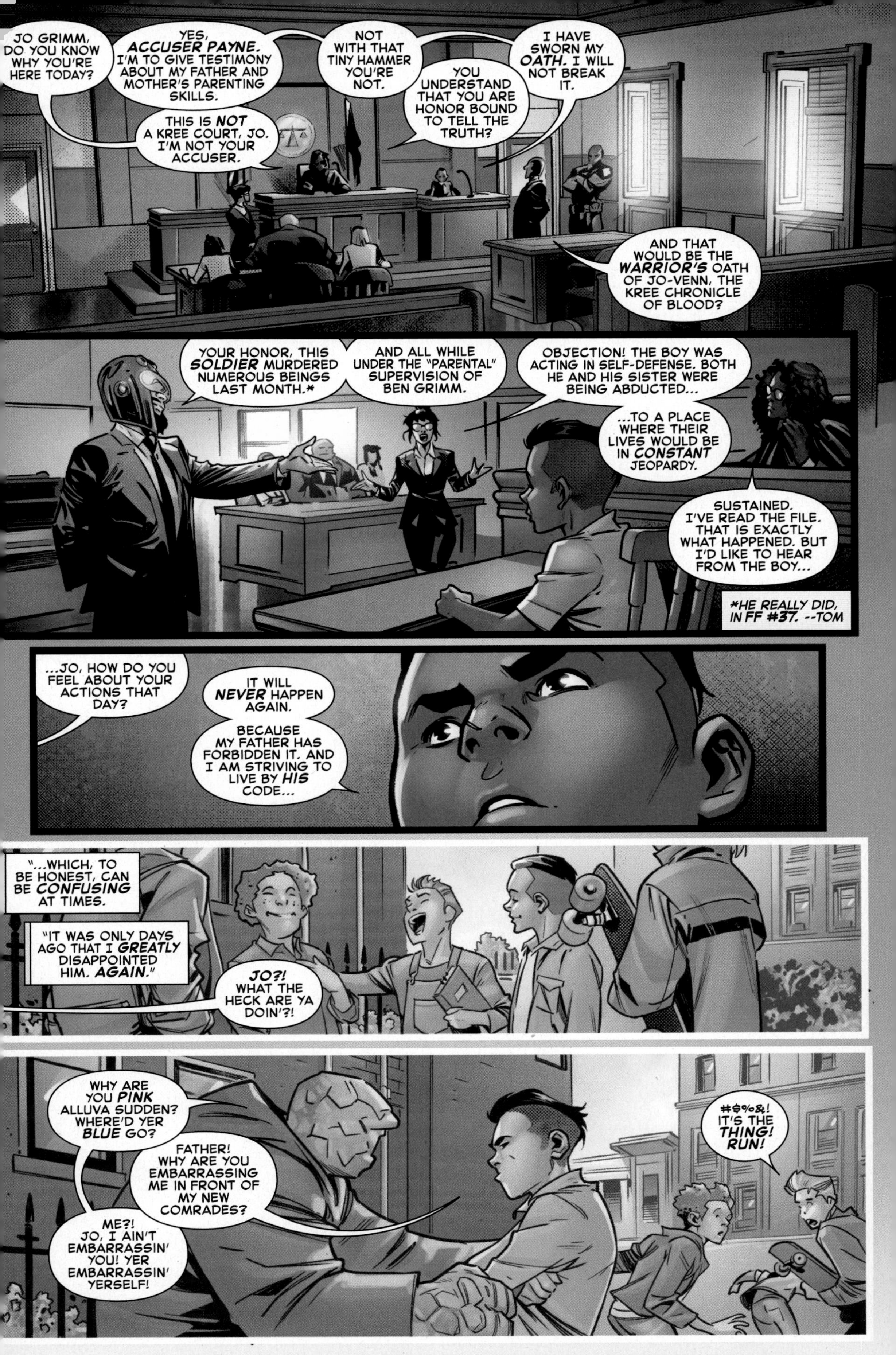

JO GRIMM, DO YOU KNOW WHY YOU'RE HERE TODAY?
YES, ACCUSER PAYNE. I'M TO GIVE TESTIMONY ABOUT MY FATHER AND MOTHER'S PARENTING SKILLS.
THIS IS NOT A KREE COURT, JO. I'M NOT YOUR ACCUSER.
NOT WITH THAT TINY HAMMER YOU'RE NOT.
YOU UNDERSTAND THAT YOU ARE HONOR BOUND TO TELL THE TRUTH?
I HAVE SWORN MY OATH. I WILL NOT BREAK IT.
AND THAT WOULD BE THE WARRIOR'S OATH OF JO-VENN, THE KREE CHRONICLE OF BLOOD?
YOUR HONOR, THIS SOLDIER MURDERED NUMEROUS BEINGS LAST MONTH.*
AND ALL WHILE UNDER THE "PARENTAL" SUPERVISION OF BEN GRIMM.
OBJECTION! THE BOY WAS ACTING IN SELF-DEFENSE. BOTH HE AND HIS SISTER WERE BEING ABDUCTED...
...TO A PLACE WHERE THEIR LIVES WOULD BE IN CONSTANT JEOPARDY.
SUSTAINED. I'VE READ THE FILE. THAT IS EXACTLY WHAT HAPPENED. BUT I'D LIKE TO HEAR FROM THE BOY...
*HE REALLY DID, IN FF #37. --TOM
...JO, HOW DO YOU FEEL ABOUT YOUR ACTIONS THAT DAY?
IT WILL NEVER HAPPEN AGAIN.
BECAUSE MY FATHER HAS FORBIDDEN IT. AND I AM STRIVING TO LIVE BY HIS CODE...
"...WHICH, TO BE HONEST, CAN BE CONFUSING AT TIMES.
"IT WAS ONLY DAYS AGO THAT I GREATLY DISAPPOINTED HIM. AGAIN."
JO?! WHAT THE HECK ARE YA DOIN'?!
WHY ARE YOU PINK ALLUVA SUDDEN? WHERE'D YER BLUE GO?
FATHER! WHY ARE YOU EMBARRASSING ME IN FRONT OF MY NEW COMRADES?
ME?! JO, I AIN'T EMBARRASSIN' YOU! YER EMBARRASSIN' YERSELF!
#$%&! IT'S THE THING! RUN!

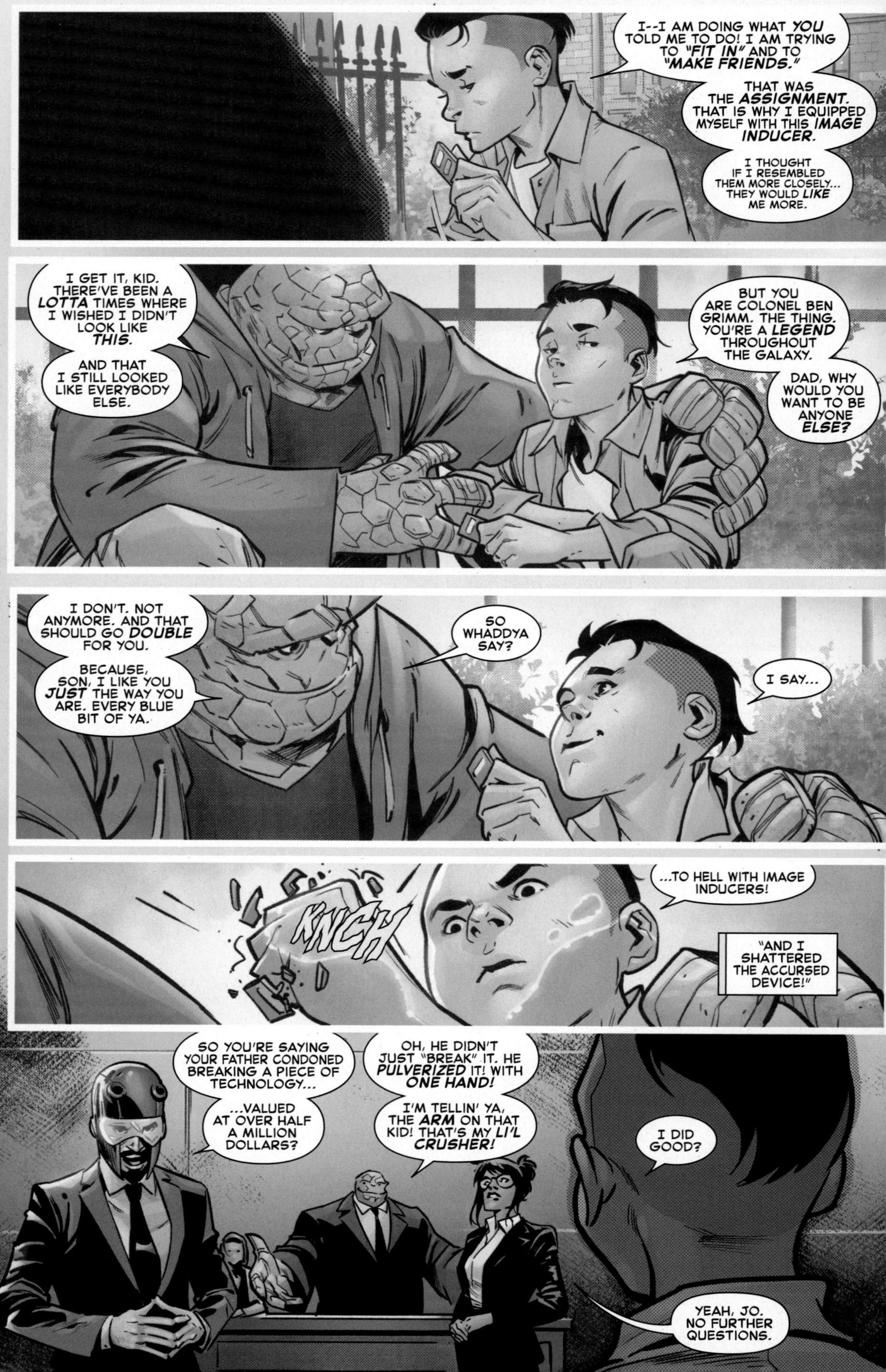
I--I AM DOING WHAT YOU TOLD ME TO DO! I AM TRYING TO "FIT IN" AND TO "MAKE FRIENDS."
THAT WAS THE ASSIGNMENT. THAT IS WHY I EQUIPPED MYSELF WITH THIS IMAGE INDUCER.
I THOUGHT IF I RESEMBLED THEM MORE CLOSELY... THEY WOULD LIKE ME MORE.
I GET IT, KID. THERE'VE BEEN A LOTTA TIMES WHERE I WISHED I DIDN'T LOOK LIKE THIS.
AND THAT I STILL LOOKED LIKE EVERYBODY ELSE.
BUT YOU ARE COLONEL BEN GRIMM. THE THING. YOU'RE A LEGEND THROUGHOUT THE GALAXY.
DAD, WHY WOULD YOU WANT TO BE ANYONE ELSE?
I DON'T. NOT ANYMORE. AND THAT SHOULD GO DOUBLE FOR YOU.
BECAUSE, SON, I LIKE YOU JUST THE WAY YOU ARE. EVERY BLUE BIT OF YA.
SO WHADDYA SAY?
I SAY...
KNCH
...TO HELL WITH IMAGE INDUCERS!
"AND I SHATTERED THE ACCURSED DEVICE!"
SO YOU'RE SAYING YOUR FATHER CONDONED BREAKING A PIECE OF TECHNOLOGY...
...VALUED AT OVER HALF A MILLION DOLLARS?
OH, HE DIDN'T JUST "BREAK" IT. HE PULVERIZED IT! WITH ONE HAND!
I'M TELLIN' YA, THE ARM ON THAT KID! THAT'S MY LI'L CRUSHER!
I DID GOOD?
YEAH, JO. NO FURTHER QUESTIONS.

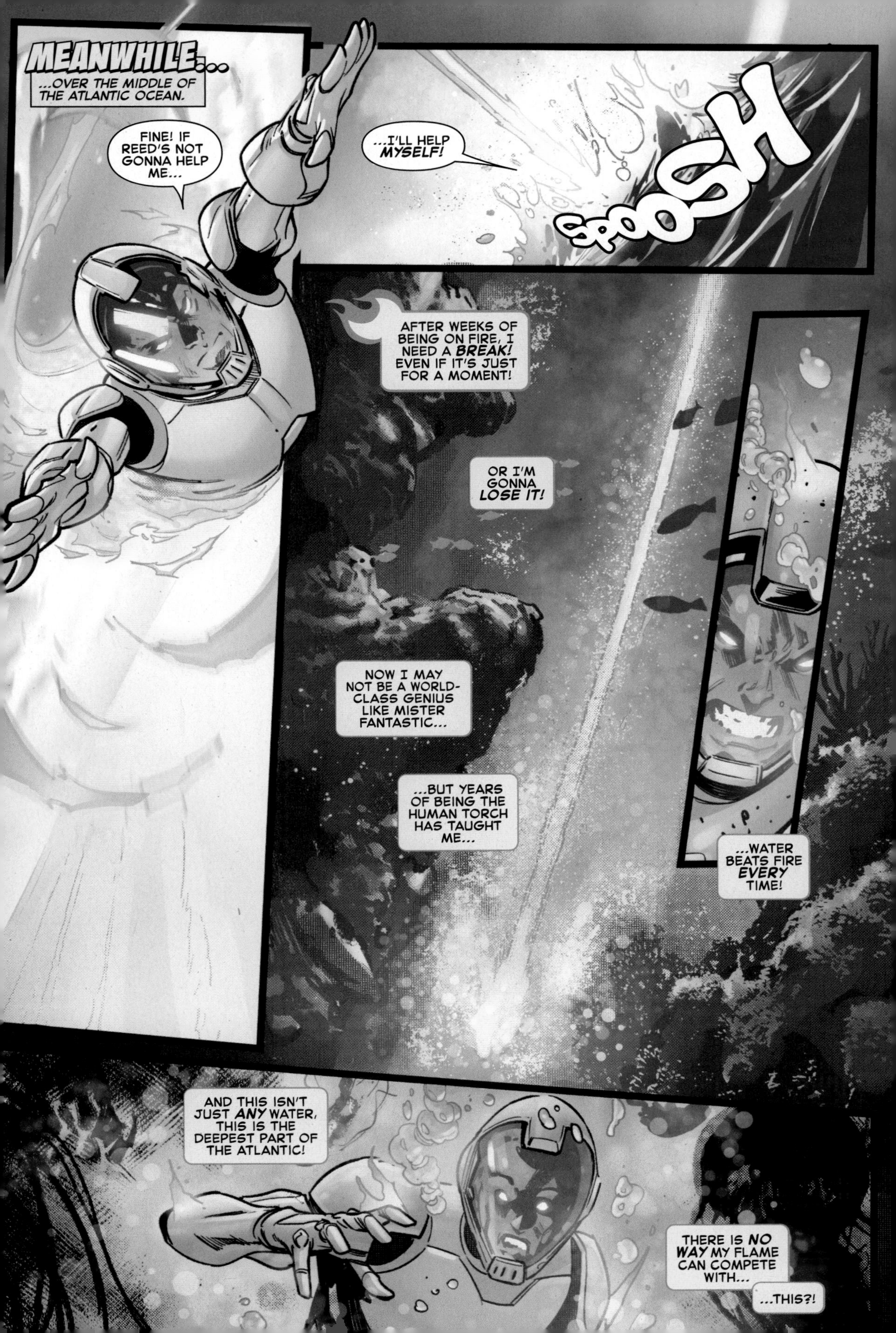
MEANWHILE...
...OVER THE MIDDLE OF THE ATLANTIC OCEAN.
FINE! IF REED'S NOT GONNA HELP ME...
...I'LL HELP MYSELF!
SPOOSH
AFTER WEEKS OF BEING ON FIRE, I NEED A BREAK! EVEN IF IT'S JUST FOR A MOMENT!
OR I'M GONNA LOSE IT!
NOW I MAY NOT BE A WORLD-CLASS GENIUS LIKE MISTER FANTASTIC...
...BUT YEARS OF BEING THE HUMAN TORCH HAS TAUGHT ME...
...WATER BEATS FIRE EVERY TIME!
AND THIS ISN'T JUST ANY WATER, THIS IS THE DEEPEST PART OF THE ATLANTIC!
THERE IS NO WAY MY FLAME CAN COMPETE WITH...
...THIS?!

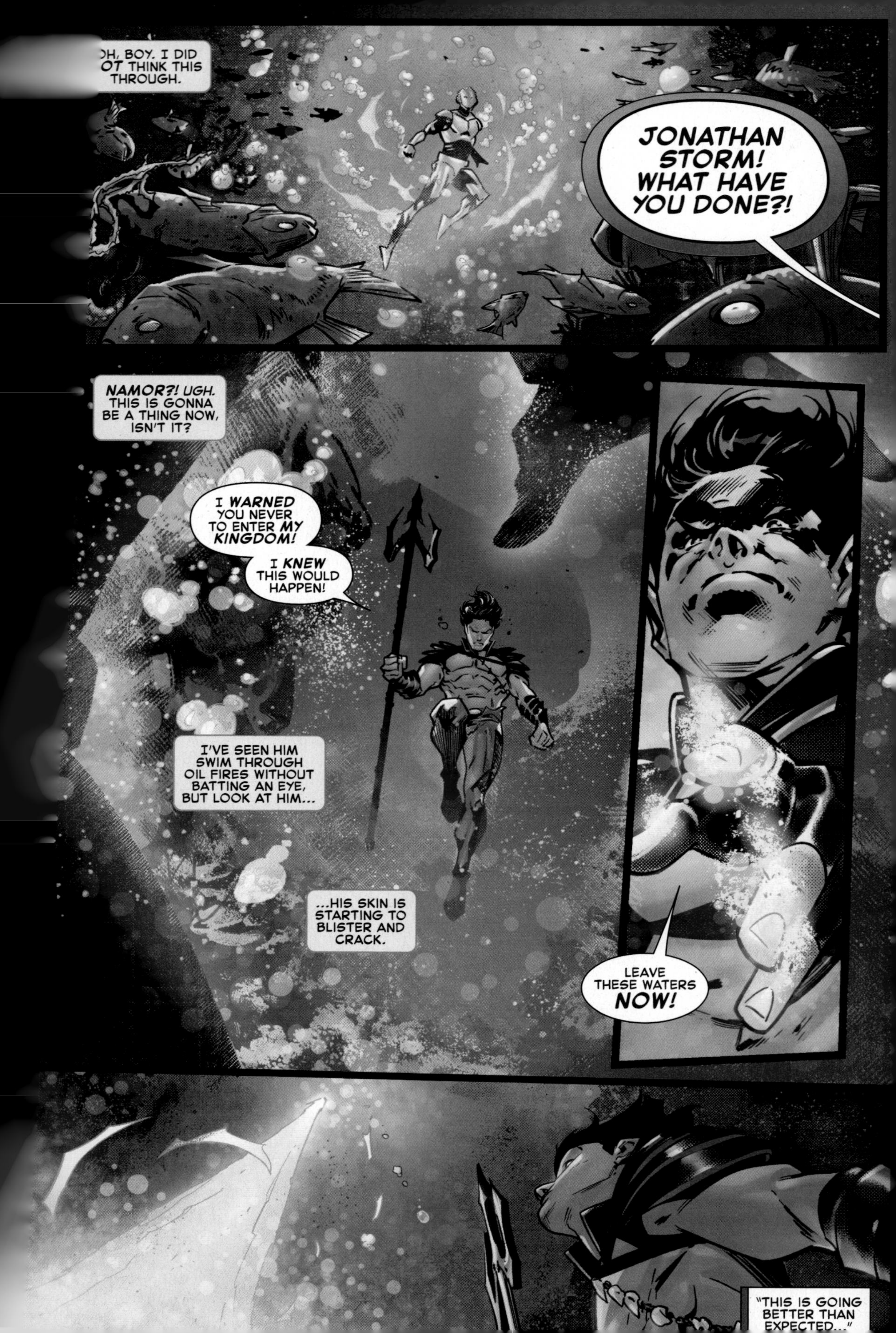
OH, BOY. I DID NOT THINK THIS THROUGH.
JONATHAN STORM! WHAT HAVE YOU DONE?!
NAMOR?! UGH. THIS IS GONNA BE A THING NOW, ISN'T IT?
I WARNED YOU NEVER TO ENTER MY KINGDOM!
I KNEW THIS WOULD HAPPEN!
I'VE SEEN HIM SWIM THROUGH OIL FIRES WITHOUT BATTING AN EYE, BUT LOOK AT HIM...
...HIS SKIN IS STARTING TO BLISTER AND CRACK.
LEAVE THESE WATERS NOW!
"THIS IS GOING BETTER THAN EXPECTED..."

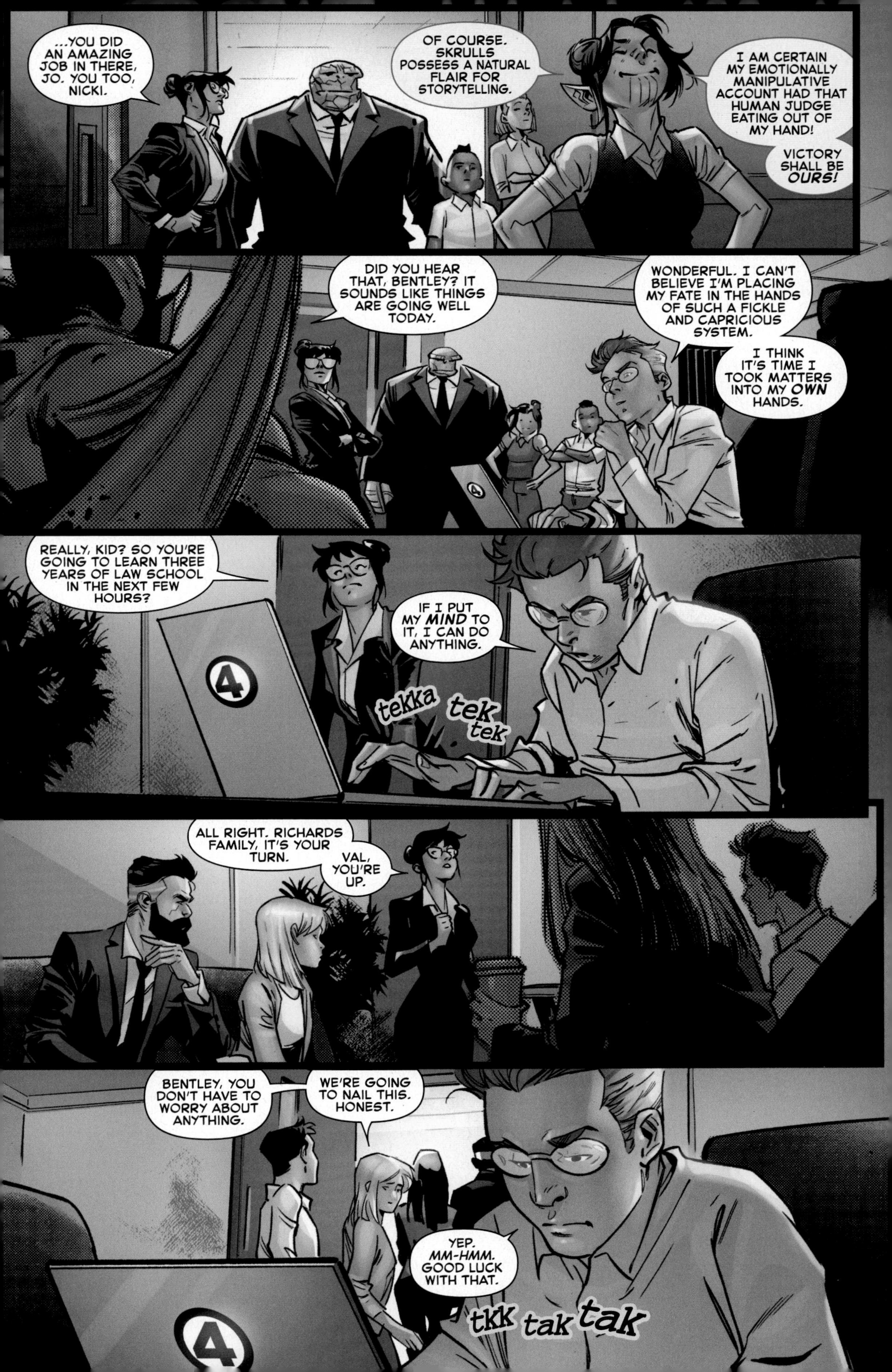
...YOU DID AN AMAZING JOB IN THERE, JO. YOU TOO, NICKI.
OF COURSE. SKRULLS POSSESS A NATURAL FLAIR FOR STORYTELLING.
I AM CERTAIN MY EMOTIONALLY MANIPULATIVE ACCOUNT HAD THAT HUMAN JUDGE EATING OUT OF MY HAND!
VICTORY SHALL BE OURS!
DID YOU HEAR THAT, BENTLEY? IT SOUNDS LIKE THINGS ARE GOING WELL TODAY.
WONDERFUL. I CAN'T BELIEVE I'M PLACING MY FATE IN THE HANDS OF SUCH A FICKLE AND CAPRICIOUS SYSTEM.
I THINK IT'S TIME I TOOK MATTERS INTO MY OWN HANDS.
REALLY, KID? SO YOU'RE GOING TO LEARN THREE YEARS OF LAW SCHOOL IN THE NEXT FEW HOURS?
IF I PUT MY MIND TO IT, I CAN DO ANYTHING.
tekka tek tek
ALL RIGHT. RICHARDS FAMILY, IT'S YOUR TURN.
VAL, YOU'RE UP.
BENTLEY, YOU DON'T HAVE TO WORRY ABOUT ANYTHING.
WE'RE GOING TO NAIL THIS. HONEST.
YEP. MM-HMM. GOOD LUCK WITH THAT.
tkk tak tak

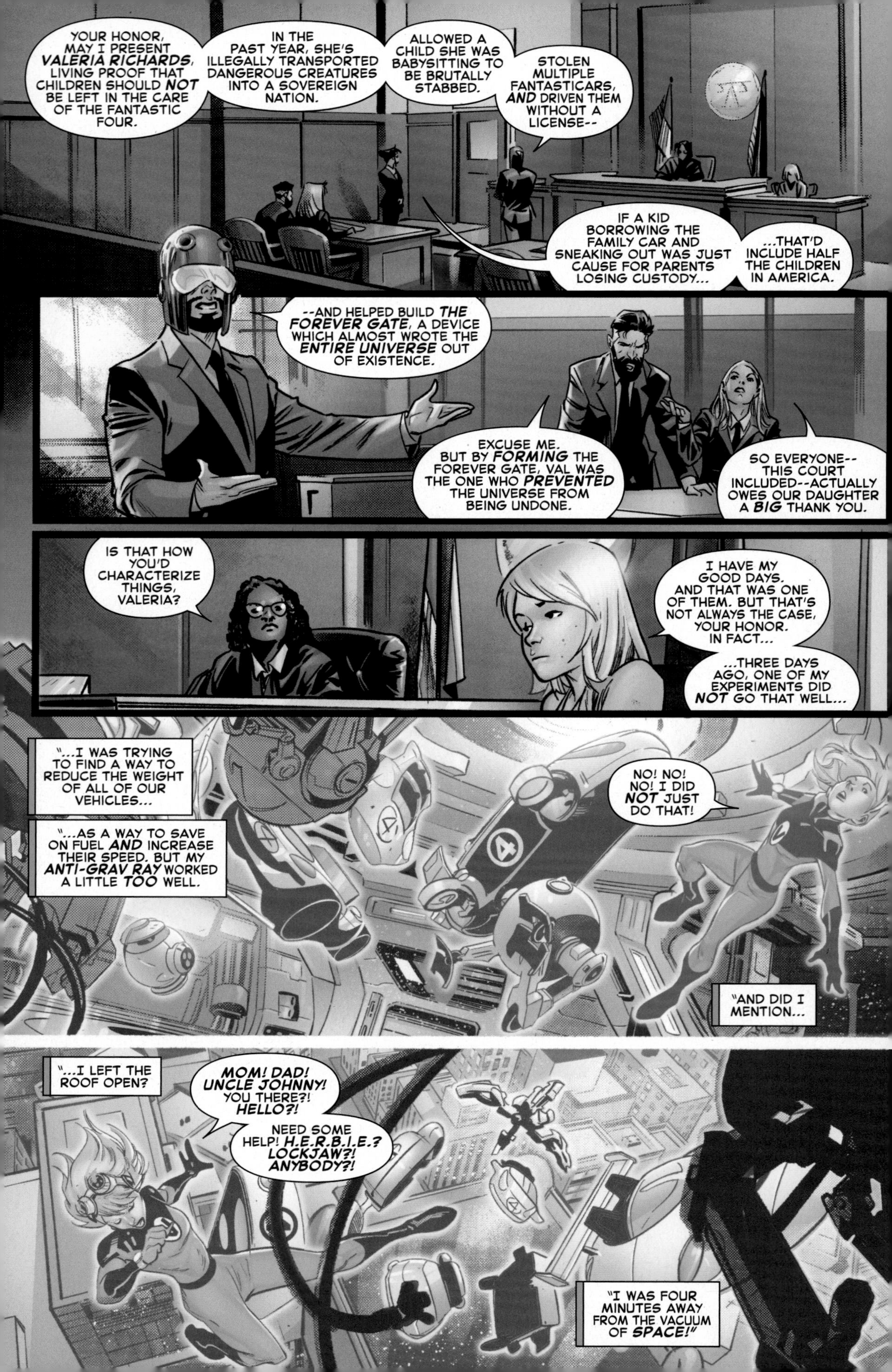
YOUR HONOR, MAY I PRESENT VALERIA RICHARDS, LIVING PROOF THAT CHILDREN SHOULD NOT BE LEFT IN THE CARE OF THE FANTASTIC FOUR.
IN THE PAST YEAR, SHE'S ILLEGALLY TRANSPORTED DANGEROUS CREATURES INTO A SOVEREIGN NATION.
ALLOWED A CHILD SHE WAS BABYSITTING TO BE BRUTALLY STABBED.
STOLEN MULTIPLE FANTASTICARS, AND DRIVEN THEM WITHOUT A LICENSE--
IF A KID BORROWING THE FAMILY CAR AND SNEAKING OUT WAS JUST CAUSE FOR PARENTS LOSING CUSTODY...
...THAT'D INCLUDE HALF THE CHILDREN IN AMERICA.
--AND HELPED BUILD THE FOREVER GATE, A DEVICE WHICH ALMOST WROTE THE ENTIRE UNIVERSE OUT OF EXISTENCE.
EXCUSE ME. BUT BY FORMING THE FOREVER GATE, VAL WAS THE ONE WHO PREVENTED THE UNIVERSE FROM BEING UNDONE.
SO EVERYONE-- THIS COURT INCLUDED--ACTUALLY OWES OUR DAUGHTER A BIG THANK YOU.
IS THAT HOW YOU'D CHARACTERIZE THINGS, VALERIA?
I HAVE MY GOOD DAYS. AND THAT WAS ONE OF THEM. BUT THAT'S NOT ALWAYS THE CASE, YOUR HONOR. IN FACT...
...THREE DAYS AGO, ONE OF MY EXPERIMENTS DID NOT GO THAT WELL...
"...I WAS TRYING TO FIND A WAY TO REDUCE THE WEIGHT OF ALL OF OUR VEHICLES...
"...AS A WAY TO SAVE ON FUEL AND INCREASE THEIR SPEED. BUT MY ANTI-GRAV RAY WORKED A LITTLE TOO WELL.
NO! NO! NO! I DID NOT JUST DO THAT!
"AND DID I MENTION...
"...I LEFT THE ROOF OPEN?
MOM! DAD! UNCLE JOHNNY! YOU THERE?! HELLO?!
NEED SOME HELP! H.E.R.B.I.E.? LOCKJAW?! ANYBODY?!
"I WAS FOUR MINUTES AWAY FROM THE VACUUM OF SPACE!"

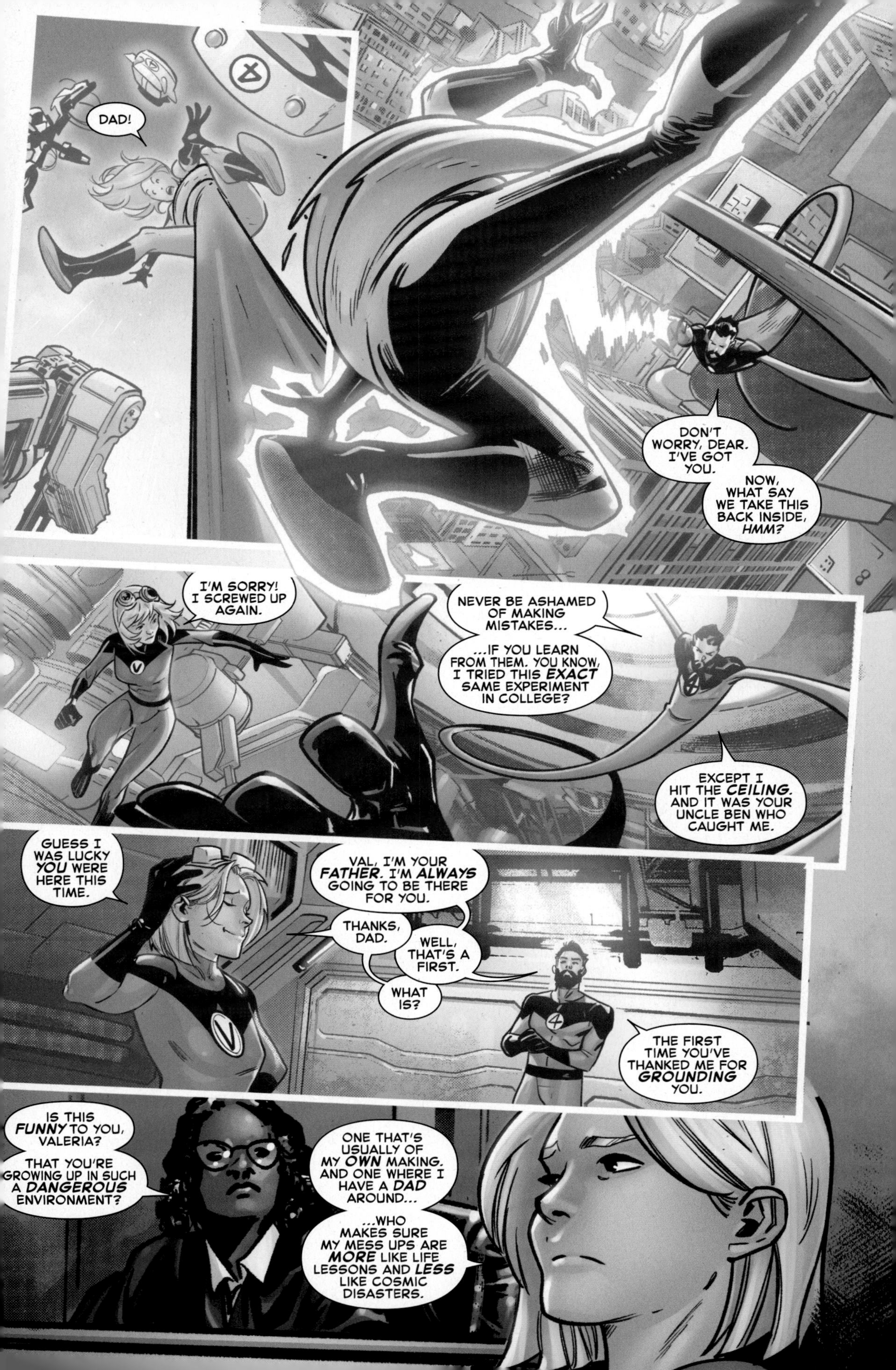
DAD!
DON'T WORRY, DEAR. I'VE GOT YOU.
NOW, WHAT SAY WE TAKE THIS BACK INSIDE, HMM?
I'M SORRY! I SCREWED UP AGAIN.
NEVER BE ASHAMED OF MAKING MISTAKES...
...IF YOU LEARN FROM THEM. YOU KNOW, I TRIED THIS EXACT SAME EXPERIMENT IN COLLEGE?
EXCEPT I HIT THE CEILING. AND IT WAS YOUR UNCLE BEN WHO CAUGHT ME.
GUESS I WAS LUCKY YOU WERE HERE THIS TIME.
VAL, I'M YOUR FATHER. I'M ALWAYS GOING TO BE THERE FOR YOU.
THANKS, DAD.
WELL, THAT'S A FIRST.
WHAT IS?
THE FIRST TIME YOU'VE THANKED ME FOR GROUNDING YOU.
IS THIS FUNNY TO YOU, VALERIA?
THAT YOU'RE GROWING UP IN SUCH A DANGEROUS ENVIRONMENT?
ONE THAT'S USUALLY OF MY OWN MAKING. AND ONE WHERE I HAVE A DAD AROUND...
...WHO MAKES SURE MY MESS UPS ARE MORE LIKE LIFE LESSONS AND LESS LIKE COSMIC DISASTERS.

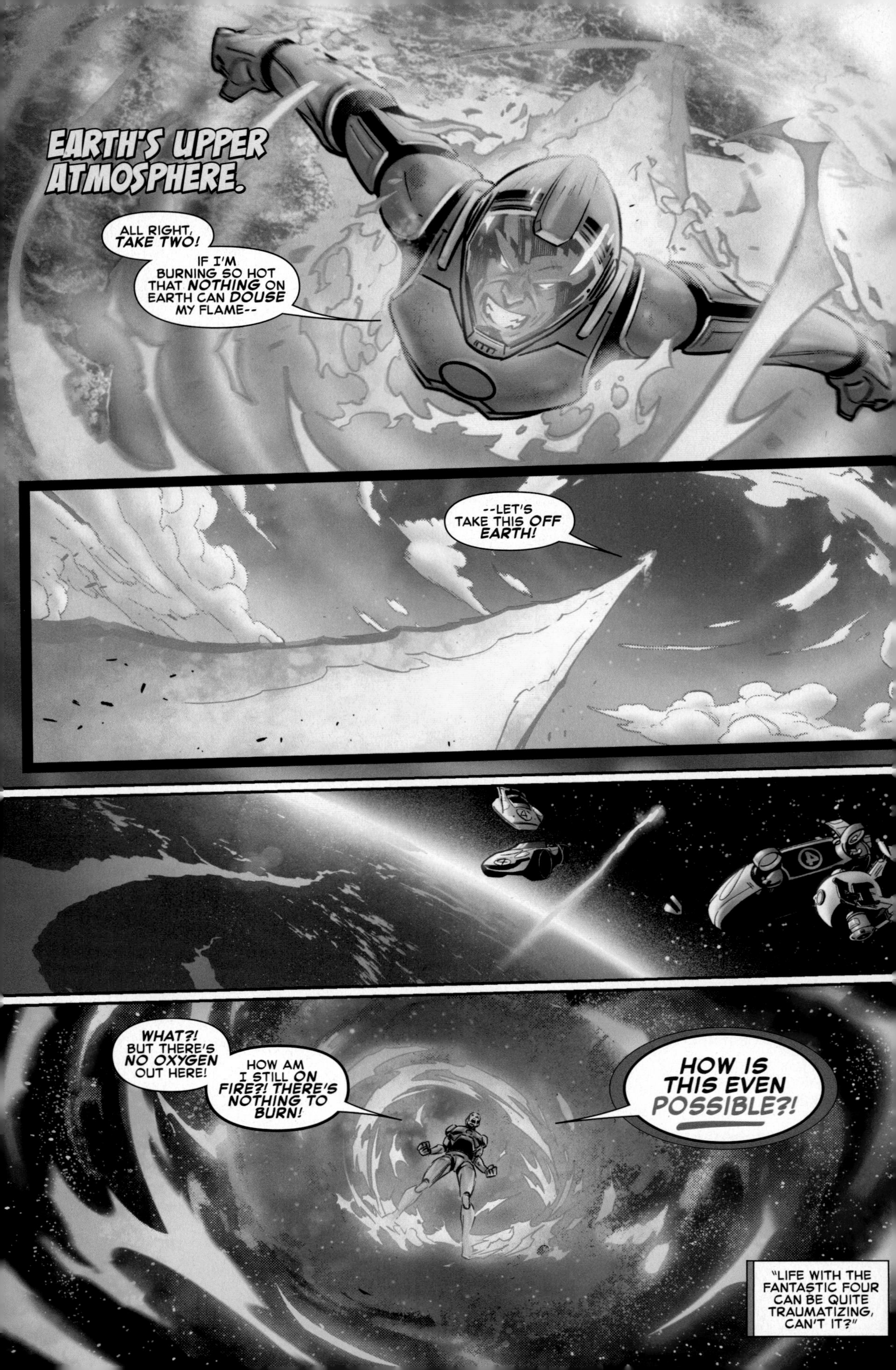
EARTH'S UPPER ATMOSPHERE.
ALL RIGHT, TAKE TWO!
IF I'M BURNING SO HOT THAT NOTHING ON EARTH CAN DOUSE MY FLAME--
--LET'S TAKE THIS OFF EARTH!
WHAT?! BUT THERE'S NO OXYGEN OUT HERE!
HOW AM I STILL ON FIRE?! THERE'S NOTHING TO BURN!
HOW IS THIS EVEN POSSIBLE?!
"LIFE WITH THE FANTASTIC FOUR CAN BE QUITE TRAUMATIZING, CAN'T IT?"

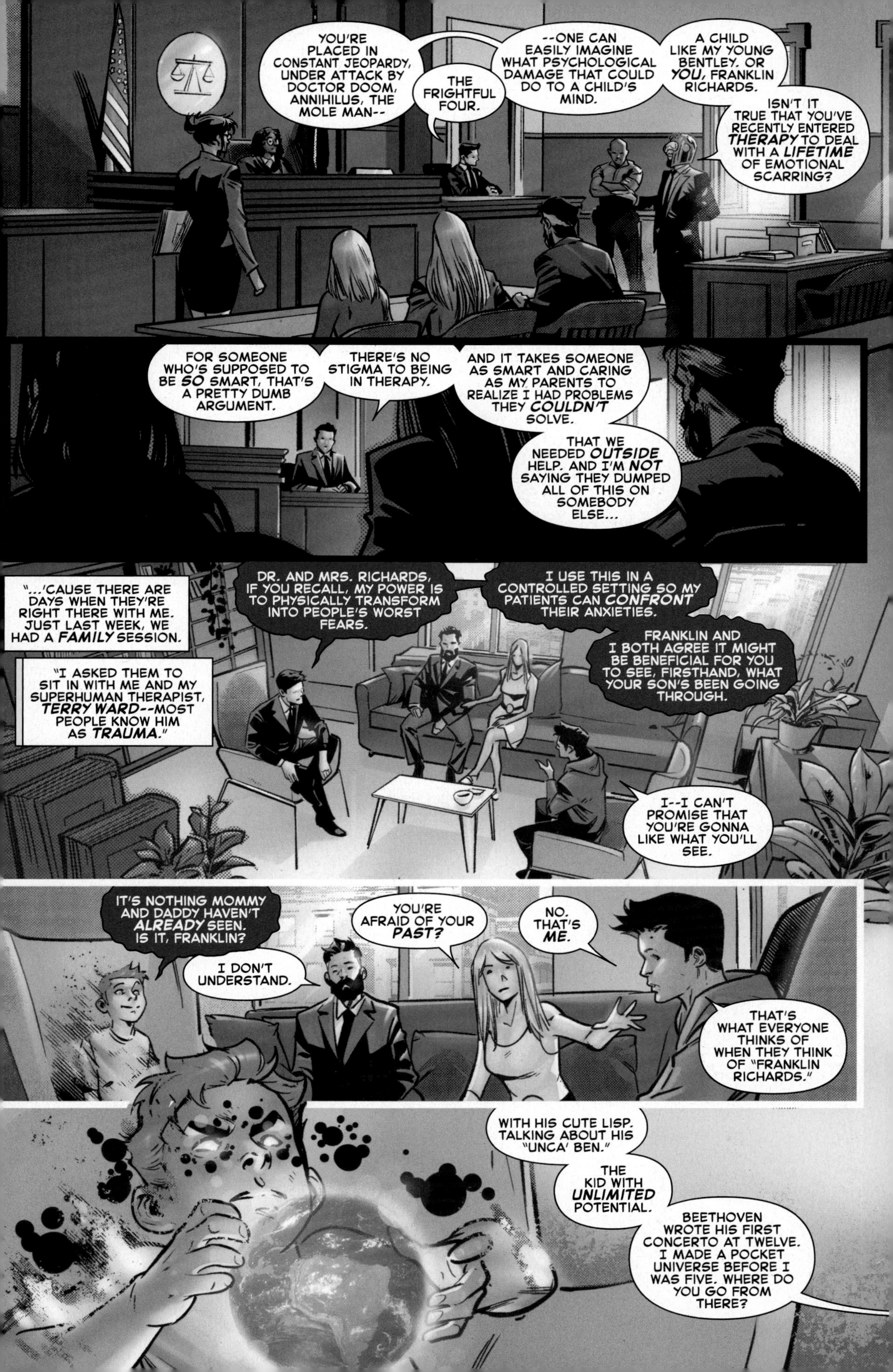
YOU'RE PLACED IN CONSTANT JEOPARDY, UNDER ATTACK BY DOCTOR DOOM, ANNIHILUS, THE MOLE MAN--
THE FRIGHTFUL FOUR.
--ONE CAN EASILY IMAGINE WHAT PSYCHOLOGICAL DAMAGE THAT COULD DO TO A CHILD'S MIND.
A CHILD LIKE MY YOUNG BENTLEY. OR YOU, FRANKLIN RICHARDS.
ISN'T IT TRUE THAT YOU'VE RECENTLY ENTERED THERAPY TO DEAL WITH A LIFETIME OF EMOTIONAL SCARRING?
FOR SOMEONE WHO'S SUPPOSED TO BE SO SMART, THAT'S A PRETTY DUMB ARGUMENT.
THERE'S NO STIGMA TO BEING IN THERAPY.
AND IT TAKES SOMEONE AS SMART AND CARING AS MY PARENTS TO REALIZE I HAD PROBLEMS THEY COULDN'T SOLVE.
THAT WE NEEDED OUTSIDE HELP. AND I'M NOT SAYING THEY DUMPED ALL OF THIS ON SOMEBODY ELSE...
"...'CAUSE THERE ARE DAYS WHEN THEY'RE RIGHT THERE WITH ME. JUST LAST WEEK, WE HAD A FAMILY SESSION.
"I ASKED THEM TO SIT IN WITH ME AND MY SUPERHUMAN THERAPIST, TERRY WARD--MOST PEOPLE KNOW HIM AS TRAUMA."
DR. AND MRS. RICHARDS, IF YOU RECALL, MY POWER IS TO PHYSICALLY TRANSFORM INTO PEOPLE'S WORST FEARS.
I USE THIS IN A CONTROLLED SETTING SO MY PATIENTS CAN CONFRONT THEIR ANXIETIES.
FRANKLIN AND I BOTH AGREE IT MIGHT BE BENEFICIAL FOR YOU TO SEE, FIRSTHAND, WHAT YOUR SON'S BEEN GOING THROUGH.
I--I CAN'T PROMISE THAT YOU'RE GONNA LIKE WHAT YOU'LL SEE.
IT'S NOTHING MOMMY AND DADDY HAVEN'T ALREADY SEEN. IS IT, FRANKLIN?
I DON'T UNDERSTAND.
YOU'RE AFRAID OF YOUR PAST?
NO. THAT'S ME.
THAT'S WHAT EVERYONE THINKS OF WHEN THEY THINK OF "FRANKLIN RICHARDS."
WITH HIS CUTE LISP. TALKING ABOUT HIS "UNCA' BEN."
THE KID WITH UNLIMITED POTENTIAL.
BEETHOVEN WROTE HIS FIRST CONCERTO AT TWELVE. I MADE A POCKET UNIVERSE BEFORE I WAS FIVE. WHERE DO YOU GO FROM THERE?

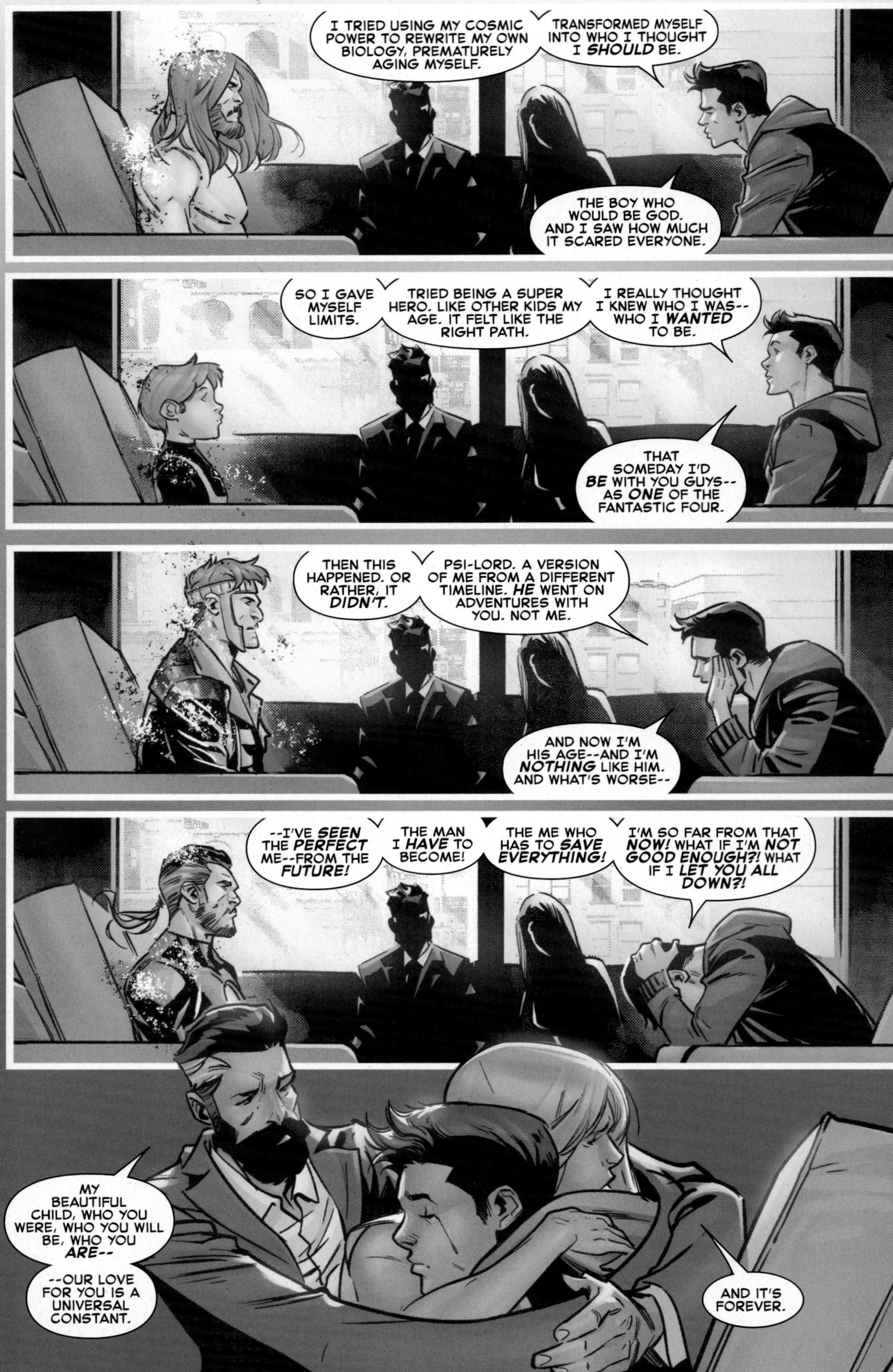
I TRIED USING MY COSMIC POWER TO REWRITE MY OWN BIOLOGY, PREMATURELY AGING MYSELF.
TRANSFORMED MYSELF INTO WHO I THOUGHT I *SHOULD* BE.
THE BOY WHO WOULD BE GOD. AND I SAW HOW MUCH IT SCARED EVERYONE.
SO I GAVE MYSELF LIMITS.
TRIED BEING A SUPER HERO. LIKE OTHER KIDS MY AGE. IT FELT LIKE THE RIGHT PATH.
I REALLY THOUGHT I KNEW WHO I WAS-- WHO I *WANTED* TO BE.
THAT SOMEDAY I'D *BE* WITH YOU GUYS-- AS *ONE* OF THE FANTASTIC FOUR.
THEN THIS HAPPENED. OR RATHER, IT *DIDN'T.*
PSI-LORD. A VERSION OF ME FROM A DIFFERENT TIMELINE. *HE* WENT ON ADVENTURES WITH YOU. NOT ME.
AND NOW I'M HIS AGE--AND I'M *NOTHING* LIKE HIM. AND WHAT'S WORSE--
--I'VE *SEEN* THE *PERFECT* ME--FROM THE *FUTURE!*
THE MAN I *HAVE* TO BECOME!
THE ME WHO HAS TO *SAVE EVERYTHING!*
I'M SO FAR FROM THAT *NOW!* WHAT IF I'M *NOT GOOD ENOUGH?!* WHAT IF I *LET YOU ALL DOWN?!*
MY BEAUTIFUL CHILD, WHO YOU WERE, WHO YOU WILL BE, WHO YOU *ARE--*
--OUR LOVE FOR YOU IS A UNIVERSAL CONSTANT.
AND IT'S FOREVER.

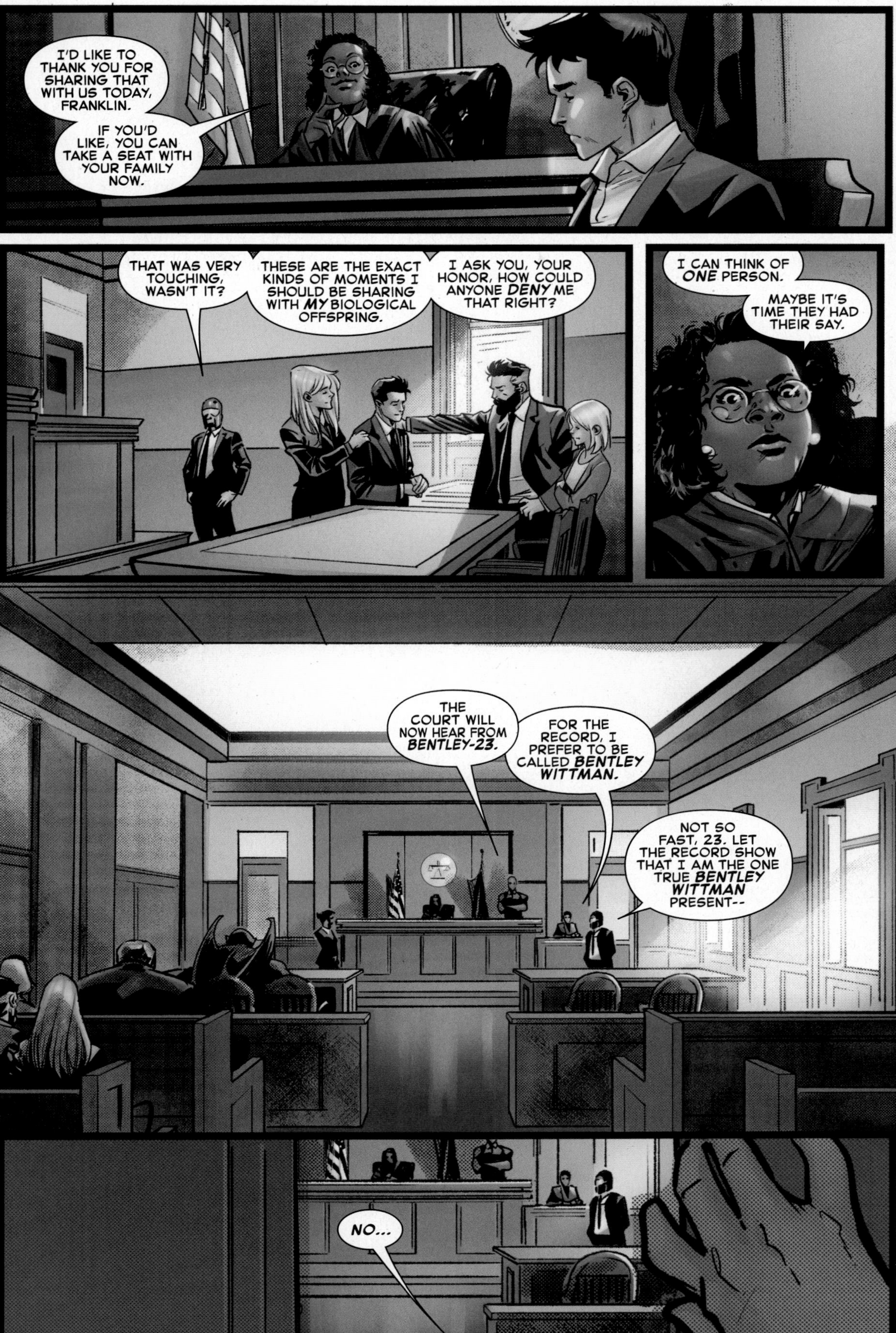
I'D LIKE TO THANK YOU FOR SHARING THAT WITH US TODAY, FRANKLIN.
IF YOU'D LIKE, YOU CAN TAKE A SEAT WITH YOUR FAMILY NOW.
THAT WAS VERY TOUCHING, WASN'T IT?
THESE ARE THE EXACT KINDS OF MOMENTS I SHOULD BE SHARING WITH MY BIOLOGICAL OFFSPRING.
I ASK YOU, YOUR HONOR, HOW COULD ANYONE DENY ME THAT RIGHT?
I CAN THINK OF ONE PERSON.
MAYBE IT'S TIME THEY HAD THEIR SAY.
THE COURT WILL NOW HEAR FROM BENTLEY-23.
FOR THE RECORD, I PREFER TO BE CALLED BENTLEY WITTMAN.
NOT SO FAST, 23. LET THE RECORD SHOW THAT I AM THE ONE TRUE BENTLEY WITTMAN PRESENT--
NO...

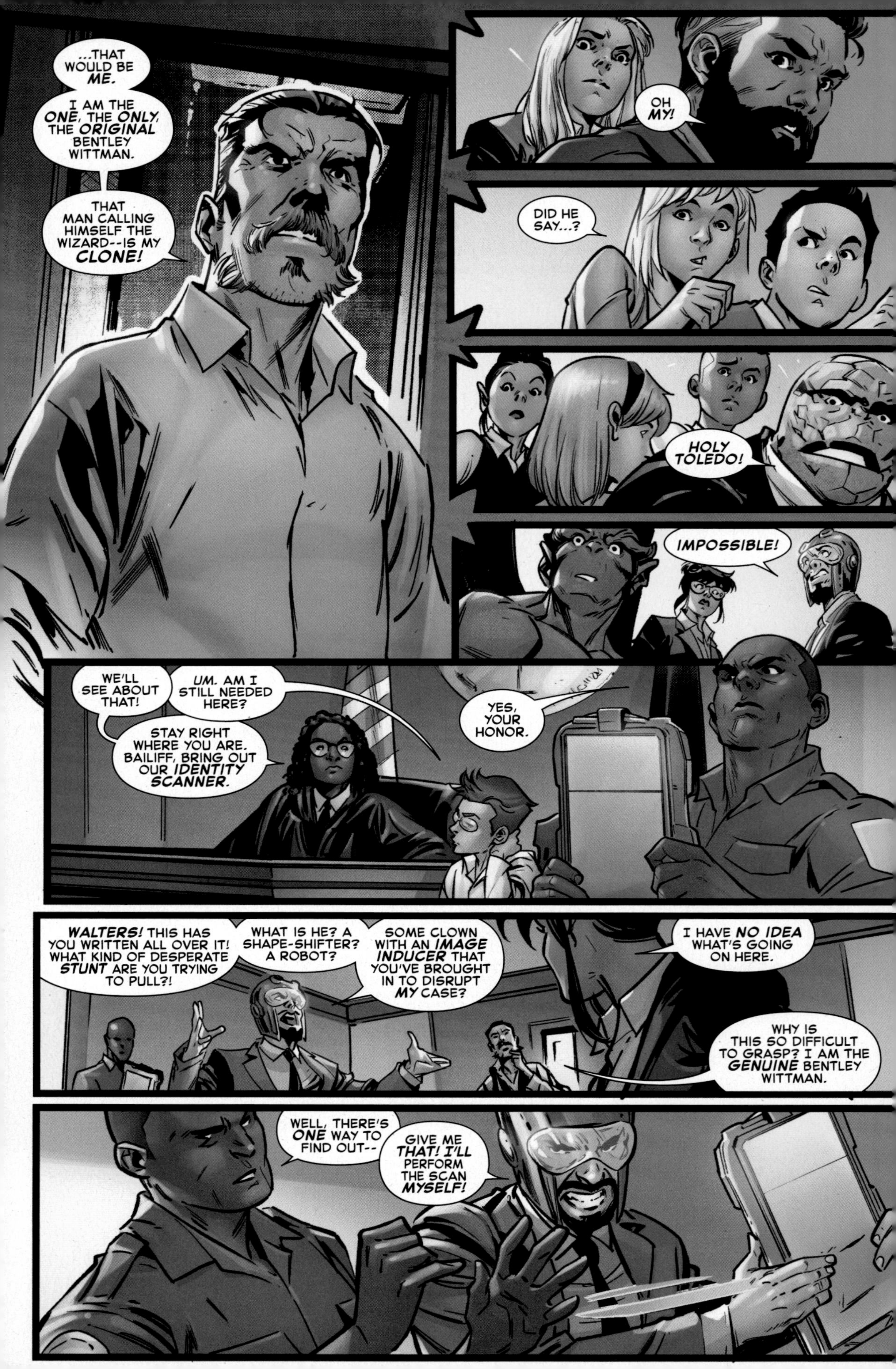
...THAT WOULD BE ME.
I AM THE ONE, THE ONLY, THE ORIGINAL BENTLEY WITTMAN.
THAT MAN CALLING HIMSELF THE WIZARD--IS MY CLONE!
OH MY!
DID HE SAY...?
HOLY TOLEDO!
IMPOSSIBLE!
WE'LL SEE ABOUT THAT!
UM. AM I STILL NEEDED HERE?
STAY RIGHT WHERE YOU ARE. BAILIFF, BRING OUT OUR IDENTITY SCANNER.
YES, YOUR HONOR.
WALTERS! THIS HAS YOU WRITTEN ALL OVER IT! WHAT KIND OF DESPERATE STUNT ARE YOU TRYING TO PULL?!
WHAT IS HE? A SHAPE-SHIFTER? A ROBOT?
SOME CLOWN WITH AN IMAGE INDUCER THAT YOU'VE BROUGHT IN TO DISRUPT MY CASE?
I HAVE NO IDEA WHAT'S GOING ON HERE.
WHY IS THIS SO DIFFICULT TO GRASP? I AM THE GENUINE BENTLEY WITTMAN.
WELL, THERE'S ONE WAY TO FIND OUT--
GIVE ME THAT! I'LL PERFORM THE SCAN MYSELF!

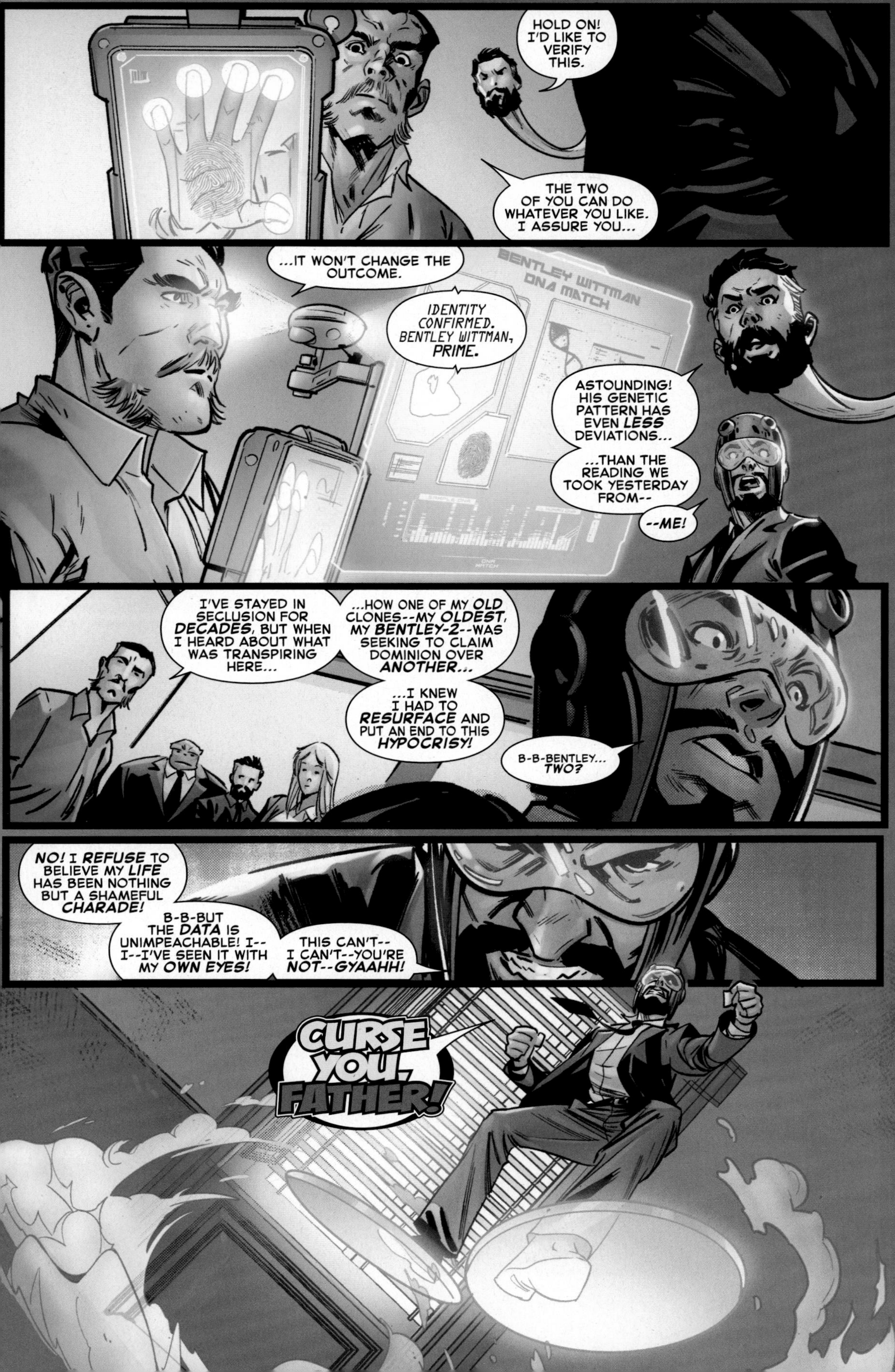
HOLD ON! I'D LIKE TO VERIFY THIS.
THE TWO OF YOU CAN DO WHATEVER YOU LIKE. I ASSURE YOU...
...IT WON'T CHANGE THE OUTCOME.
BENTLEY WITTMAN DNA MATCH
IDENTITY CONFIRMED. BENTLEY WITTMAN, PRIME.
ASTOUNDING! HIS GENETIC PATTERN HAS EVEN LESS DEVIATIONS...
...THAN THE READING WE TOOK YESTERDAY FROM--
--ME!
I'VE STAYED IN SECLUSION FOR DECADES, BUT WHEN I HEARD ABOUT WHAT WAS TRANSPIRING HERE...
...HOW ONE OF MY OLD CLONES--MY OLDEST, MY BENTLEY-2--WAS SEEKING TO CLAIM DOMINION OVER ANOTHER...
...I KNEW I HAD TO RESURFACE AND PUT AN END TO THIS HYPOCRISY!
B-B-BENTLEY... TWO?
NO! I REFUSE TO BELIEVE MY LIFE HAS BEEN NOTHING BUT A SHAMEFUL CHARADE!
B-B-BUT THE DATA IS UNIMPEACHABLE! I-- I--I'VE SEEN IT WITH MY OWN EYES!
THIS CAN'T-- I CAN'T--YOU'RE NOT--GYAAHH!
CURSE YOU, FATHER!

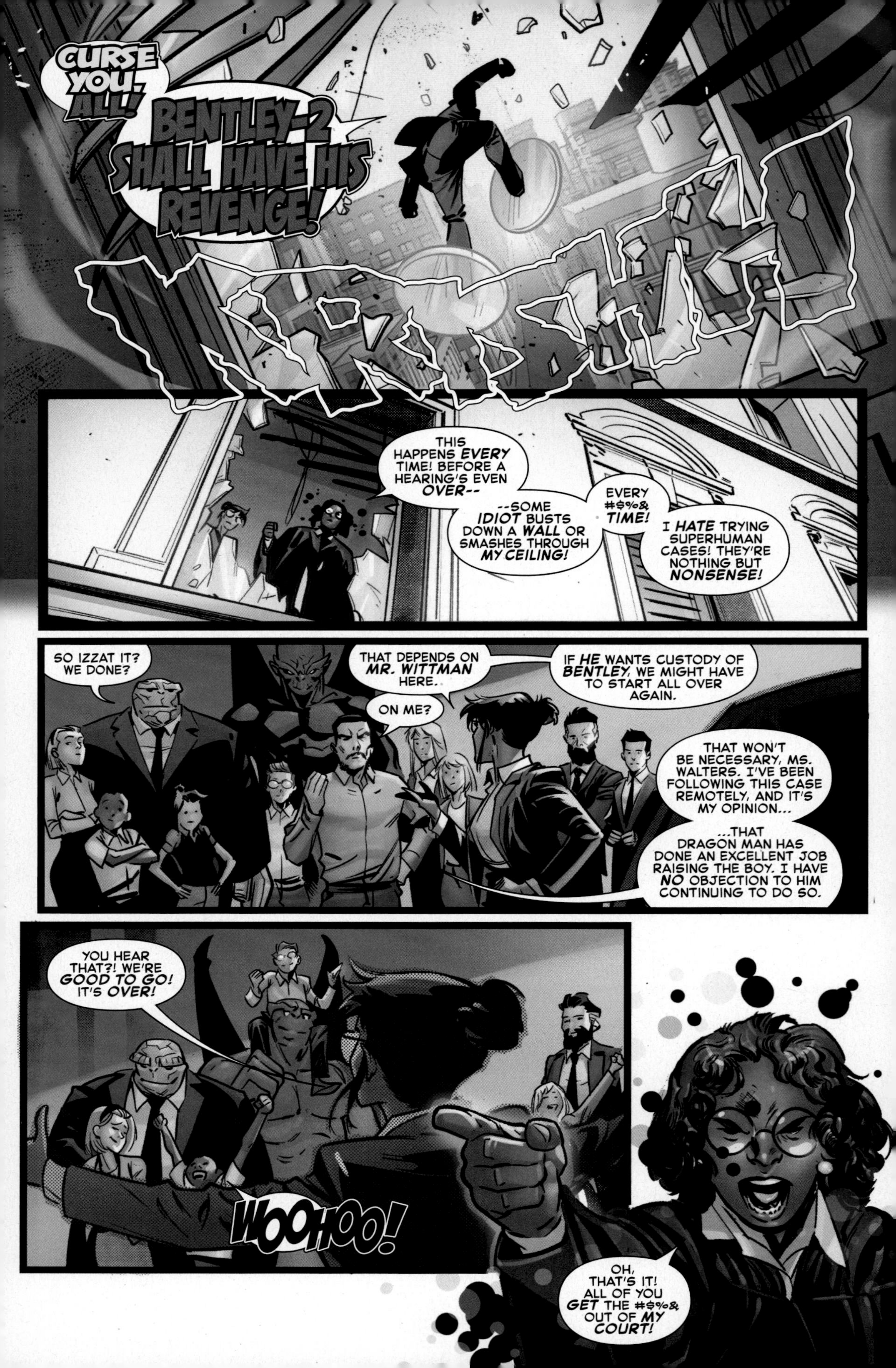
CURSE YOU, ALL!
BENTLEY-2 SHALL HAVE HIS REVENGE!
THIS HAPPENS EVERY TIME! BEFORE A HEARING'S EVEN OVER--
--SOME IDIOT BUSTS DOWN A WALL OR SMASHES THROUGH MY CEILING!
EVERY #$%& TIME!
I HATE TRYING SUPERHUMAN CASES! THEY'RE NOTHING BUT NONSENSE!
SO IZZAT IT? WE DONE?
THAT DEPENDS ON MR. WITTMAN HERE.
ON ME?
IF HE WANTS CUSTODY OF BENTLEY, WE MIGHT HAVE TO START ALL OVER AGAIN.
THAT WON'T BE NECESSARY, MS. WALTERS. I'VE BEEN FOLLOWING THIS CASE REMOTELY, AND IT'S MY OPINION...
...THAT DRAGON MAN HAS DONE AN EXCELLENT JOB RAISING THE BOY. I HAVE NO OBJECTION TO HIM CONTINUING TO DO SO.
YOU HEAR THAT?! WE'RE GOOD TO GO! IT'S OVER!
WOOHOO!
OH, THAT'S IT! ALL OF YOU GET THE #$%& OUT OF MY COURT!

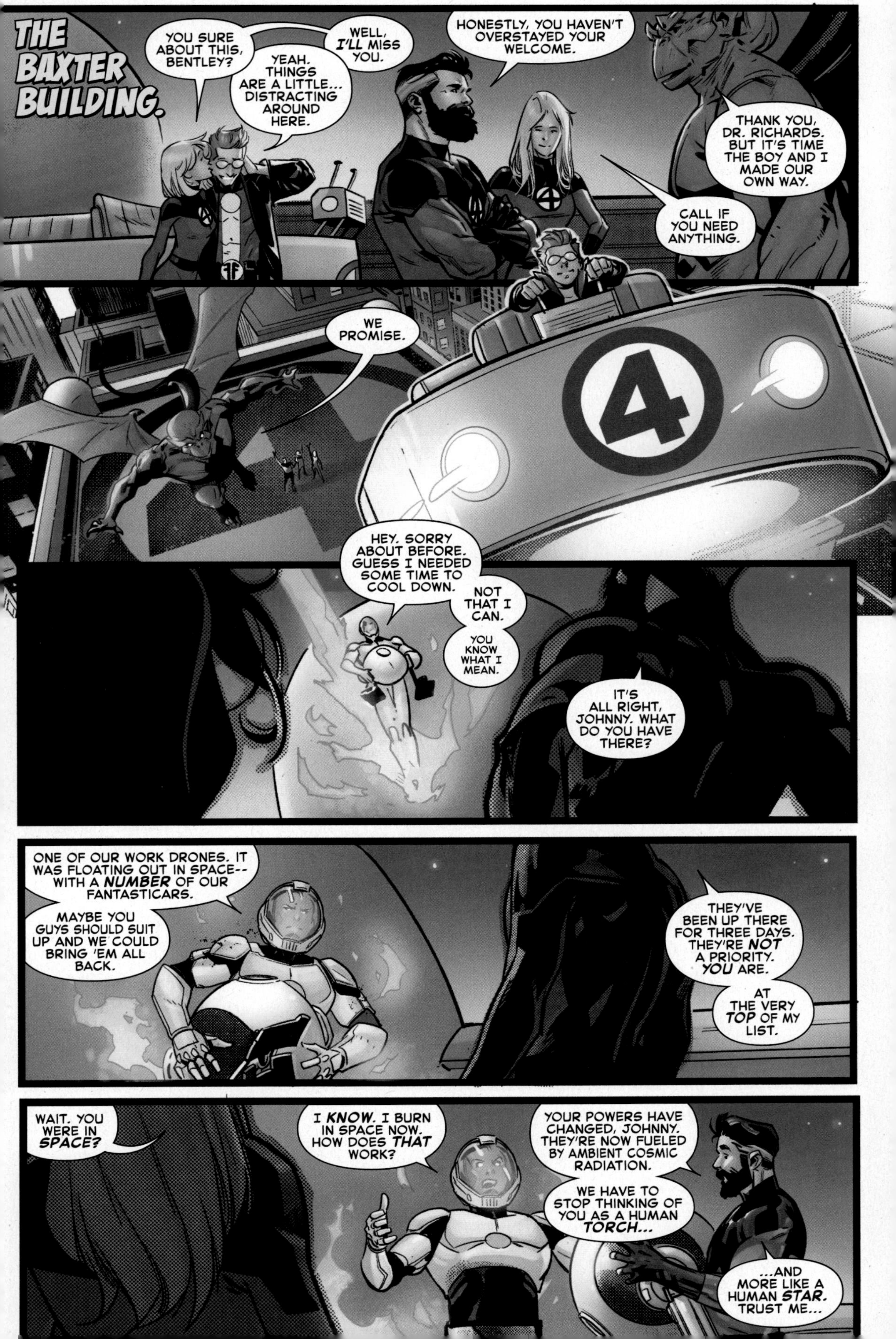
THE BAXTER BUILDING.
YOU SURE ABOUT THIS, BENTLEY?
YEAH. THINGS ARE A LITTLE... DISTRACTING AROUND HERE.
WELL, I'LL MISS YOU.
HONESTLY, YOU HAVEN'T OVERSTAYED YOUR WELCOME.
THANK YOU, DR. RICHARDS. BUT IT'S TIME THE BOY AND I MADE OUR OWN WAY.
CALL IF YOU NEED ANYTHING.
WE PROMISE.
HEY. SORRY ABOUT BEFORE. GUESS I NEEDED SOME TIME TO COOL DOWN.
NOT THAT I CAN.
YOU KNOW WHAT I MEAN.
IT'S ALL RIGHT, JOHNNY. WHAT DO YOU HAVE THERE?
ONE OF OUR WORK DRONES. IT WAS FLOATING OUT IN SPACE-- WITH A NUMBER OF OUR FANTASTICARS.
MAYBE YOU GUYS SHOULD SUIT UP AND WE COULD BRING 'EM ALL BACK.
THEY'VE BEEN UP THERE FOR THREE DAYS. THEY'RE NOT A PRIORITY. YOU ARE.
AT THE VERY TOP OF MY LIST.
WAIT. YOU WERE IN SPACE?
I KNOW. I BURN IN SPACE NOW. HOW DOES THAT WORK?
YOUR POWERS HAVE CHANGED, JOHNNY. THEY'RE NOW FUELED BY AMBIENT COSMIC RADIATION.
WE HAVE TO STOP THINKING OF YOU AS A HUMAN TORCH...
...AND MORE LIKE A HUMAN STAR. TRUST ME...

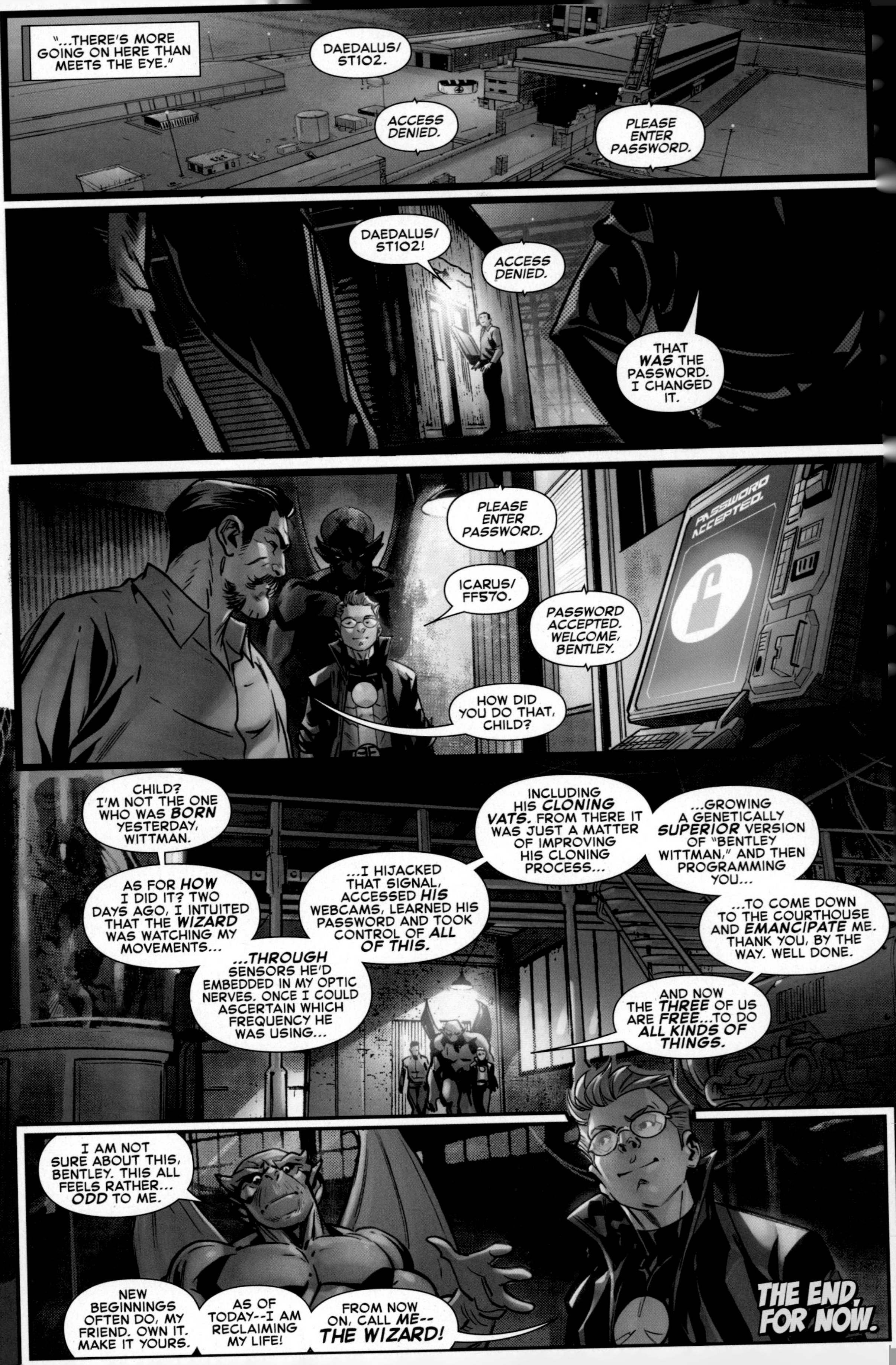
"...THERE'S MORE GOING ON HERE THAN MEETS THE EYE."
DAEDALUS/ ST102.
ACCESS DENIED.
PLEASE ENTER PASSWORD.
DAEDALUS/ ST102!
ACCESS DENIED.
THAT WAS THE PASSWORD. I CHANGED IT.
PLEASE ENTER PASSWORD.
ICARUS/ FF570.
PASSWORD ACCEPTED. WELCOME, BENTLEY.
PASSWORD ACCEPTED.
HOW DID YOU DO THAT, CHILD?
CHILD? I'M NOT THE ONE WHO WAS BORN YESTERDAY, WITTMAN.
AS FOR HOW I DID IT? TWO DAYS AGO, I INTUITED THAT THE WIZARD WAS WATCHING MY MOVEMENTS...
...THROUGH SENSORS HE'D EMBEDDED IN MY OPTIC NERVES. ONCE I COULD ASCERTAIN WHICH FREQUENCY HE WAS USING...
...I HIJACKED THAT SIGNAL, ACCESSED HIS WEBCAMS, LEARNED HIS PASSWORD AND TOOK CONTROL OF ALL OF THIS.
INCLUDING HIS CLONING VATS. FROM THERE IT WAS JUST A MATTER OF IMPROVING HIS CLONING PROCESS...
...GROWING A GENETICALLY SUPERIOR VERSION OF "BENTLEY WITTMAN," AND THEN PROGRAMMING YOU...
...TO COME DOWN TO THE COURTHOUSE AND EMANCIPATE ME. THANK YOU, BY THE WAY. WELL DONE.
AND NOW THE THREE OF US ARE FREE...TO DO ALL KINDS OF THINGS.
I AM NOT SURE ABOUT THIS, BENTLEY. THIS ALL FEELS RATHER... ODD TO ME.
NEW BEGINNINGS OFTEN DO, MY FRIEND. OWN IT. MAKE IT YOURS.
AS OF TODAY--I AM RECLAIMING MY LIFE!
FROM NOW ON, CALL ME-- THE WIZARD!
THE END, FOR NOW.

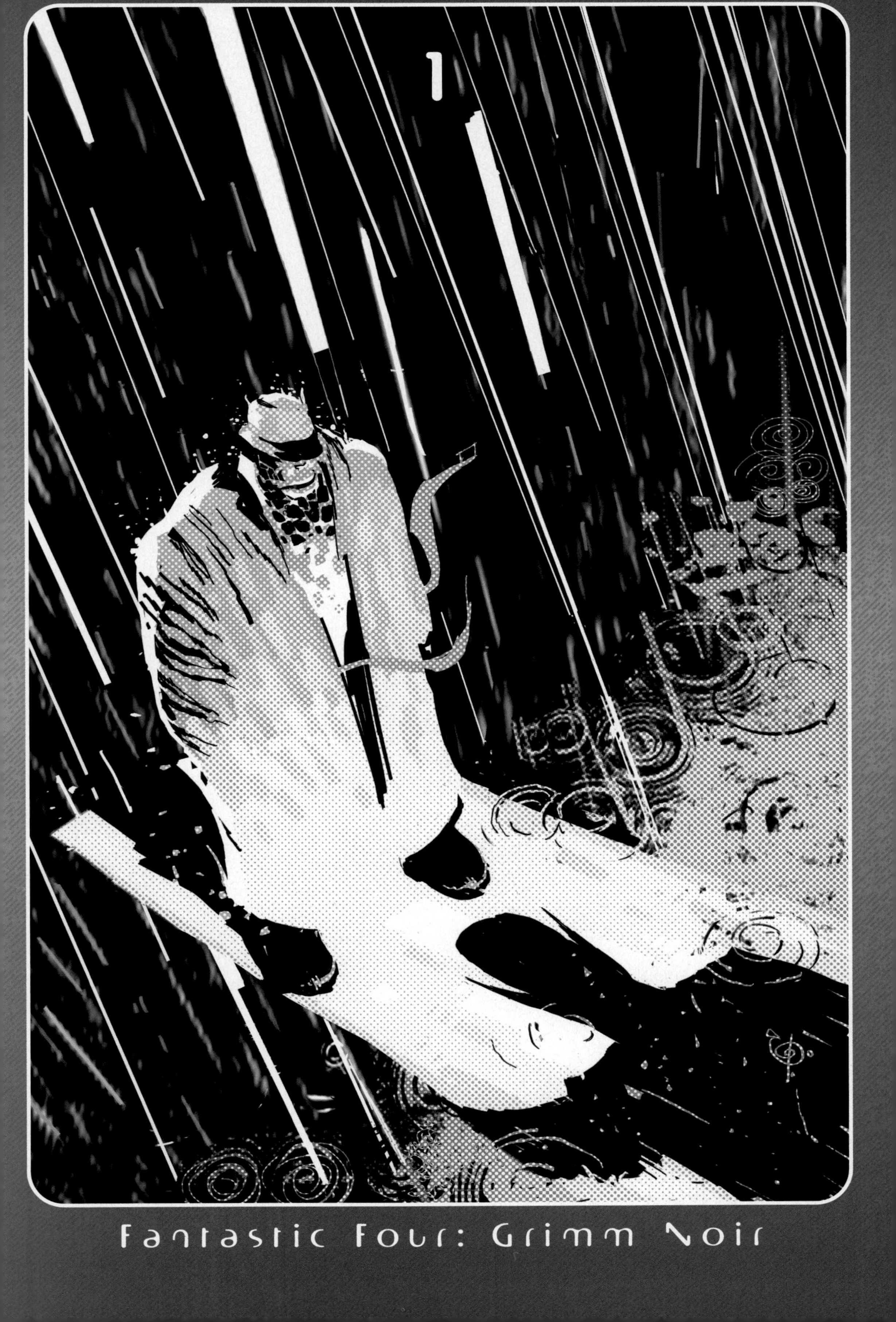
1

Fantastic Four: Grimm Noir

Fantastic Four
GRIMM NOIR

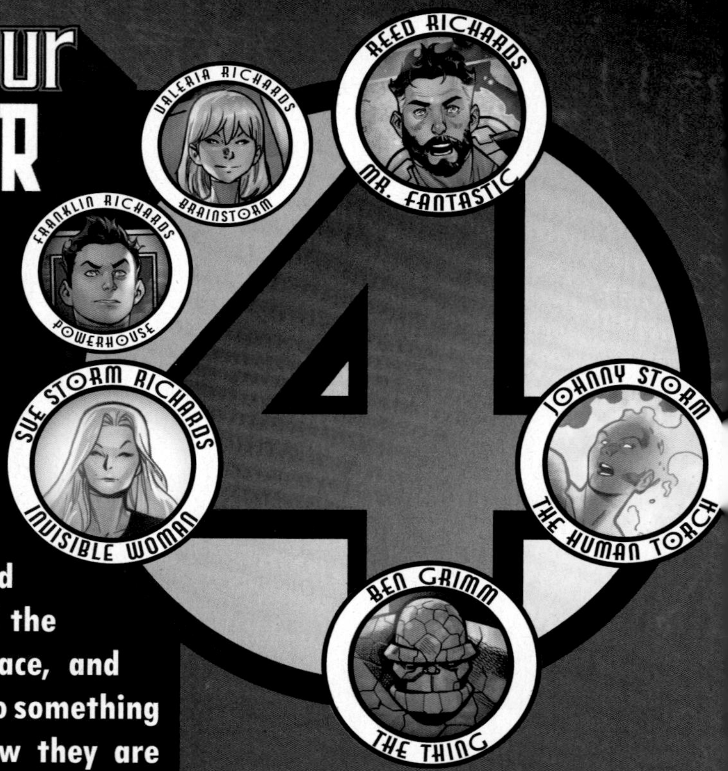
REED RICHARDS
MR. FANTASTIC
VALERIA RICHARDS
BRAINSTORM
FRANKLIN RICHARDS
POWERHOUSE
SUE STORM RICHARDS
INVISIBLE WOMAN
JOHNNY STORM
THE HUMAN TORCH
BEN GRIMM
THE THING

A brilliant scientist--his best friend--the woman he loves--and her fiery-tempered kid brother! Together, they braved the unknown terrors of outer space, and were changed by cosmic rays into something more than merely human! Now they are THE FANTASTIC FOUR--and the world will never be the same again!

Ben Grimm recently married his longtime flame, Alicia Masters--but between Doctor Doom interrupting their wedding and the Hulk crashing their honeymoon, they haven't had much time to settle into married life. And while their future is still bright, there's something sinister looming in the shadows of Yancy Street...

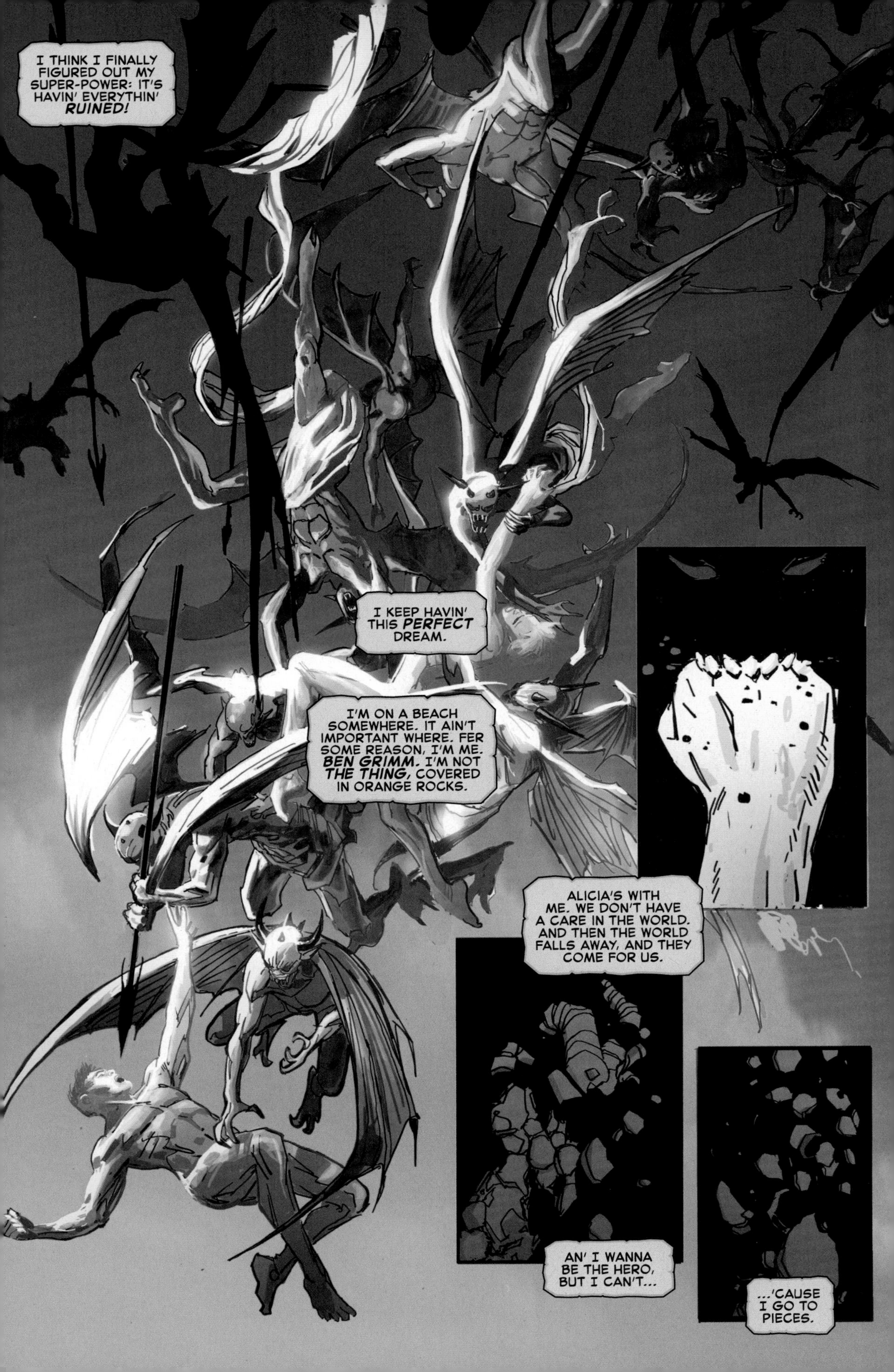

I THINK I FINALLY FIGURED OUT MY SUPER-POWER: IT'S HAVIN' EVERYTHIN' RUINED!
I KEEP HAVIN' THIS PERFECT DREAM.
I'M ON A BEACH SOMEWHERE. IT AIN'T IMPORTANT WHERE. FER SOME REASON, I'M ME. BEN GRIMM. I'M NOT THE THING, COVERED IN ORANGE ROCKS.
ALICIA'S WITH ME. WE DON'T HAVE A CARE IN THE WORLD. AND THEN THE WORLD FALLS AWAY, AND THEY COME FOR US.
AN' I WANNA BE THE HERO, BUT I CAN'T...
...'CAUSE I GO TO PIECES.

I GOT A LOT OF MILEAGE ON THE ODOMETER, YOU KNOW?
I BEEN TO SPACE AND BACK MORE TIMES THAN I CAN COUNT. OTHER DIMENSIONS, UNIVERSES, YADA YADA...
...I KNOW THIS IS JUST A NIGHTMARE...
...BUT I'M STILL MORE SCARED THAN I EVER BEEN.

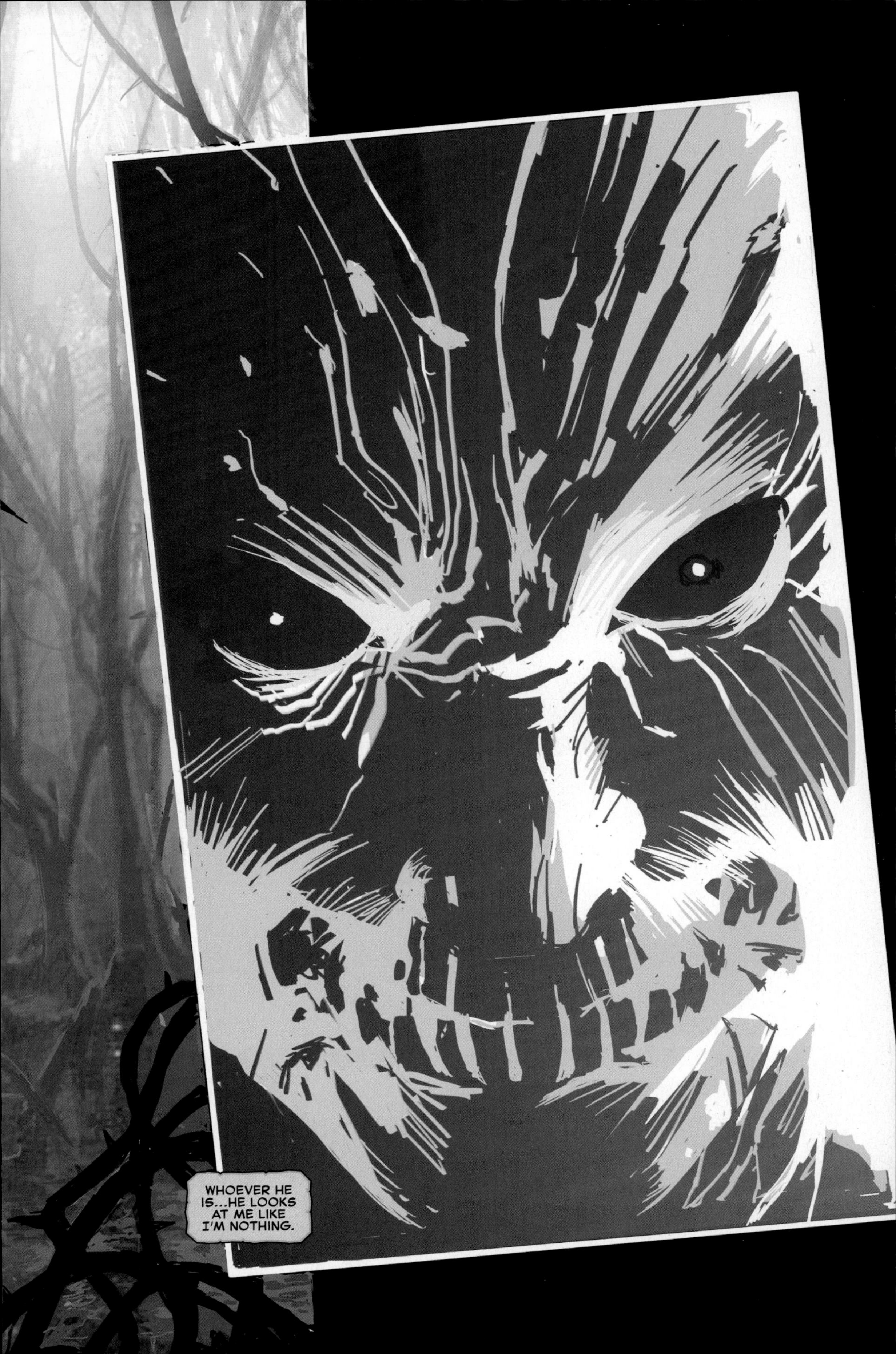
WHOEVER HE IS...HE LOOKS AT ME LIKE I'M NOTHING.

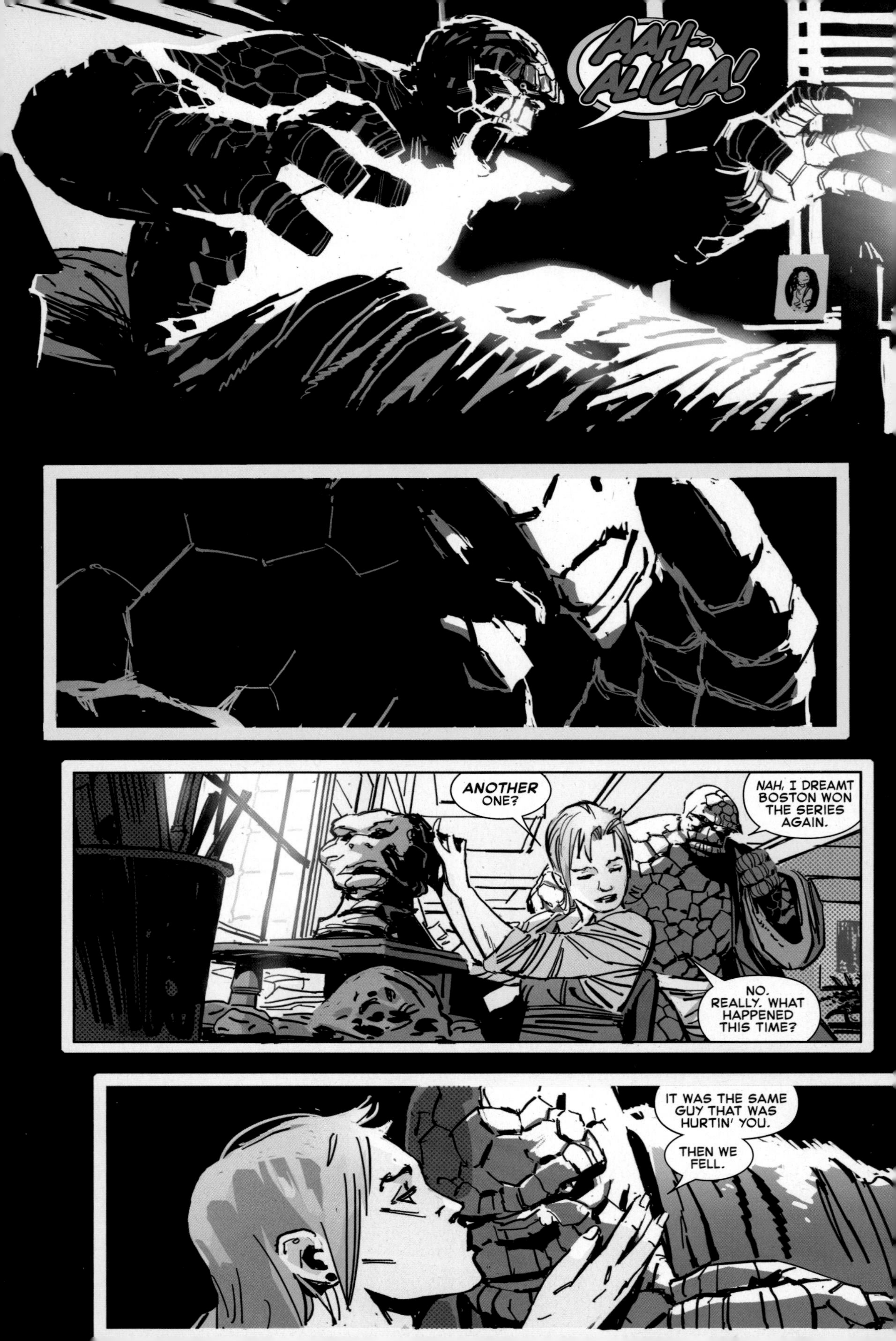
AAH--ALICIA!
ANOTHER ONE?
NAH, I DREAMT BOSTON WON THE SERIES AGAIN.
NO. REALLY. WHAT HAPPENED THIS TIME?
IT WAS THE SAME GUY THAT WAS HURTIN' YOU.
THEN WE FELL.

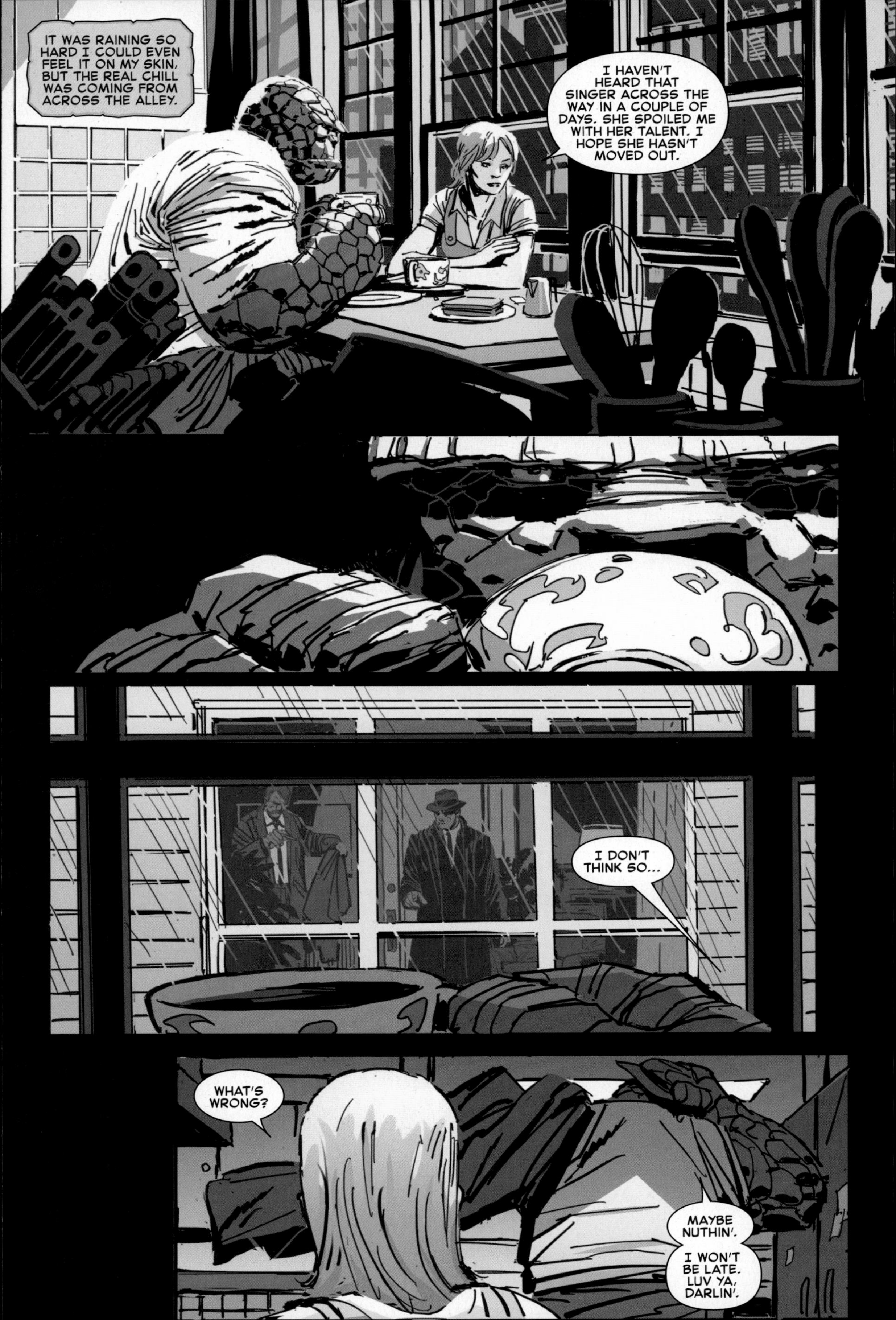
IT WAS RAINING SO HARD I COULD EVEN FEEL IT ON MY SKIN, BUT THE REAL CHILL WAS COMING FROM ACROSS THE ALLEY.
I HAVEN'T HEARD THAT SINGER ACROSS THE WAY IN A COUPLE OF DAYS. SHE SPOILED ME WITH HER TALENT. I HOPE SHE HASN'T MOVED OUT.
I DON'T THINK SO...
WHAT'S WRONG?
MAYBE NUTHIN'.
I WON'T BE LATE. LUV YA, DARLIN'.

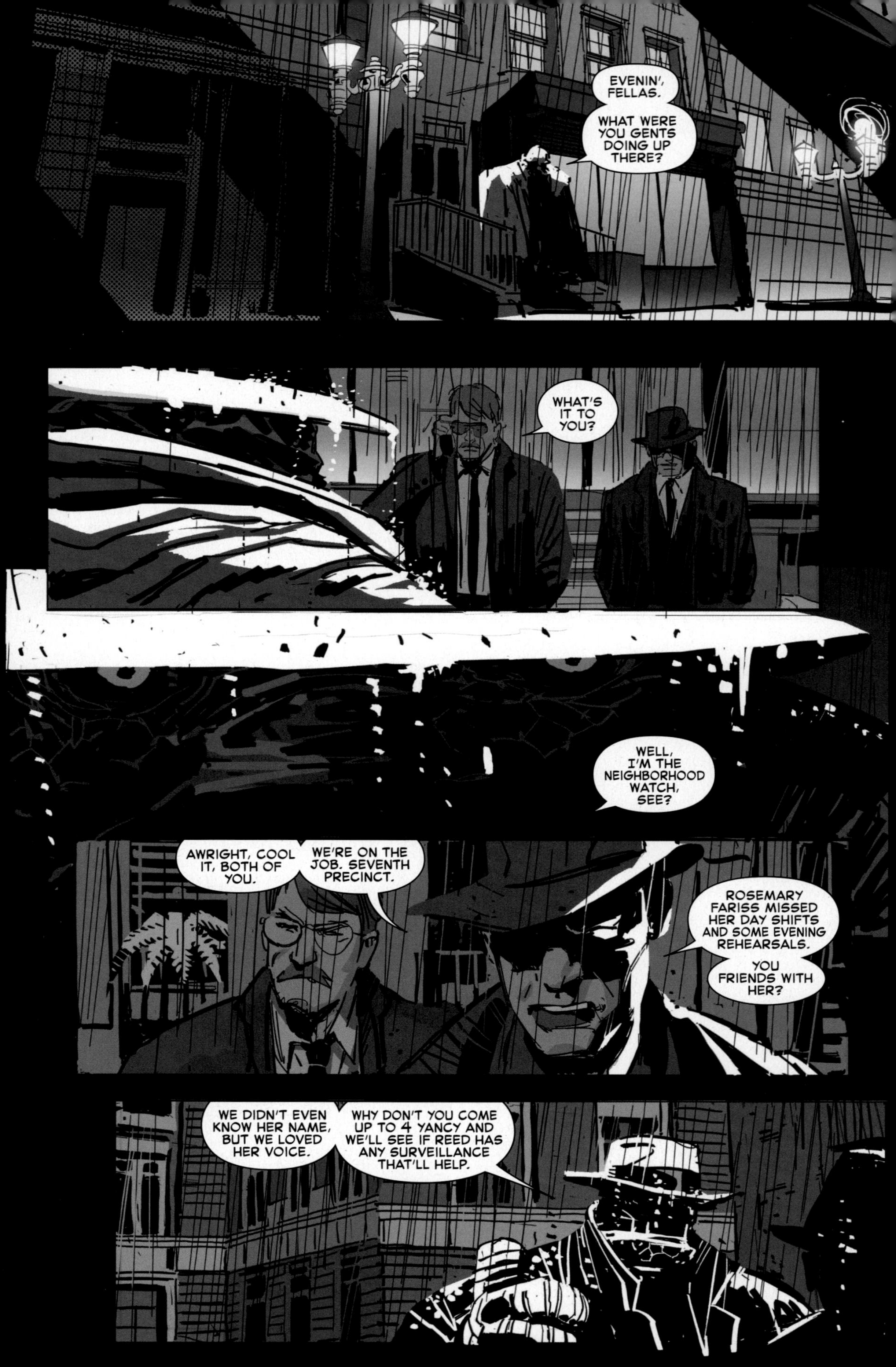
EVENIN', FELLAS.
WHAT WERE YOU GENTS DOING UP THERE?
WHAT'S IT TO YOU?
WELL, I'M THE NEIGHBORHOOD WATCH, SEE?
AWRIGHT, COOL IT, BOTH OF YOU.
WE'RE ON THE JOB. SEVENTH PRECINCT.
ROSEMARY FARISS MISSED HER DAY SHIFTS AND SOME EVENING REHEARSALS.
YOU FRIENDS WITH HER?
WE DIDN'T EVEN KNOW HER NAME, BUT WE LOVED HER VOICE.
WHY DON'T YOU COME UP TO 4 YANCY AND WE'LL SEE IF REED HAS ANY SURVEILLANCE THAT'LL HELP.

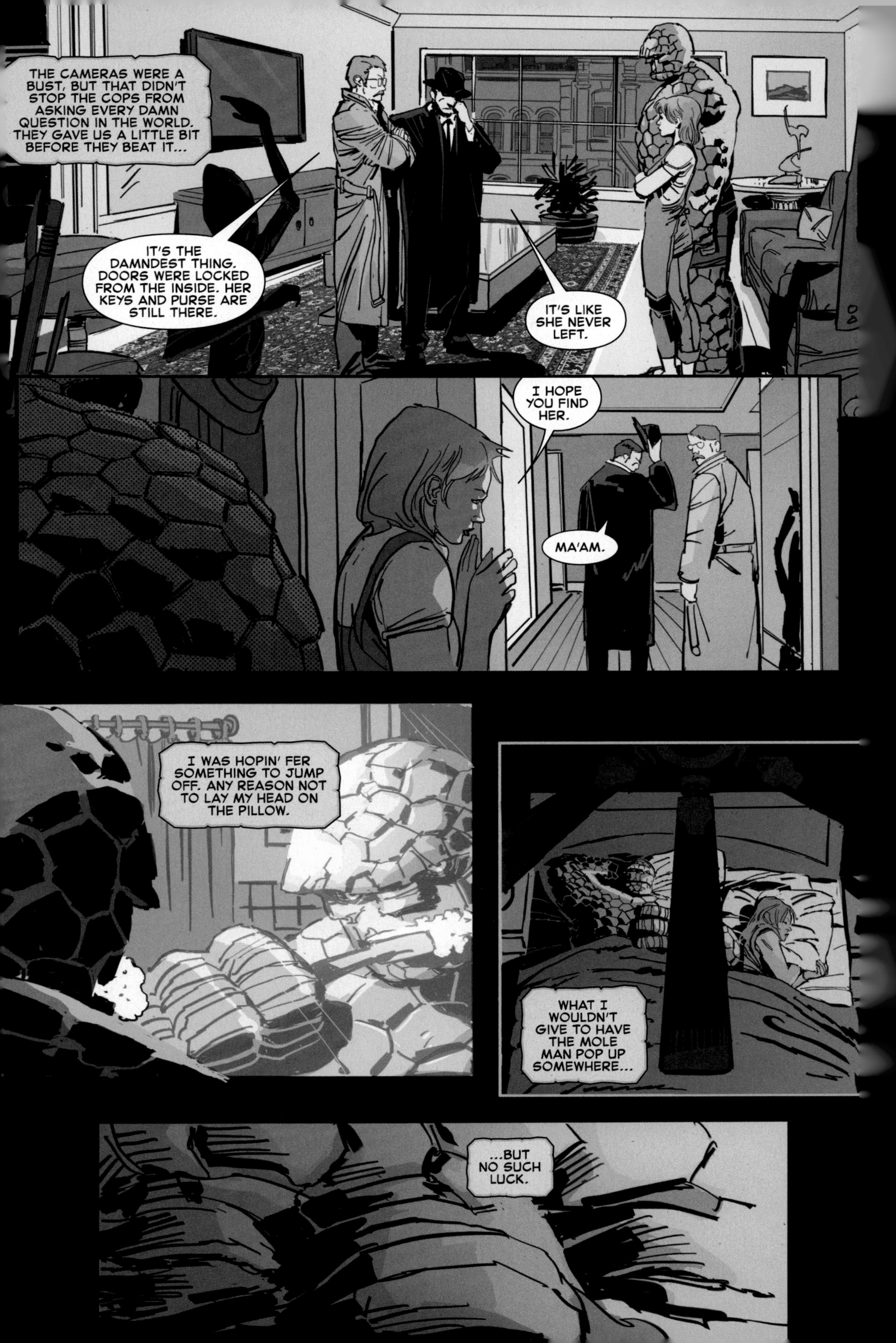
THE CAMERAS WERE A BUST, BUT THAT DIDN'T STOP THE COPS FROM ASKING EVERY DAMN QUESTION IN THE WORLD. THEY GAVE US A LITTLE BIT BEFORE THEY BEAT IT...
IT'S THE DAMNDEST THING. DOORS WERE LOCKED FROM THE INSIDE. HER KEYS AND PURSE ARE STILL THERE.
IT'S LIKE SHE NEVER LEFT.
I HOPE YOU FIND HER.
MA'AM.
I WAS HOPIN' FER SOMETHING TO JUMP OFF. ANY REASON NOT TO LAY MY HEAD ON THE PILLOW.
WHAT I WOULDN'T GIVE TO HAVE THE MOLE MAN POP UP SOMEWHERE...
...BUT NO SUCH LUCK.

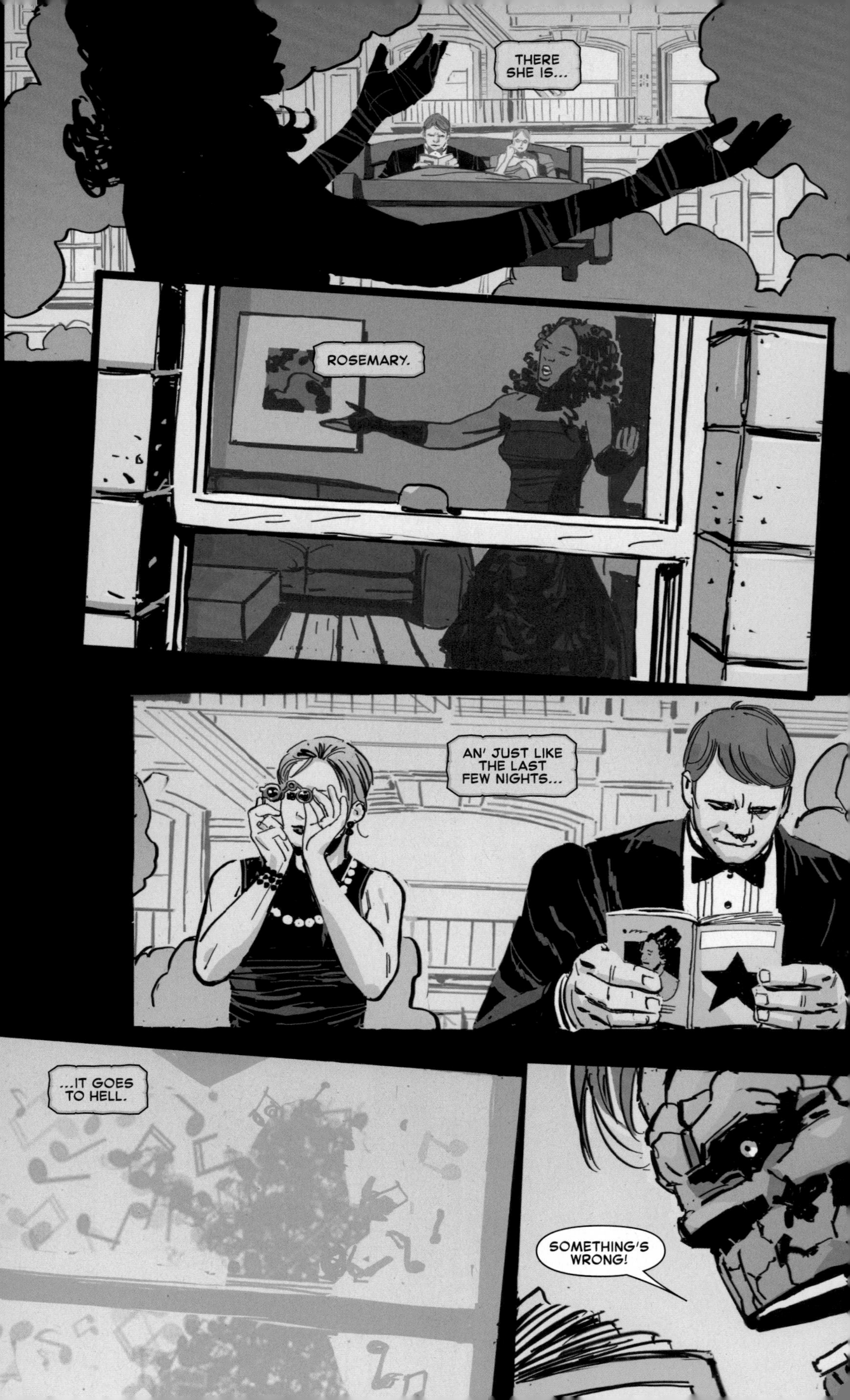
THERE SHE IS...
ROSEMARY.
AN' JUST LIKE THE LAST FEW NIGHTS...
...IT GOES TO HELL.
SOMETHING'S WRONG!

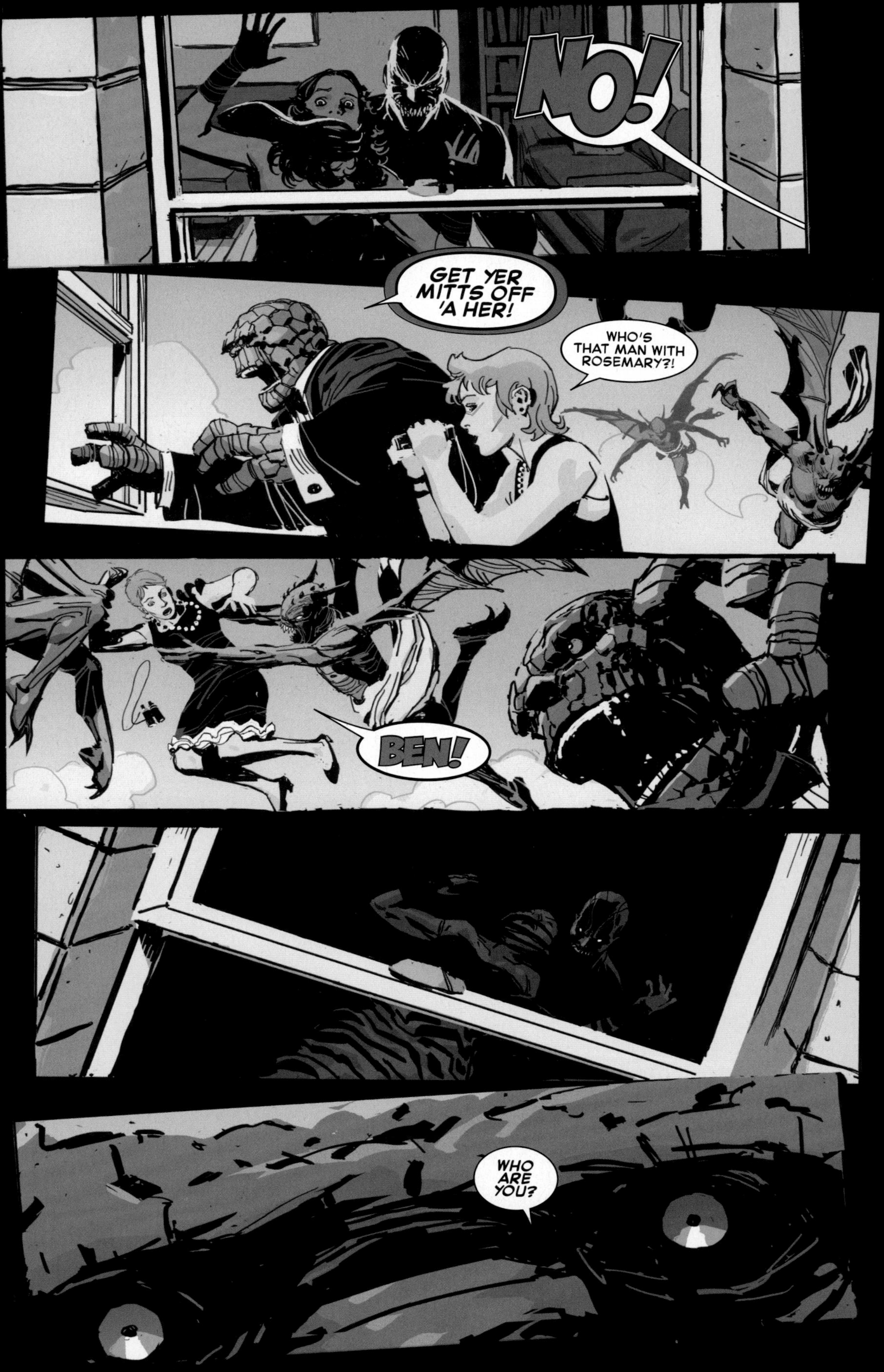
NO!
GET YER MITTS OFF 'A HER!
WHO'S THAT MAN WITH ROSEMARY?!
BEN!
WHO ARE YOU?

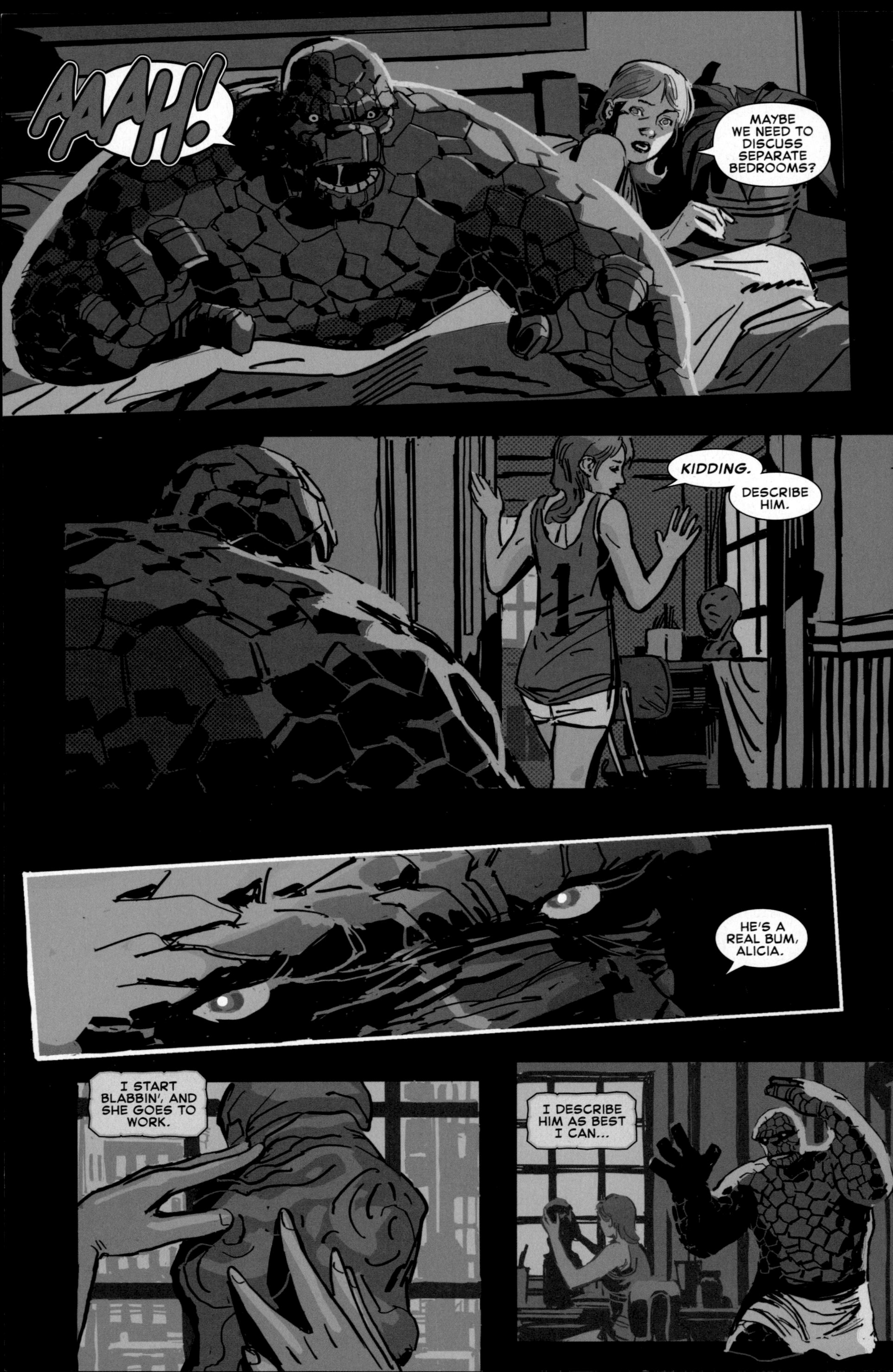
AAAH!
MAYBE WE NEED TO DISCUSS SEPARATE BEDROOMS?
KIDDING.
DESCRIBE HIM.
HE'S A REAL BUM, ALICIA.
I START BLABBIN', AND SHE GOES TO WORK.
I DESCRIBE HIM AS BEST I CAN...

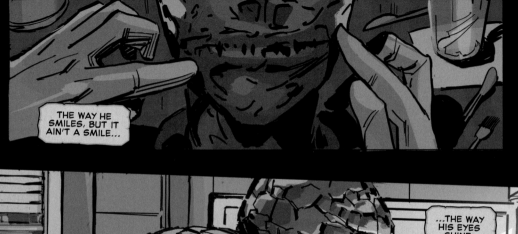

THE WAY HE SMILES, BUT IT AIN'T A SMILE...

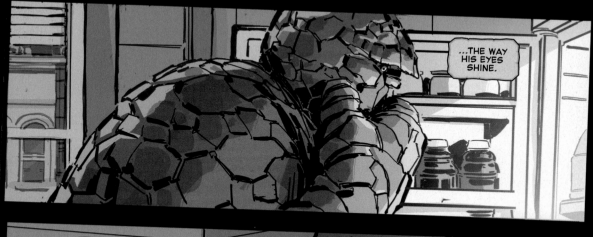

...THE WAY HIS EYES SHINE.

MAYBE I NEED A HOAGIE TO CALM DOWN?

IS THIS YOUR BAD GUY?

HOLY COW!

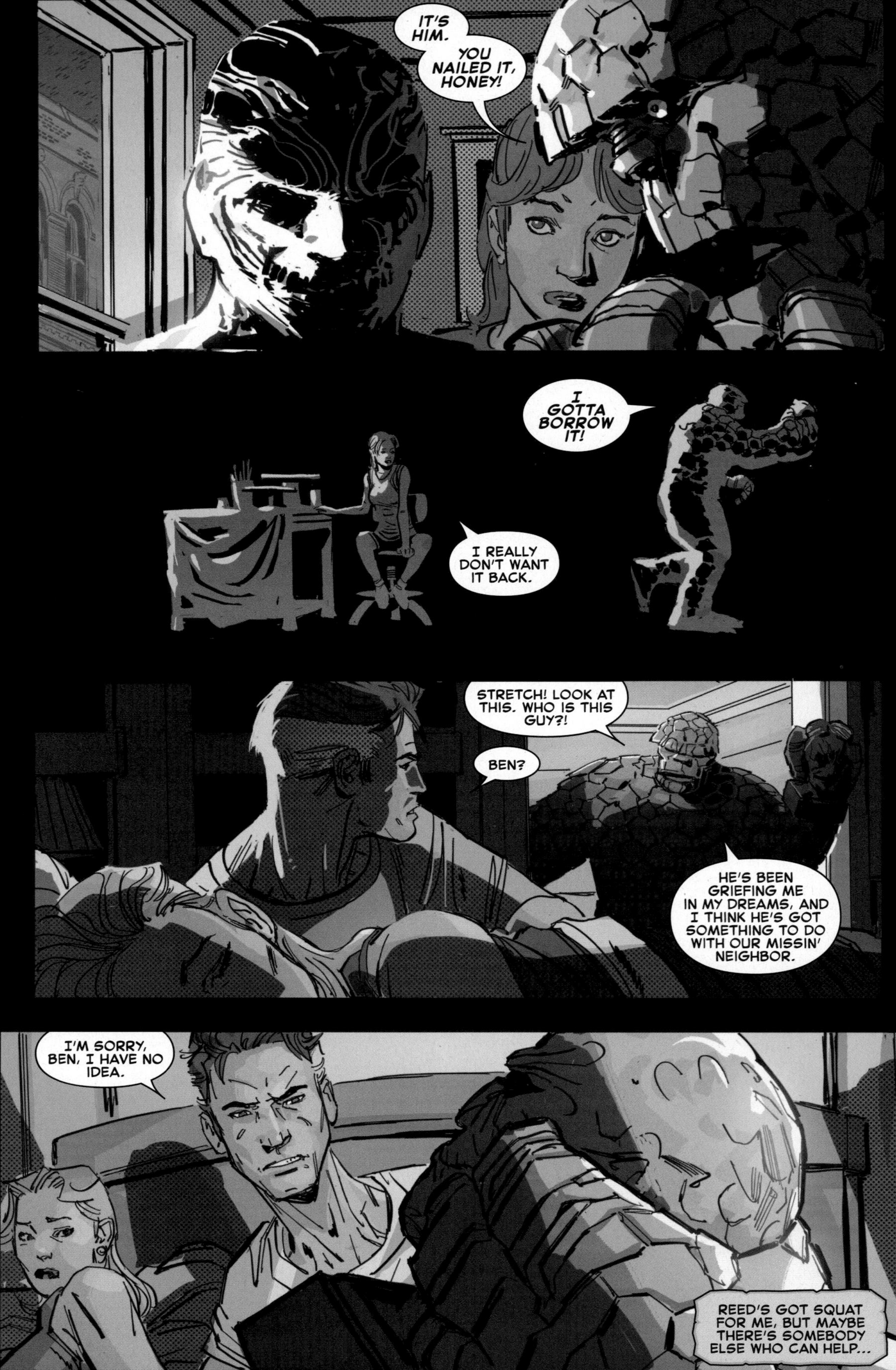
IT'S HIM.
YOU NAILED IT, HONEY!
I GOTTA BORROW IT!
I REALLY DON'T WANT IT BACK.
STRETCH! LOOK AT THIS. WHO IS THIS GUY?!
BEN?
HE'S BEEN GRIEFING ME IN MY DREAMS, AND I THINK HE'S GOT SOMETHING TO DO WITH OUR MISSIN' NEIGHBOR.
I'M SORRY, BEN, I HAVE NO IDEA.
REED'S GOT SQUAT FOR ME, BUT MAYBE THERE'S SOMEBODY ELSE WHO CAN HELP...

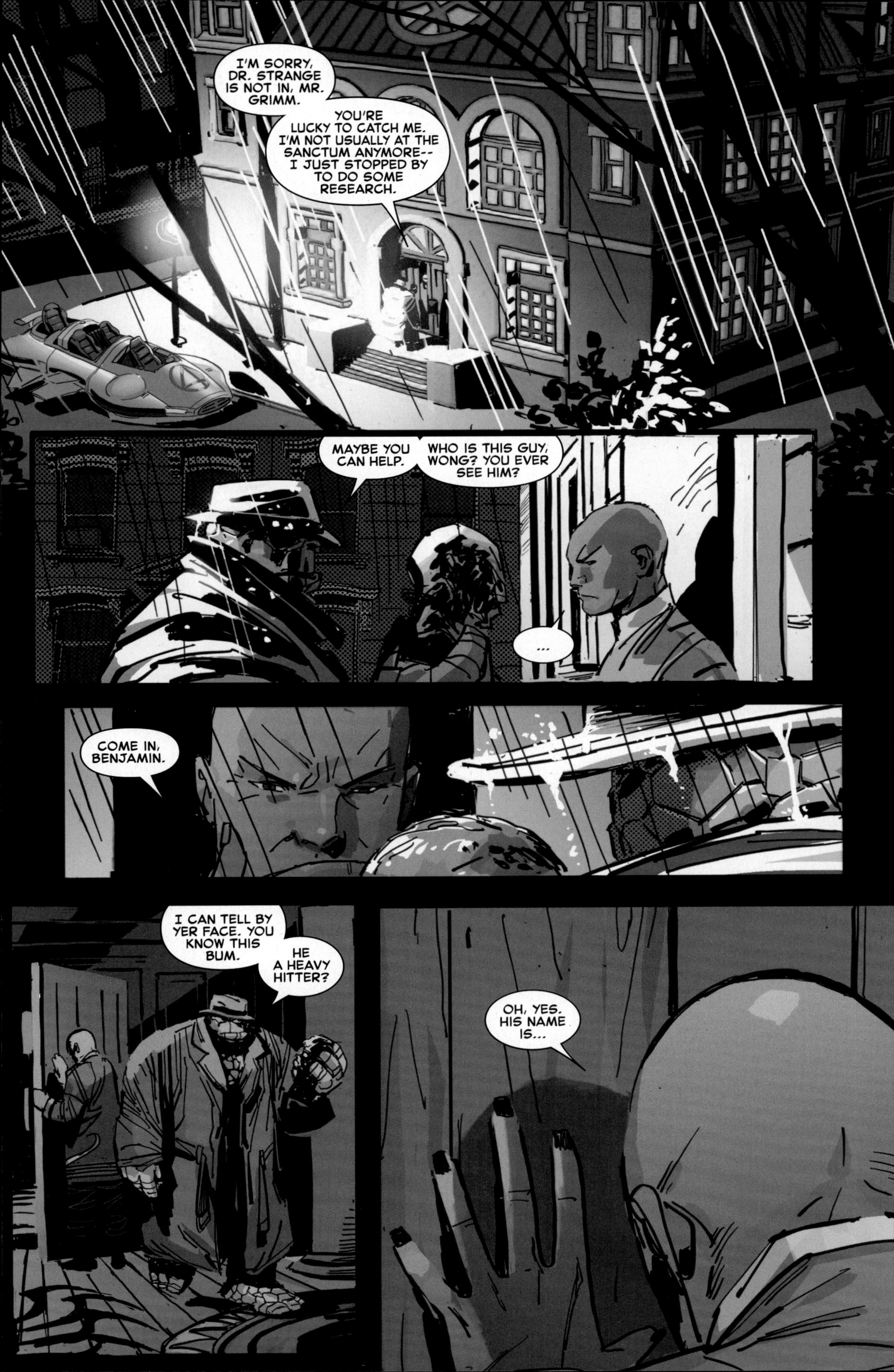

I'M SORRY, DR. STRANGE IS NOT IN, MR. GRIMM.
YOU'RE LUCKY TO CATCH ME. I'M NOT USUALLY AT THE SANCTUM ANYMORE-- I JUST STOPPED BY TO DO SOME RESEARCH.
MAYBE YOU CAN HELP.
WHO IS THIS GUY, WONG? YOU EVER SEE HIM?
...
COME IN, BENJAMIN.
I CAN TELL BY YER FACE. YOU KNOW THIS BUM.
HE A HEAVY HITTER?
OH, YES. HIS NAME IS...

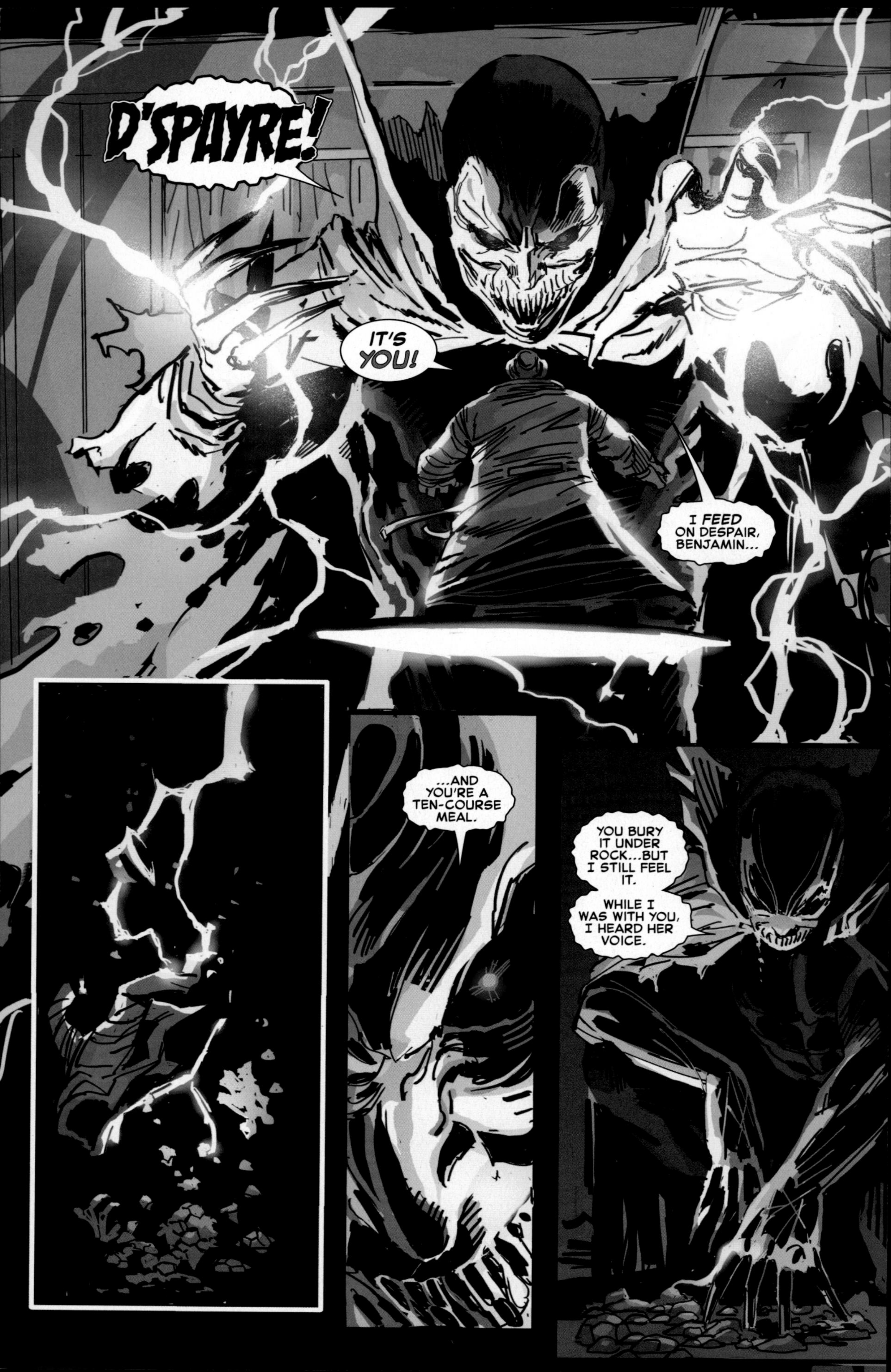
D'SPAYRE!
IT'S YOU!
I FEED ON DESPAIR, BENJAMIN...
...AND YOU'RE A TEN-COURSE MEAL.
YOU BURY IT UNDER ROCK...BUT I STILL FEEL IT.
WHILE I WAS WITH YOU, I HEARD HER VOICE.

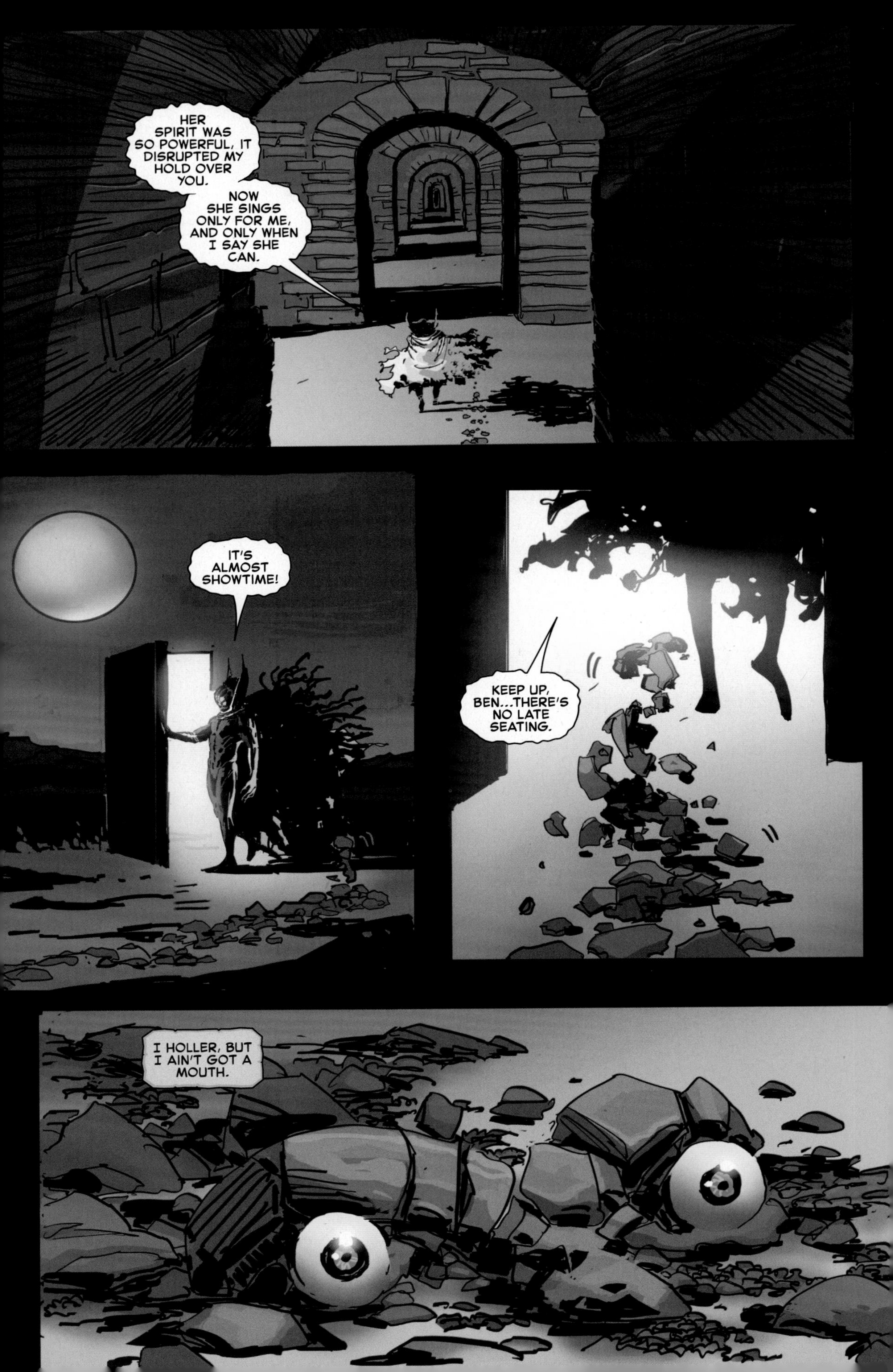
HER SPIRIT WAS SO POWERFUL, IT DISRUPTED MY HOLD OVER YOU.
NOW SHE SINGS ONLY FOR ME, AND ONLY WHEN I SAY SHE CAN.
IT'S ALMOST SHOWTIME!
KEEP UP, BEN...THERE'S NO LATE SEATING.
I HOLLER, BUT I AIN'T GOT A MOUTH.

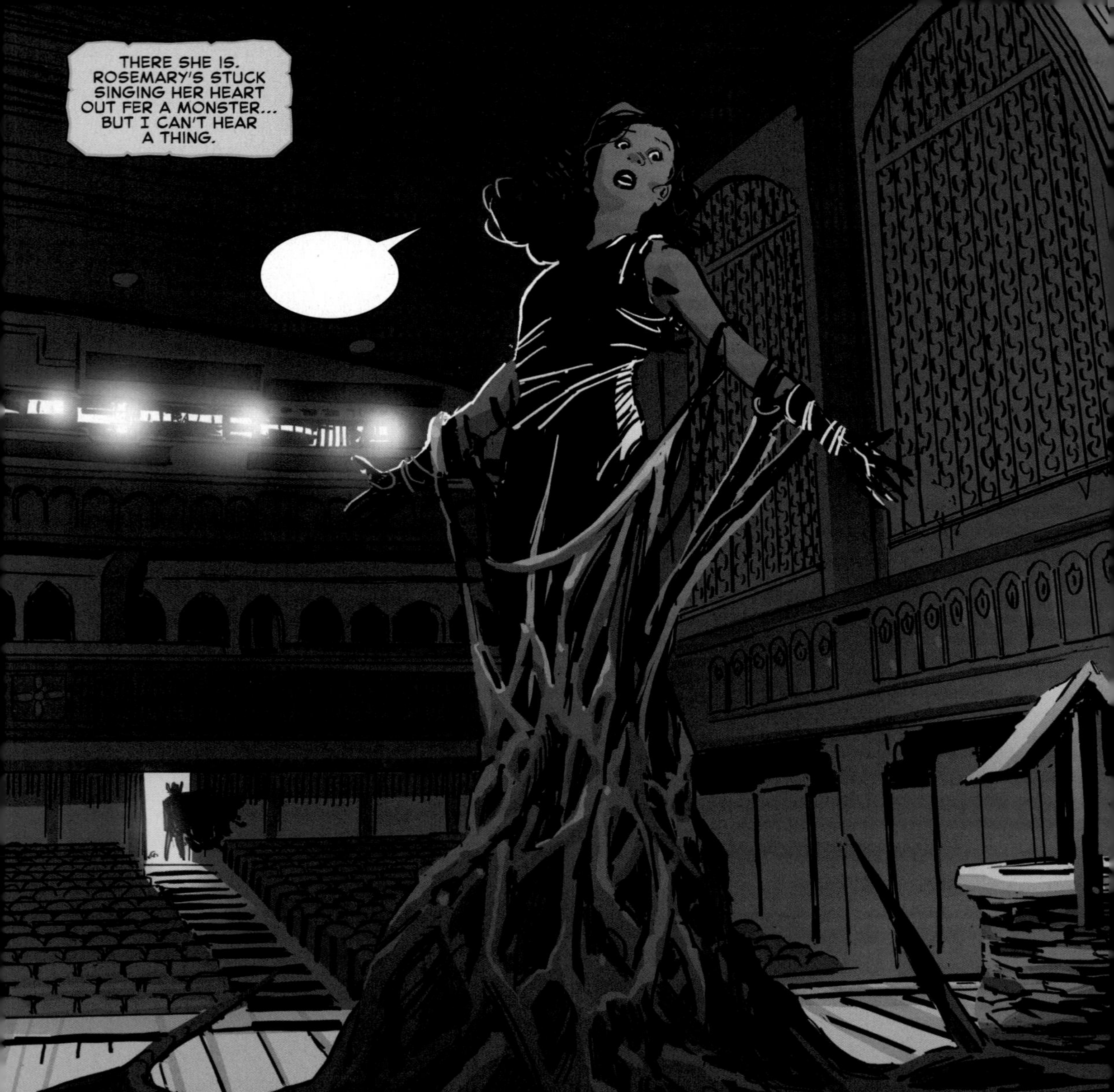
THERE SHE IS. ROSEMARY'S STUCK SINGING HER HEART OUT FER A MONSTER... BUT I CAN'T HEAR A THING.
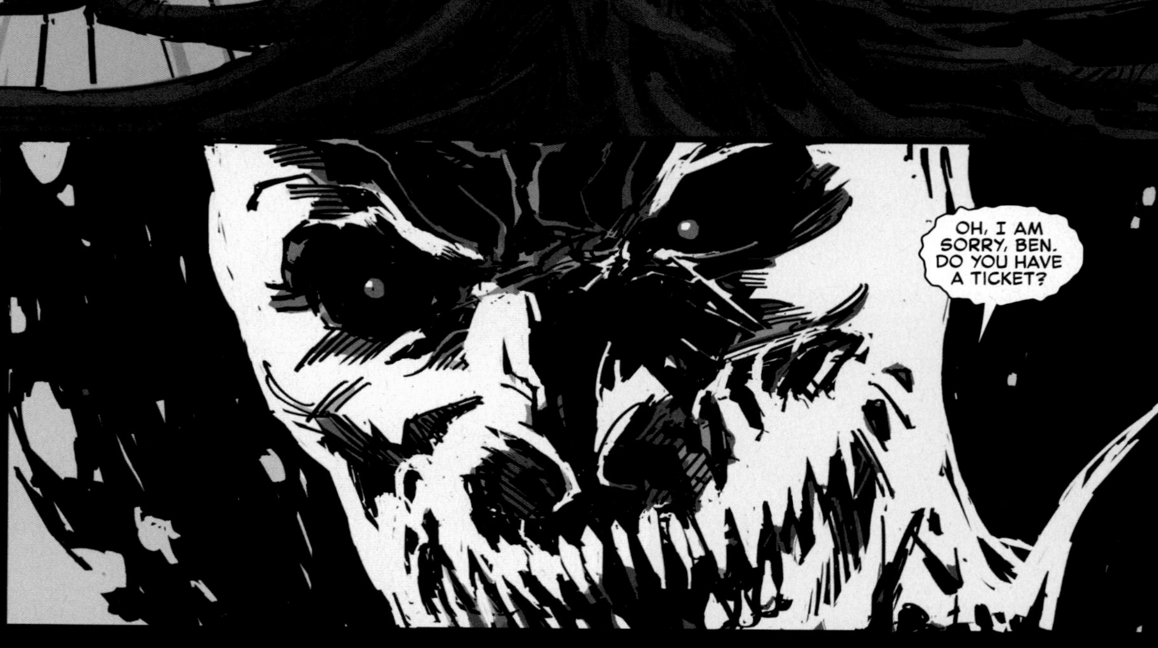
OH, I AM SORRY, BEN. DO YOU HAVE A TICKET?

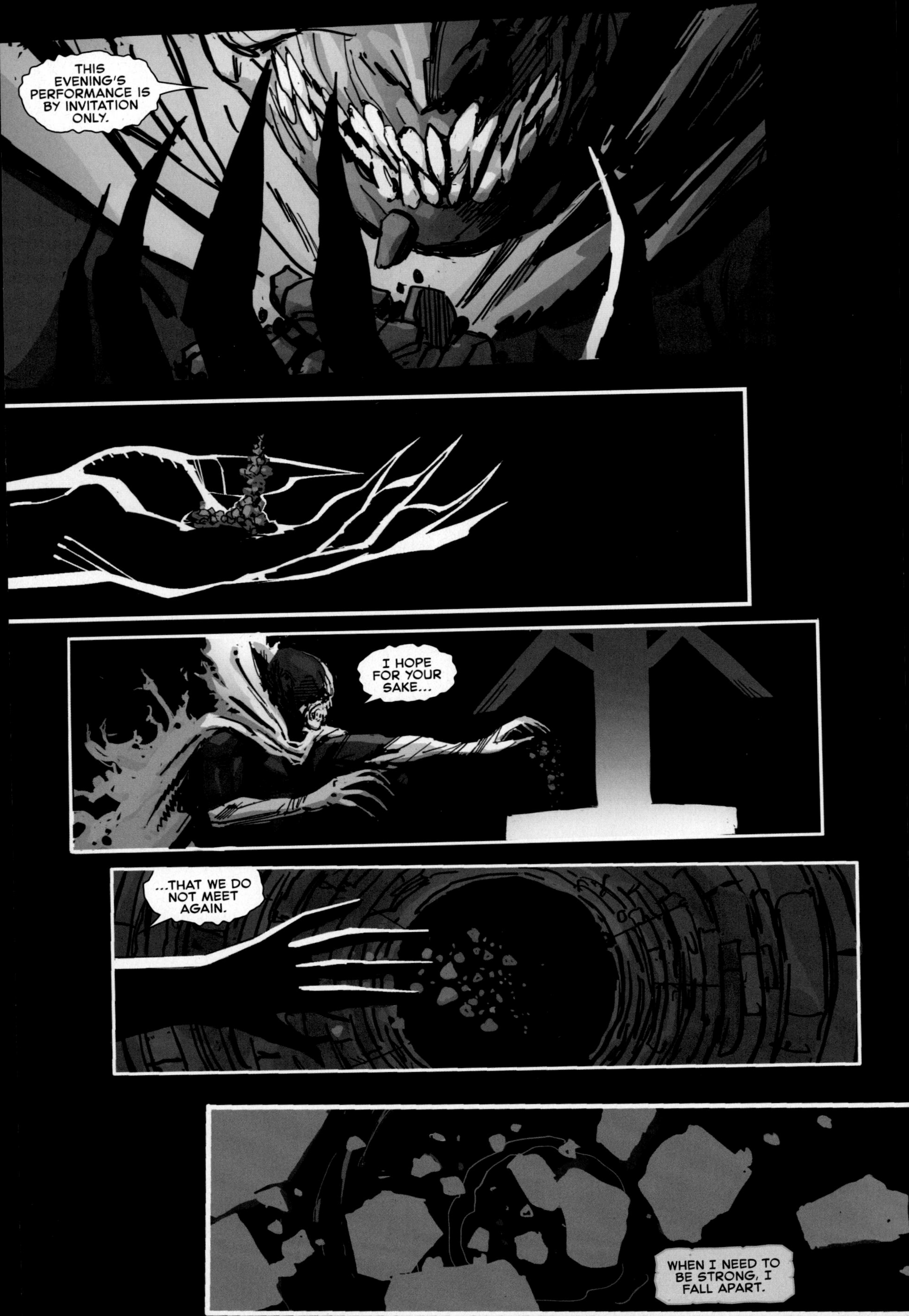
THIS EVENING'S PERFORMANCE IS BY INVITATION ONLY.
I HOPE FOR YOUR SAKE...
...THAT WE DO NOT MEET AGAIN.
WHEN I NEED TO BE STRONG, I FALL APART.

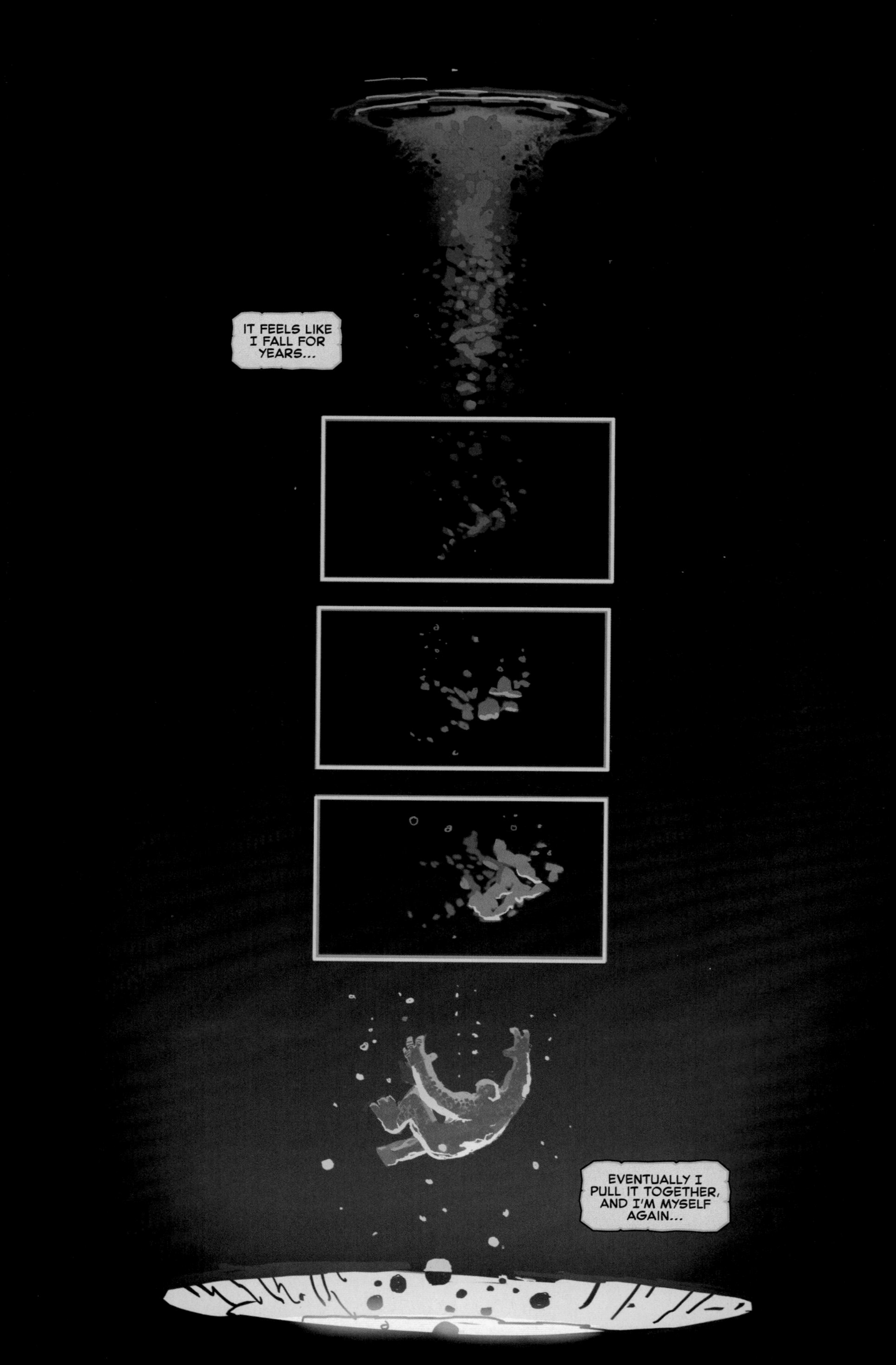
IT FEELS LIKE I FALL FOR YEARS...
EVENTUALLY I PULL IT TOGETHER, AND I'M MYSELF AGAIN...

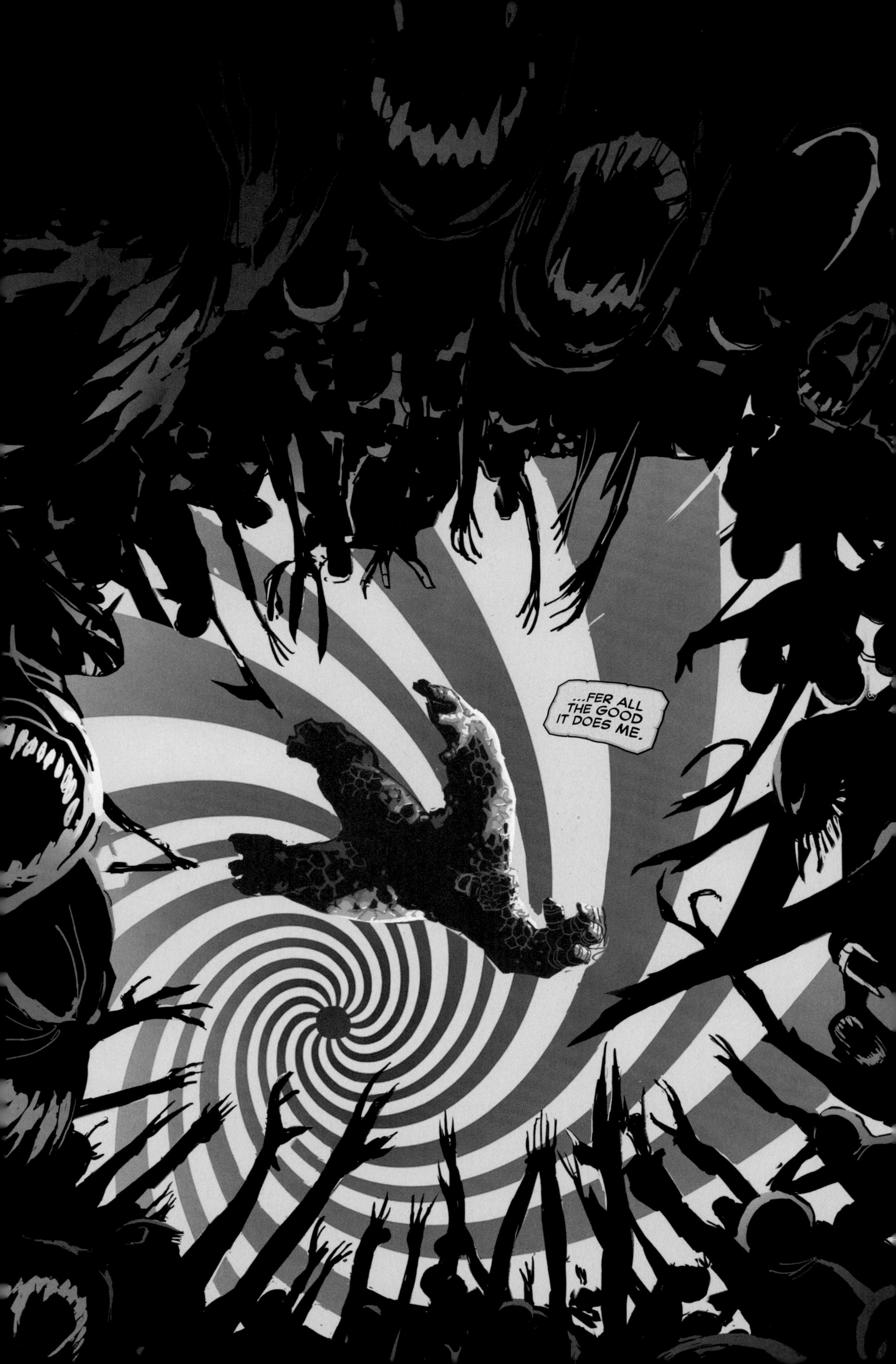
...FER ALL THE GOOD IT DOES ME.

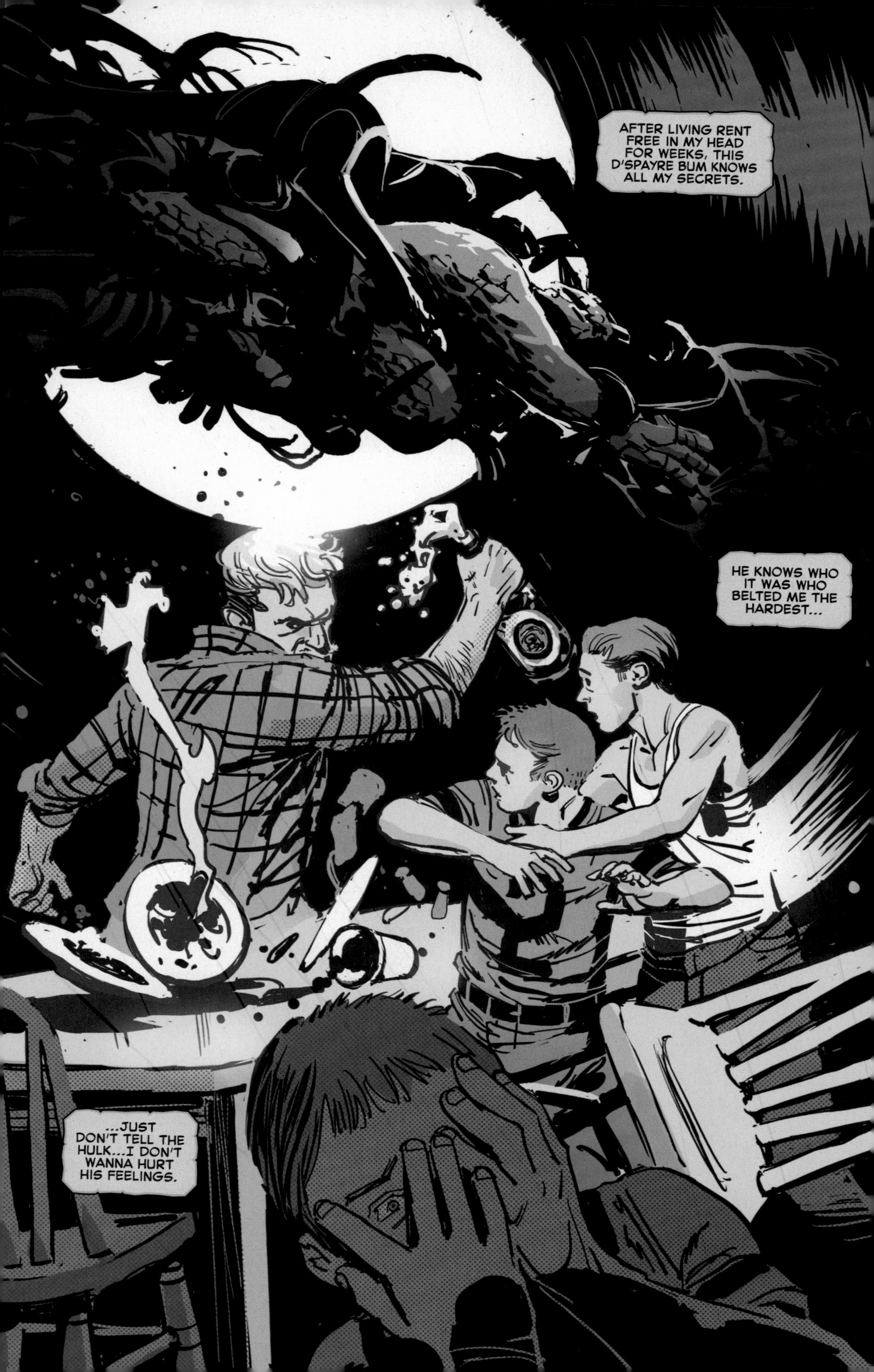
AFTER LIVING RENT FREE IN MY HEAD FOR WEEKS, THIS D'SPAYRE BUM KNOWS ALL MY SECRETS.
HE KNOWS WHO IT WAS WHO BELTED ME THE HARDEST...
...JUST DON'T TELL THE HULK...I DON'T WANNA HURT HIS FEELINGS.

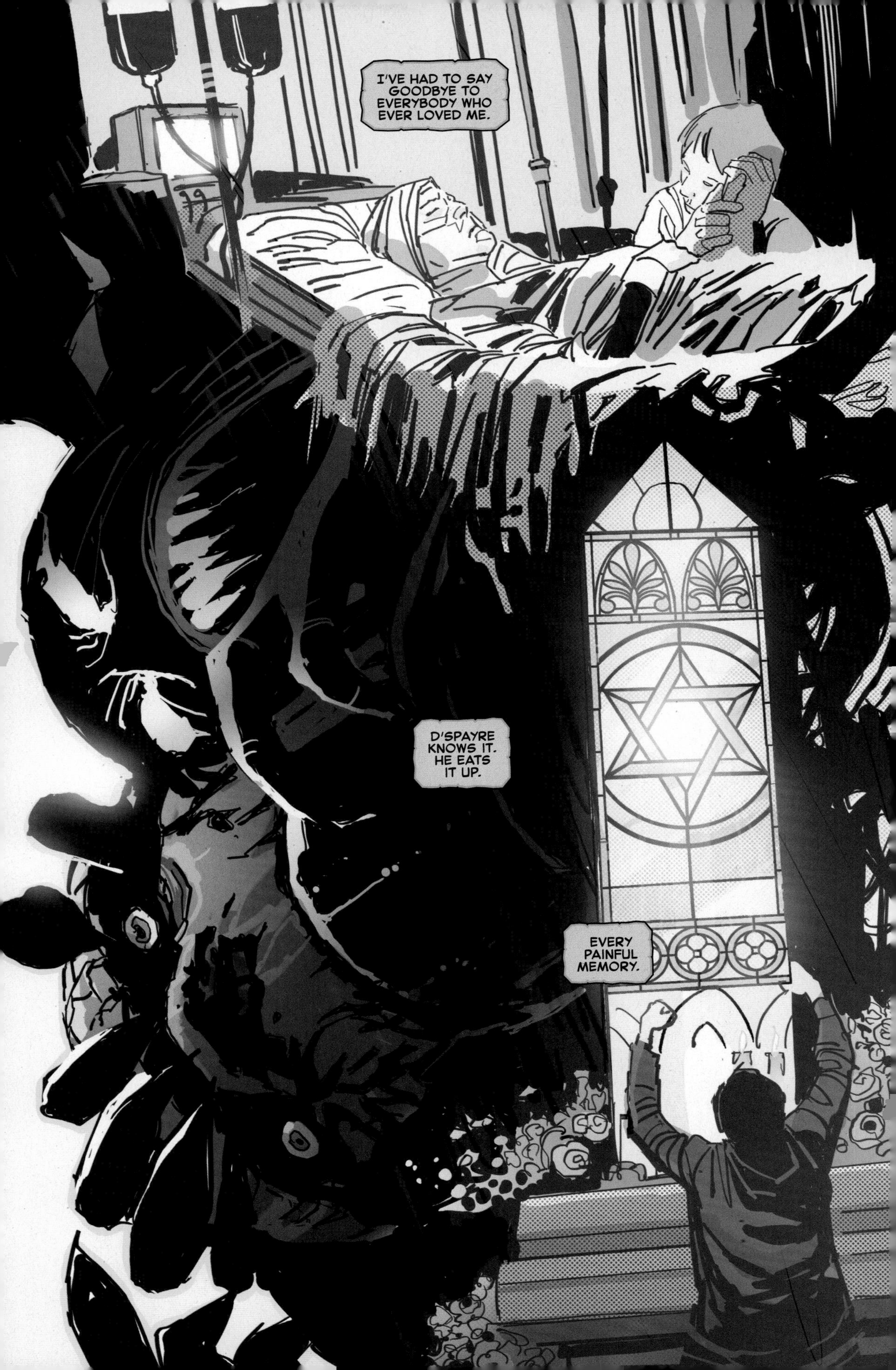
I'VE HAD TO SAY GOODBYE TO EVERYBODY WHO EVER LOVED ME.
D'SPAYRE KNOWS IT. HE EATS IT UP.
EVERY PAINFUL MEMORY.

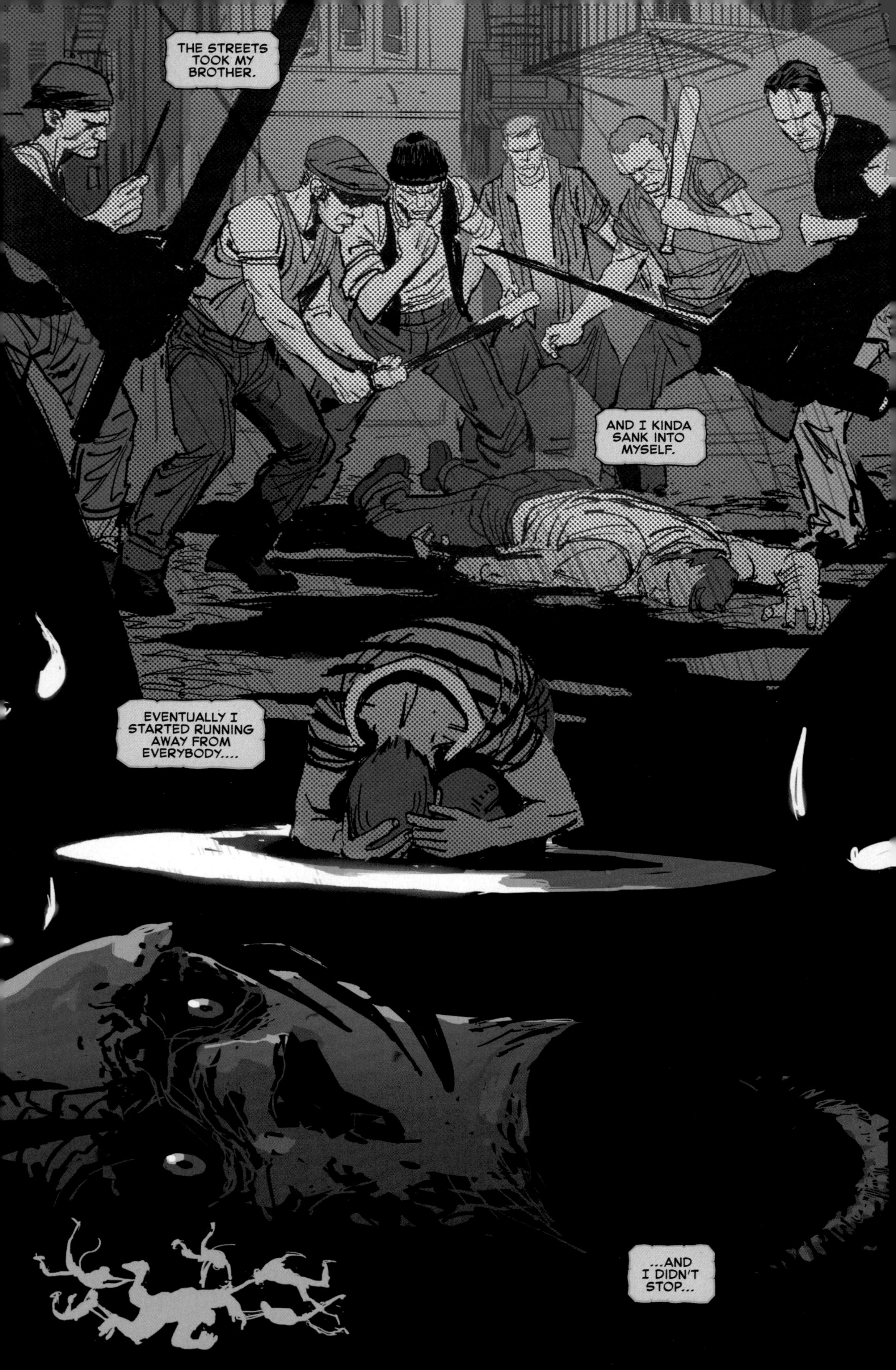
THE STREETS TOOK MY BROTHER.
AND I KINDA SANK INTO MYSELF.
EVENTUALLY I STARTED RUNNING AWAY FROM EVERYBODY....
...AND I DIDN'T STOP...

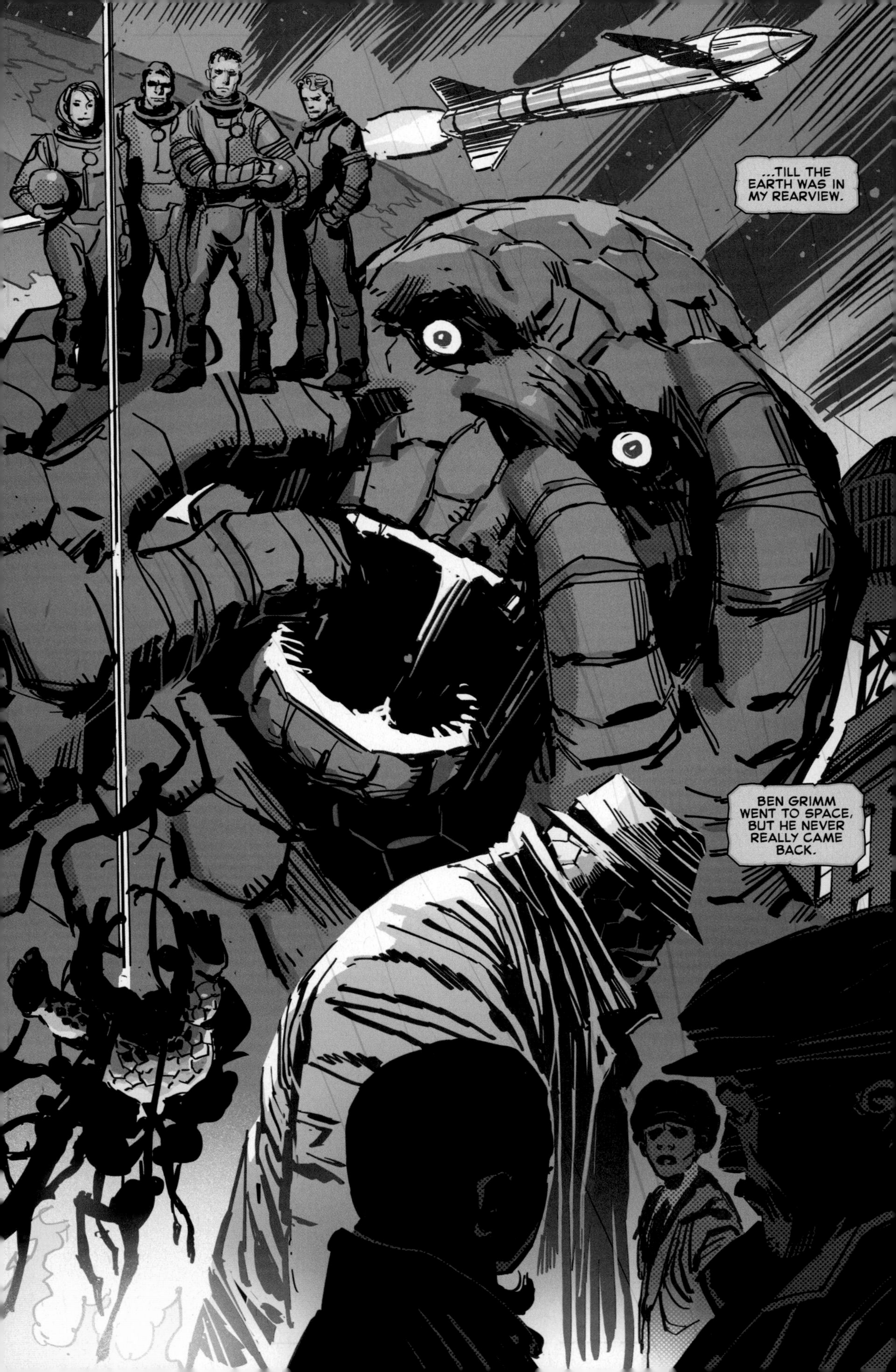
...TILL THE EARTH WAS IN MY REARVIEW.
BEN GRIMM WENT TO SPACE, BUT HE NEVER REALLY CAME BACK.

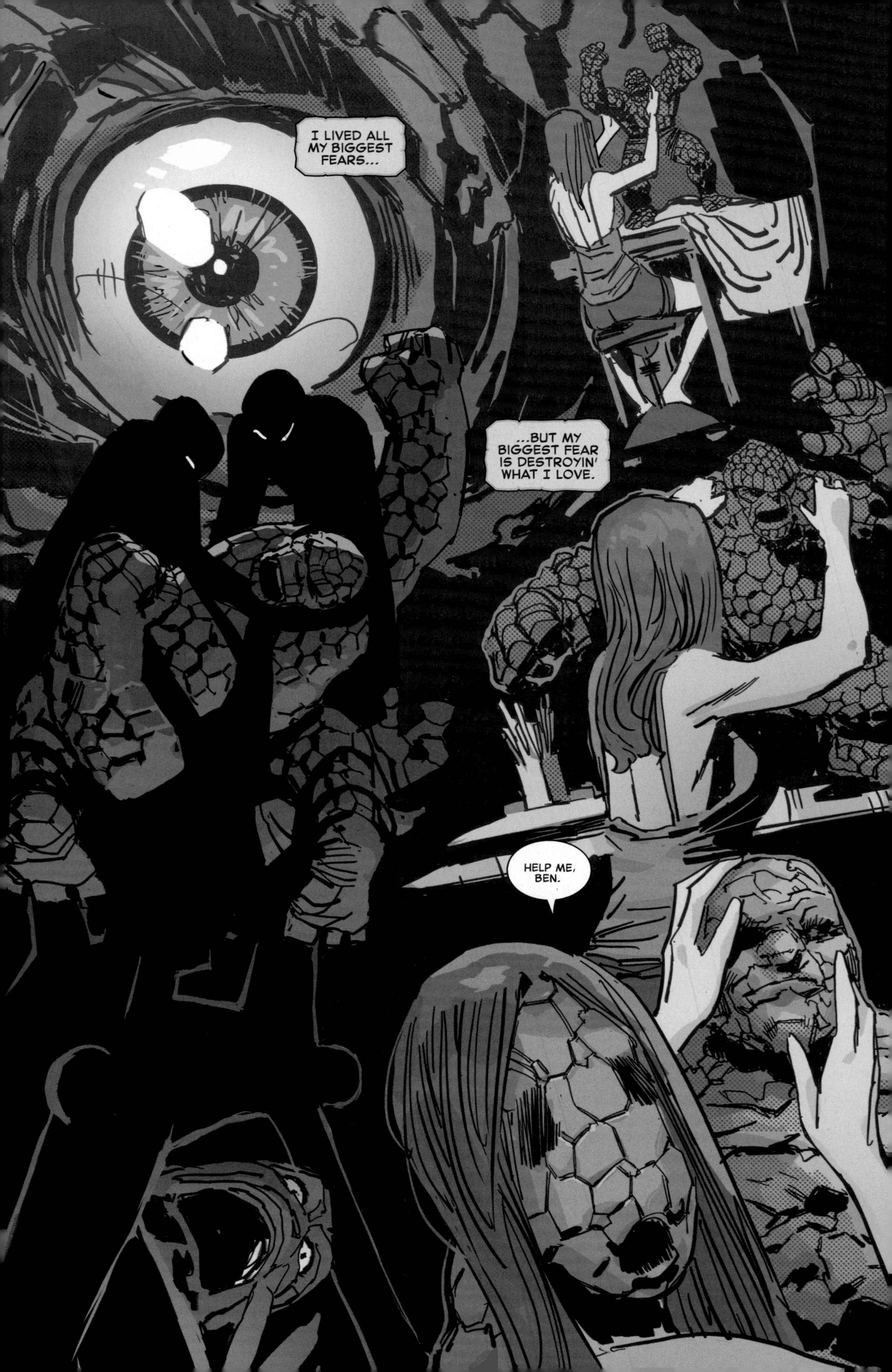
I LIVED ALL MY BIGGEST FEARS...
...BUT MY BIGGEST FEAR IS DESTROYIN' WHAT I LOVE.
HELP ME, BEN.

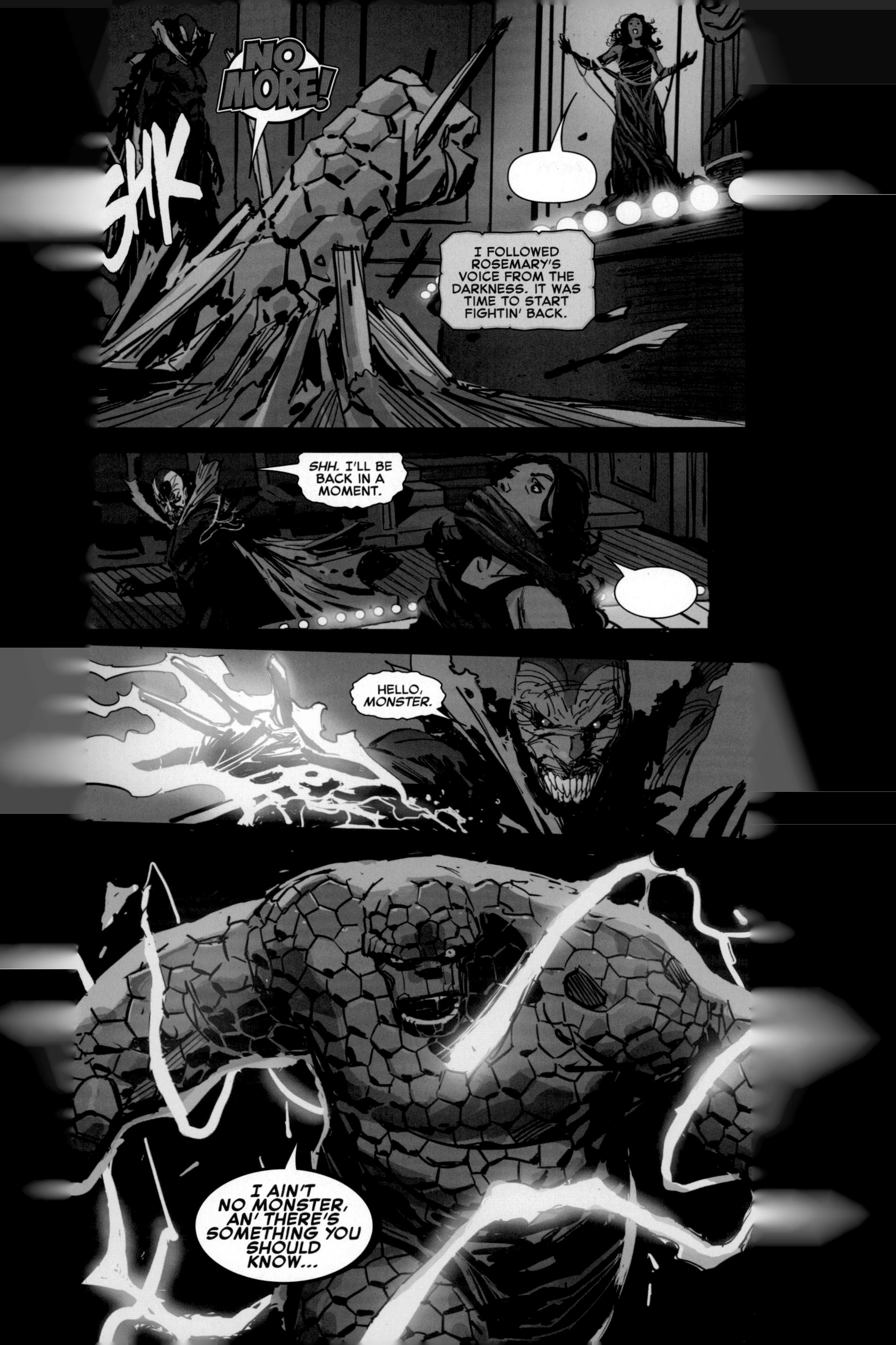
NO MORE!
SHK
I FOLLOWED ROSEMARY'S VOICE FROM THE DARKNESS. IT WAS TIME TO START FIGHTIN' BACK.
SHH. I'LL BE BACK IN A MOMENT.
HELLO, MONSTER.
I AIN'T NO MONSTER, AN' THERE'S SOMETHING YOU SHOULD KNOW...

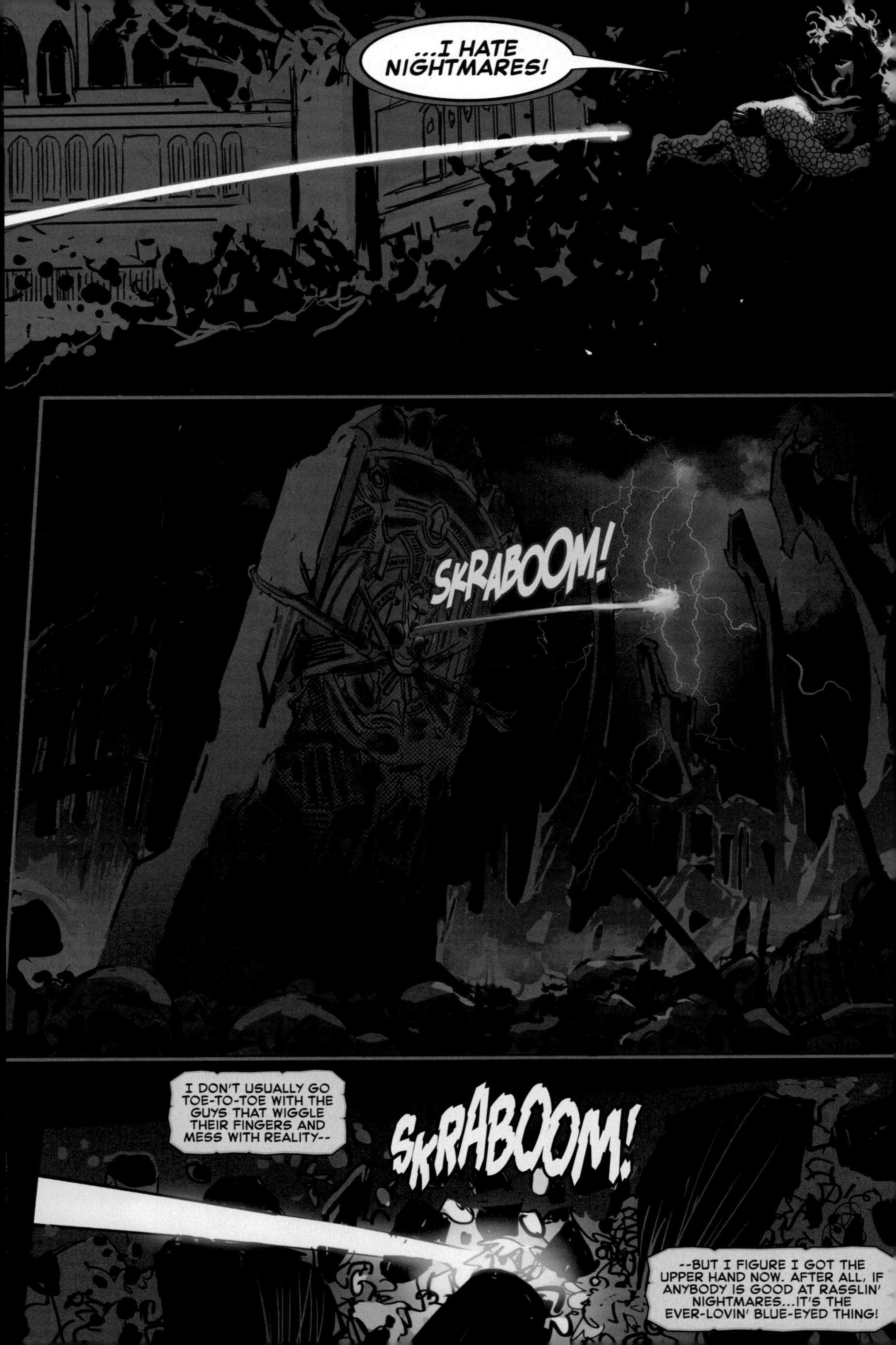
...I HATE NIGHTMARES!
SKRABOOM!
I DON'T USUALLY GO TOE-TO-TOE WITH THE GUYS THAT WIGGLE THEIR FINGERS AND MESS WITH REALITY--
SKRABOOM!
--BUT I FIGURE I GOT THE UPPER HAND NOW. AFTER ALL, IF ANYBODY IS GOOD AT RASSLIN' NIGHTMARES...IT'S THE EVER-LOVIN' BLUE-EYED THING!

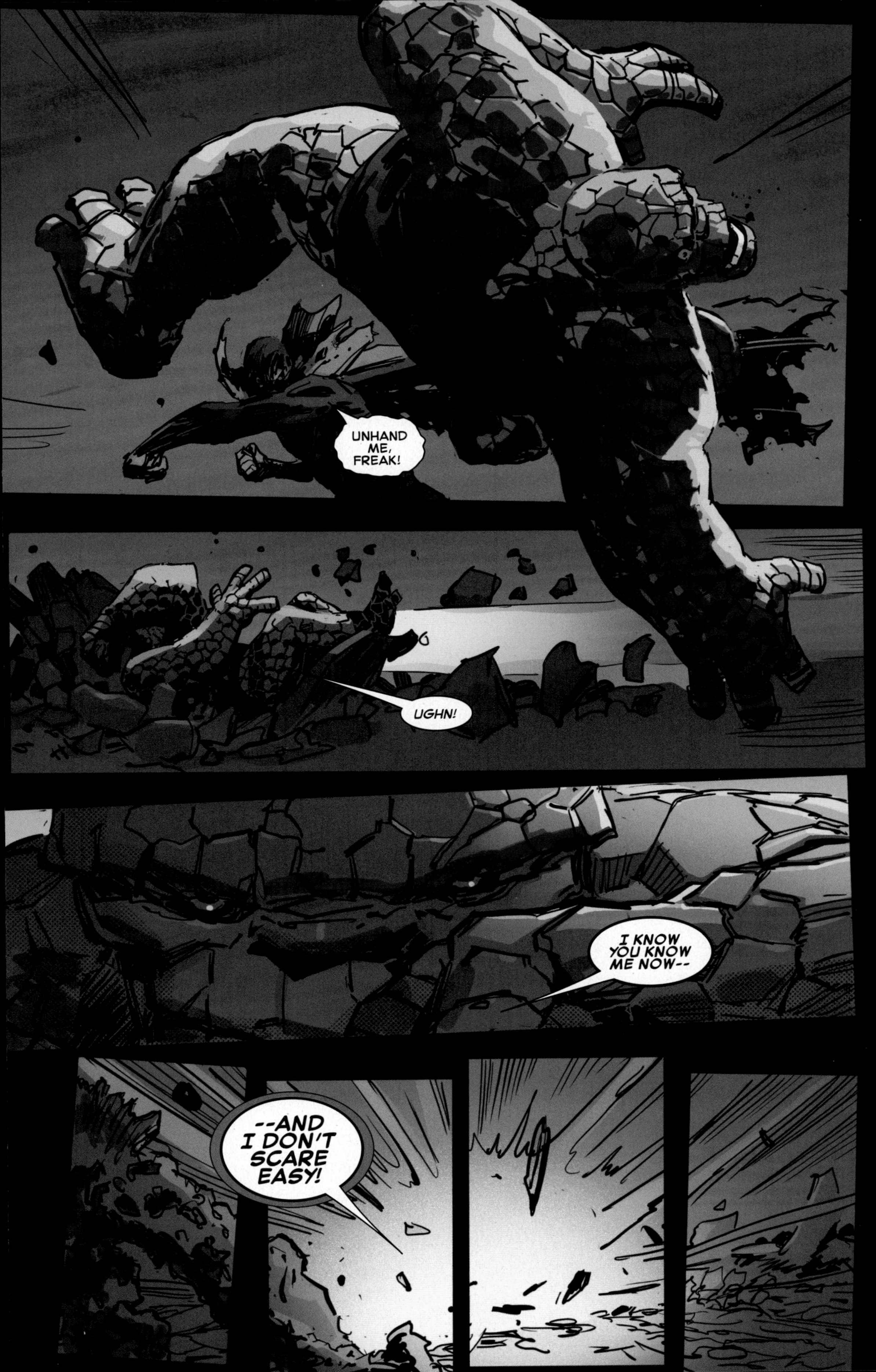
UNHAND ME, FREAK!
UGHN!
I KNOW YOU KNOW ME NOW--
--AND I DON'T SCARE EASY!

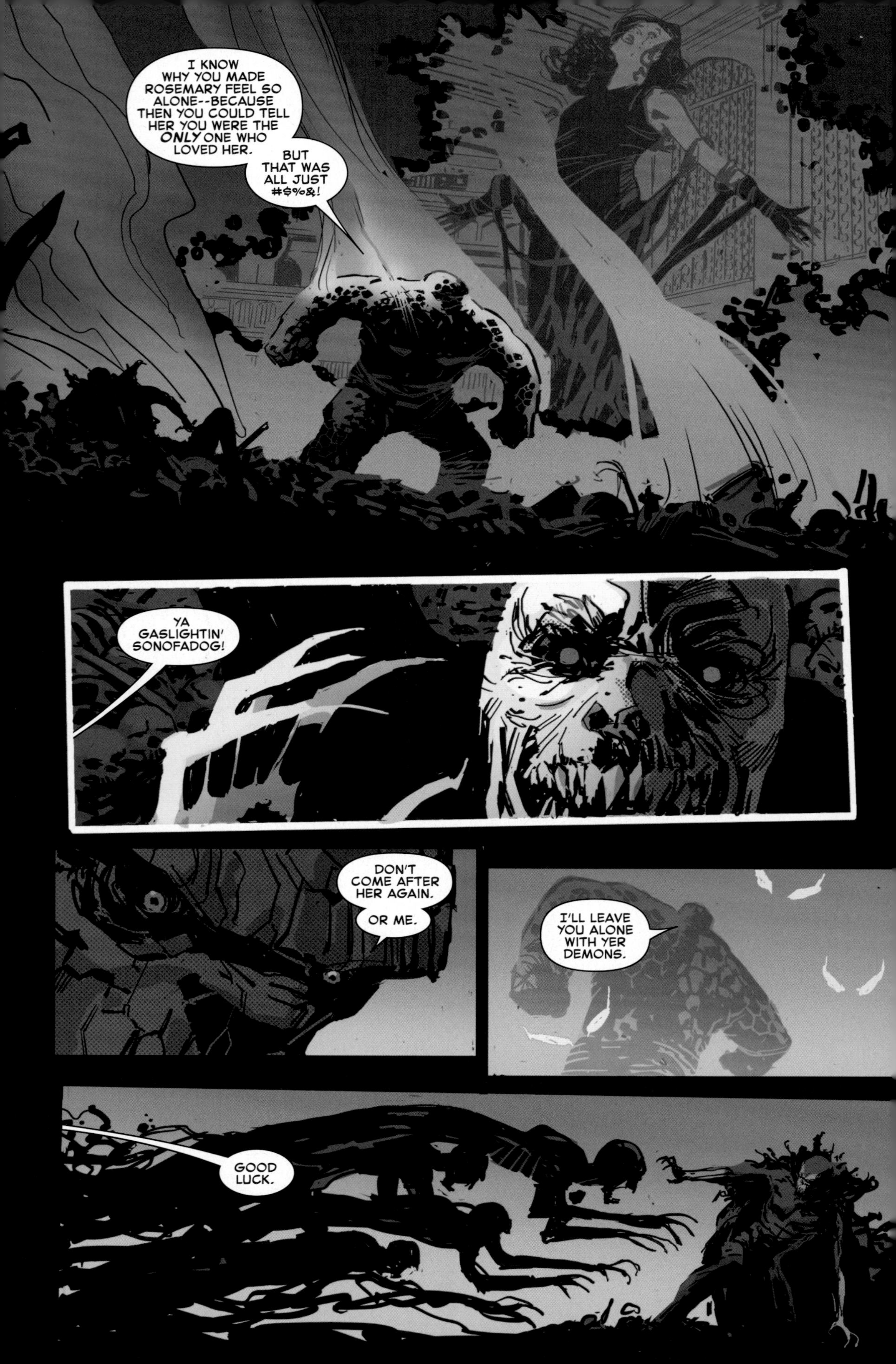
I KNOW WHY YOU MADE ROSEMARY FEEL SO ALONE--BECAUSE THEN YOU COULD TELL HER YOU WERE THE ONLY ONE WHO LOVED HER.
BUT THAT WAS ALL JUST #$%&!
YA GASLIGHTIN' SONOFADOG!
DON'T COME AFTER HER AGAIN.
OR ME.
I'LL LEAVE YOU ALONE WITH YER DEMONS.
GOOD LUCK.

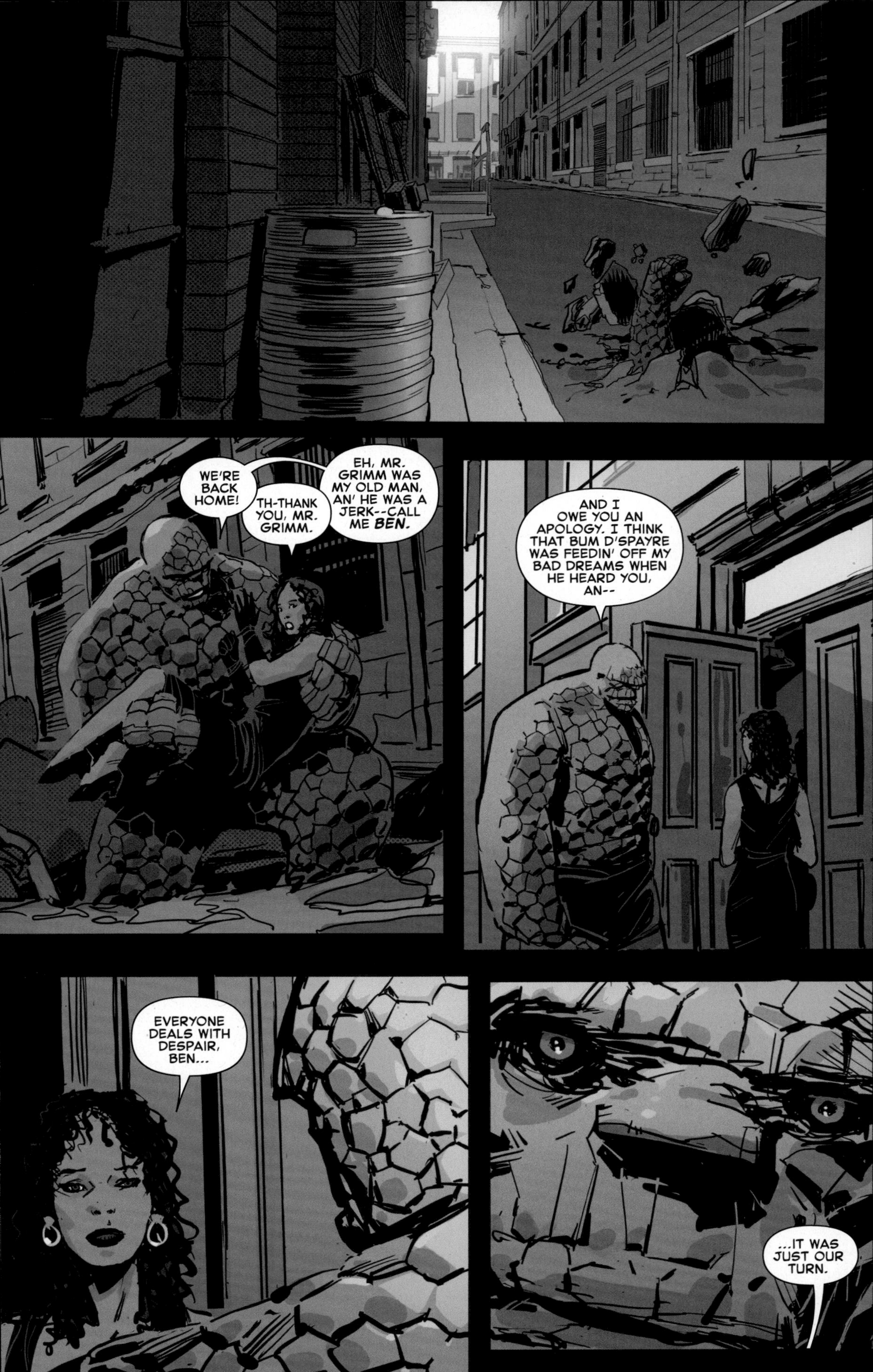
WE'RE BACK HOME!
TH-THANK YOU, MR. GRIMM.
EH, MR. GRIMM WAS MY OLD MAN, AN' HE WAS A JERK--CALL ME BEN.
AND I OWE YOU AN APOLOGY. I THINK THAT BUM D'SPAYRE WAS FEEDIN' OFF MY BAD DREAMS WHEN HE HEARD YOU, AN--
EVERYONE DEALS WITH DESPAIR, BEN...
...IT WAS JUST OUR TURN.

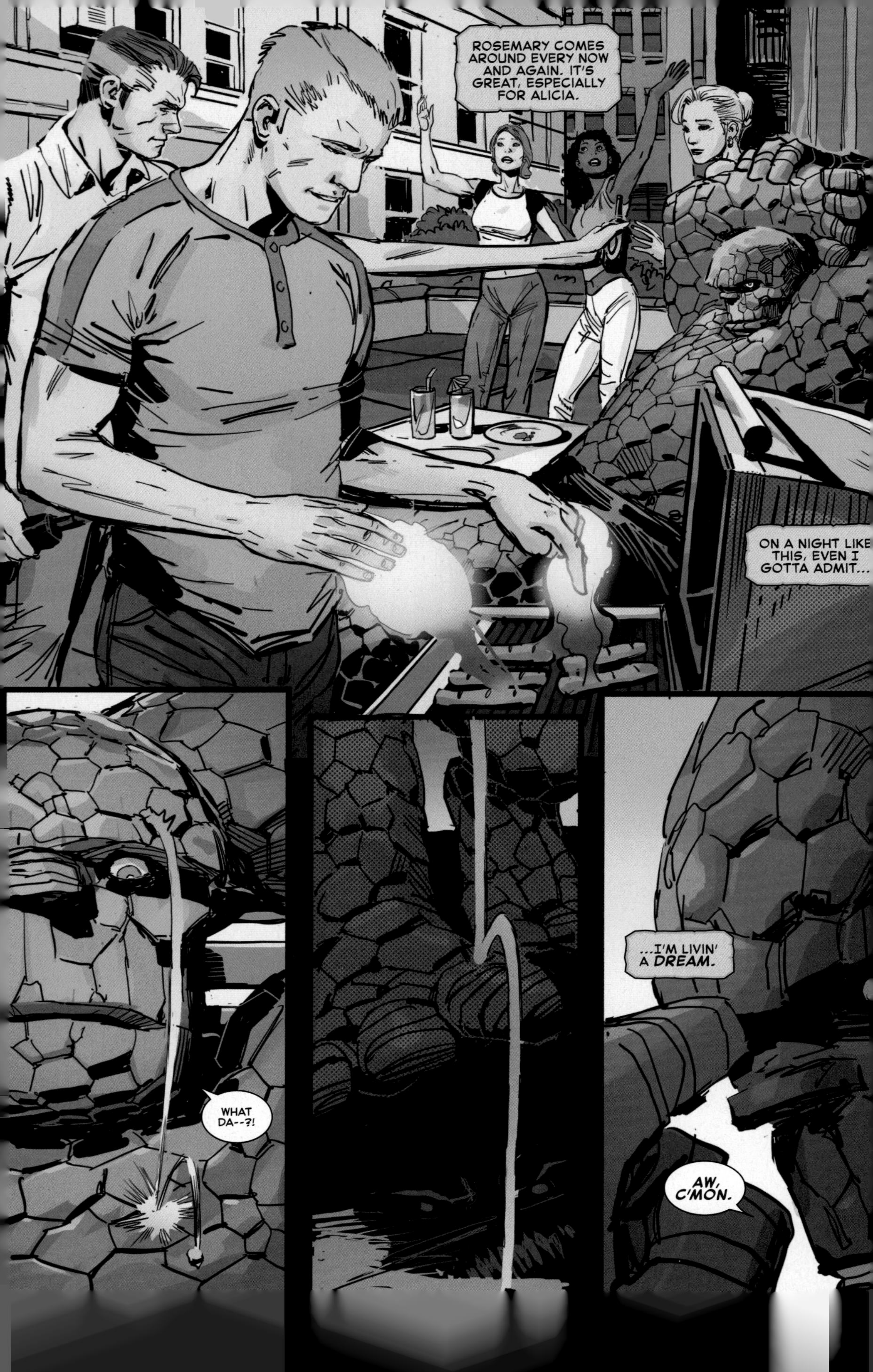
ROSEMARY COMES AROUND EVERY NOW AND AGAIN. IT'S GREAT, ESPECIALLY FOR ALICIA.
ON A NIGHT LIKE THIS, EVEN I GOTTA ADMIT...
WHAT DA--?!
...I'M LIVIN' A DREAM.
AW, C'MON.

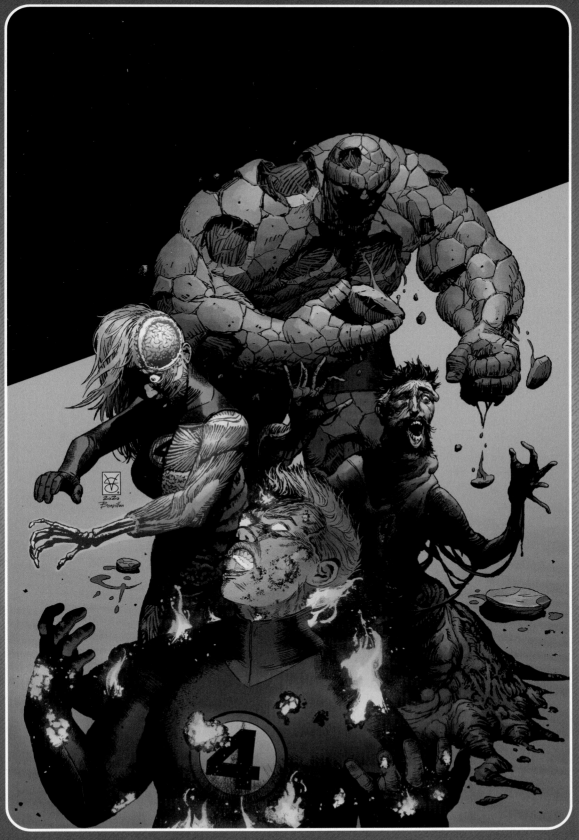

Fantastic Four: Road Trip

"We traveled to the stars and flew through a storm of cosmic energy... We became something more than human, but we were still the same people. We still are."

--Reed Richards

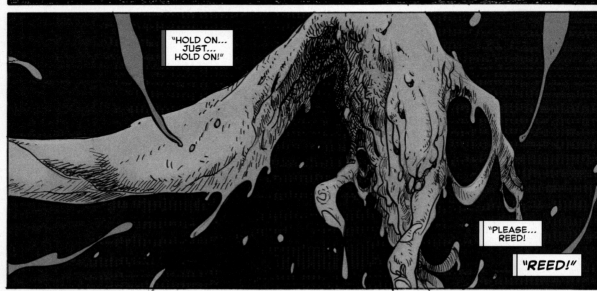

"HOLD ON... JUST... HOLD ON!"

"PLEASE... REED!"

"REED!"

ONE DAY EARLIER.

ARE WE THERE YET?

NORTH 87

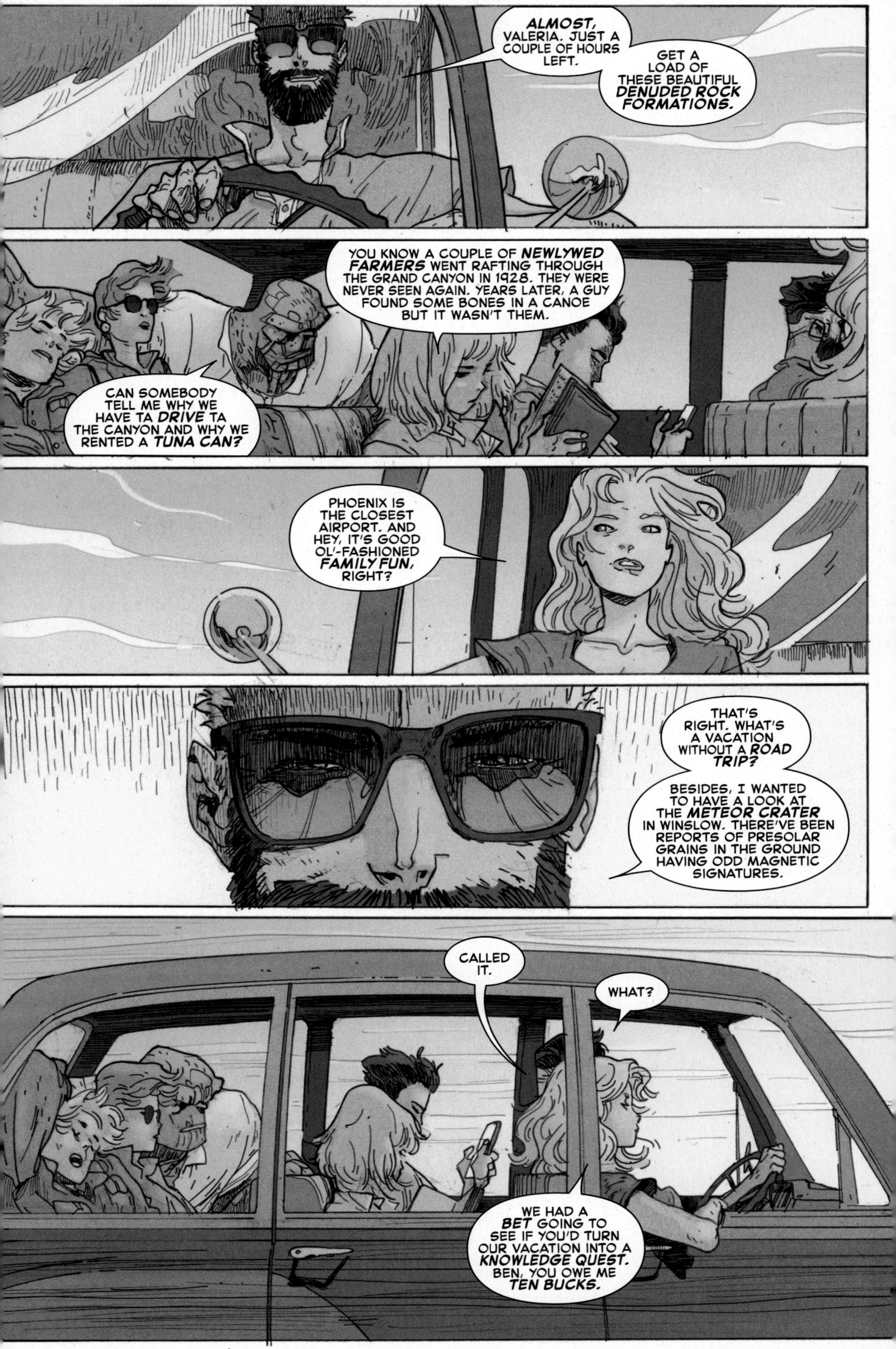
ALMOST, VALERIA. JUST A COUPLE OF HOURS LEFT.
GET A LOAD OF THESE BEAUTIFUL DENUDED ROCK FORMATIONS.
YOU KNOW A COUPLE OF NEWLYWED FARMERS WENT RAFTING THROUGH THE GRAND CANYON IN 1928. THEY WERE NEVER SEEN AGAIN. YEARS LATER, A GUY FOUND SOME BONES IN A CANOE BUT IT WASN'T THEM.
CAN SOMEBODY TELL ME WHY WE HAVE TA DRIVE TA THE CANYON AND WHY WE RENTED A TUNA CAN?
PHOENIX IS THE CLOSEST AIRPORT. AND HEY, IT'S GOOD OL'-FASHIONED FAMILY FUN, RIGHT?
THAT'S RIGHT. WHAT'S A VACATION WITHOUT A ROAD TRIP?
BESIDES, I WANTED TO HAVE A LOOK AT THE METEOR CRATER IN WINSLOW. THERE'VE BEEN REPORTS OF PRESOLAR GRAINS IN THE GROUND HAVING ODD MAGNETIC SIGNATURES.
CALLED IT.
WHAT?
WE HAD A BET GOING TO SEE IF YOU'D TURN OUR VACATION INTO A KNOWLEDGE QUEST. BEN, YOU OWE ME TEN BUCKS.

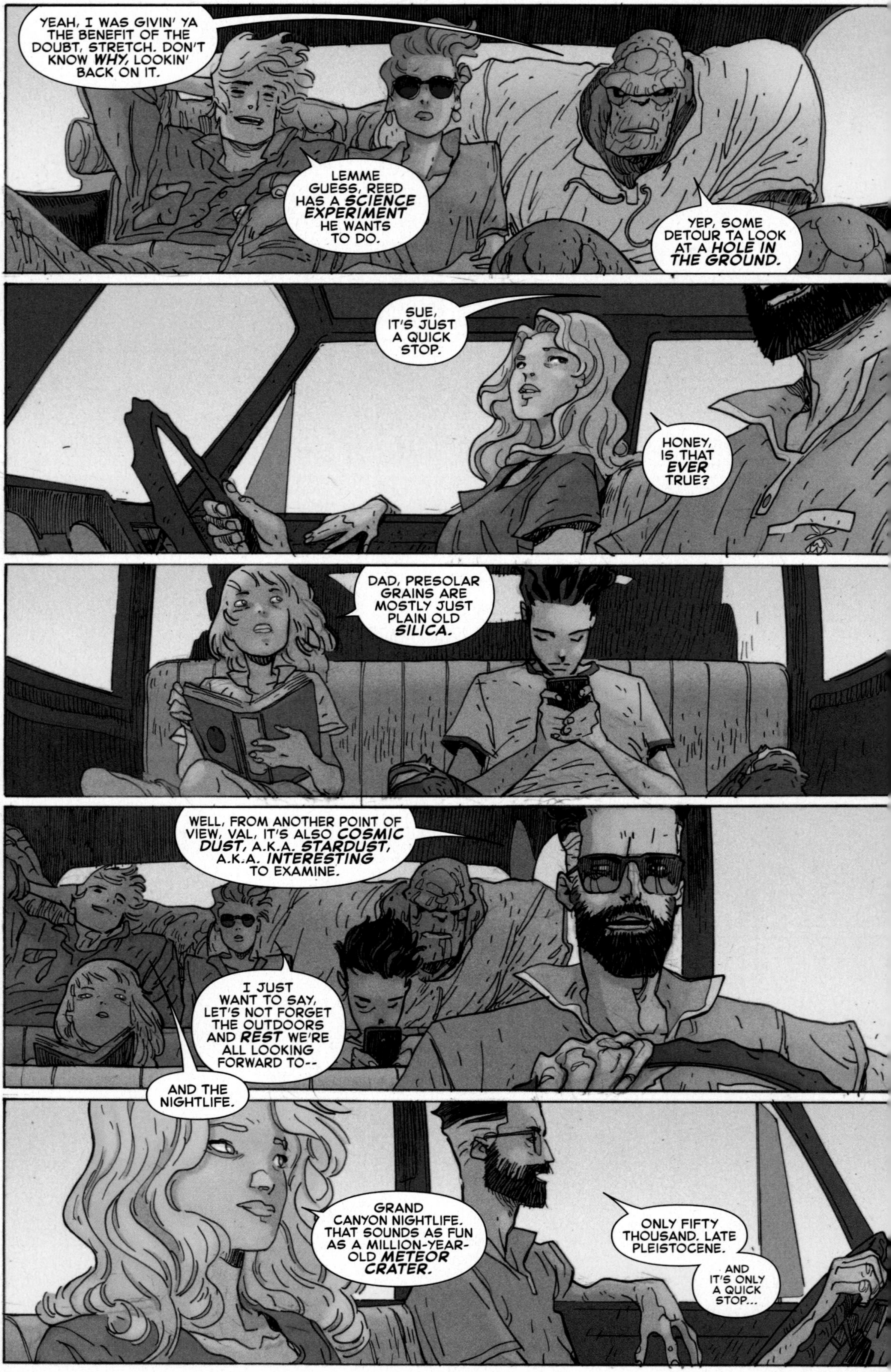
YEAH, I WAS GIVIN' YA THE BENEFIT OF THE DOUBT, STRETCH. DON'T KNOW WHY, LOOKIN' BACK ON IT.
LEMME GUESS, REED HAS A SCIENCE EXPERIMENT HE WANTS TO DO.
YEP, SOME DETOUR TA LOOK AT A HOLE IN THE GROUND.
SUE, IT'S JUST A QUICK STOP.
HONEY, IS THAT EVER TRUE?
DAD, PRESOLAR GRAINS ARE MOSTLY JUST PLAIN OLD SILICA.
WELL, FROM ANOTHER POINT OF VIEW, VAL, IT'S ALSO COSMIC DUST, A.K.A. STARDUST, A.K.A. INTERESTING TO EXAMINE.
I JUST WANT TO SAY, LET'S NOT FORGET THE OUTDOORS AND REST WE'RE ALL LOOKING FORWARD TO--
AND THE NIGHTLIFE.
GRAND CANYON NIGHTLIFE. THAT SOUNDS AS FUN AS A MILLION-YEAR-OLD METEOR CRATER.
ONLY FIFTY THOUSAND. LATE PLEISTOCENE.
AND IT'S ONLY A QUICK STOP...

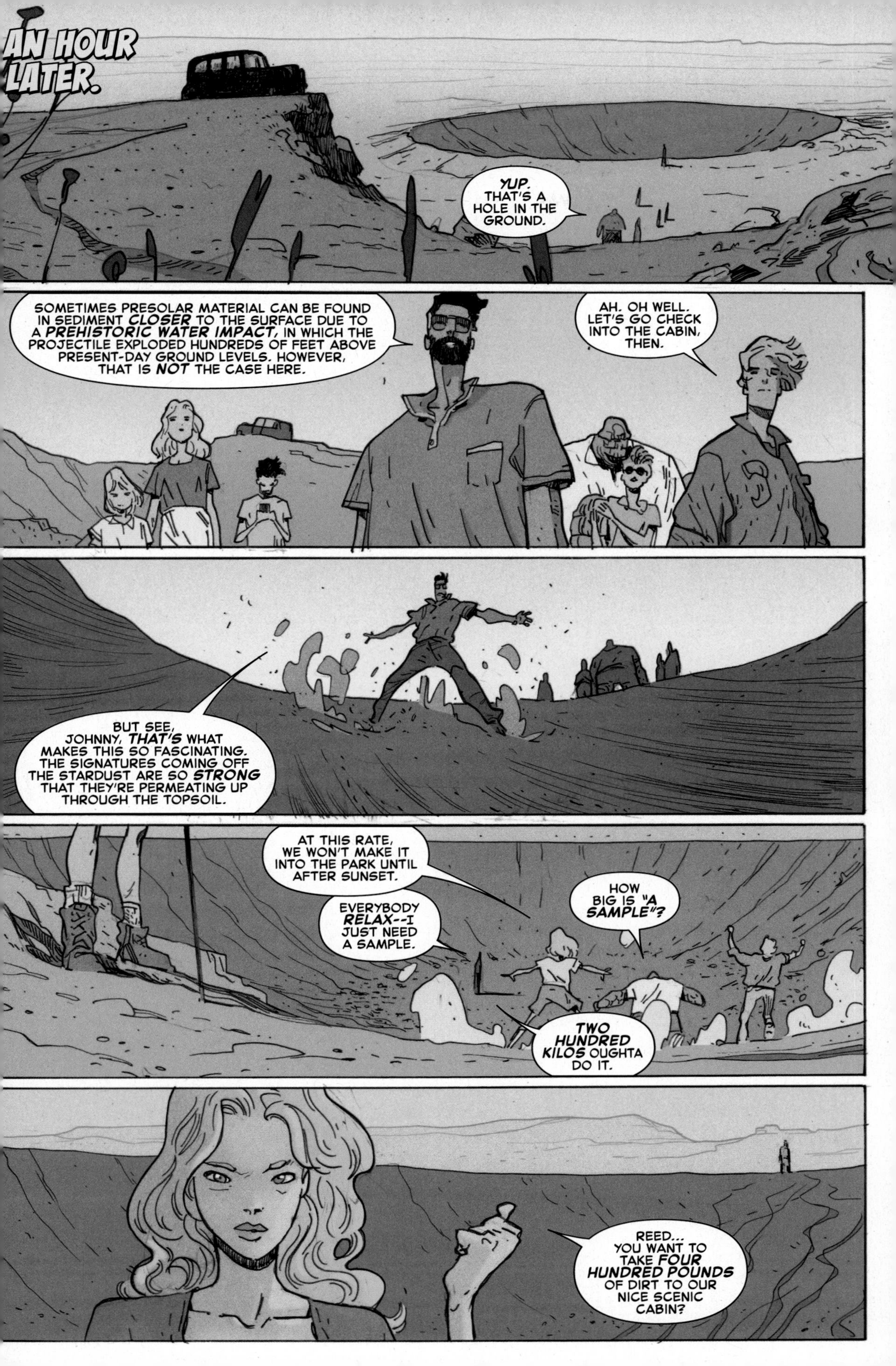
AN HOUR LATER.
YUP. THAT'S A HOLE IN THE GROUND.
SOMETIMES PRESOLAR MATERIAL CAN BE FOUND IN SEDIMENT CLOSER TO THE SURFACE DUE TO A PREHISTORIC WATER IMPACT, IN WHICH THE PROJECTILE EXPLODED HUNDREDS OF FEET ABOVE PRESENT-DAY GROUND LEVELS. HOWEVER, THAT IS NOT THE CASE HERE.
AH. OH WELL. LET'S GO CHECK INTO THE CABIN, THEN.
BUT SEE, JOHNNY, THAT'S WHAT MAKES THIS SO FASCINATING. THE SIGNATURES COMING OFF THE STARDUST ARE SO STRONG THAT THEY'RE PERMEATING UP THROUGH THE TOPSOIL.
AT THIS RATE, WE WON'T MAKE IT INTO THE PARK UNTIL AFTER SUNSET.
EVERYBODY RELAX--I JUST NEED A SAMPLE.
HOW BIG IS "A SAMPLE"?
TWO HUNDRED KILOS OUGHTA DO IT.
REED... YOU WANT TO TAKE FOUR HUNDRED POUNDS OF DIRT TO OUR NICE SCENIC CABIN?

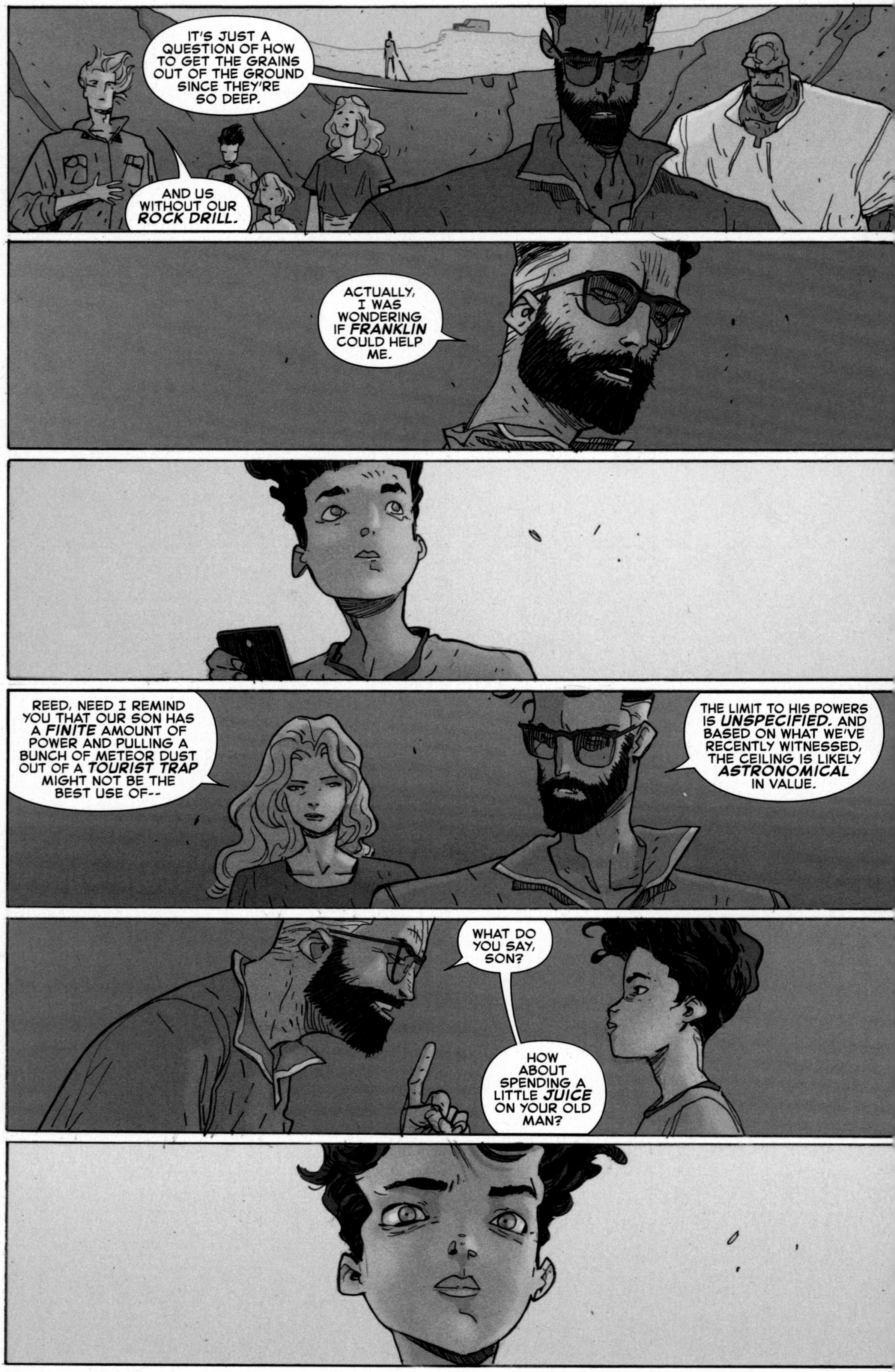
IT'S JUST A QUESTION OF HOW TO GET THE GRAINS OUT OF THE GROUND SINCE THEY'RE SO DEEP.
AND US WITHOUT OUR ROCK DRILL.
ACTUALLY, I WAS WONDERING IF FRANKLIN COULD HELP ME.
REED, NEED I REMIND YOU THAT OUR SON HAS A FINITE AMOUNT OF POWER AND PULLING A BUNCH OF METEOR DUST OUT OF A TOURIST TRAP MIGHT NOT BE THE BEST USE OF--
THE LIMIT TO HIS POWERS IS UNSPECIFIED. AND BASED ON WHAT WE'VE RECENTLY WITNESSED, THE CEILING IS LIKELY ASTRONOMICAL IN VALUE.
WHAT DO YOU SAY, SON?
HOW ABOUT SPENDING A LITTLE JUICE ON YOUR OLD MAN?

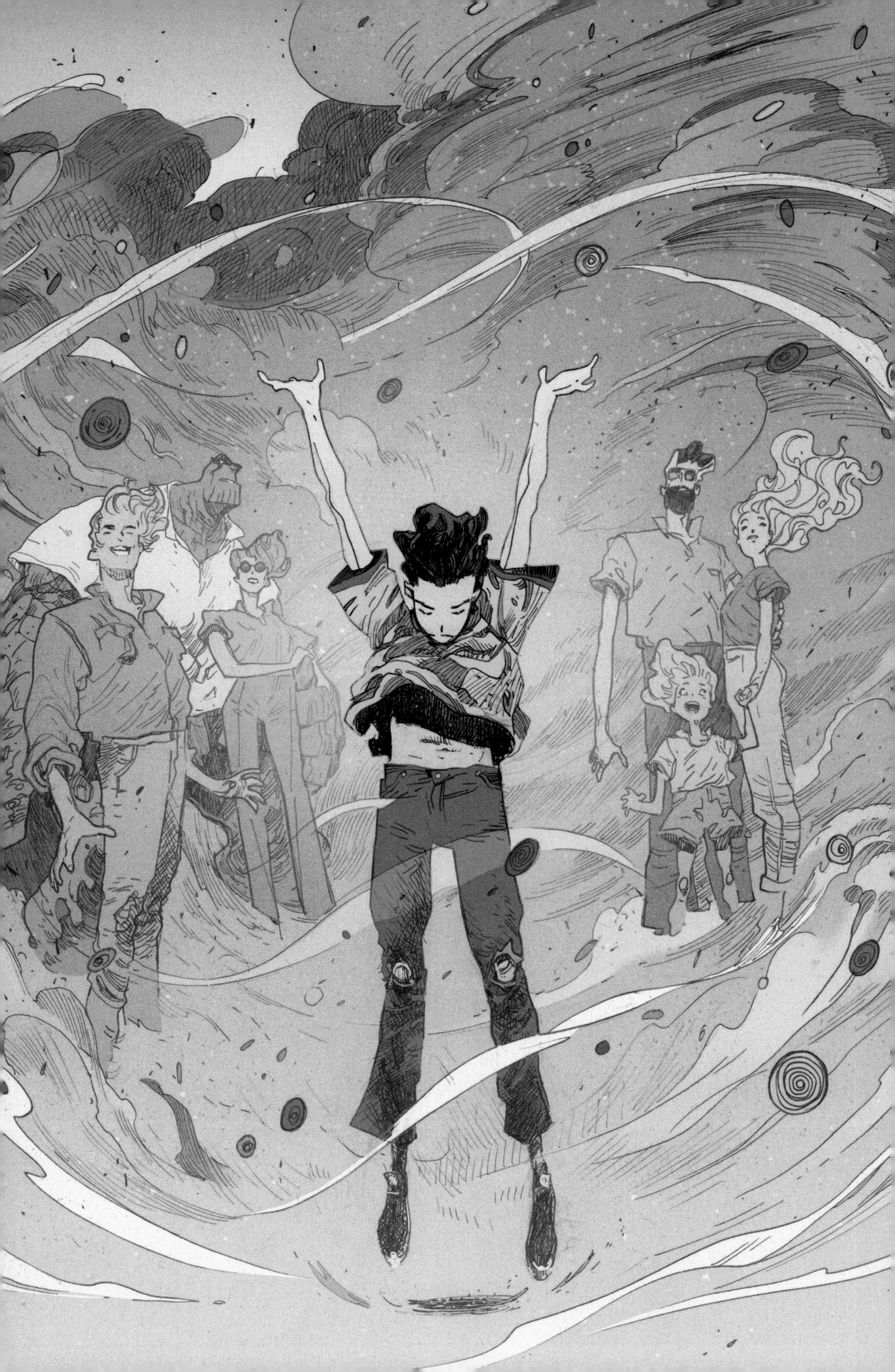

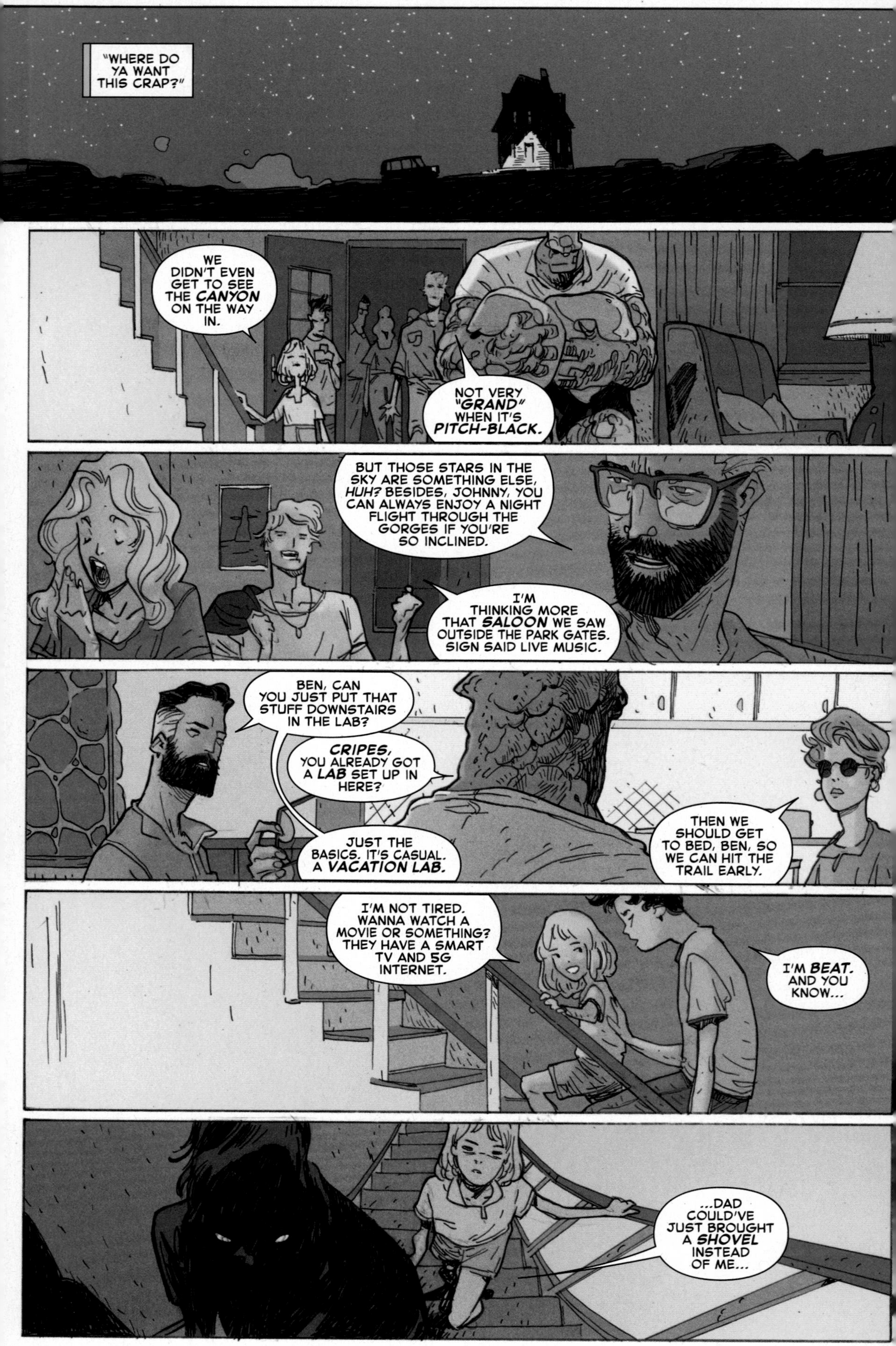
"WHERE DO YA WANT THIS CRAP?"
WE DIDN'T EVEN GET TO SEE THE *CANYON* ON THE WAY IN.
NOT VERY *"GRAND"* WHEN IT'S *PITCH-BLACK.*
BUT THOSE STARS IN THE SKY ARE SOMETHING ELSE, *HUH?* BESIDES, JOHNNY, YOU CAN ALWAYS ENJOY A NIGHT FLIGHT THROUGH THE GORGES IF YOU'RE SO INCLINED.
I'M THINKING MORE THAT *SALOON* WE SAW OUTSIDE THE PARK GATES. SIGN SAID LIVE MUSIC.
BEN, CAN YOU JUST PUT THAT STUFF DOWNSTAIRS IN THE LAB?
CRIPES, YOU ALREADY GOT A *LAB* SET UP IN HERE?
JUST THE BASICS. IT'S CASUAL. A *VACATION LAB.*
THEN WE SHOULD GET TO BED, BEN, SO WE CAN HIT THE TRAIL EARLY.
I'M NOT TIRED. WANNA WATCH A MOVIE OR SOMETHING? THEY HAVE A SMART TV AND 5G INTERNET.
I'M *BEAT.* AND YOU KNOW...
...DAD COULD'VE JUST BROUGHT A *SHOVEL* INSTEAD OF ME...

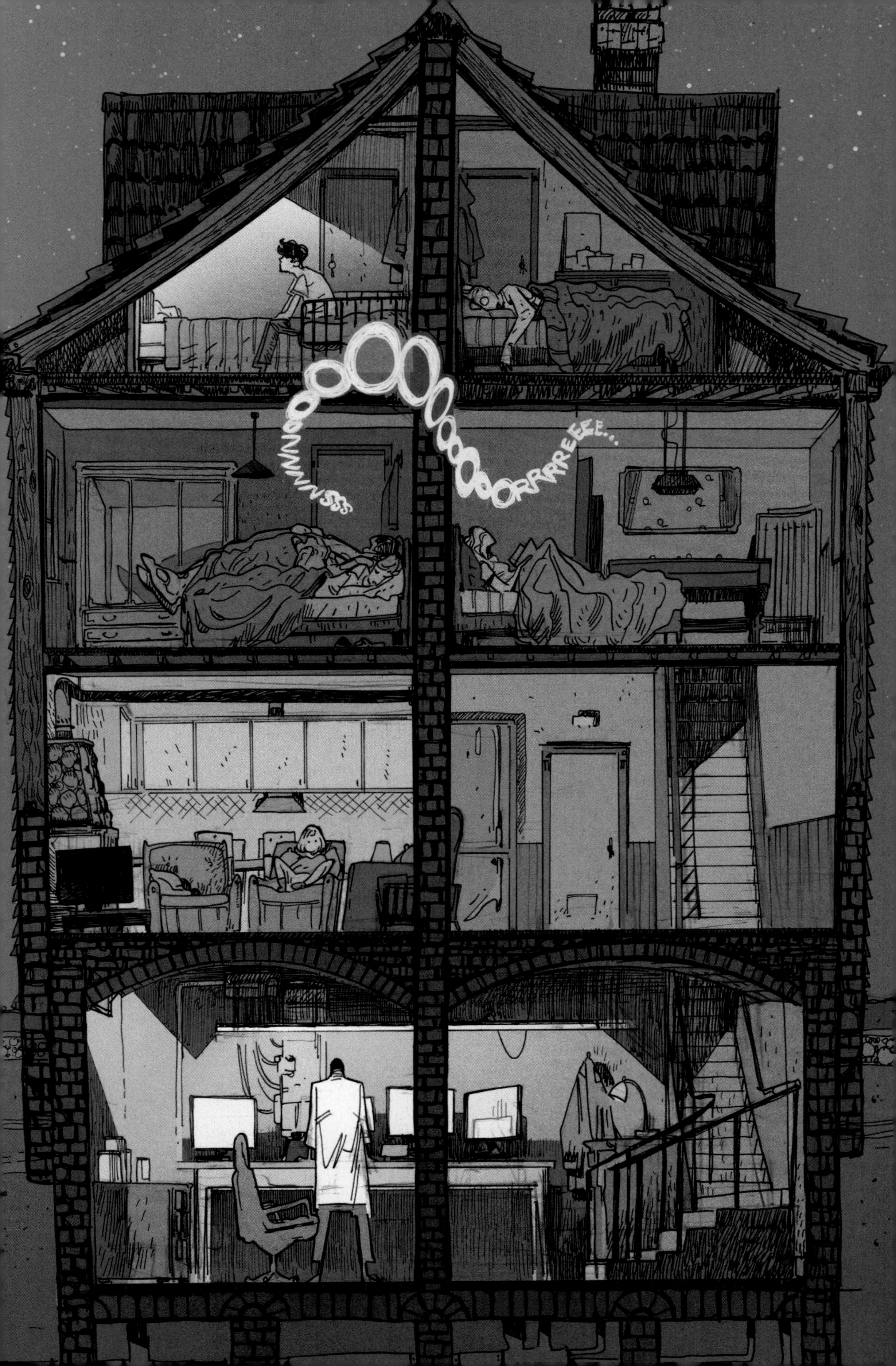
SSSNNNNNOOOOOOOOOOOORRRRREEEE...

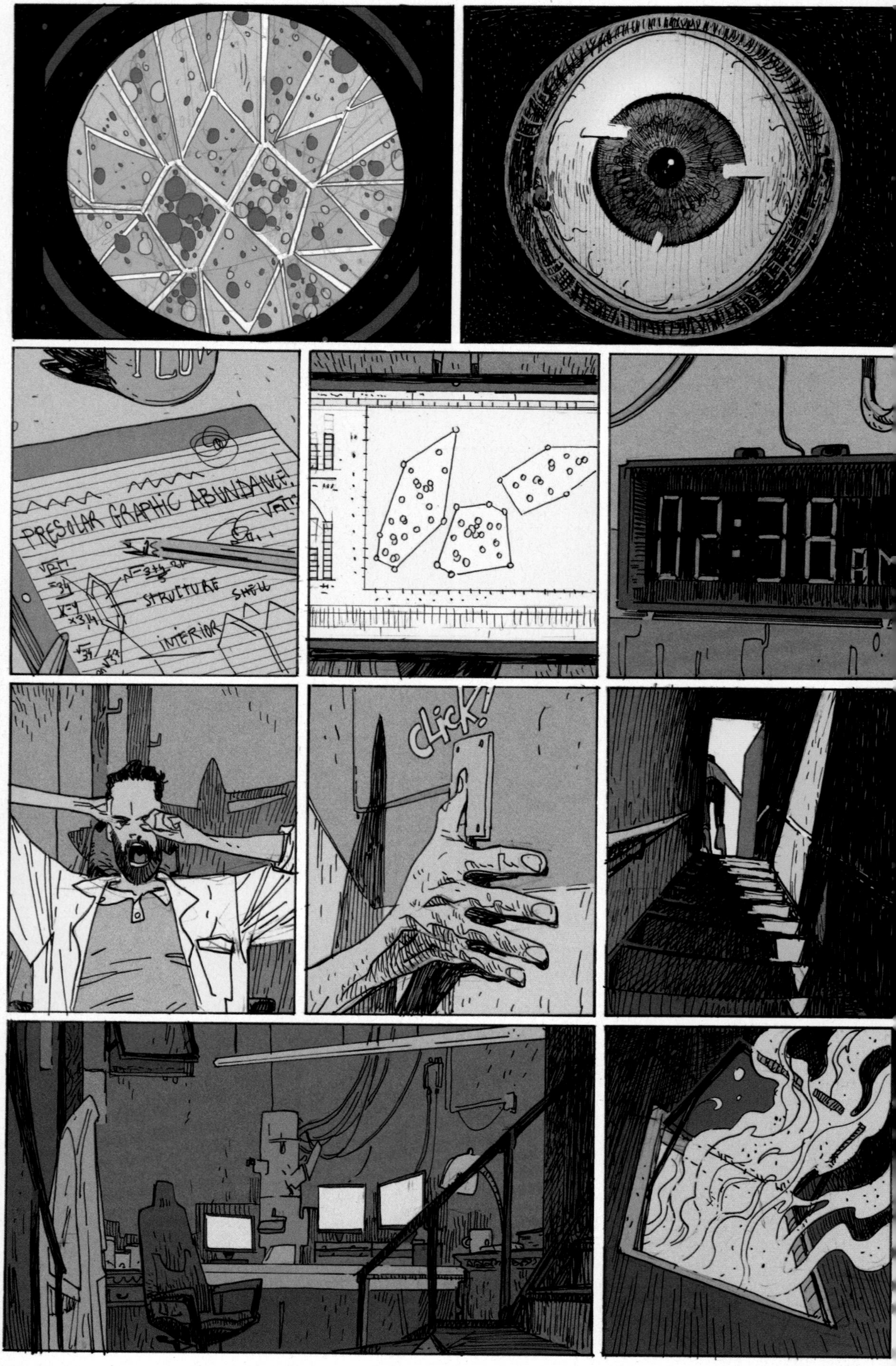
PRESOLAR GRAPHIC ABUNDANCE!
STRUCTURE
SHELL
INTERIOR
12:38
CLICK!

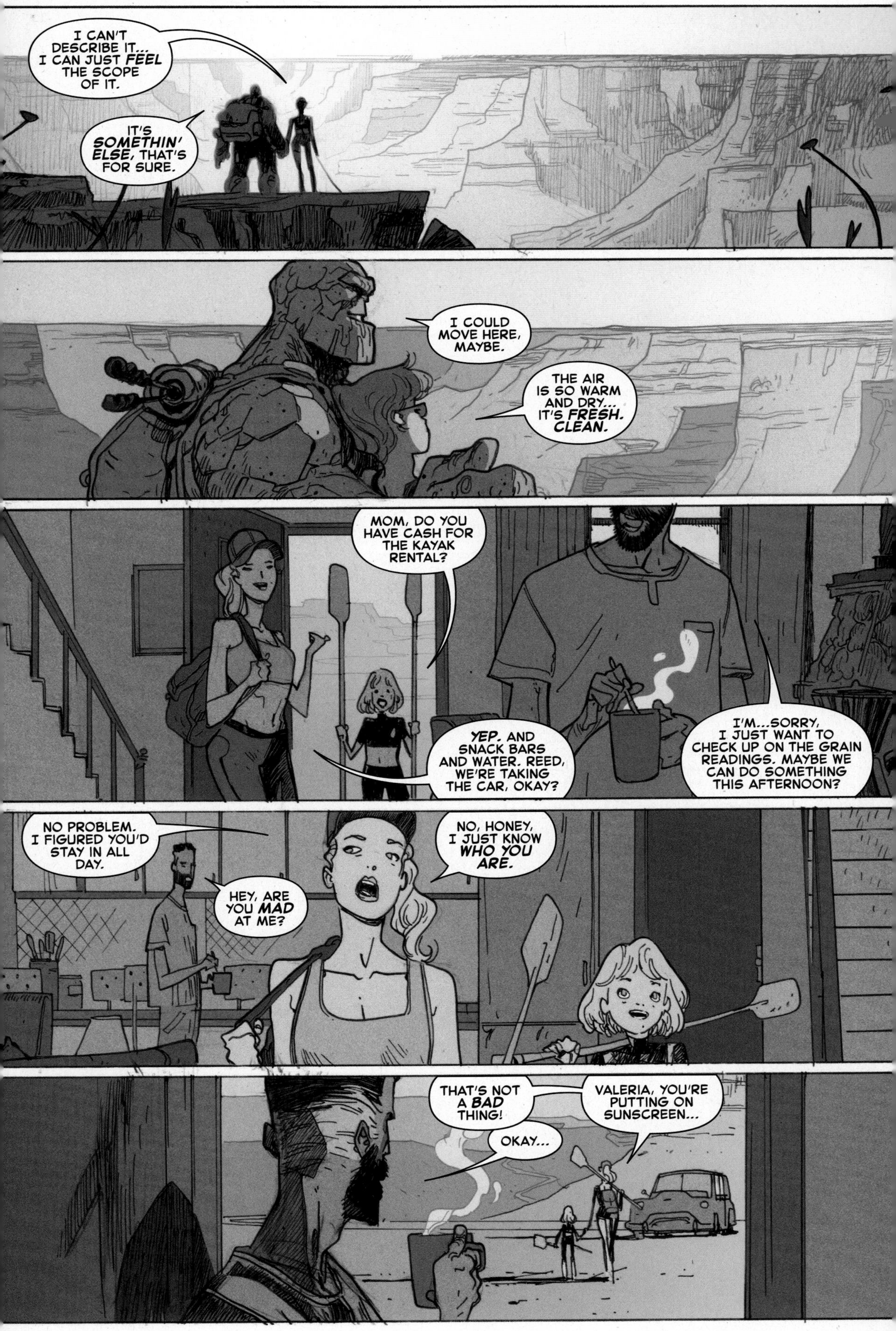
I CAN'T DESCRIBE IT... I CAN JUST FEEL THE SCOPE OF IT.
IT'S SOMETHIN' ELSE, THAT'S FOR SURE.
I COULD MOVE HERE, MAYBE.
THE AIR IS SO WARM AND DRY... IT'S FRESH. CLEAN.
MOM, DO YOU HAVE CASH FOR THE KAYAK RENTAL?
YEP. AND SNACK BARS AND WATER. REED, WE'RE TAKING THE CAR, OKAY?
I'M...SORRY, I JUST WANT TO CHECK UP ON THE GRAIN READINGS. MAYBE WE CAN DO SOMETHING THIS AFTERNOON?
NO PROBLEM. I FIGURED YOU'D STAY IN ALL DAY.
HEY, ARE YOU MAD AT ME?
NO, HONEY, I JUST KNOW WHO YOU ARE.
THAT'S NOT A BAD THING!
OKAY...
VALERIA, YOU'RE PUTTING ON SUNSCREEN...

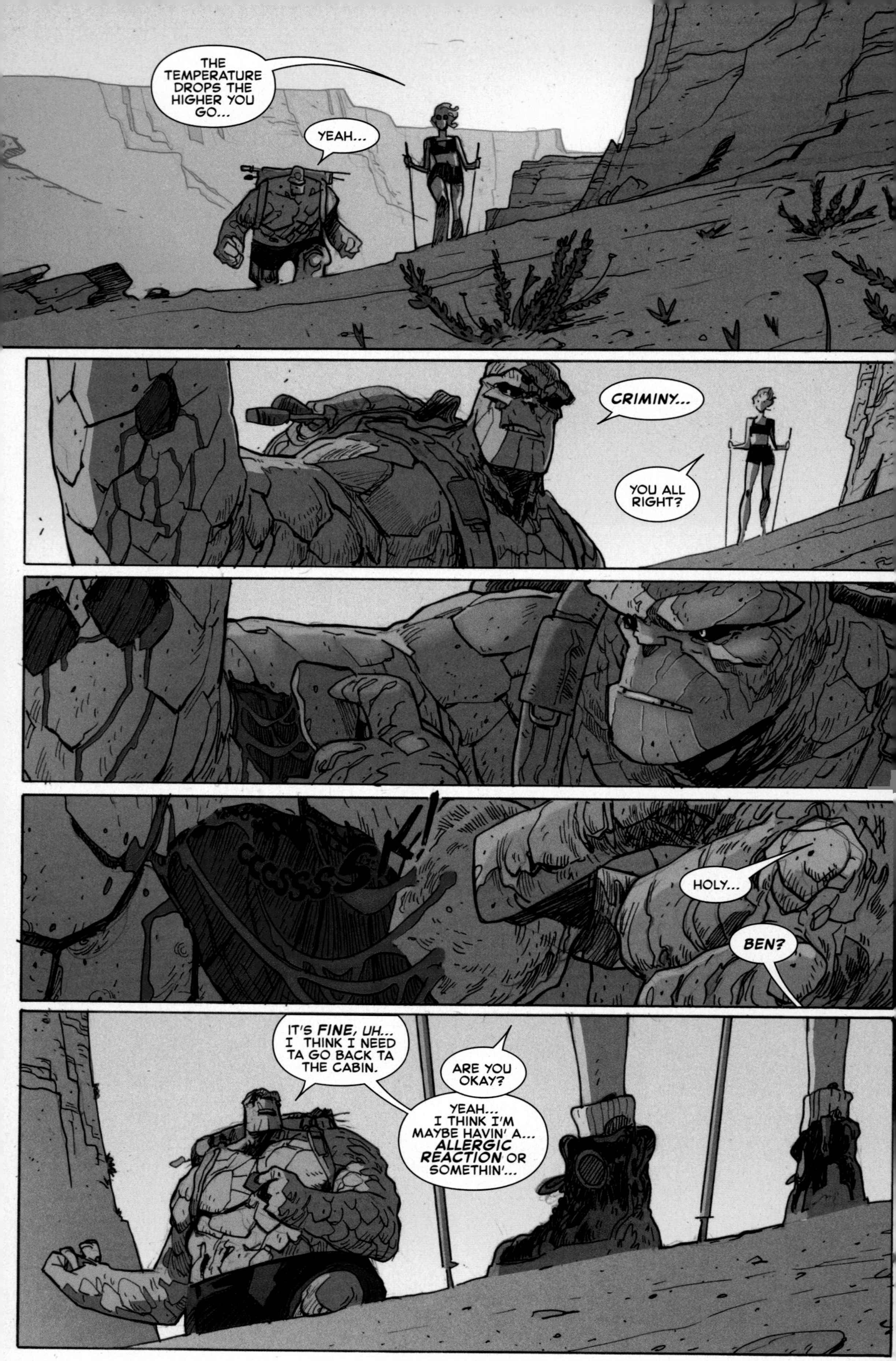
THE TEMPERATURE DROPS THE HIGHER YOU GO...
YEAH...
CRIMINY...
YOU ALL RIGHT?
HOLY...
BEN?
IT'S FINE, UH... I THINK I NEED TA GO BACK TA THE CABIN.
ARE YOU OKAY?
YEAH... I THINK I'M MAYBE HAVIN' A... ALLERGIC REACTION OR SOMETHIN'...

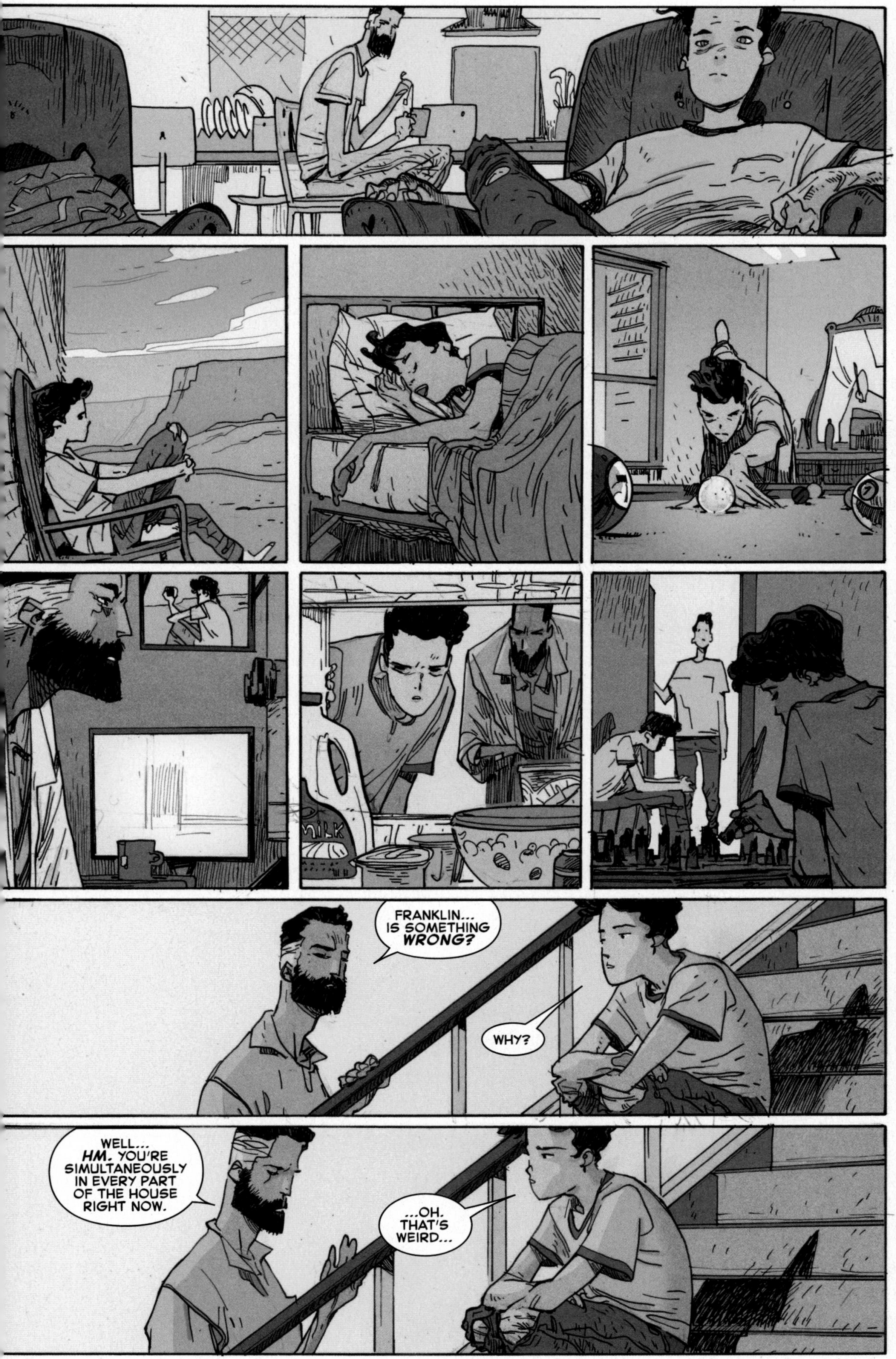
FRANKLIN... IS SOMETHING WRONG?
WHY?
WELL... HM. YOU'RE SIMULTANEOUSLY IN EVERY PART OF THE HOUSE RIGHT NOW.
...OH. THAT'S WEIRD...

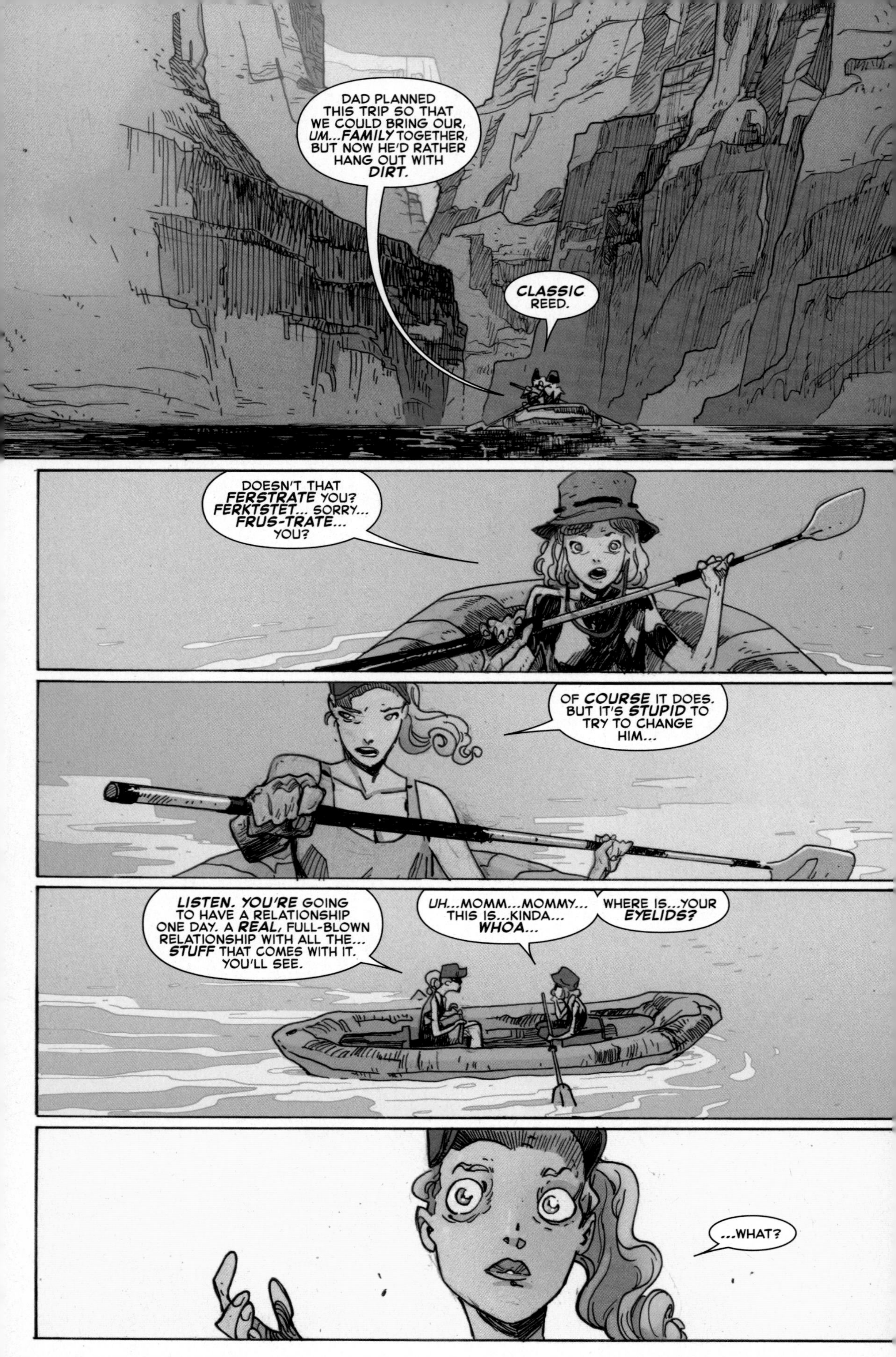
DAD PLANNED THIS TRIP SO THAT WE COULD BRING OUR, UM...FAMILY TOGETHER, BUT NOW HE'D RATHER HANG OUT WITH DIRT.
CLASSIC REED.
DOESN'T THAT FERSTRATE YOU? FERKTSTET... SORRY... FRUS-TRATE... YOU?
OF COURSE IT DOES. BUT IT'S STUPID TO TRY TO CHANGE HIM...
LISTEN. YOU'RE GOING TO HAVE A RELATIONSHIP ONE DAY. A REAL, FULL-BLOWN RELATIONSHIP WITH ALL THE... STUFF THAT COMES WITH IT. YOU'LL SEE.
UH...MOMM...MOMMY... THIS IS...KINDA... WHOA...
WHERE IS...YOUR EYELIDS?
...WHAT?

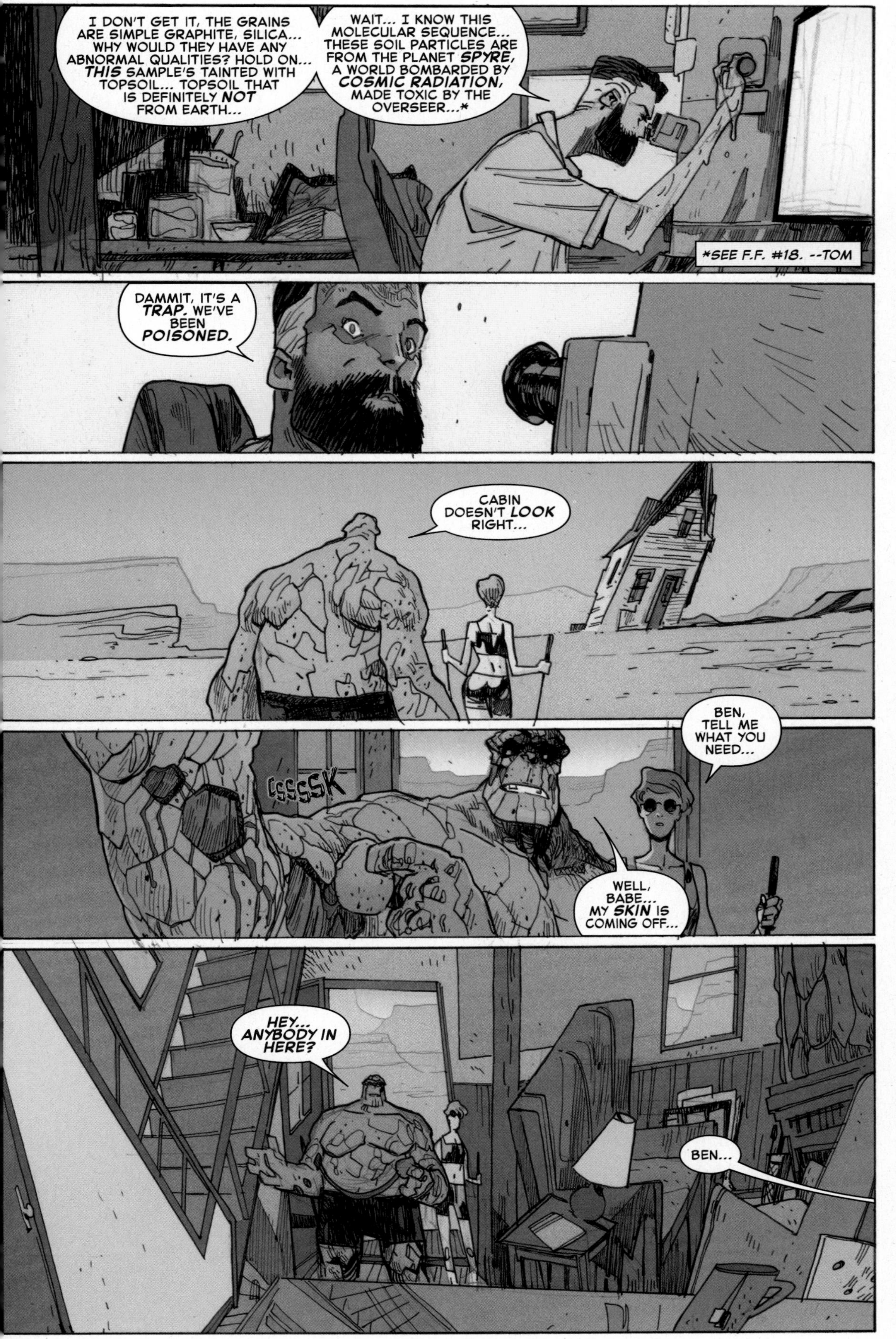
I DON'T GET IT, THE GRAINS ARE SIMPLE GRAPHITE, SILICA... WHY WOULD THEY HAVE ANY ABNORMAL QUALITIES? HOLD ON... THIS SAMPLE'S TAINTED WITH TOPSOIL... TOPSOIL THAT IS DEFINITELY NOT FROM EARTH...
WAIT... I KNOW THIS MOLECULAR SEQUENCE... THESE SOIL PARTICLES ARE FROM THE PLANET SPYRE, A WORLD BOMBARDED BY COSMIC RADIATION, MADE TOXIC BY THE OVERSEER...*
*SEE F.F. #18. --TOM
DAMMIT, IT'S A TRAP. WE'VE BEEN POISONED.
CABIN DOESN'T LOOK RIGHT...
BEN, TELL ME WHAT YOU NEED...
CSSSSK
WELL, BABE... MY SKIN IS COMING OFF...
HEY... ANYBODY IN HERE?
BEN...

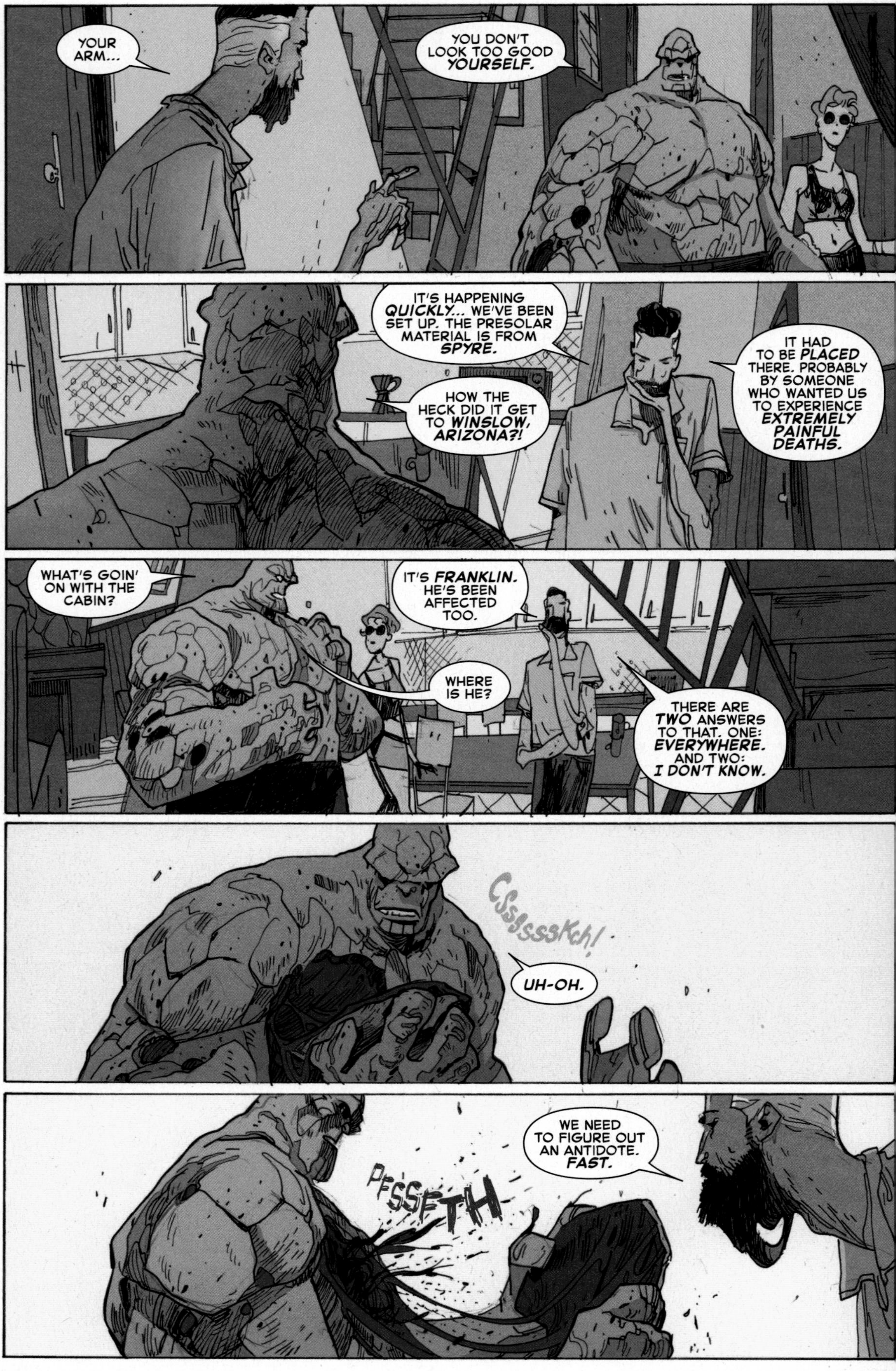
YOUR ARM...
YOU DON'T LOOK TOO GOOD *YOURSELF.*
IT'S HAPPENING *QUICKLY...* WE'VE BEEN SET UP. THE PRESOLAR MATERIAL IS FROM *SPYRE.*
HOW THE HECK DID IT GET TO *WINSLOW, ARIZONA?!*
IT HAD TO BE *PLACED* THERE. PROBABLY BY SOMEONE WHO WANTED US TO EXPERIENCE *EXTREMELY PAINFUL DEATHS.*
WHAT'S GOIN' ON WITH THE CABIN?
IT'S *FRANKLIN.* HE'S BEEN AFFECTED TOO.
WHERE IS HE?
THERE ARE *TWO* ANSWERS TO THAT. ONE: *EVERYWHERE.* AND TWO: *I DON'T KNOW.*
CSSSSSSKCH!
UH-OH.
WE NEED TO FIGURE OUT AN ANTIDOTE. *FAST.*
PFSSFTH

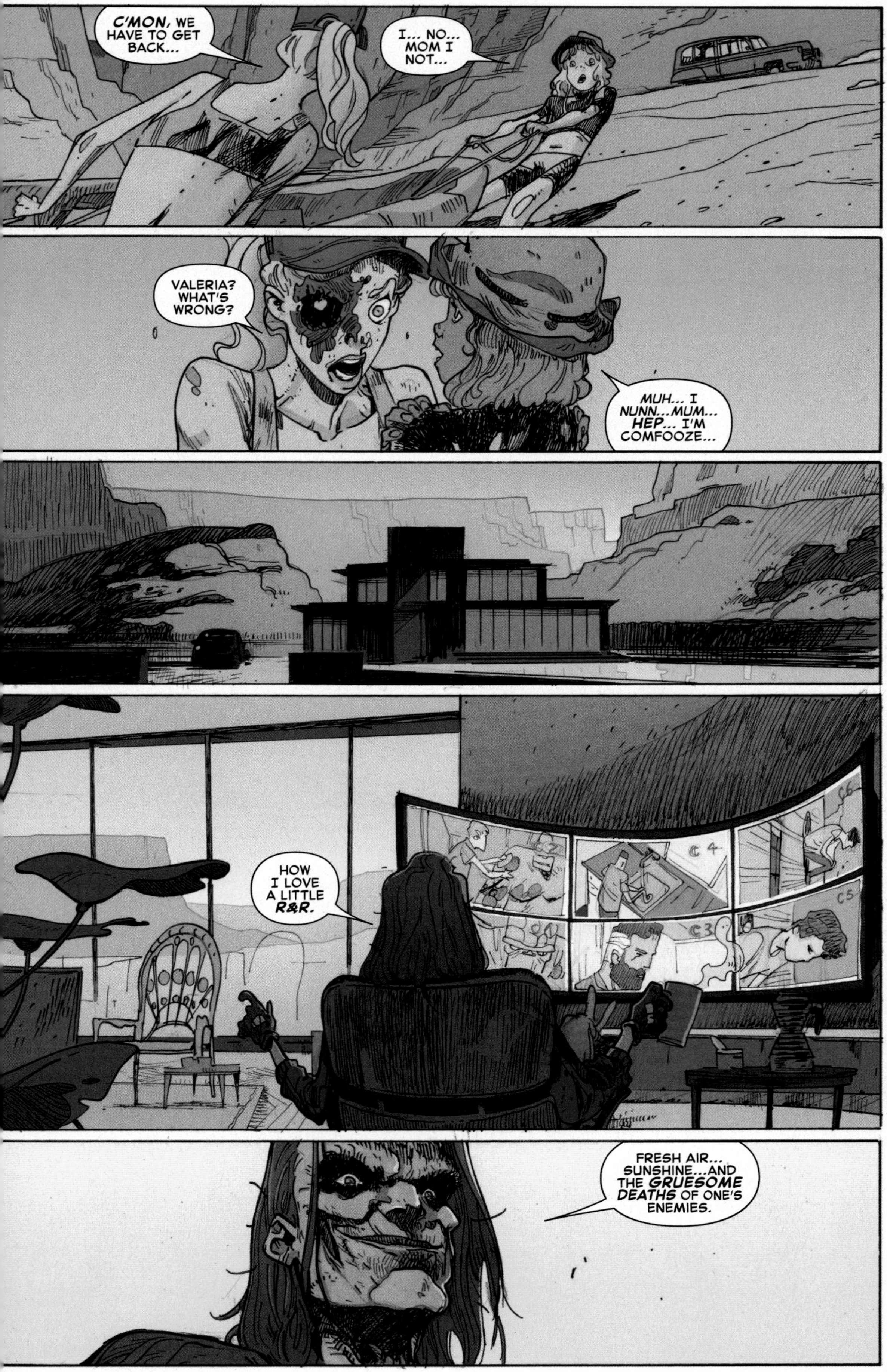
C'MON, WE HAVE TO GET BACK...
I... NO... MOM I NOT...
VALERIA? WHAT'S WRONG?
MUH... I NUNN...MUM... HEP... I'M COMFOOZE...
HOW I LOVE A LITTLE R&R.
FRESH AIR... SUNSHINE...AND THE GRUESOME DEATHS OF ONE'S ENEMIES.

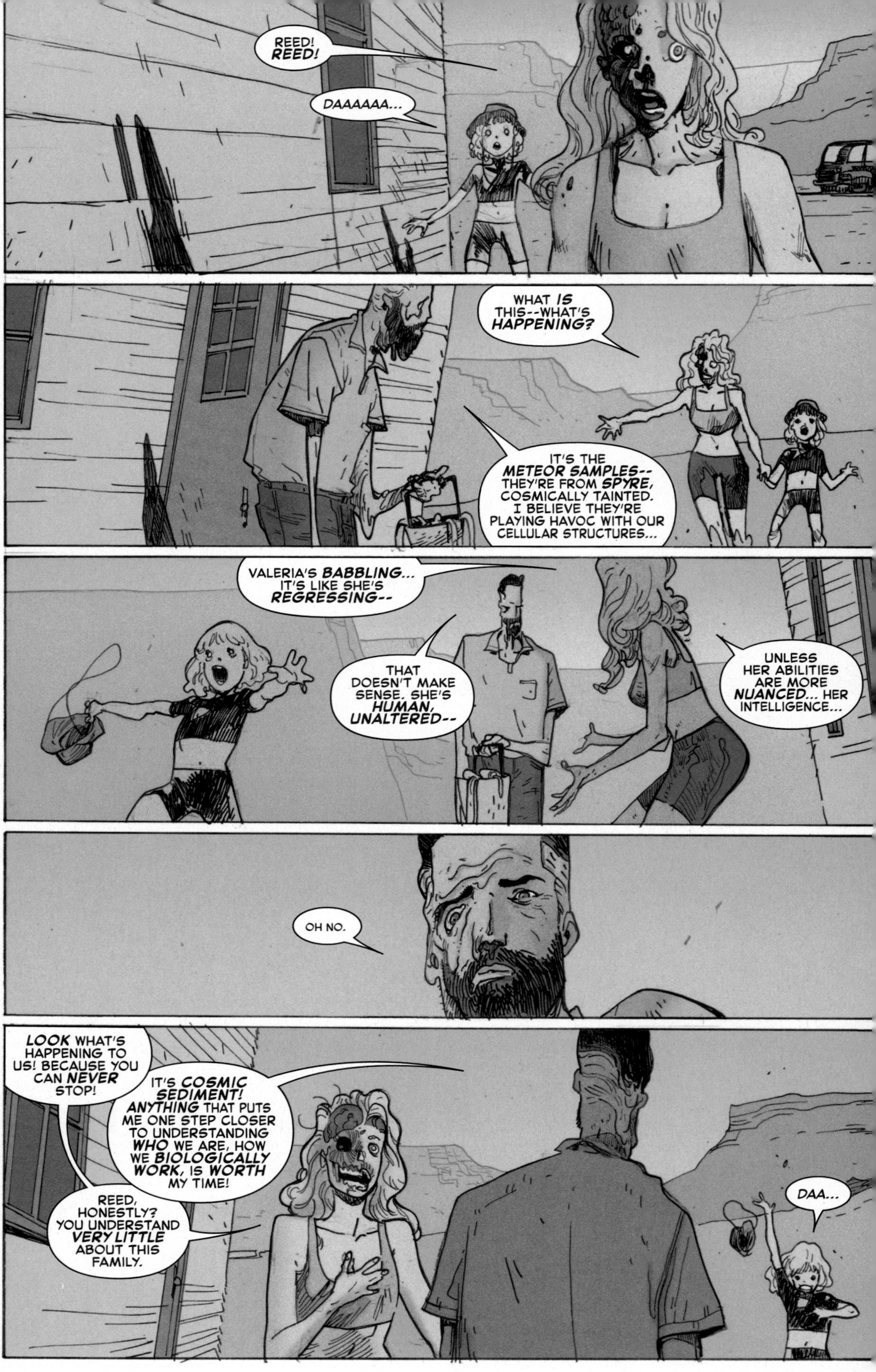
REED! REED!
DAAAAAA...
WHAT IS THIS--WHAT'S HAPPENING?
IT'S THE METEOR SAMPLES-- THEY'RE FROM SPYRE, COSMICALLY TAINTED. I BELIEVE THEY'RE PLAYING HAVOC WITH OUR CELLULAR STRUCTURES...
VALERIA'S BABBLING... IT'S LIKE SHE'S REGRESSING--
THAT DOESN'T MAKE SENSE. SHE'S HUMAN, UNALTERED--
UNLESS HER ABILITIES ARE MORE NUANCED... HER INTELLIGENCE...
OH NO.
LOOK WHAT'S HAPPENING TO US! BECAUSE YOU CAN NEVER STOP!
IT'S COSMIC SEDIMENT! ANYTHING THAT PUTS ME ONE STEP CLOSER TO UNDERSTANDING WHO WE ARE, HOW WE BIOLOGICALLY WORK, IS WORTH MY TIME!
REED, HONESTLY? YOU UNDERSTAND VERY LITTLE ABOUT THIS FAMILY.
DAA...

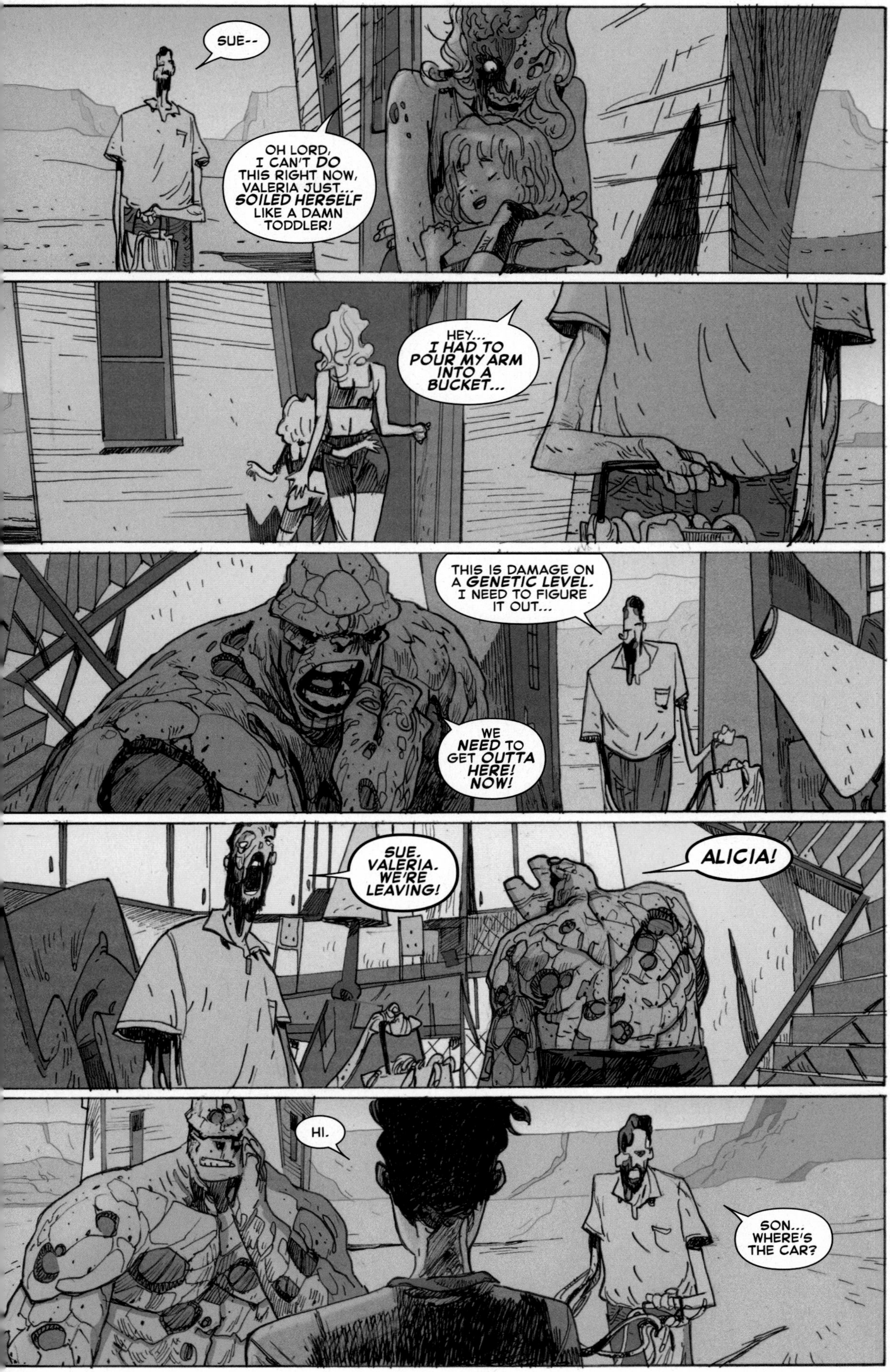
SUE--
OH LORD, I CAN'T DO THIS RIGHT NOW, VALERIA JUST... SOILED HERSELF LIKE A DAMN TODDLER!
HEY... I HAD TO POUR MY ARM INTO A BUCKET...
THIS IS DAMAGE ON A GENETIC LEVEL. I NEED TO FIGURE IT OUT...
WE NEED TO GET OUTTA HERE! NOW!
SUE. VALERIA. WE'RE LEAVING!
ALICIA!
HI.
SON... WHERE'S THE CAR?

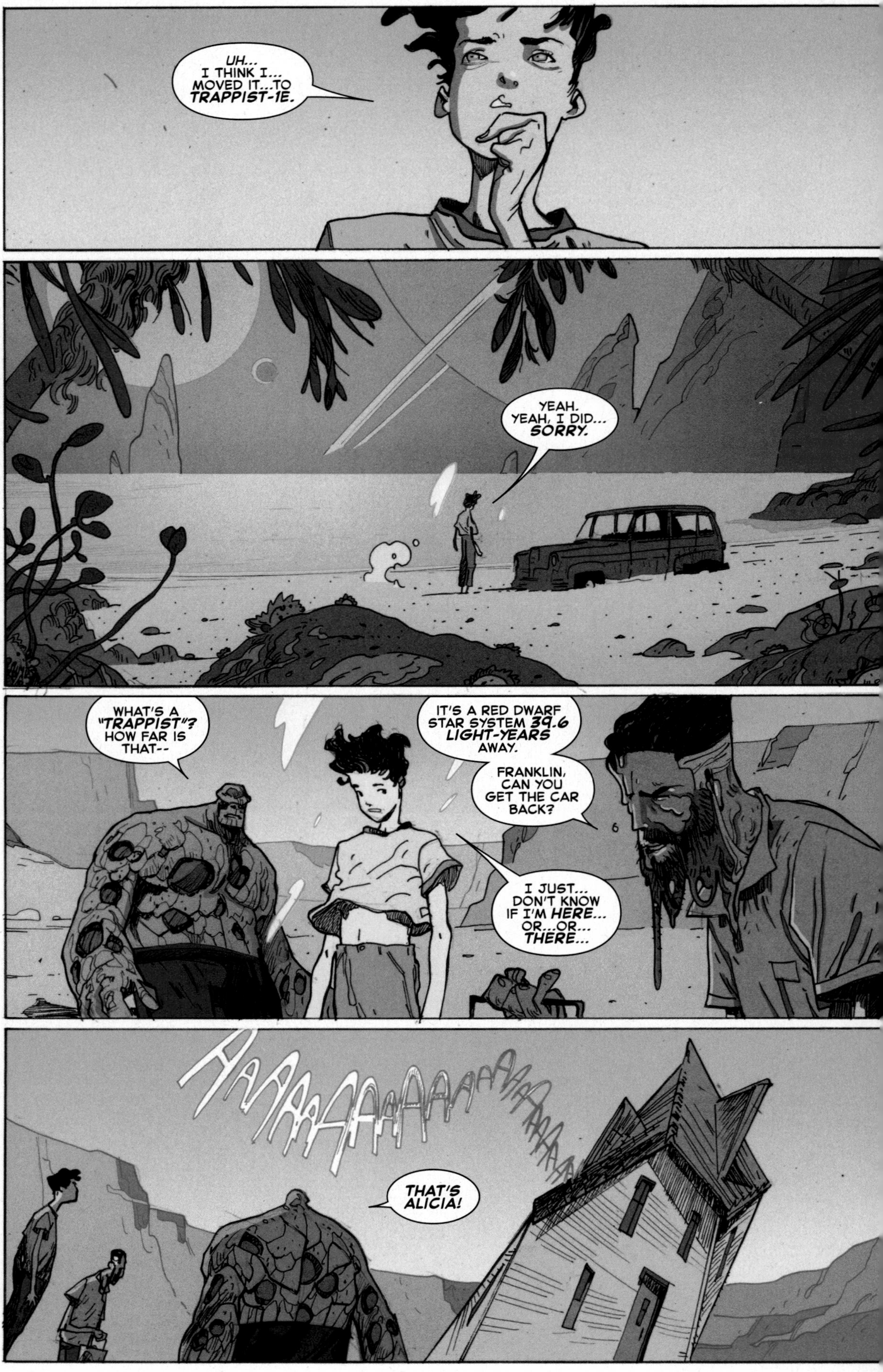
UH... I THINK I... MOVED IT...TO TRAPPIST-1E.
YEAH. YEAH, I DID... SORRY.
WHAT'S A "TRAPPIST"? HOW FAR IS THAT--
IT'S A RED DWARF STAR SYSTEM 39.6 LIGHT-YEARS AWAY.
FRANKLIN, CAN YOU GET THE CAR BACK?
I JUST... DON'T KNOW IF I'M HERE... OR...OR... THERE...
AAAAAAAAAAAAAAAAAAAAA
THAT'S ALICIA!

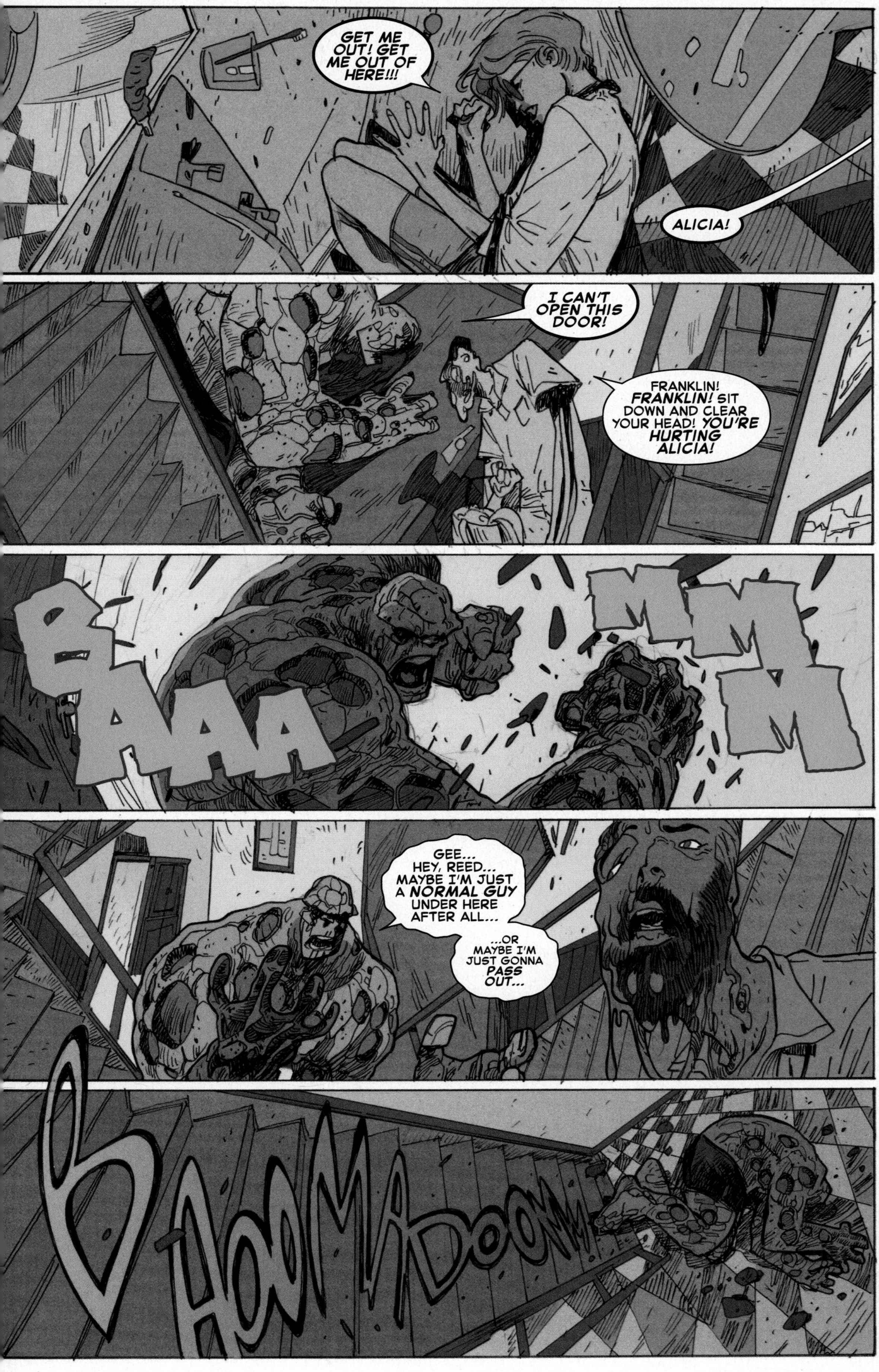
GET ME OUT! GET ME OUT OF HERE!!!
ALICIA!
I CAN'T OPEN THIS DOOR!
FRANKLIN! FRANKLIN! SIT DOWN AND CLEAR YOUR HEAD! YOU'RE HURTING ALICIA!
BAAAMMM
GEE... HEY, REED... MAYBE I'M JUST A NORMAL GUY UNDER HERE AFTER ALL...
...OR MAYBE I'M JUST GONNA PASS OUT...
BAOOMADOOM

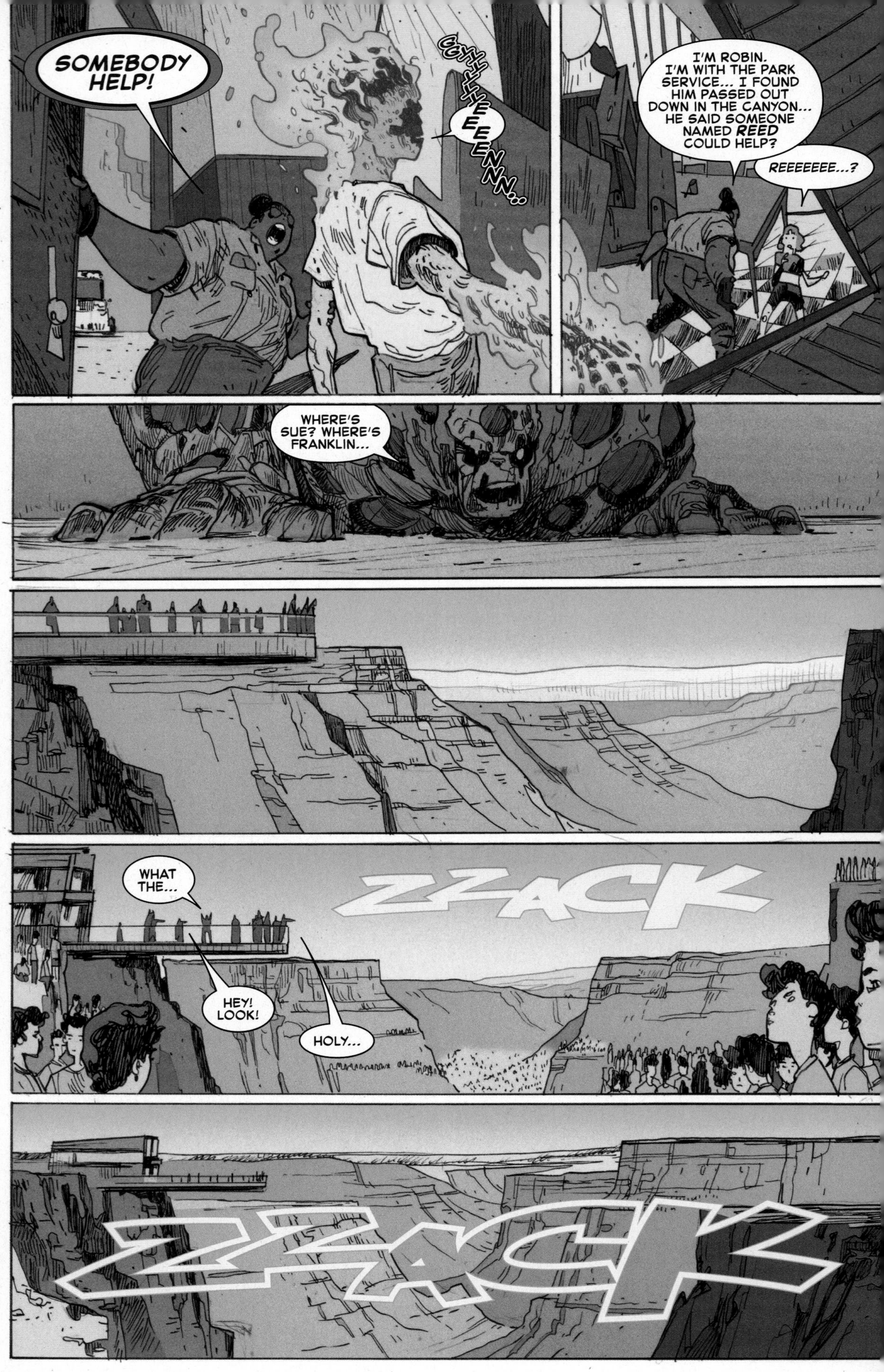

SOMEBODY HELP!
GGYYYYYYEEEENNN..
I'M ROBIN. I'M WITH THE PARK SERVICE... I FOUND HIM PASSED OUT DOWN IN THE CANYON... HE SAID SOMEONE NAMED REED COULD HELP?
REEEEEEE...?
WHERE'S SUE? WHERE'S FRANKLIN...
WHAT THE...
ZZACK
HEY! LOOK!
HOLY...
ZZACK

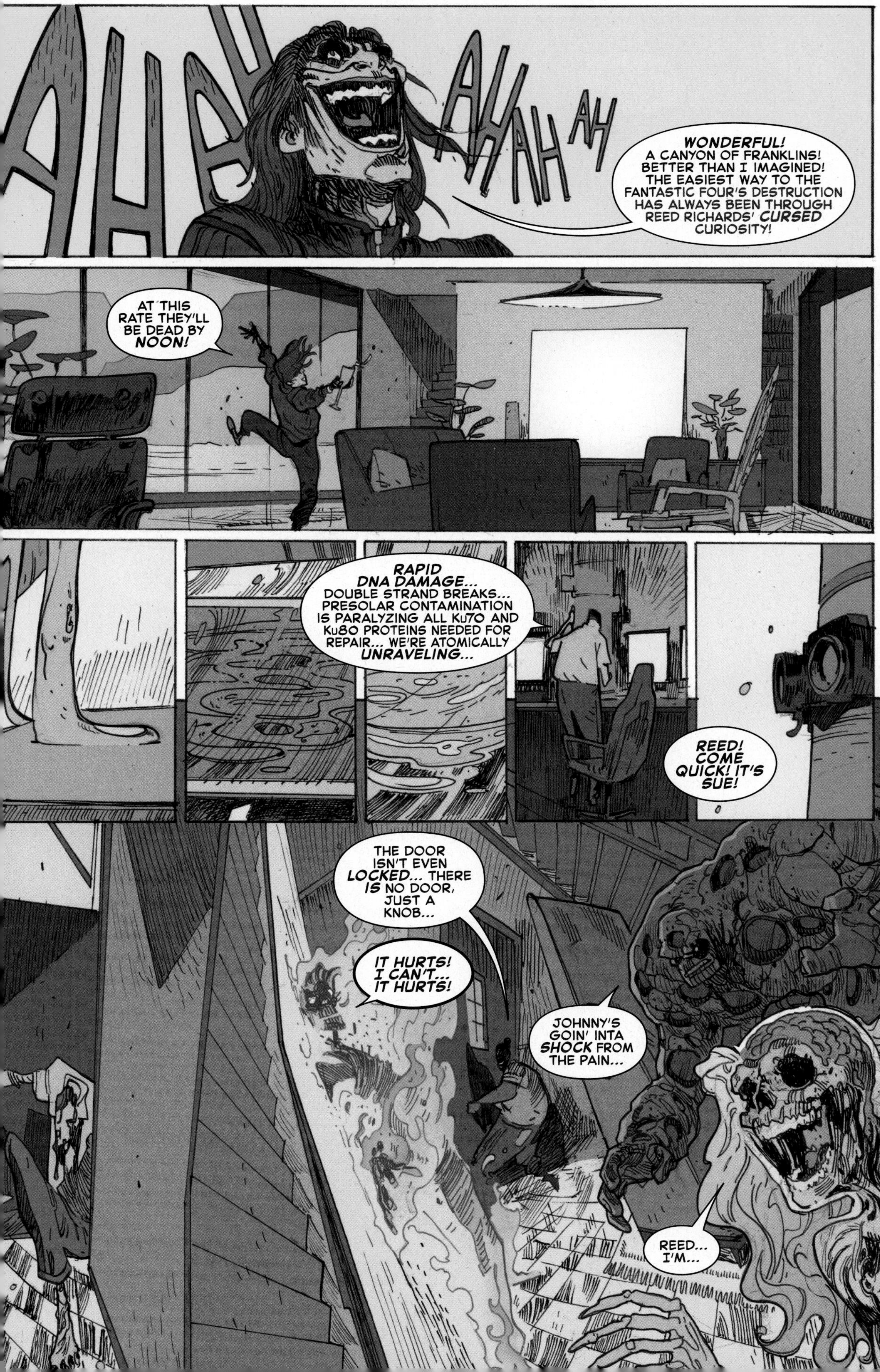

AAHAH
AHAHAH AH
WONDERFUL! A CANYON OF FRANKLINS! BETTER THAN I IMAGINED! THE EASIEST WAY TO THE FANTASTIC FOUR'S DESTRUCTION HAS ALWAYS BEEN THROUGH REED RICHARDS' CURSED CURIOSITY!
AT THIS RATE THEY'LL BE DEAD BY NOON!
RAPID DNA DAMAGE... DOUBLE STRAND BREAKS... PRESOLAR CONTAMINATION IS PARALYZING ALL Ku70 AND Ku80 PROTEINS NEEDED FOR REPAIR... WE'RE ATOMICALLY UNRAVELING...
REED! COME QUICK! IT'S SUE!
THE DOOR ISN'T EVEN LOCKED... THERE IS NO DOOR, JUST A KNOB...
IT HURTS! I CAN'T... IT HURTS!
JOHNNY'S GOIN' INTA SHOCK FROM THE PAIN...
REED... I'M...

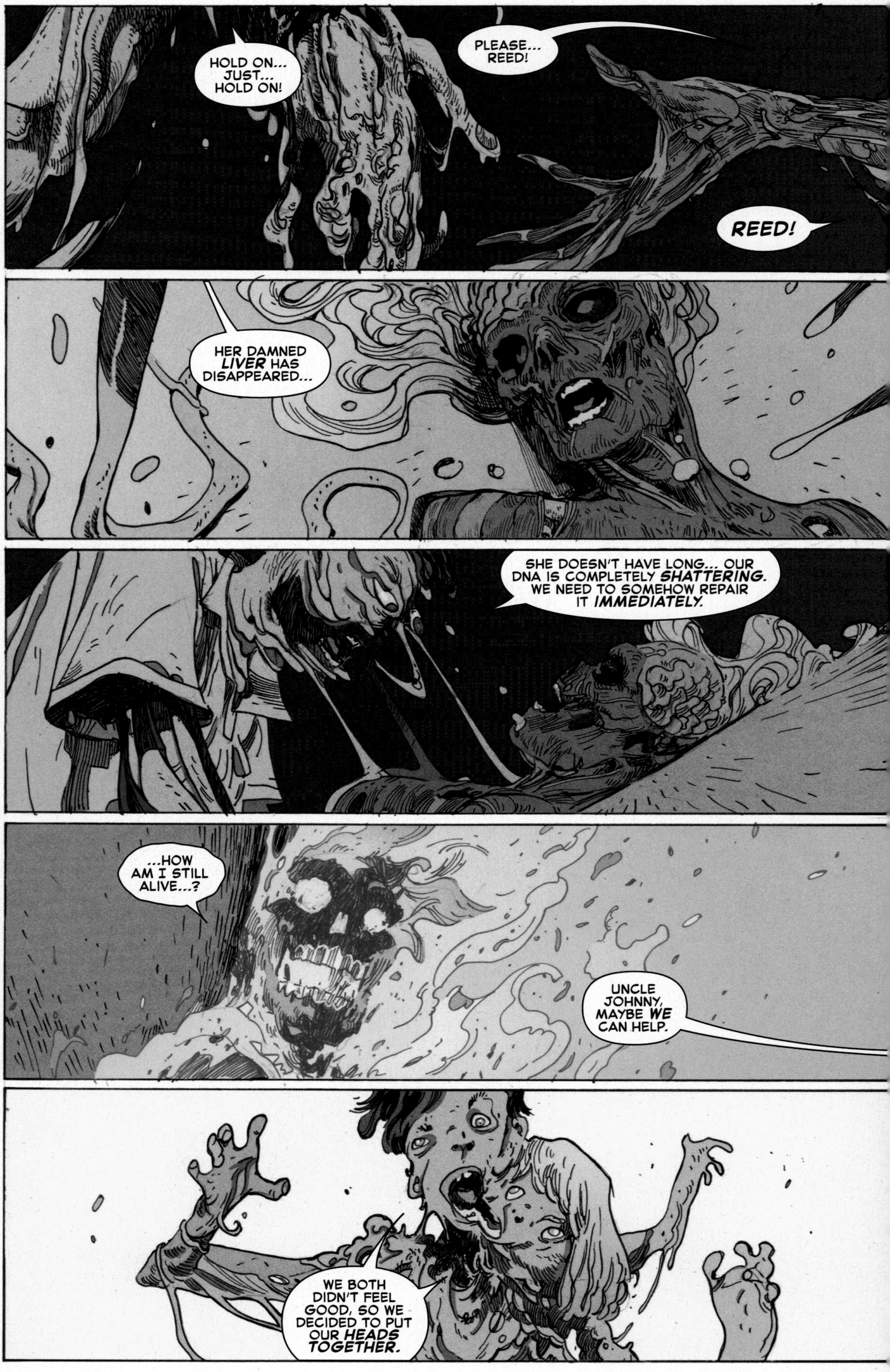
HOLD ON... JUST... HOLD ON!
PLEASE... REED!
REED!
HER DAMNED LIVER HAS DISAPPEARED...
SHE DOESN'T HAVE LONG... OUR DNA IS COMPLETELY SHATTERING. WE NEED TO SOMEHOW REPAIR IT IMMEDIATELY.
...HOW AM I STILL ALIVE...?
UNCLE JOHNNY, MAYBE WE CAN HELP.
WE BOTH DIDN'T FEEL GOOD, SO WE DECIDED TO PUT OUR HEADS TOGETHER.

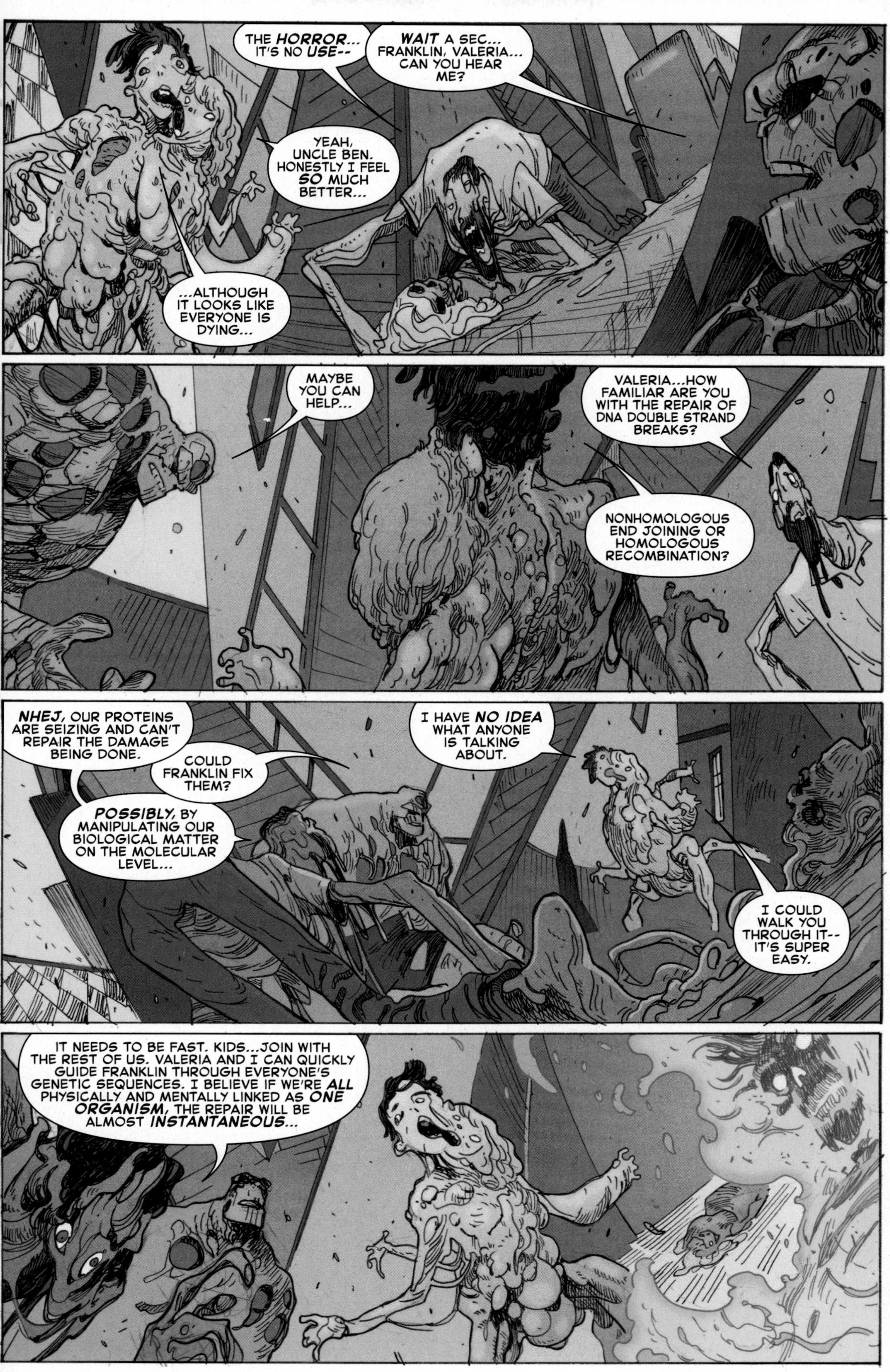
THE HORROR... IT'S NO USE--
WAIT A SEC... FRANKLIN, VALERIA... CAN YOU HEAR ME?
YEAH, UNCLE BEN. HONESTLY I FEEL SO MUCH BETTER...
...ALTHOUGH IT LOOKS LIKE EVERYONE IS DYING...
MAYBE YOU CAN HELP...
VALERIA...HOW FAMILIAR ARE YOU WITH THE REPAIR OF DNA DOUBLE STRAND BREAKS?
NONHOMOLOGOUS END JOINING OR HOMOLOGOUS RECOMBINATION?
NHEJ, OUR PROTEINS ARE SEIZING AND CAN'T REPAIR THE DAMAGE BEING DONE.
COULD FRANKLIN FIX THEM?
POSSIBLY, BY MANIPULATING OUR BIOLOGICAL MATTER ON THE MOLECULAR LEVEL...
I HAVE NO IDEA WHAT ANYONE IS TALKING ABOUT.
I COULD WALK YOU THROUGH IT-- IT'S SUPER EASY.
IT NEEDS TO BE FAST. KIDS...JOIN WITH THE REST OF US. VALERIA AND I CAN QUICKLY GUIDE FRANKLIN THROUGH EVERYONE'S GENETIC SEQUENCES. I BELIEVE IF WE'RE ALL PHYSICALLY AND MENTALLY LINKED AS ONE ORGANISM, THE REPAIR WILL BE ALMOST INSTANTANEOUS...

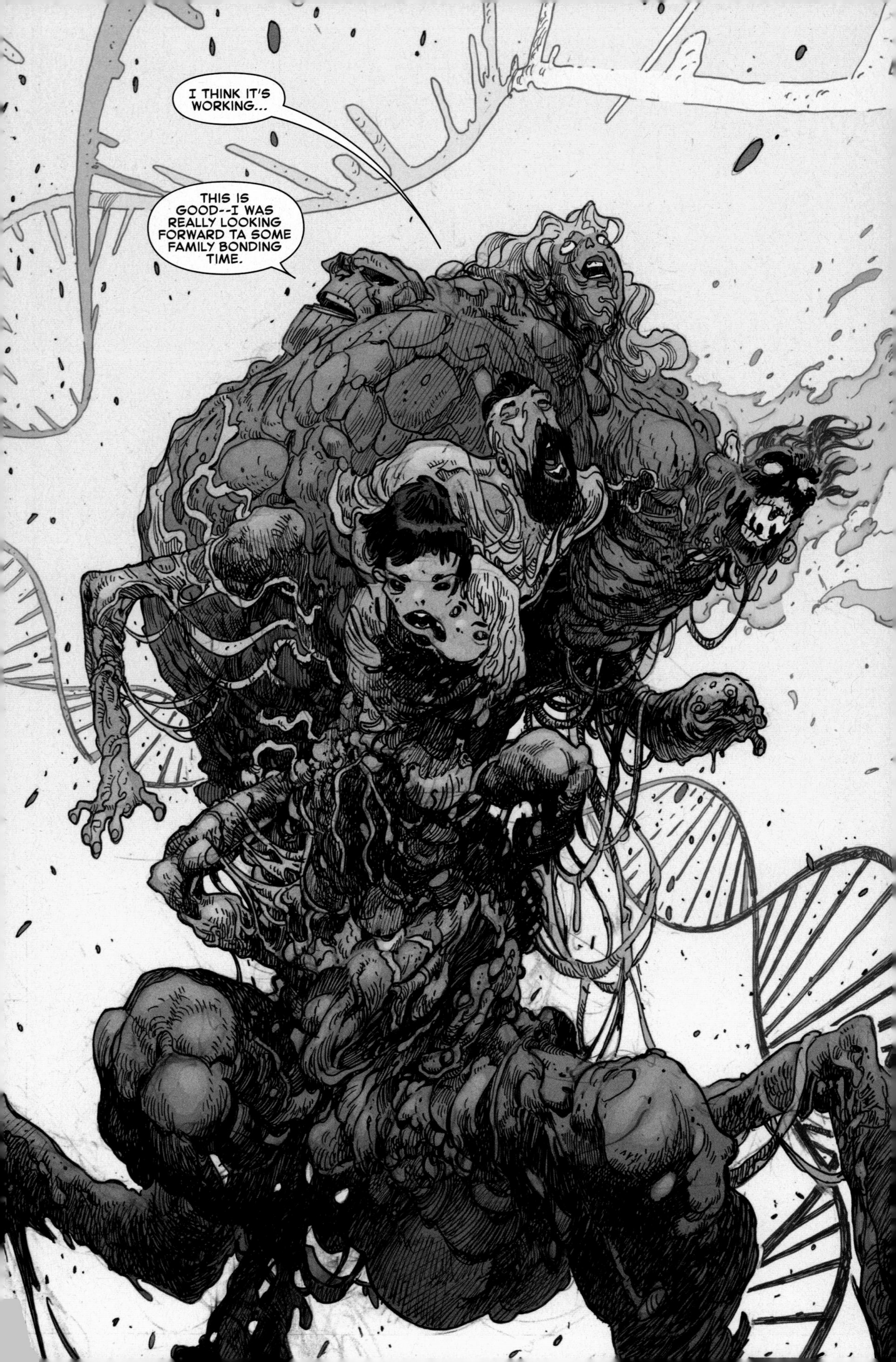
I THINK IT'S WORKING...
THIS IS GOOD--I WAS REALLY LOOKING FORWARD TA SOME FAMILY BONDING TIME.

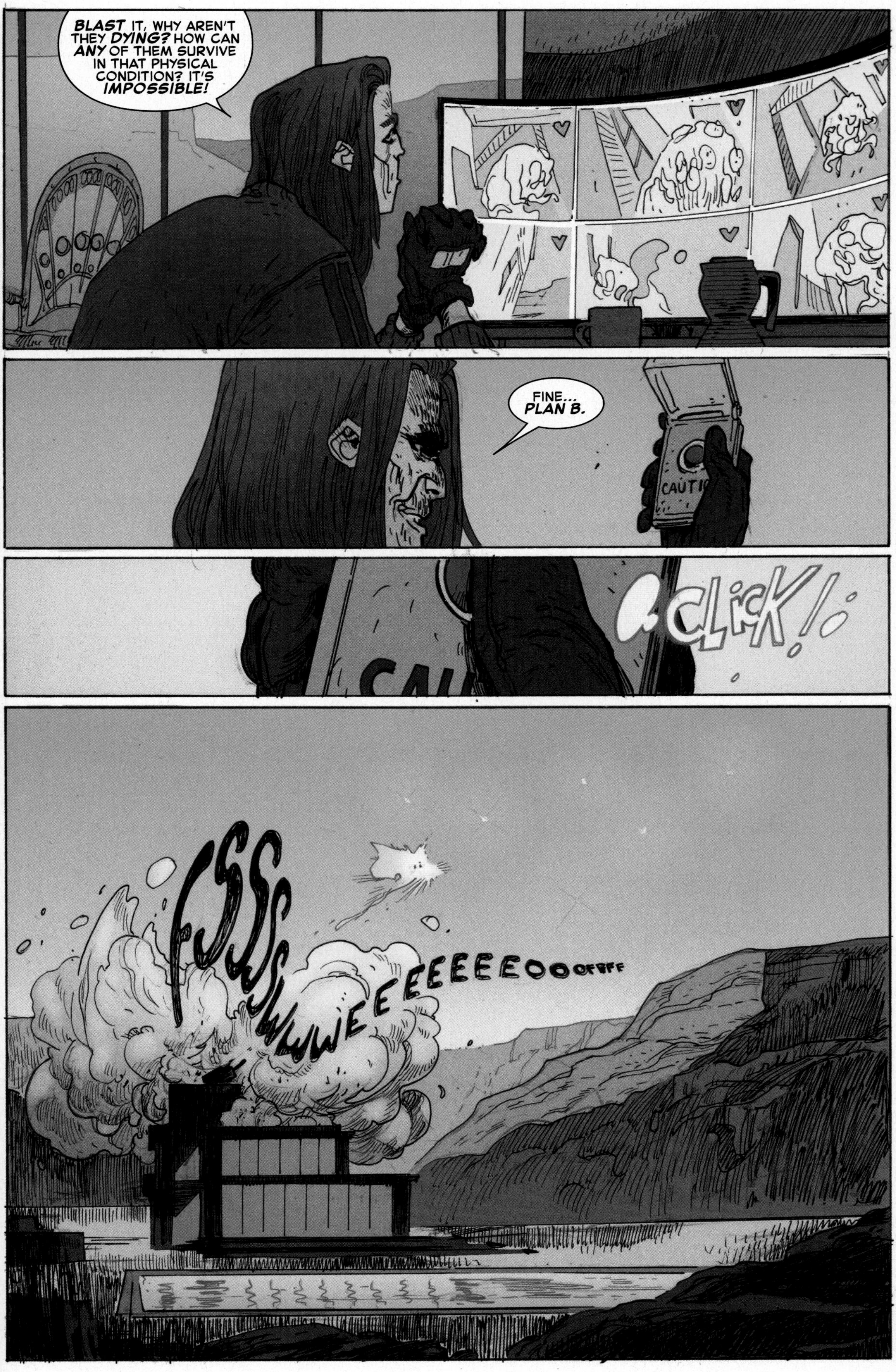

BLAST IT, WHY AREN'T THEY DYING? HOW CAN ANY OF THEM SURVIVE IN THAT PHYSICAL CONDITION? IT'S IMPOSSIBLE!
FINE... PLAN B.
CAUTI
CLICK!
CAU
FSSSWWWEEEEEEEEEOOOOFFFF

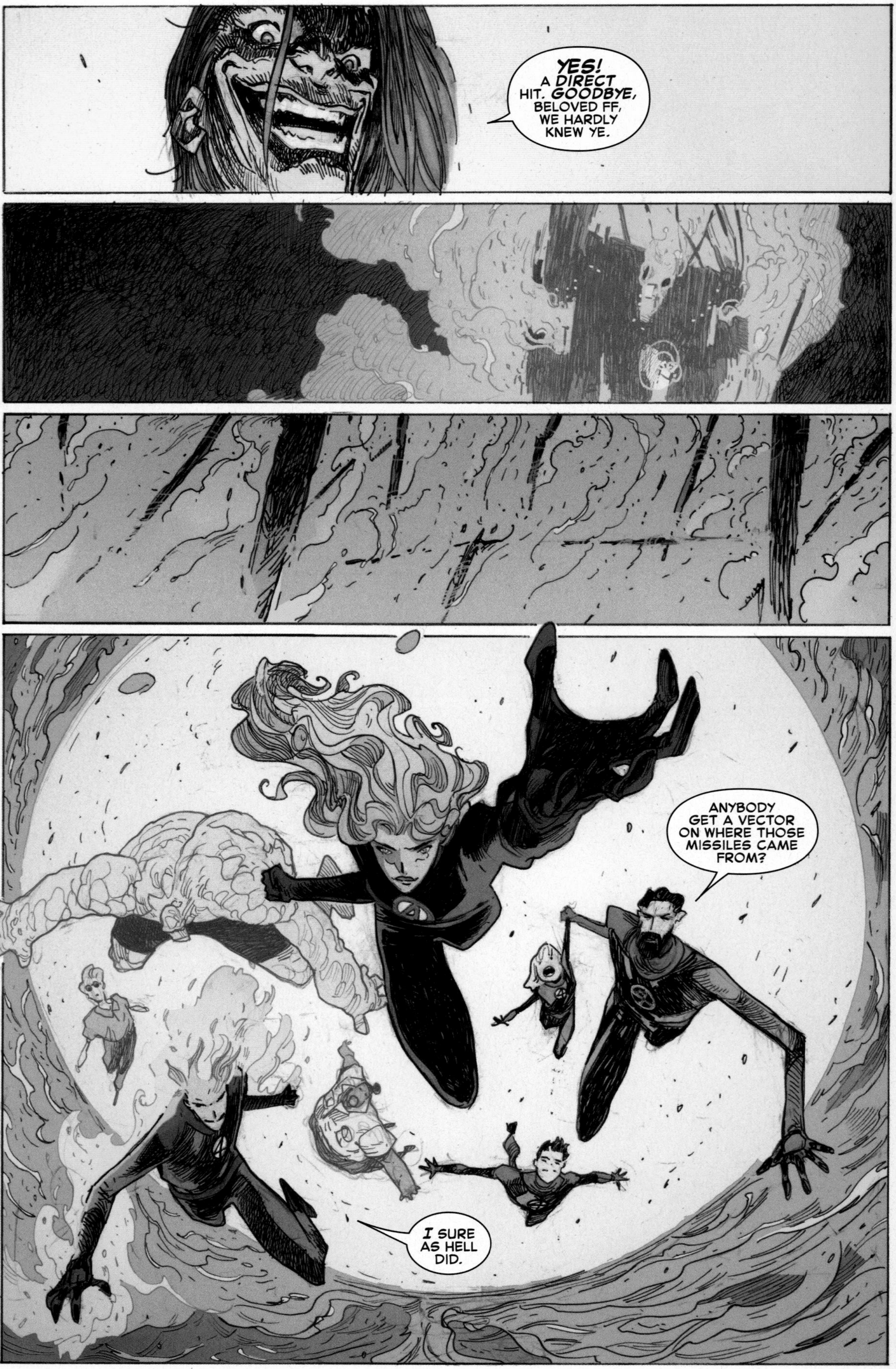
YES! A DIRECT HIT. GOODBYE, BELOVED FF, WE HARDLY KNEW YE.
ANYBODY GET A VECTOR ON WHERE THOSE MISSILES CAME FROM?
I SURE AS HELL DID.

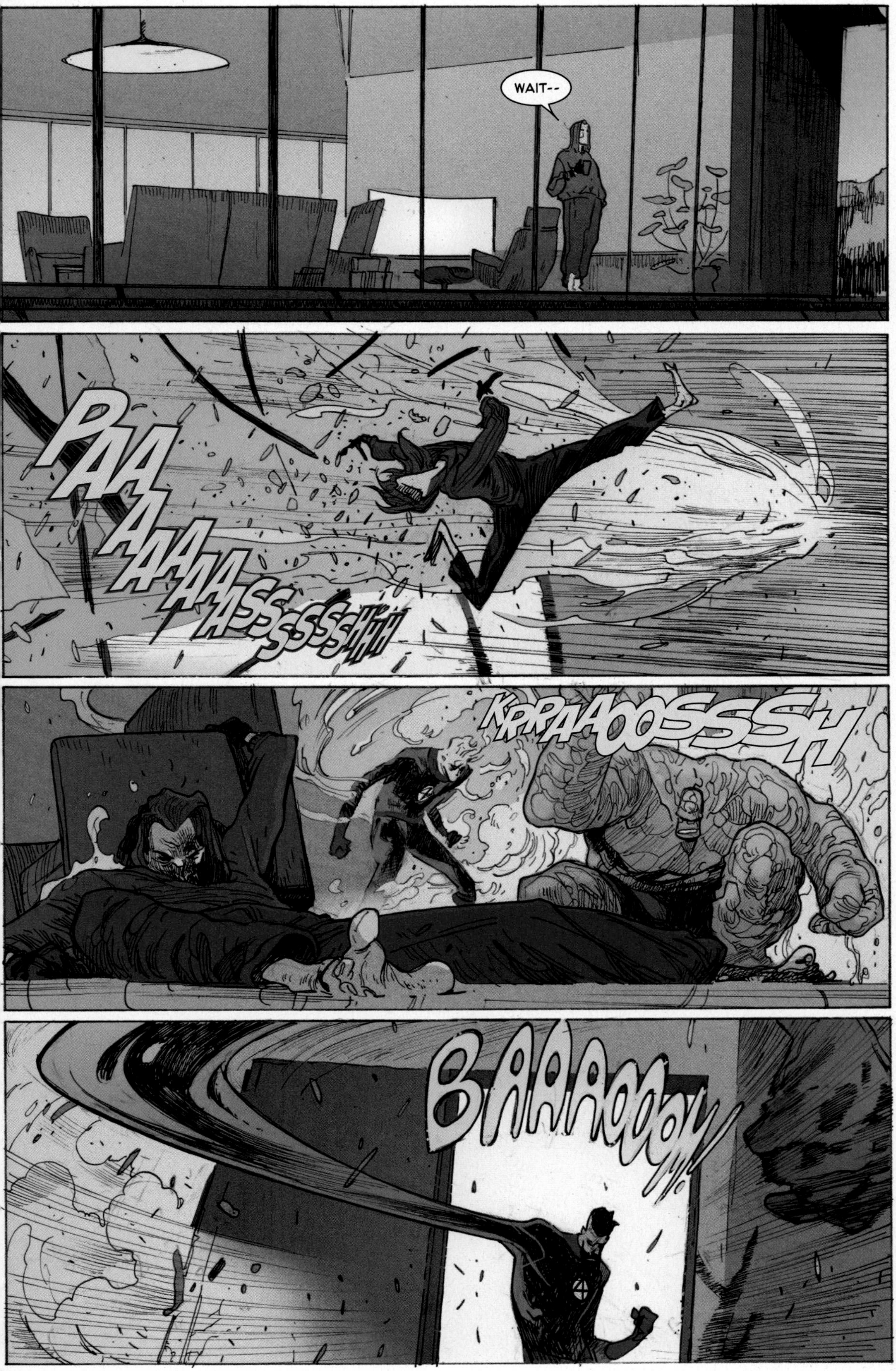
WAIT--
PAAAAAAASSSSSHH
KRRAAOOSSSSH

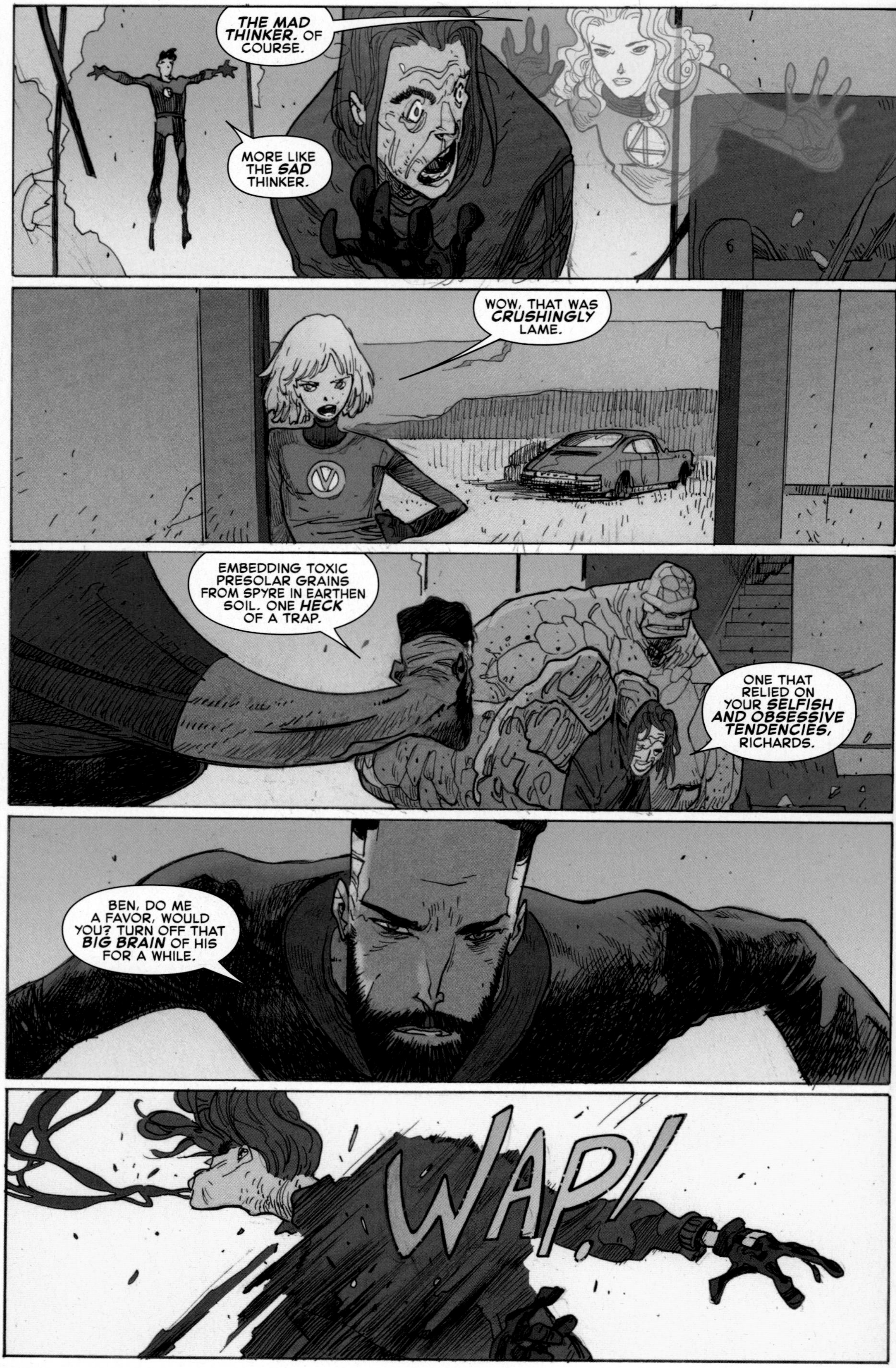
THE MAD THINKER. OF COURSE.
MORE LIKE THE SAD THINKER.
WOW, THAT WAS CRUSHINGLY LAME.
EMBEDDING TOXIC PRESOLAR GRAINS FROM SPYRE IN EARTHEN SOIL. ONE HECK OF A TRAP.
ONE THAT RELIED ON YOUR SELFISH AND OBSESSIVE TENDENCIES, RICHARDS.
BEN, DO ME A FAVOR, WOULD YOU? TURN OFF THAT BIG BRAIN OF HIS FOR A WHILE.
WAP!

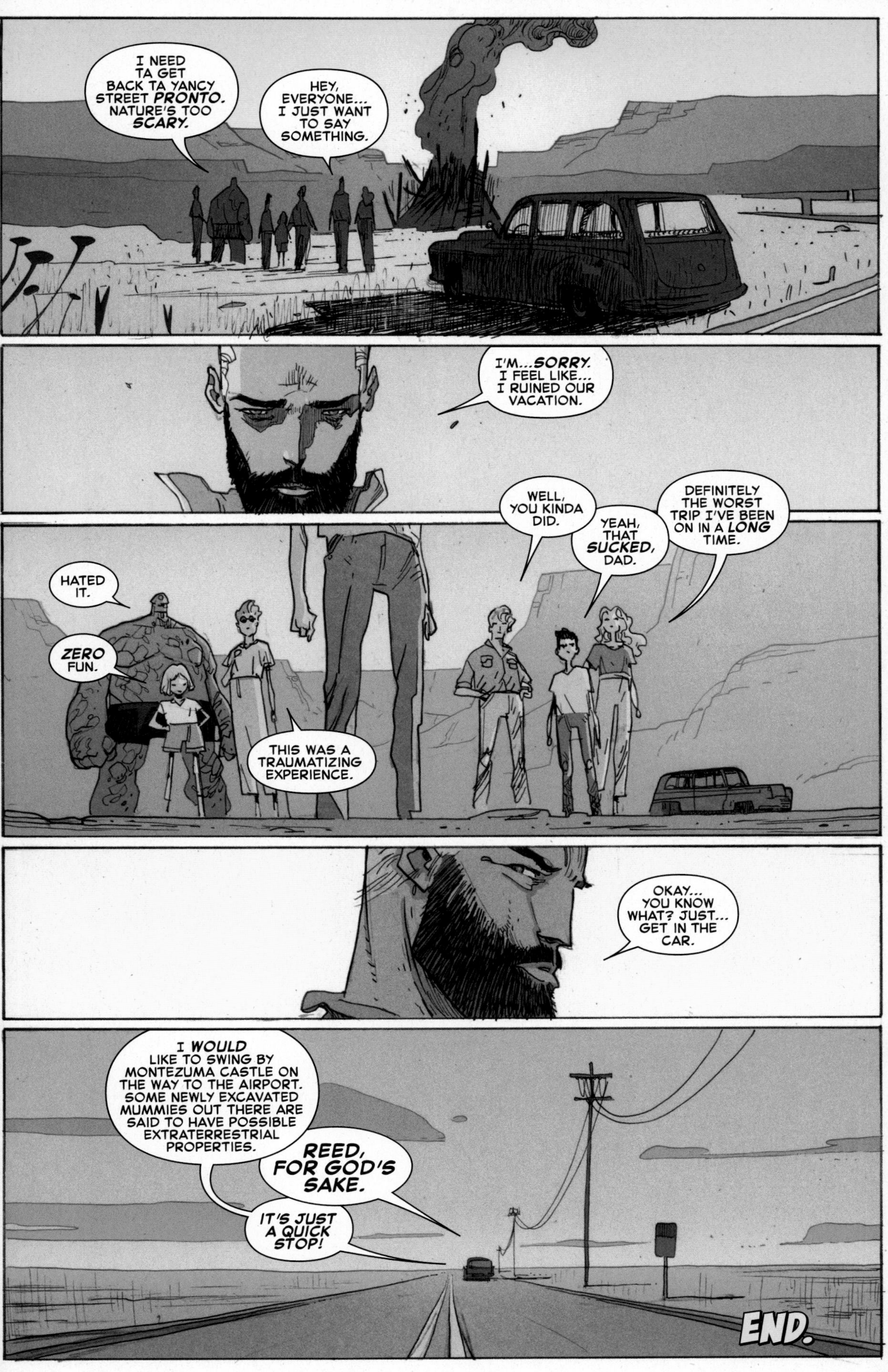
I NEED TA GET BACK TA YANCY STREET PRONTO. NATURE'S TOO SCARY.
HEY, EVERYONE... I JUST WANT TO SAY SOMETHING.
I'M...SORRY. I FEEL LIKE... I RUINED OUR VACATION.
HATED IT.
ZERO FUN.
THIS WAS A TRAUMATIZING EXPERIENCE.
WELL, YOU KINDA DID.
YEAH, THAT SUCKED, DAD.
DEFINITELY THE WORST TRIP I'VE BEEN ON IN A LONG TIME.
OKAY... YOU KNOW WHAT? JUST... GET IN THE CAR.
I WOULD LIKE TO SWING BY MONTEZUMA CASTLE ON THE WAY TO THE AIRPORT. SOME NEWLY EXCAVATED MUMMIES OUT THERE ARE SAID TO HAVE POSSIBLE EXTRATERRESTRIAL PROPERTIES.
REED, FOR GOD'S SAKE.
IT'S JUST A QUICK STOP!
END.

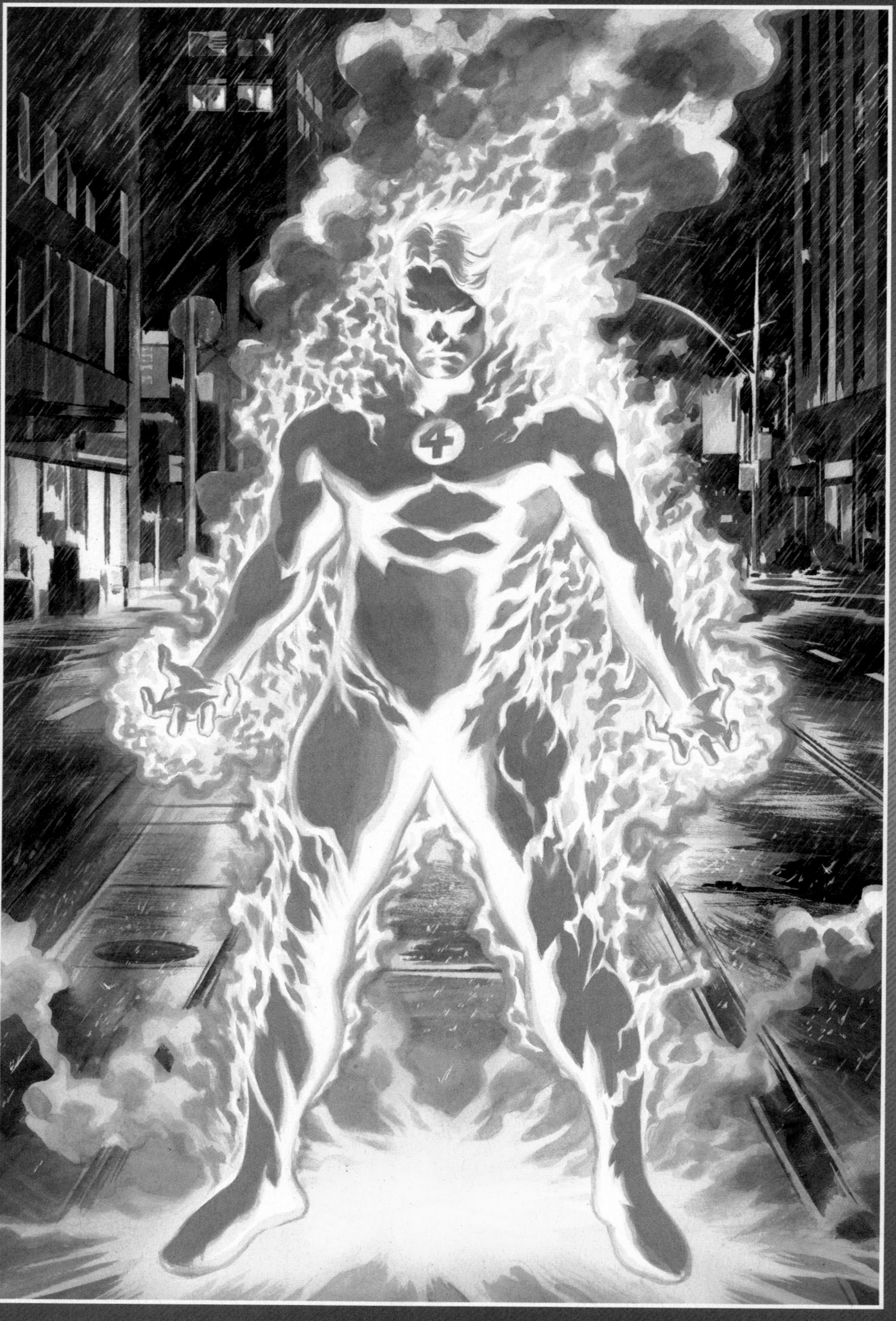

#37 Variant by **Felipe Massafera**

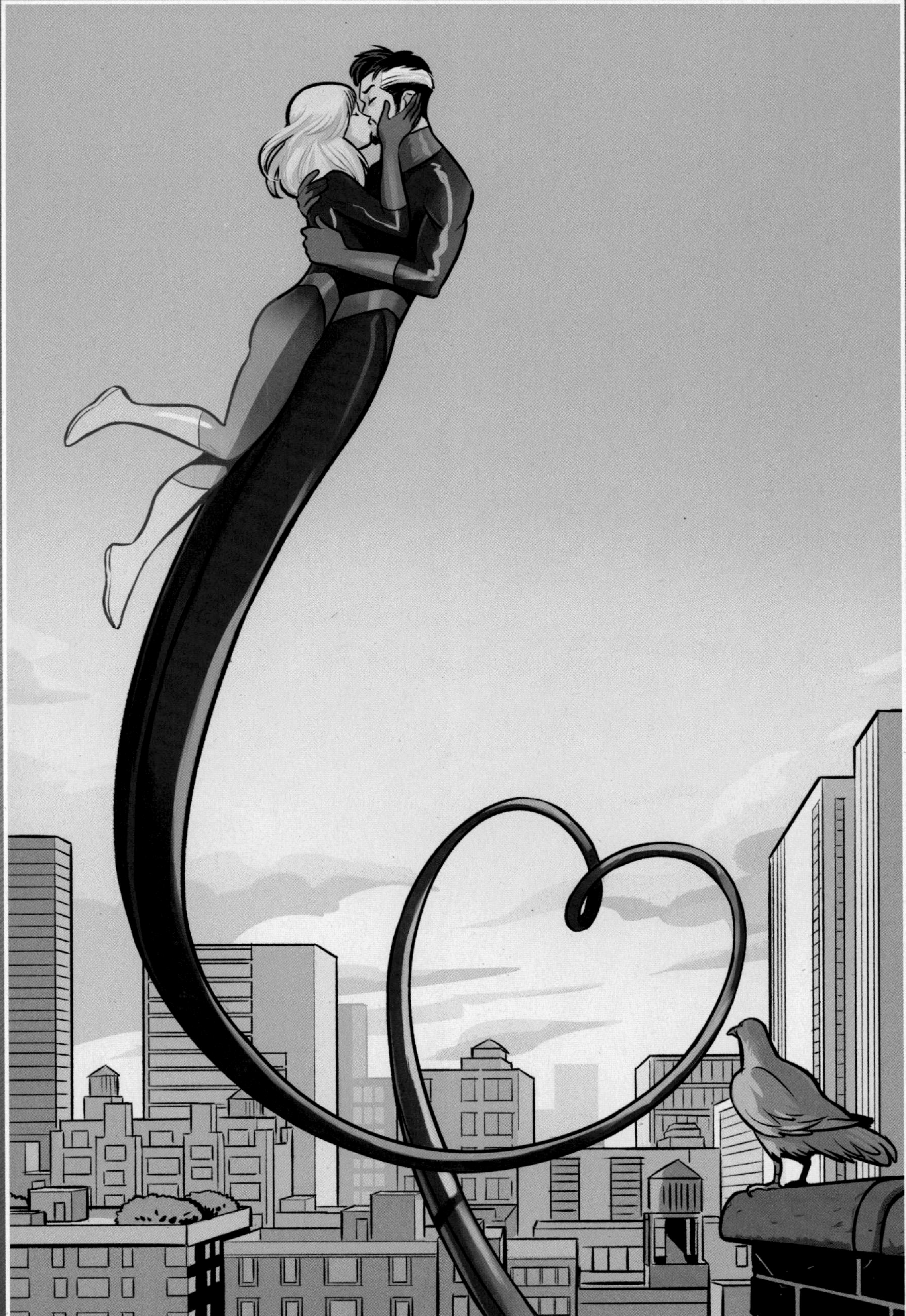

#38 Stormbreakers Variant by **Natacha Bustos**

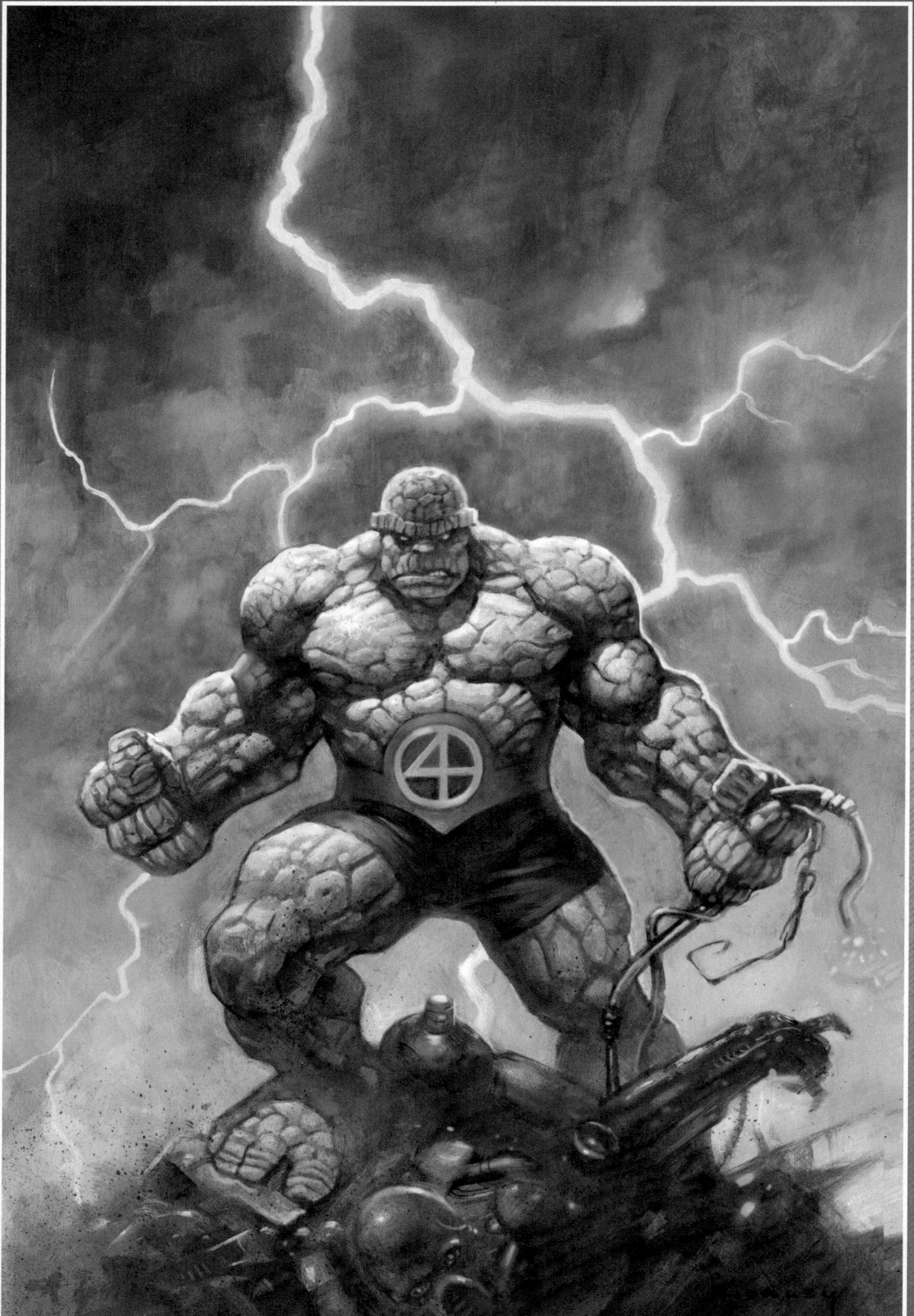

#38 Variant by **Alex Horley**

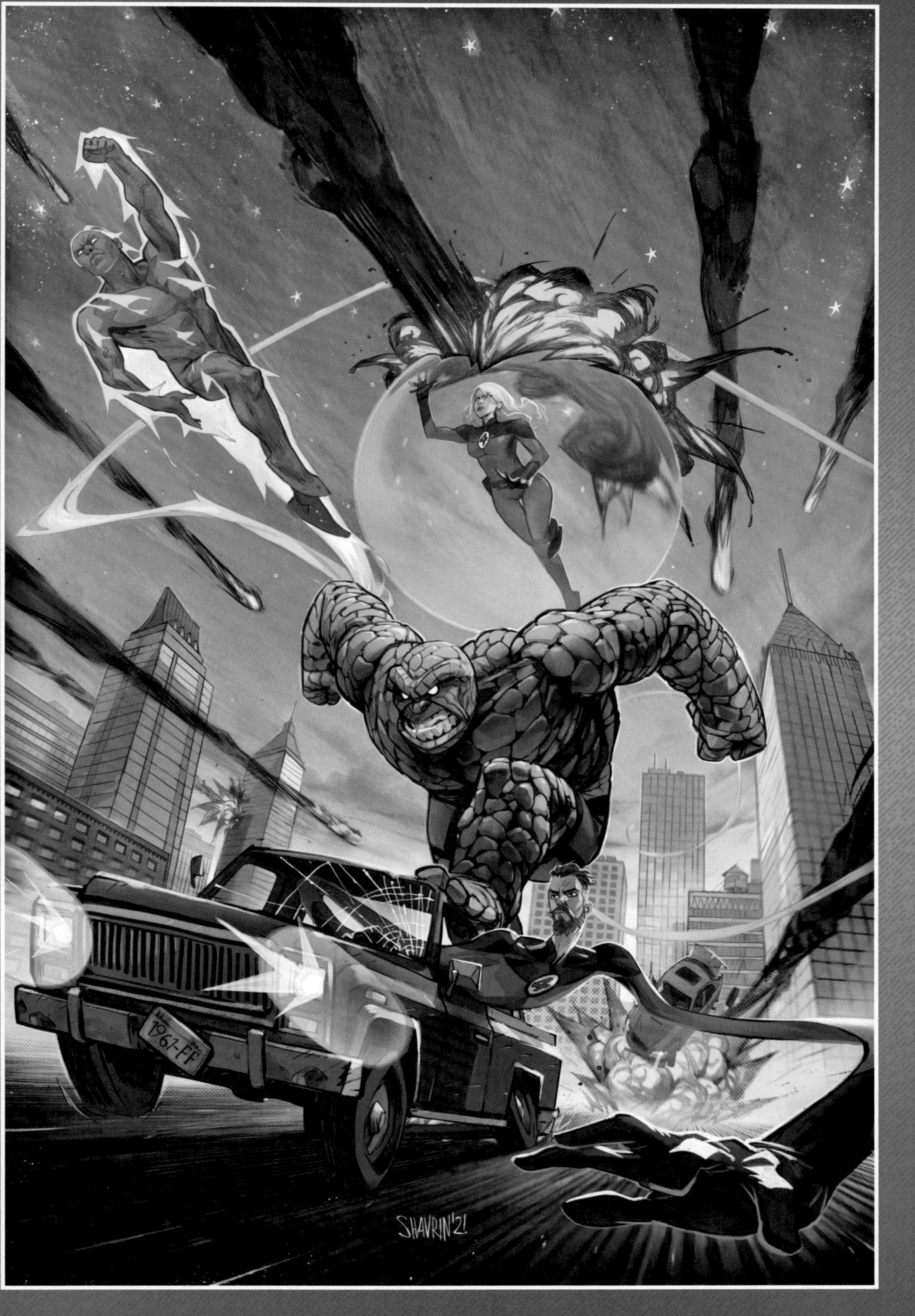
1961-FF
SHAVRIN'21

#39 Variant by **Ivan Shavrin**

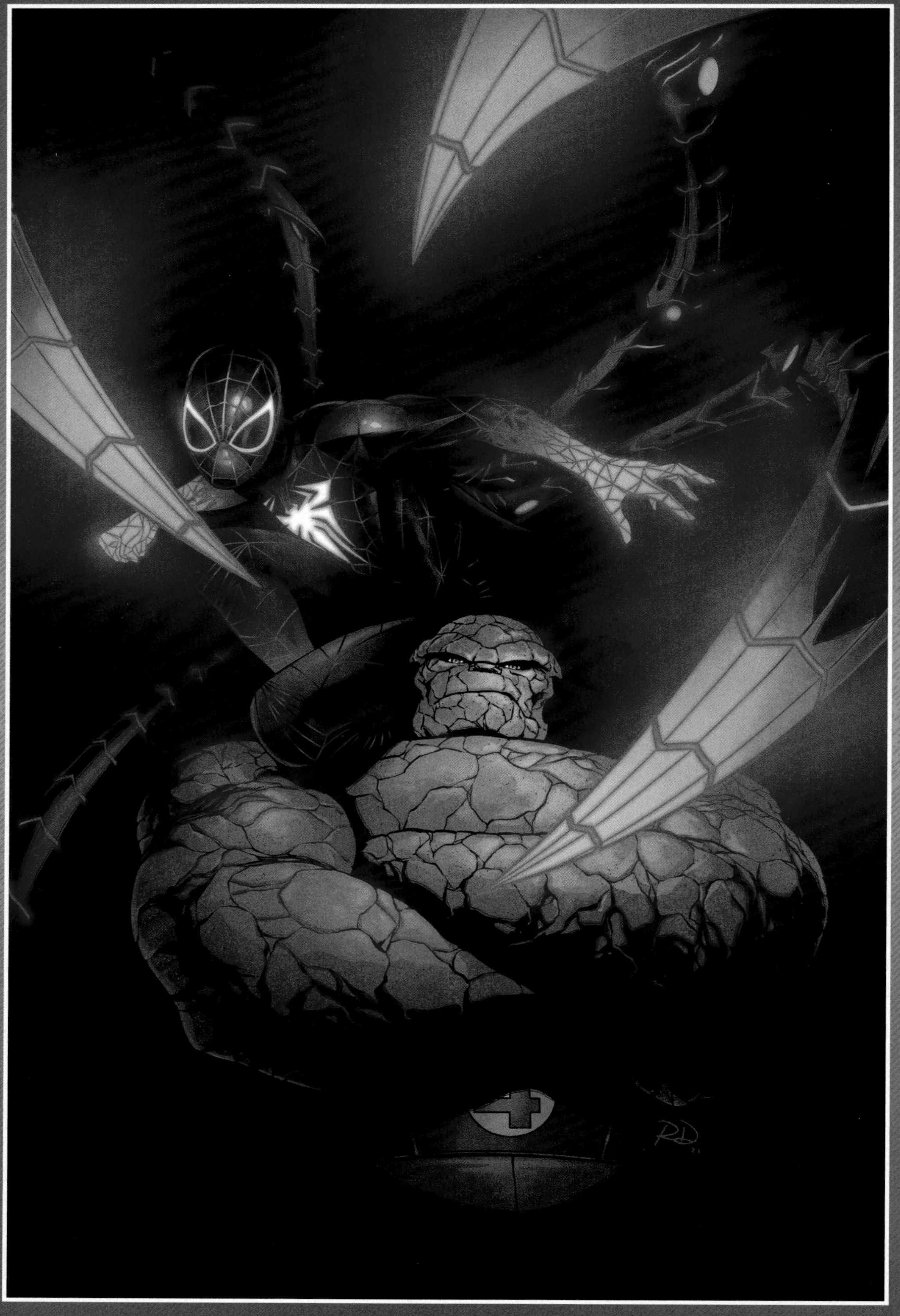

#36 Miles Morales: Spider-Man 10th Anniversary Variant by **Russell Dauterman**

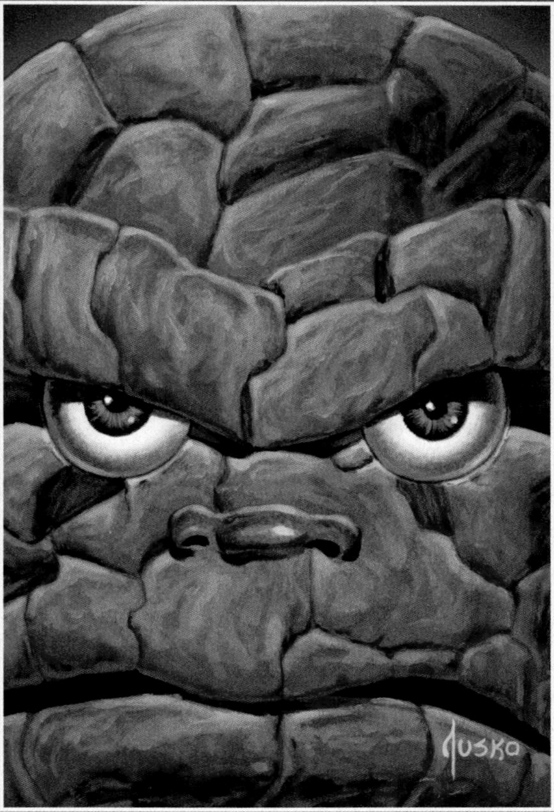
JUSKO

#37 Marvel Masterpieces Variant
by **Joe Jusko**

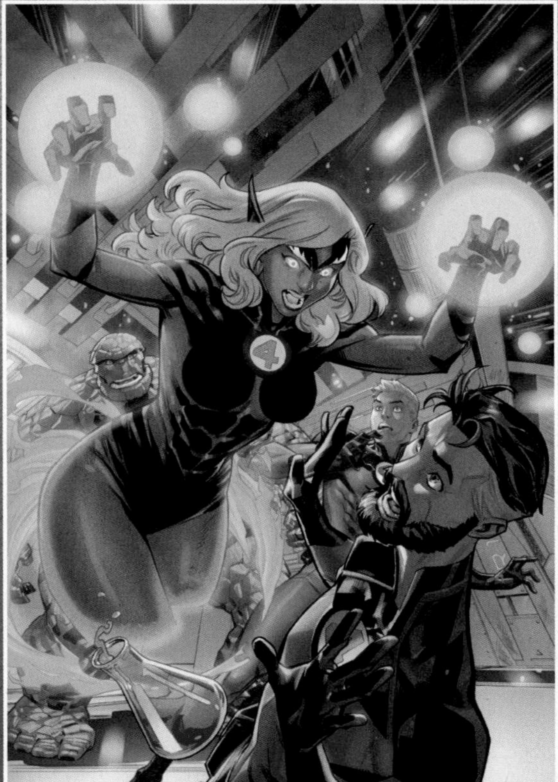

#39 Devil's Reign Variant by
Carlos Gomez & **Jesus Aburtov**

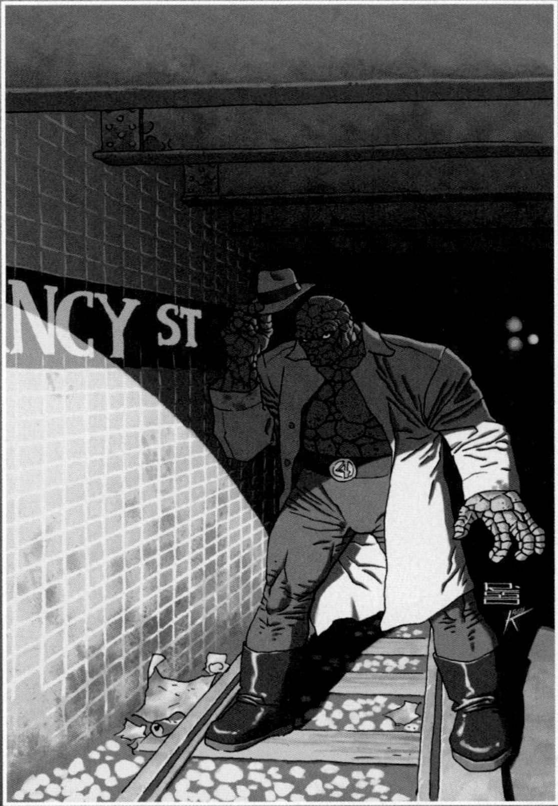
NCY ST

Fantastic Four: Grimm Noir Variant by
Eduardo Risso & **Kristian Rossi**

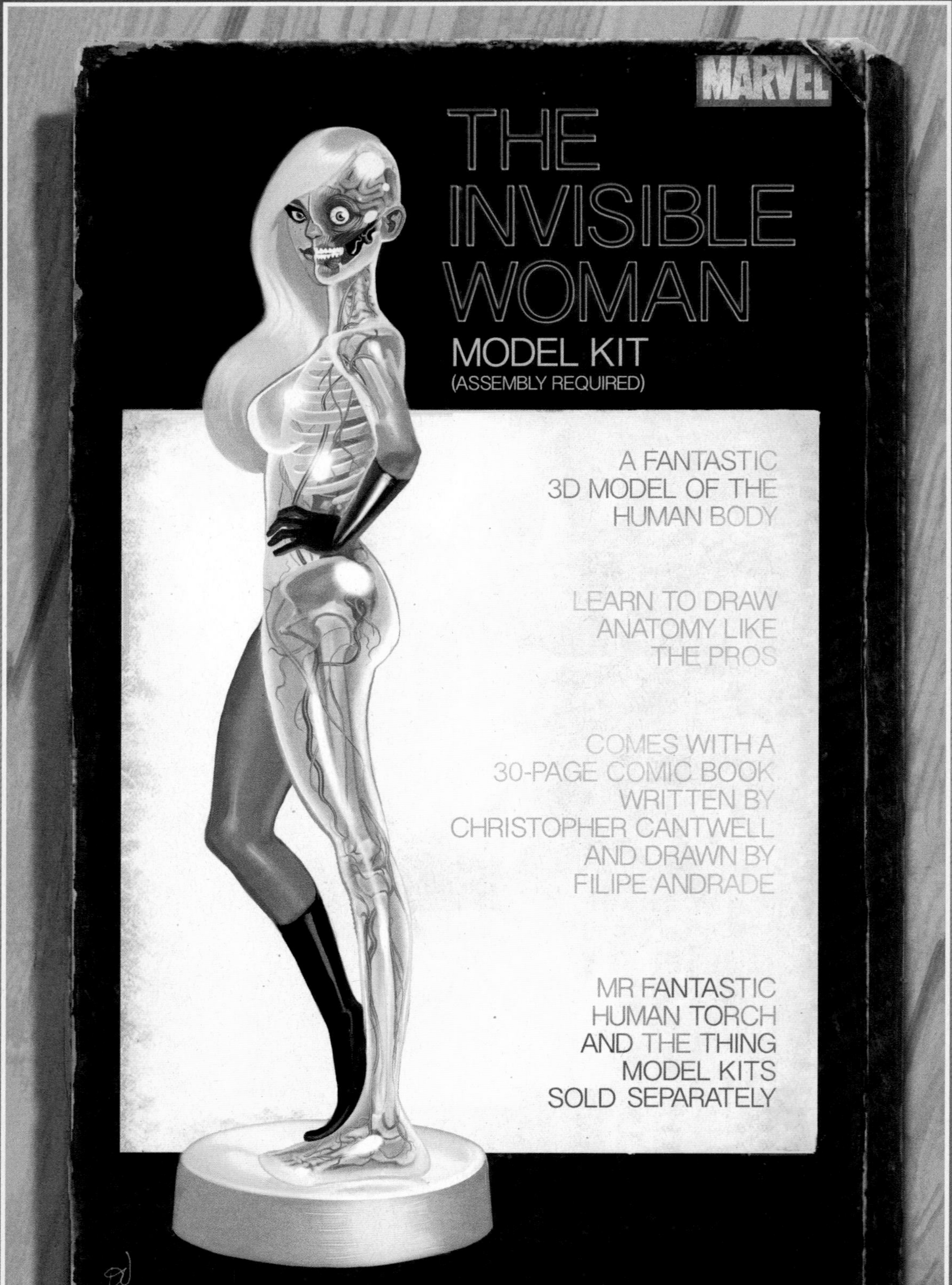

Fantastic Four: Road Trip Variant by **Mike del Mundo**

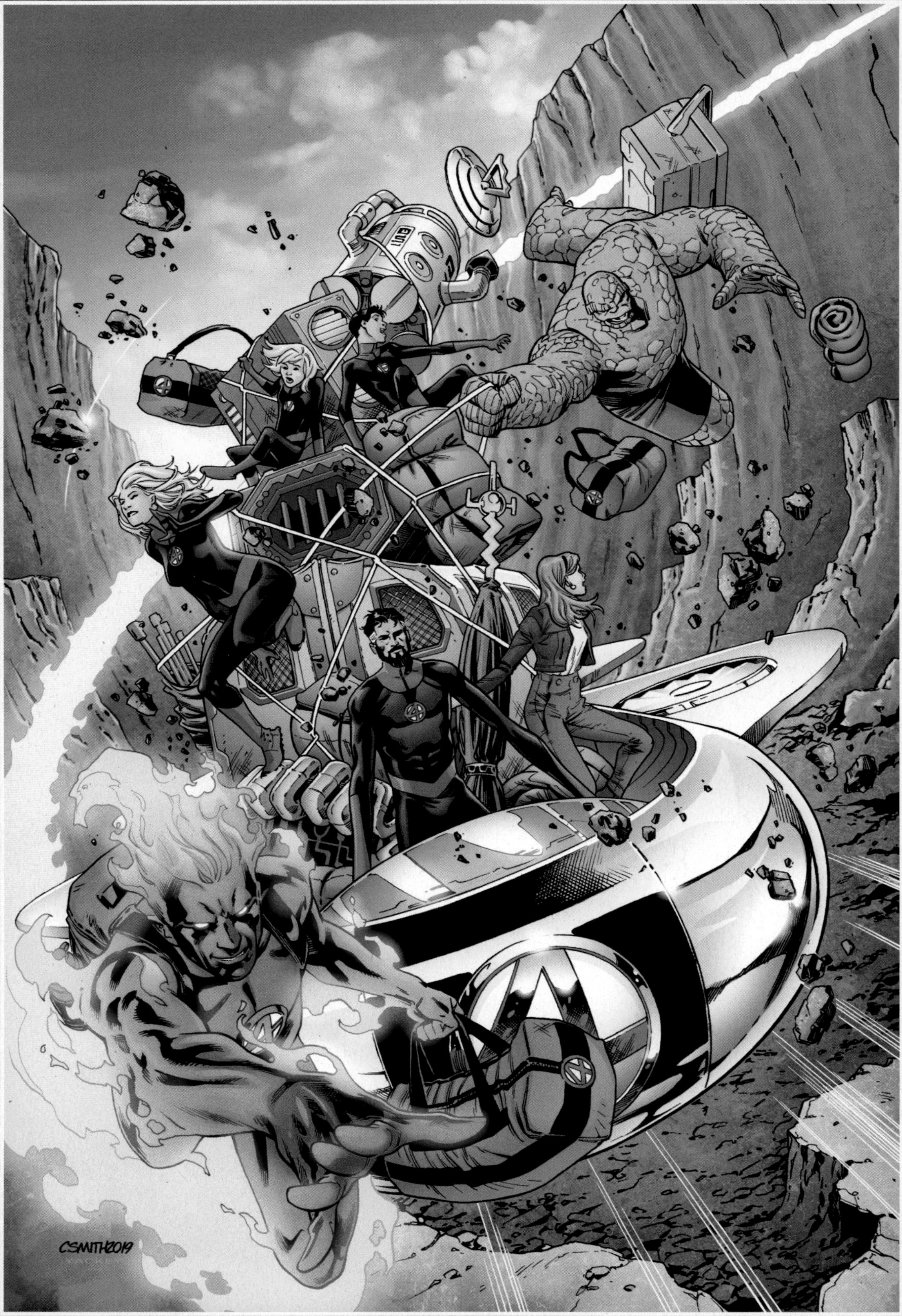
CSMITH2019

Fantastic Four: Road Trip Variant by **Cory Smith** & **Matt Yackey**

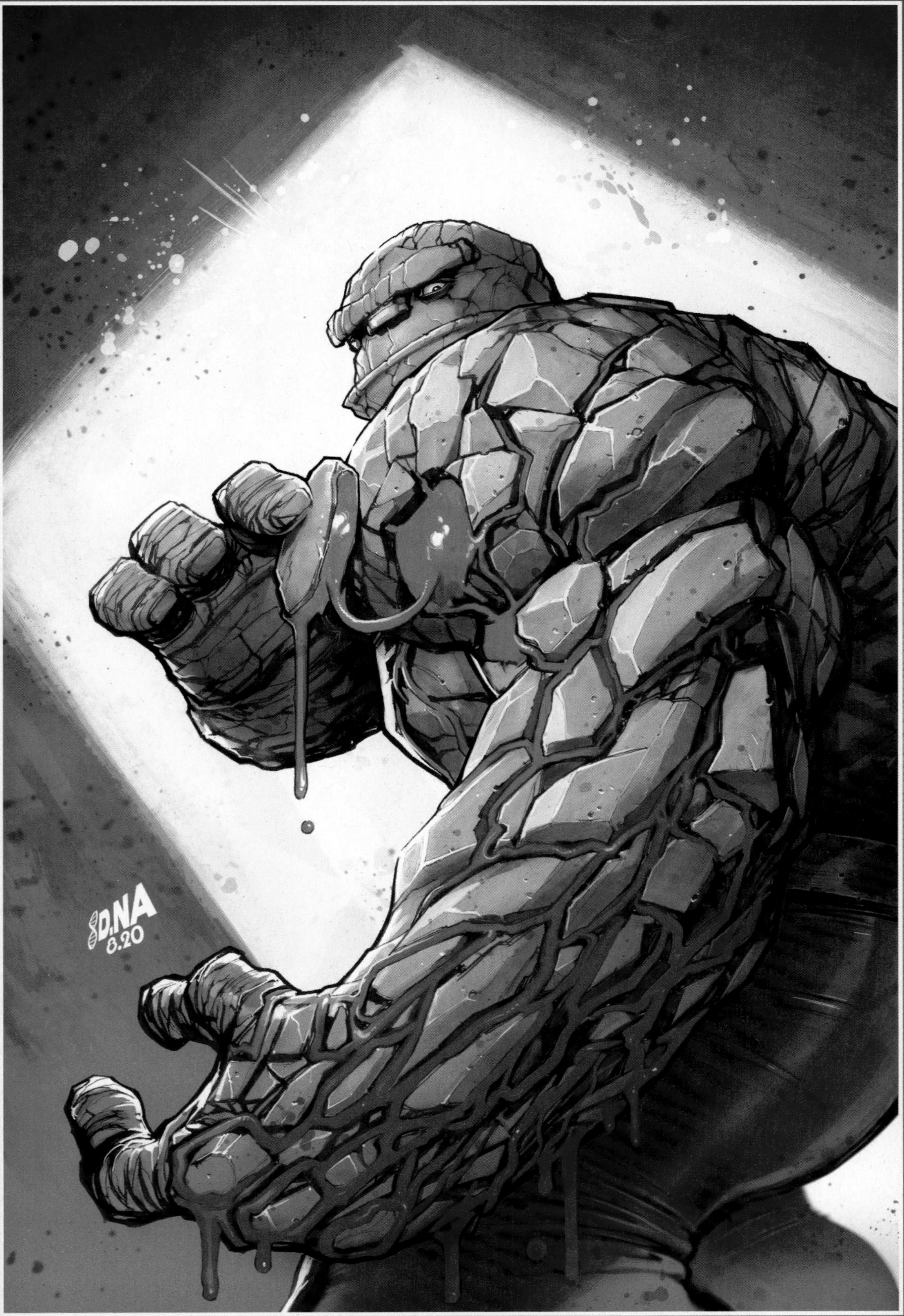
D.NA
8.20

Fantastic Four: Road Trip Variant by **David Nakayama**